# STRONG
# AND
# FEARLESS

The secret of health for both mind and body
is not to mourn for the past,
not to worry about the future,
not to anticipate troubles,
but to live in the present moment
wisely and earnestly.

—Buddha—

# STRONG
# AND
# FEARLESS

## THE QUEST
## FOR
## PERSONAL POWER

PHIL NUERNBERGER, PH.D.

YES INTERNATIONAL PUBLISHERS

SAINT PAUL, MN

Yes International Publishers
1317 Summit Avenue
Saint Paul, MN 55105
www.yespublishers.com

Library of Congress Cataloging in Publication Data
Nuernberger, Phil, date.
Strong and fearless: the quest for personal power
by Phil Nuernberger.
p. cm.
ISBN 0-936663-34-0
1. Self-control.  2. Self-perception.  3. Mind and body.
4. Stress (Psychology)  I. Title.
BFBF632.N84 2003      95-33633 CIP
158'.1-dc20

Cover design by Anton Crane
Illustrations by Kit Wray and Anton Crane

Printed in the United States of America

# Contents

INTRODUCTION                                                        7

PART I: THE KNOWLEDGE OF SELF-MASTERY                              13
1.    Power, Wisdom, Serenity: The Dimensions of Identity          17
2.    Trouble in Paradise: Stress and the Dragons of the Mind      46
3.    Our All Too Human Mind: Home of the Dragons                  77
4.    Skill: Taking Charge of the Power                           103

PART II: THE SKILLS OF SELF-MASTERY                               121
5.    Body Skills: Relaxation, Diet, and Exercise                 125
6.    The Breath of Life                                          161
7.    Mind and Mastery: Taking on the Dragons                     193
8.    Moving from Power to Wisdom                                 221
9.    Spiritual Strength: The End of Loneliness                   257

Addendum: On the Way to Self-Mastery: Starting Your
          Self-Training Program                                   282
Appendix A: Summary of Exercise                                  290
Appendix B: Details of a Muscle-Relaxation Exercise              294
Appendix C: Detail of Deep-State Breath Relaxation               296
Appendix D: Detail of "61 Points" Concentration Exercise         298

This book is dedicated to my parents,
Irvin and Dolores,
my first teachers.
Your love became my strength,
giving me the freedom to make my journey.

# ACKNOWLEDGEMENTS

I would like to acknowledge my debt to the ancient tradition of tantra yoga, from which my knowledge derives. While my experience is my own, without the loving guidance of my spiritual master over the past thirty-three years, I would have little to say. He has been, and continues to be, the embodiment of the tradition, the unerring guide who continues to lead me deeper into the mysteries of the inner source. Whatever is of value in this book is a result of his love. Whatever mistakes have been made are my own.

I would like to thank an old friend who taught me much about writing: Anne Mazer. I value the feedback and suggestions from Diane Bemel and Bob Bostrom, good friends and wonderful human beings. I also would like to thank John Duff for his direction, knowledge, and support. I am grateful for his vision for the book. Kit Wray, a friend and sparring partner, provided the artwork and always was willing to go another step to meet unexpected deadlines.

I also owe a great deal to my brothers and sisters in the tradition who have nourished and supported me on the journey. Last, but certainly first in my heart, I wish to honor my wife and children for their continuing love and support.

# INTRODUCTION

## SELF-MASTERY: THE WISDOM PATH TO FEARLESSNESS

*First of all a human being should learn to understand himself on all levels.*
*Then he can understand the Self of all, the absolute Self,*
*which is the absolute Truth.*
—His Holiness Swami Rama—

I went to my first meditation class because a friend coerced me into going. I thought yoga was a fermented dairy product that health nuts ate, and wasn't interested in meditation. I had successfully completed my doctoral coursework in psychology, but was very disillusioned by the superficiality of the knowledge, the egocentric theory, and the preoccupation with trivia that characterized my chosen profession. Psychology seemed to offer few practical tools, and even less wisdom. And the professors were more interested in getting their next publication than in exploring the depth of the human mind.

But the meditation class quickly captured my attention. The instructor, a brahmin priest who taught Indian philosophy at the university, presented a completely different perspective on personal psychology, one that I had never even heard mentioned before. One evening before class, the meditation teacher announced with great pleasure that his newly met guru, a great tantric spiritual master from the Himalayan Mountains, had arrived and would talk to the class.

At six-feet, two-inches tall, with a powerful physique, the tantric master certainly didn't look like any stereotype of a sage that I had ever seen or imagined. Throughout the entire lecture that evening, my attention was riveted to him. After what was to me one of the most insightful discussions of human nature I had ever heard, he opened the discussion to the audience. I jumped to my feet and asked if yoga was ever used as a therapy. "Of course," he replied. "But perhaps you had better heal yourself first!"

As difficult as it was to hear, his instruction to heal myself was right on the money. I was suffering from bleeding ulcers and had labile hypertension. I was an expert at creating stress for others and myself. I knew all the answers, I could tell you the theories and the research, even which books to read. But I couldn't help myself. I had no idea how to stay calm and balanced or how to stop worrying so much. In short, even with all my credentials and accomplishments, I was just like the professors – full of intellectual knowledge but powerless, unable to take control of my life.

That lecture was the beginning of a close personal relationship with my master, and a long search that has taken me to India, Nepal, and the Himalayan Mountains. It has been a journey of synthesis, integrating my western scientific background with tantra yoga, a 5,000-year-old science of physical, mental, and spiritual self-mastery. He also encouraged me to study the martial arts, first Washin Ryu Karate and currently, Shaolin Taijiquan. These ancient disciplines have proven to be powerful antidotes for the pervasive stress, disease, and unhappiness that are so endemic in this modern, fast-paced age. But above all, they have provided others and me with the knowledge and techniques of self-mastery, giving us the power to transform stress and unhappiness into wellness, self-confidence, and joy.

## Tantra Yoga: Science in Mythic Form

Nothing could have seemed stranger than this ancient tantric tradition with its gods and goddesses, demons and saints. But, the dramatic and colorful symbolism of the tantra yoga tradition is necessary where knowledge has been passed as an oral tradition from master to disciple, from teacher to student, without the aid of computers, books or tape recorders. The stories and myths, heroes and villains are remembered far more easily than facts and figures. However, my rigorous scientific and academic background with its overwhelming emphasis on logic and objectivism left me ill-prepared to listen from my own experience and heart, to discern the subtle meanings hidden within the symbolism. As I struggled to understand the mythology, I began to see that underneath the images and stories lies a powerful and systematic science of human development, the details of how body, mind, and spirit all successfully come together in human form. As I discovered, tantra yoga is nothing less than the science of inner life, a practical prescription for personal power and excellence.

Tantra yoga is based on the most critical elements of science. It is an experimental, verifiable, and highly empirical introspective science in which the object of study is not a material object but one's mind and consciousness. It is a sophisticated systems approach to human functioning, and as such, deals with all aspects of life – spiritual, mental, and physical. Self-knowledge and self-discipline are the foundation; awareness created through rigorous introspection is the methodology; the body and mind are the laboratory; and the goal is complete knowledge of human functioning, from the most mundane physiological response through the more subtle mental activities, to the highest expression of human consciousness. And like any science, achieving results requires discipline, significant effort and patience.

Tantra yoga is the practical path of fearlessness and non-attachment. It is the path of fire and light, confronting ignorance and fear until both are eliminated completely , and one is free of egoism. Tantra yoga is a set of spiritual practices, an inner technology, so to speak, not a philosophical school or religion. The focus of training is to gain control over the ego and other functions of the mind. These practices are designed to access and develop the unlimited self-confidence that lies deep within the mind of each individual. Consequently, the skilled tantric is fearless, unafraid of other's opinions, and not driven by the need for acceptance and approval. In tantra, there is a commitment to truth that leads to impeccable personal integrity, free from the dictates of "common knowledge." We learn to be fully responsible for our lives. We are, in the words of my master, the architects of our lives.

Sadly, the information available to most westerners about tantra yoga has been grossly distorted. Look in any bookstore under tantra yoga and you will find the shelves lined with books about so-called "tantric sex." "So-called" because that's the only relationship with the tradition of tantra yoga that these books have. For the most part, the authors of these books proclaim themselves to be heirs to secret teachings on sexual energy from the tantric masters. Not a single one references any traditional tantric text or tradition, nor do they defer to any living or past tantric sage who endorses, or even condones, this imaginary meandering of their libidos as having anything remotely to do with tantra yoga. The reader can, and will, draw his or her conclusions about the value of these books. However, from a traditional tantric point of view, all these books are nothing more than western trash.

Instead of sensuality, the tantrica's purpose is the development of spiritual knowledge. The real tantric is a practical mystic, engaged fully in living in the world, but seeing the divinity in every aspect of it. The goal of a tantrica is complete knowledge, an unalloyed will, and the capacity for skillful action. Skillful action means to have the ability to act free from historical (*karmic*) and emotional attachment, without disturbing one's self or others. It is focused, effective action guided by wisdom and will.

As I became more knowledgeable and skilled in the tools and techniques of tantra yoga, I realized that the demons and dragons of tantric mythology represented distortions of the powerful creative force of my own mind. I was an unconscious but active participant in creating my own misery. Like most people, I wasn't consciously malicious to myself, but my unconscious habits were creating chronic problems. My mind and its habits had control of me, and I really didn't know how to help myself.

In our education, we learn what to think and do. We learn all sorts of useless information, but we don't learn how to be. We are not taught how to consciously use the control systems of the body, we aren't taught about emotions and how to regulate them, and we aren't taught how to use the mind. Because we are uneducated about our inner resources, we use only the smallest fraction of the mind's power. Since we are not aware of our inner strengths, we have no idea how to teach our children how to be aware of their inner strengths.

Like most people, I grew up learning to look outside myself to find answers to my problems. Doctors and medicines would cure my disease, friends and lovers would end my loneliness, attaining status, position, and power would bring me self-esteem and fulfillment, and money and all the things it could buy would bring me security and happiness. The kid who had it all, or at least as much as he or she could grab from life, would win.

You and I both know that this doesn't work. But we don't know what else to do. We are so externally oriented that we know very little about what happens within our inner world. It is an unknown region, a scary place filled with the terrible things the psychiatrists talk about, all the things we struggle to forget, all the powerful desires and fears that we work desperately to suppress.

## Face to Face with Yourself

Suddenly, I was face-to-face with an alternative, a tradition of inner mastery that could teach me how to tap into my inner strength, create balance between body, mind, and spirit, and live in harmony with myself and with others – the kind of life we all want. But the catch was that I had to become responsible for myself. I had to become a skilled human being. In other words, I had to become master of myself.

Under the personal guidance of my tantric master, I learned to pay attention to what was happening in my mind and inside my body. I saw how my habits distorted the creative force of the mind and created two very powerful dragons, fear and self-hatred. The real source of my stress was not the problems I faced or the people I knew, but these two dragons. It wasn't life that created my stress and unhappiness, it was I. Rather, it was my inability to manage my powerful inner resources. I also discovered that loneliness had nothing to do with whether or not I had friends, family, or lovers. It was another dragon in my mind, only more sneaky and subtle. It would hide in the smoke and mirrors of my mind as I would focus on having friends and lovers, never recognizing the real source of loneliness.

As I practiced the breathing and relaxation exercises, my body began to heal. And, as I learned to calm and quiet my mind through concentration and meditation techniques, I discovered an inner strength that dissipated my anger and dissolved my fears. As I reached deeper into myself, I discovered a source of unlimited strength and wholeness, a spiritual core or Self that put an end to the loneliness.

As I slowly gained self-awareness, I could see how my thoughts, feelings, and habits created disturbances. This allowed me to take charge of them and stop the disturbances. As I became more and more skilled, my inner balance returned and my stress diminished. I felt better, and so I was easier to get along with. I became less aggressive and hostile, and my relationships deepened. My thinking became clearer, and I was more effective at my work.

The more inner awareness and skill I gained, the greater was my ability to live without worry, stress, and disease. My health improved, and life became more joyful. As my knowledge and power unfolded, I began to see just how connected I was to the world around me, my sense of isolation began to disappear, and I experienced a deep sense of commitment to and compassion for those around me.

As I continued my journey, I began to teach others the tools and techniuqes my master had taught me. It wasn't long before they, too, began to access their inner strength. It wasn't necessary for them to travel to the Himalayan Mountains, or even know that what they had learned had its foundation in tantra yoga. What was important was that they too discovered their inner strength and became strong human beings, free from the fear, stress, and unhappiness created by their own inner dragons.

## Returning to the Source

The way that most of us deal with the problems of life is more than a little misdirected. We basically ignore our inner resources. We are so caught up in the world around us that we don't even see that both the cause and the cure of our suffering lie within ourselves. Because we look in the wrong direction, we have a distorted view of ourselves, and very little ability to use our powerful inner resources. As a consequence, our human skills have not kept pace with our technological skills. We have become so enamored with the power and speed of our technology that we ignore the nearly infinite power of our minds. In so doing, we become dependent on external means to solve internal problems. We overuse drugs, blame others for our own choices, and become victims of circumstance. The more things we have, the more disturbed we seem to become. With all our technical and scientific knowledge we still feel powerless, alienated from each other, and fearful of the world around us.

It's time to come home. It's time to take back the power, to live without fear, self-hatred, and loneliness. It's time to be free from stress and stress-related disease. It's time to become all that we truly are. It isn't a question of belief, but one of knowlege and skill. Fortunately, the yogic tradition doesn't demand that you believe in a certain way or in a certain individual. It asks only that you approach yourself with a healthy, curious skepticism and willingness to experiment and practice.

Contrary to what most people believe, genuine tantra yoga masters (like Zen, Sufi, and Taoist masters) have no interest in collecting large gatherings of followers. The whole thrust of the tradition is to become free – of self-doubt, of neuroses, of self-imposed suffering of all sorts. But this freedom is not something that can be given by the master or teacher. Having done the research and practice themselves, they serve as guides, helping you understand and nagivate through the labyrinth of your mind. Through example and methods, they bring you face-to-face with your greatest resource, yourself. But they can't make it work for you; only you can become master of yourself.

## The Marriage of East and West

Over a hundred years ago Rudyard Kipling wrote in "The Ballad of East and West" that "East is East, and West is West, and never the twain shall meet." Rudyard Kipling was wrong. Two great traditions, the material science and advanced technology of the West, and the wisdom and inner science of self-mastery of the East, must come together if we are to achieve the promise of our destiny.

That doesn't mean that we should wear ocher robes, shave our heads, or burn incense in our homes. There is absolutely no reason to become mock Indian, mock Chinese, or mock anything! We may be intrigued, shocked, or amused by eastern cultures, but we cannot afford to dismiss their knowledge and tools for self-mastery, inner strength, and wisdom.

It doesn't matter what culture we live in, which religion we practice, or which political party we endorse; nor does it matter what calling in life – doctor, lawyer, or Indian chief. We all want to live without worry and fear, we all want to have self-respect and be self-confident, and we all want to share joy and life with others. In other words, we all want to be successful human beings.

We can accomplish this if we understand the fundamental truth that lies at the heart of our humanity: self-knowledge and self-discipline (skill) lead to self-mastery; self-mastery alone leads to freedom, to happiness, to success in life.

These two essential elements of self-mastery, self-knowledge and skill, are like two sides of a coin. We cannot have one without the other. Self-knowledge is not self-analysis. It's awareness of who we are at all levels – body, mind, and spirit – and in all the different dimensions of the self. When we have self-knowledge but no skill, we become paper tigers – we know all the answers, but we can't live any of them. Self-knowledge without self-discipline is an empty bag.

On the other hand, self-discipline without self-knowledge leads to fanaticism. We become rigid, inflexible, unable to adapt to the rapidly changing circumstances that characterize modern life. Genuine self-discipline is not harsh or abusive, but the freedom to do what we really choose to do.

Without self-knowledge and skill, belief systems become rigid and inflexible, stifling creativity, and the ability to understand others and ourselves. We believe that our way is the only way, which leads only to intolerance and fear. Our world becomes smaller and smaller as our habits makes us slaves to unproductive and unhealthy reactions. And life passes us by. As we age we find fear instead of wisdom, loneliness instead of family and friends, and disease instead of health and comfort.

## The Book

The structure of this book reflects the two elements of self-mastery. The first four chapters are concerned with self-knowledge, exploring, and understanding the different dimensions of our human experience. Here you will find a road map of your inner realities, and the powerful inner resources available to you. You will also see how these resources are mismanaged and how the dragons of the mind – fear, self-hatred, and loneliness – are created. But it isn't enough to only *think* about the different dimensions. It is important that as you read the material you also do the exercises that allow you to experience the different levels. True self-knowledge comes from direct experience, not belief or intellectual analysis. These two tools of the mind are very limited if used without direct experience.

The five chapters of Part II focus on self-discipline, or skill, and provide the techniques and tools necessary to explore and take command of your inner resources. The exercises are basicaly of two different kinds.

The first type is designed to illustrate a point, to help you become aware of a certain inner experience so that you understand it more completely. These exercises and techniques are integrated into the text, and four are found in Part I. They will provide you with insight, and make reading the book far more interesting and engaging.

The other exercises are designed to create specific skills. Several of them, such as Diaphragmatic Breathing, Meditation, and Centering, must be practiced on a consistent basis in order to build the skills necessary for self-mastery. Others, such as the Insight Exercise (Chapter 9) to make better decisions, or the Sleep Exercise (Chapter 6) to help you fall asleep, can be used when they are needed. As you come across these exercises in your reading, go ahead and try them.

The purpose of the book is to provide you with the knowledge and skills you need to achieve true self-mastery. Simply reading the book, however, will not accomplish this. Unless you actually use these tools and techniques, unless you practice what you learn, nothing happens. But even if you take only one technique, and practice it every day until it becomes a habit, you will gain the benefits in greater strength, less stress and unhappiness, and more joy and self-confidence. The addendum will help you develop a practical self-training program that will fit your own unique needs, and Appendix A will make it easy for you to find a specific exercise in the book.

I know that whatever effort you put into your own development will bring you great rewards. Don't hesitate, but don't overdo. Remember, the key is balance, practice, and patience. From the very beginning I was taught to experiment, to discover who I really am, and to develop my inner strength. Without asking me for a single thing except that I practice what I was taught, my master led me step-by-step into the tradition, step- by-step into my inner strength and wisdom.

I can never repay him for his love and guidance, or the tantra yoga tradition for the knowledge and freedom that I have gained. But I can share what I have learned, and pass on to you the practical knowledge and tools that will lead you to your wisdom, self-mastery, and joy.

PART I

# The
# Knowledge
# of
# Self-Mastery

1

# POWER, WISDOM, SERENITY: THE DIMENSIONS OF IDENTITY

*Know then thyself, presume not God to scan;*
*The proper study of mankind is man.*
—Alexander Pope—

Human beings, the most powerful of all living creatures, are very often the most troubled, confused and disturbed of all creatures. The great sages of all spiritual traditions tell us that we are literally children of God, yet we worry ourselves to death about the most insignificant of things. We sense that we are part of something far greater and more profound than ourselves, but we live more like guilt-ridden serfs. Unaware of the infinite Divinity within ourselves, we constantly hunt for something to make us feel important, powerful, and loved. The human mind is the most powerful of creative forces, and yet, we struggle with stress, impotence, failure, and loneliness. We know *what* to do, but *how* to do seems just beyond our grasp.

The sages are right. We are truly the architects of our lives. We alone have the power to create success, joy, and love. We have everything we need *except* the self-knowledge and self-discipline to use this power. Most of us have no idea of the power, wisdom, and serenity that lie within let alone the discipline and skill to use this power. Although proud of our mastery of nature, we cannot master ourselves. We explore outer space and the deepest seas, but not the inner space of our own being where all endeavors, great and small, begin. We use the mind in every science, but we have only the slightest knowledge about how the mind creates meaning in the first place. No matter where we go or what we do, the two tools that we use are the mind and body. Yet, what do we know about these two essential instruments?

We must become as skilled in our inner knowledge as we are in our knowledge of the material world around us. Self-mastery is an inner journey, an exploration of the subtle but unlimited power of body, mind, and spirit. The goal is conscious access and skillful use of the powerful inner resources of the body, mind, and spirit. To be whole, to fulfill the destiny of our humanity, we must take this journey. You will find the journey difficult at times, and easy at other times, but it is always fascinating. It is a journey leading to power, wisdom, and serenity, a journey that takes you to yourself.

## AWARENESS AND SKILL: DISTILLING POWER OF SELF-MASTERY

Like two sides of a coin, self-mastery has two aspects that cannot be separated: self-awareness and skill (self-discipline). It is the dynamic interaction of these two elements that gives us the power to live the way we choose. Having one without the other is like trying to eat milk with a fork. Self-awareness without the ability to act on our knowledge leads to frustration and neurotic impotency. We know what we should do, but we have no power to do it. On the other hand, when we have all the discipline and skill in the world but no self-awareness, we become fanatics or egomaniacs, our skills driven by fears and desires.

### Self-Awareness: The Experience of Power

Self-awareness is not what we *think* about ourselves, it is what we are *aware* of about ourselves. Often what we think about ourselves is quite different from who we really are and what our experience really is. I may think that I am relaxed, cool under pressure, even have a wonderful sense of humor, but what I experience is the pain from the chronic tension in my shoulder and neck muscles, frustration and anger from the deadlines I face, and a rigidity that prevents me from being playful and able to laugh at myself and the situations I find myself in.

Self-awareness is an ongoing process where we learn to be a witness, an observer to ourselves as well as the world around us. This is not self-analysis, where you constantly ask yourself, "Why did I do that?" As most of us know, this quickly leads to depression or leaves us feeling crazy and incompetent. Nor is it being self-centered where we inflate our egos to make ourselves the most important person. This ego problem has its roots in self-condemnation and fears of being unimportant.

To see myself clearly, I must give up being judgmental about myself as well as being overly impressed with myself. Self-awareness means becoming an observer, simply watching the mind and body work together. The more I judge myself or the more I try to impress myself and others, the less able I am to see myself clearly. I don't want to be distracted by all the dumb things I might do, or by all the wonderful things that I might accomplish. In order to see myself clearly, I must look beyond all the colors of the ego, and see beyond the fear, judgment or pride.

In fact, genuine self-awareness has nothing at all to do with the ego. Self-awareness is an open, observational process that allows us to watch the ego perform its functions. Through awareness we see (hear, feel, smell, touch) just what the mind and body are doing. Being an observer, we witness both strengths and weaknesses with the same equanimity. It is like being a court reporter, the individual in the courtroom who must listen to and record everything said without making any interpretation. We must become a court reporter to our personality, a witness who listens without making judgments or interpretations.

This act of awareness (called mindfulness in Zen) has power in and of itself. If someone pinches you on the arm, you quickly feel the pain and pull your arm back. Identifying with your body, you experience the pain directly and sharply. But if you relax, become an observer, you find that when your arm is pinched the pain begins to diminish and has little effect on you. The impact on the body is the same, but by being a witness or observer, you break your identity with the pain. This gives you greater ability to understand and control the pain. You can use this principle to eliminate or control any kind of pain.

For instance, you can often eliminate a headache by creating a relaxed focus and paying attention to the headache as an object. By becoming a witness to the pain instead of identifying with the pain, you change the conditions that allow the headache to exist. The next time you have a headache, or you are with someone who has a headache, try the following Shrinking Headache Exercise. It usually works better if someone takes you through the exercise while you focus on doing it. In the exercise on page 20, a series of periods...indicates a pause, and words in parentheses (e.g., verbal answer) are only used the first time and not repeated as you continue to repeat the exercise.

As self-awareness deepens, we become aware of the enormous power we have within ourselves for health and wellness, emotional fulfillment, and knowledge. We experience our inner wisdom to direct our lives and fulfill our destinies. We discover an inner strength that is unaffected by the circumstances that surround us. And we experience a power within us that goes beyond the limits of mind and body. Self-awareness means to consciously experience the different dimensions of our finest instruments, the mind and body, and experience at the deepest level their relationship to our true Self, the spiritual core of our being. We have all that we need to be complete, to experience wholeness and joy, and create the kind of life we choose.

## Skill: The Ability to Choose

All this awareness is useless without the skill to use it. Self-discipline is the other half of self-mastery. We often use the concept of self-discipline to beat up on ourselves. But in truth, self-discipline is simply the ability to do what you choose to do. Each of us has skill, and every day we use self-discipline. But because we aren't aware of what we do, we become skilled in ways that create problems for ourselves.

## SHRINKING HEADACHE EXERCISE

*When doing an exercise, a series of periods . . . indicates a pause.*

Sit quietly, let your breath become very smooth and even...Picture your forehead becoming very smooth and even, with all the lines and bumps becoming as smooth as a piece of glass...Bring your attention to your breath at the opening of your nostrils...Clear your mind by focusing on the feeling of the breath going in and out of the nostrils...You will feel a slight coolness on the inhalation and a very subtle feeling of warmth on the exhalation at the opening of the nostrils...

Tell me how long is your headache? (Indicate by using your hands)...
How wide is your headache? (Again, indicate with your hands)...
How deep is your headache? (Again, indicate with your hands)...
What shape is your headache? (Verbal answer: round, square, triangle, oblong,
What color is your headache? (Verbal answer)...

Now, clear your mind by focusing on the feeling of your breath at the openings of the nostrils... (Repeat the relaxation paragraph above. After a few moments of relaxing, again repeat the questions. Continue alternating the set of questions with focused relaxation until the headache or other pain is gone. It will seem a bit peculiar to describe head pain by size, shape, and color, but this creates the objective focus necessary to break the identity with the pain.)

Let's take a simple example. Think about the things that you worried about today. Most of our worries are about small things, and hardly worth the notice. But how many times did you fret about something? Now think about all the things you worried about yesterday – and the day before. Look at the discipline you have. Every day you practice worrying. No wonder you get so good at it. Yet, you don't think of yourself as being disciplined. After all, you know all the things you would accomplish if only you had more self-discipline.

Every day we act with discipline. We do the same things day-in and day-out. Only the disciplines we practice aren't ones that we consciously choose for ourselves. They simply arise out of our unconscious habits. If I have the habit of slouching when I sit in front of my computer, then every day I practice slouching. I have become self-disciplined in the art of slouching. When I begin to realize that sitting in this way doesn't feel good, then I begin sitting up straight. Every day I practice sitting up straight until that becomes an unconscious habit. Now I have a discipline that helps me physically and mentally.

To be skilled means to practice a particular set of behaviors until it becomes a habit. The key word is practice, but practice what? If you want to be a skilled tennis player, you practice tennis. If you want to become a skilled accountant, you practice accounting. But what do you practice when you want to become a skilled human being? Unfortunately we seldom think in these terms. Formal education fills our head with acts, figures, and systems, but it doesn't teach us how to use the most important tools that we have, the powerful resources of our own minds.

We need a systematic, practical approach to develop our inner skills. This is the essence of the tantric tradition. It provides us with the concepts and tools that allow us to live our daily lives with awareness and discipline, with skill and power. It is the practical science of self-responsibility.

## PERSONAL RESPONSIBILITY: POWER THROUGH SELF-MASTERY

Because we aren't skilled human beings, we feel powerless and ineffectual, and become more dissatisfied and cynical about ourselves and our ability to make a real difference in life. Instead of responding effectively and confidently to the pressures and challenges we face, we all too often find ourselves playing the role of victim. To compensate, we turn even more aggressively to external resources – technology, therapists, medicines, and laws. And when these disappoint us, we turn to magic crystals, subliminal tapes, herbal teas, and New Age brain machines.

We have an untapped resource of power and abilities, but it doesn't come in a book or a pill, it isn't dispensed by a doctor or therapist, and it isn't activated by crystals hung around the neck. We are the resource and the key to this resource is self-mastery, creating and acting with personal responsibility. To be responsible does not mean accepting "blame" or finding fault. Think of responsibility as two distinct concepts: "response" and "ability." One obvious dimension of response ability is the capacity to respond rather than react. When we react to something, we are not making a conscious choice, but acting out of habit. Imagine that you had one of those work days when nothing seemed to go right. No matter what you tried to do, something or somebody would come along and throw a monkey-wrench into your plans and frustrate your efforts. Finally, you leave for home. You get into your car, pull out on the highway, and some jerk pulls out right in front of you. You crowd up behind him, lay on the horn, scream obscenities, and give hand signals expressing your anger. It's only then you notice that there are several antennas on the car and a license plate that says "State Police" in small letters before the numbers.

If you hadn't been in reaction, you probably would have chosen to act differently with that unmarked police car. Your emotional state not only inhibited your perceptual abilities (you didn't notice critical information), it also provoked you into reacting in ways that might very well prove to be troublesome. The stronger the emotional reaction, the more rigid and predictable our behavior becomes, the less creative we are, and the less freedom we experience. To have "response-ability" means that we have both the awareness and the skill to take effective action, which will have the freedom to consciously determine our behavior. The more knowledgeable and skilled we become, the greater our response-ability.

Emotional reactivity is an important dimension and an easy example to illustrate. But response ability refers to our capacity to use all the resources at our command. Self-mastery means that we have the knowledge and skill to use all dimensions of our humanity – physical, mental/emotional, and spiritual – in a conscious, skillful way.

You don't have to be an intellectual genius to develop your power as a human being. Anyone can learn to use all his or her inner resources. Nor does it matter what kind of work you do, whether or not you have a college degree, whether you are single, married, divorced or widowed. Becoming a skilled human being doesn't depend on external things, but on what we do with ourselves. There are senior executives, as well as plumbers, chefs, and housewives, who have become skilled human beings. How we choose to use the skills that we develop is a matter of individual choice and opportunity. But anyone can become skilled; anyone can develop his or her strength.

When I first met Jerry, he was forty-two years old, and had been out of prison for only a short time. Growing up poor, Jerry learned to steal at an early age as a way to provide food for the family. Over the years, he stole millions of dollars, but he also spent sixteen years in prison. With each new prison term, he would immediately do something that would land him in solitary confinement. He found that this was the safest way to do the time. The biggest problem for him there was never having enough to eat. Since he was in solitary confinement, his food was brought to him, as he wasn't allowed to pass through a cafeteria line with other prisoners where he could help himself. During his last time in prison, he began to read books on yoga that talked about eating as a way of discipline. He read that if you chew your food thoroughly, you would eat far less and digest your food more completely.

Intrigued, Jerry began to follow this small discipline. Soon, he was leaving food on his plate, no longer requiring the large amounts he was used to. Through this one small act of discipline, Jerry realized that he had the power to make choices for himself. If he could control his appetite, he certainly could control the choices he made. He didn't have to continue being a thief and risk spending his life in prison. He began to use the relaxation and breathing exercises to help him gain greater self-awareness and self-control. When he finished serving his time, he returned to Minneapolis and continued to practice his exercises and develop his inner balance and self-discipline. He married, fathered a beautiful child who is now a teenager, and became a loving, supportive husband and father. The past twenty years have not always been easy. Jerry is certainly not wealthy, but he continues to develop his self-awareness and discipline, and his life is free of worry and crime. My friend's power is in the kind of person he has become.

Prison didn't change Jerry. He did that himself. Instead of reacting like he always did, he decided to do something different. The more he learned about himself, the more choices he realized he had. The more he practiced the exercises, the more able he was to make choices. Like him, we must look within to discover our strength. To take charge of our lives, we must take charge of ourselves. But what is this "self"? This question has as many answers as there are people who ask it.

## BEING HUMAN: THE WHOLE PICTURE

As human beings, we are complex organizations of physical events, energy, perceptions, thoughts, feelings and emotions, and something more that we will simply call for now the spirit. What others see in us, and how we see ourselves, is what we often refer to as our personality. But there is far more to us than meets the eye.

We tend to define ourselves in many different ways: We are rich or poor, male or female, liberal or conservative, smart or dumb, successful or unsuccessful. The labels we use often limit self-awareness and keep us from overcoming our fear, self-hatre,d and loneliness. We can analyze ourselves in biochemical and/or genetic terms, but that doesn't help us understand our thoughts. We could use psychiatric concepts, but the focus of psychiatry is on pathology, not strengths, and we end up with one-sided, distorted pictures of ourselves.

Enchanted with technology, we often think of ourselves as biocomputers, sophisticated biological machines. But machines are closed systems. They don't think, they don't feel, they cannot move beyond their own parameters. We can take them apart and put them back together again. We can switch parts from one machine to another, and then back again. We can build a computer piece-by-piece, adding up parts to create a system. If we don't like the system we build, we change it around and create a new system.

But we can never add up the parts and pieces to get a human being. Human beings are more than the physical parts of the body. While some scientists would have us believe that we are only the body, our experience tells us another story.

If we lose a finger, an arm or a leg, we don't think of ourselves as being less of a human being. We may see ourselves as less capable, even less lovable, but inside there is something that still insists that we are a person, a complete human being. We can think, we can dream about the future and take actions based on those dreams. We can live in the past, totally ignoring the present reality. We have other dimensions that go far beyond the physical body. Even without having a mystical experience, most of us believe there is a spiritual dimension, a soul or consciousness that transcends both the mind and body.

We are living "open systems." We constantly interact with our environment, change it, and in turn, are changed by it. Open systems are characterized by options and creative expression. Human beings have the capacity to create chaos or harmony, to be self-destructive or create wellness and fulfillment. We can choose to eat to excess, drive too fast, work too hard, or lose control of our emotions. Or we can eat properly, drive carefully, balance our work with leisure time, and take control of our emotional lives. We may cure disease by altering our emotional condition, by stimulating the immune system through imagery, by taking herbs and natural medicines, or by using synthetic medicines.

Similarly, we can solve problems in a variety of ways. We may draw upon our past experience, base our decision on instinct, use intuitive knowledge, rely on logic and intellect, or combine these methods. The mind has unlimited creative capacity to structure knowledge, insights, and creative expression. No technology comes even close to matching human creativity, adaptability, and flexibility. We have infinite opportunities, ways and means to achieve what we want, *if we develop the knowledge and skill to use them.*

Open systems are also characterized by *harmonization,* the ability to achieve and maintain harmony of energy and effort. We have an innate ability to maintain inner balance, or harmony, which allows us to function efficiently and effectively. A good example is the resting heartbeat when the heart pumps blood and performs its duties, but does so in a state of balance. No one dies from a resting heartbeat. But if we do something to disrupt the system – bad diet, improper breathing, lack of exercise, inappropriate emotional reactions – we destabilize the system and the heart becomes unstable. Instead of a balanced heart rhythm, we end up with irregular heartbeats or high blood pressure.

We create that same harmony of energy and effort when we totally focus on our task and work seems effortless. When we do this, we don't create excess tension, worry about something else, or doubt ourselves. The mind is calm and our thoughts are clear. But if we destabilize the system – start doubting ourselves, worrying about what someone will think of our efforts, recall all the times when we failed – then we create a chaotic situation, our work suffers, and we finish the day with a headache or feeling worn out.

We are not simply biochemical reactions, but *living* systems. We are sustained by a life force that cannot be flipped on and off. A computer "comes alive" when you plug it in and run an electric current through it. You can switch the computer, or any machine, on and off without doing any harm. It's very difficult to do that with a human being. Our life force is an essential part of who we are, and plays a vital function in our ability to live without stress. On still another level, we think, we feel, we dream – our rich mental and emotional life plays a crucial role in determining our health and well being.

When we act as if the different elements of our life are separate from each other, we lose our human power. For example, when the cardiologist treats high blood pressure with medication and ignores the role of diet, exercise, emotions, family and work life, he treats the patient as a machine. When we ignore our intuitive knowledge, deny our emotions and rely solely on so-called logic, we act as if we are machines. We must look to all aspects of our personality system if we want to achieve self-mastery. We come as a complete package. Any action we take involves all aspects of the personality. We do not make decisions without our memory playing a role, nor do we play handball without our liver functioning. Just as teamwork makes a world-class team, it's teamwork within the personality that makes a world-class human being.

## THE SIX DIMENSIONS OF IDENTITY

Instead of labels, we need a simple, practical way of seeing ourselves, one that allows us to recognize and explore all the different aspects and resources at our disposal. Tantric psychology provides a conceptual framework of six dimensions to define how body, mind, and spirit relate and interact with each other. These are illustrated and briefly described in Figure 1.1. The outer five dimensions are like sheaths that fit over the core sixth dimension, the spiritual Self. These five sheaths are called *koshas* in tantra. This spiritual Self is the core identity while the other dimensions constitute the expressive vehicle, the instrument through which the spiritual Self expresses itself in the world around it. While each dimension has unique functions, one cannot be separated from the other. Each is a necessary part of being human. We always function as a whole person, not as individual, mechanical pieces. Whenever we think, or talk, or act, all parts of the body, mind, and spirit are involved. By exploring these dimensions, we can see where our resources lie and how to use them to create the magic of a beautiful life.

You can think of these five sheaths or dimensions like thin layers of glass surrounding a pure white light symbolizing the spiritual Self. The farther away from the light, the more opaque the glass sheath becomes. The most subtle sheath is the one that first surrounds the light. This sheath, which we will call the Balanced Mind, is crystalline pure, and reflects the light as a very clear mirror perfectly reflects an image. As we move farther away from the spiritual Self, each dimension becomes increasingly more clouded, or opaque, until we reach the most dense sheath, the physical body. This is the most primitive level, and the most dense form of energy.

When we look at other human beings the first thing we see is some part of the body – posture, the face, the eyes, a smile. Few have the capacity to see the shining light of the soul hidden beneath material dimension. But what if we could? How would it change our life if we had the power to know all dimensions of the individual? How would it change your interaction with others if you could relate directly to the spiritual Self in each human being? Those who have that capacity are known as sages in every culture, time, and place. These are the people who live without fear, self-hatred, and stress, who live without disturbing themselves and others. They are models for the rest of us, and we can learn to do the same.

We begin our journey with the physical dimension, the body, and then travel inward through increasingly more subtle levels of energy that make up the life

Figure 1.1
## THE DIMENSIONS OF IDENTITY

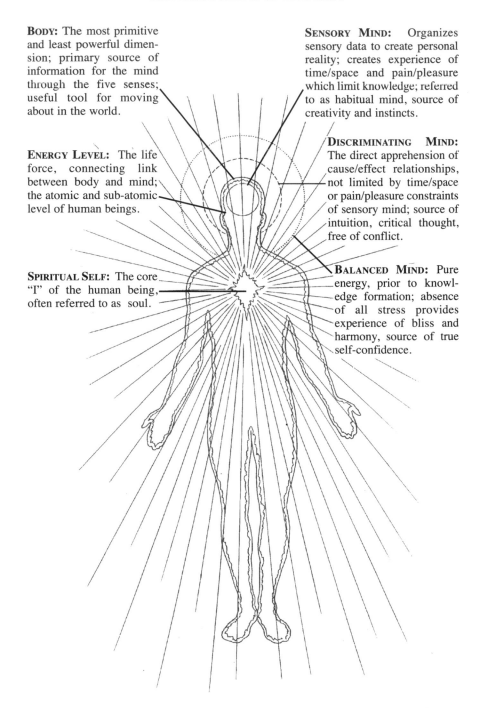

**BODY:** The most primitive and least powerful dimension; primary source of information for the mind through the five senses; useful tool for moving about in the world.

**ENERGY LEVEL:** The life force, connecting link between body and mind; the atomic and sub-atomic level of human beings.

**SPIRITUAL SELF:** The core "I" of the human being, often referred to as soul.

**SENSORY MIND:** Organizes sensory data to create personal reality; creates experience of time/space and pain/pleasure which limit knowledge; referred to as habitual mind, source of creativity and instincts.

**DISCRIMINATING MIND:** The direct apprehension of cause/effect relationships, not limited by time/space or pain/pleasure constraints of sensory mind; source of intuition, critical thought, free of conflict.

**BALANCED MIND:** Pure energy, prior to knowledge formation; absence of all stress provides experience of bliss and harmony, source of true self-confidence.

force and mind. We end with the sixth dimension of pure consciousness, the spiritual Self. Each succeeding dimension is more subtle and contains more powerful resources than the previous one. The more subtle the dimension, the greater the potential for personal power and freedom.

## The Power Functions: Tools for Self-Mastery

Each dimension contains different functions that combine to create knowledge and action. These "power functions" create and direct our thoughts and behavior. Used skillfully, they help us become successful, healthy, and happy. But when we mismanage them, we become stressed, unhappy, and diseased. For

Table 1.1
THE SIX DIMENSIONS AND SUMMARY OF POWER FUNCTIONS

| DIMENSION | POWER FUNCTION | PRACTICAL RESOURCE |
|---|---|---|
| I. Body | Sensory mechanisms<br>Neural control systems | Information,<br>health/wellness,<br>mobile home |
| II. Energy | Link between body/mind | Control mechanism<br>for body/mind<br>balance, energy,<br>power, enhanced<br>concentration |
| III. Sensory Mind | Perceptual organization,<br>language, habit, emotions | Creativity, instinct,<br>imagination |
| IV. Discriminating Mind | Discrimination, the ability<br>to discern cause/effect<br>relationships | Wisdom, intuition,<br>decisiveness<br>critical thinking |
| V. Balanced Mind | Inner harmony/peace | Inner strength<br>leads to absolute<br>self-confidence,<br>dynamic will,<br>serenity |
| VI. Spiritual Self | Pure consciousness,<br>spiritual knowledge,<br>and vision | Love, joy,<br>tranquility,<br>fearlessness, |

instance, emotional energy is a power function of the sensory level of the mind. Our emotions can inspire and motivate, or they can create fear and rigidity. We can react to a situation, become angry and blow up, or we can take control and channel our anger into determination and will. The difference lies in our ability to direct this emotional energy, to choose our response instead of reacting out of habit. These functions and their practical application are briefly summarized in Table 1.

For example, as we grow, there are periods in life when the emotions are strong and developing. Teenagers have a notorious reputation for emotional ups and downs. Whenever you mention that you have children who are entering their teens, most people roll their eyes and extend their condolences. Certainly the teenage years can be a time of surging emotions. But that doesn't mean that self-control isn't possible. If teenagers understand how to manage the powerful emotional energies that develop during these years, they have the means for great learning and accomplishment.

Raka was just becoming a teenager when she was confronted with an opportunity to develop her inner strength. Raka has a mercurial personality. Usually good-natured and easily generous, when pushed she can also explode in a fit of temper. Raka loved to play basketball, and she was very good at it. When she first started playing, she would get angry whenever someone would play rough against her. She took every competitive knock personally. Before long, she would be so mad she couldn't focus on the game, and would make mistake after mistake. The angrier she got, the worse her playing became.

She soon realized that her anger was preventing her from playing effectively, and would often result in her being benched. She knew that if she could channel her angry energy into jumping higher and moving faster instead of directing it towards an opponent, she would be able to out-play the others. With practice Raka taught herself to focus on her performance instead of the other player. It took time and effort, but the payoff was well worth it to Raka, and to the team. Raka always started out cool, calm, and in control. Instead of getting angry during a game, Raka became more intense and focused, and doubled the intensity of her play. Like any good athlete, she focused her energy on out-rebounding, out-shooting, and out-playing her opponent. Raka took control of her mind and used her emotional energy to motivate herself for even better performance.

But it doesn't matter what age we are. If we don't take control, it's all too easy to be victimized by our thoughts and emotions, and trapped by the tension in our body. The starting point is inner awareness. Raka was fortunate. Her early education included yoga and martial arts training. She had an education in self-mastery that most of us don't receive. But like Raka, our ability to skillfully use our resources develops to the degree that we become aware of them within ourselves.

The first step in self-mastery is self-knowledge. That means more than just having ideas about who we are. It is based solely on direct experience. In a moment, we will read about the different dimensions of our personality. In other words, we will have a map of the territory we want to explore. But like all maps, it can't substitute for being there. Let's start by first being there, and begin with an experiential journey through the six dimensions of the personality. First read through the Traveling Exercise a few times until you feel comfortable about the sequence, and then do it as completely as you can by memory. After a few times, you will easily remember the sequence. You can also record the exercise on a cassette tape and listen to it, or have a friend guide you through the exercise. If

### A TRAVELING EXERCISE

Sit back in your chair, close your eyes, and relax as well as you can...Let your breath become very smooth and even....Breathe without any effort on your part...Now direct your awareness to your body...Where do you feel tension in the body?... Can you feel your heart beat?...What else do you feel in your body?...What do you feel or sense, what do you hear, what do you smell?... Now bring your attention to your breath...What does the air feel like as you breathe in and breathe out?... Be aware of the lungs as they expand and contract... Be aware of your feelings of energy...Is your energy level low or high?... Is the quality of the energy calm or tense?... Now be aware of your thoughts... Don't try to think them, just be aware of your mind thinking them for you... Notice how they jump from one topic to another...Be aware of how some thoughts grab your attention more than others... Do you notice any relationship between your thoughts and your level of energy?...What happens when a worry comes to your mind?... Do you notice any relationship between your thoughts and tension in the body?... Now go to what seems to be the center of your mind and allow yourself to think of a problem you must solve...Don't allow your emotions to pull you into the problem, look at the problem as if it were quite separate from you... Examine the problem as if it had nothing at all to do with you...Do you notice anything different about the problem?...Is there any greater clarity, and do you notice any details that you may have passed over before?... Now imagine yourself going to the very center of your mind where it is very quiet and still...Allow yourself to experience this stillness and quietness for a few moments...Notice what happens to the thought...Now visualize a pure flame...Let the flame be as small, as perfect and as clear as your mind will allow... After a few moments, be aware of the stillness in the very center of your mind...Now become aware of the thoughts of your mind...Now become aware of your breathing...Are you breathing differently than when you started this exercise?... Now be aware of how your body feels...Now gently open your eyes.

you wear contact lenses, take them off before doing this or any exercise, such as deep relaxation, concentration, or meditation that requires you to close your eyes for more than a few moments.

Notice how quiet you feel after doing this exercise. Do you feel any difference in the tension levels of your muscles? Did your breathing become more quiet and stable? Almost always, simply directing your attention inwards towards the center of the mind creates a calm, restful state.

As you explore the different dimensions, you will have different experiences – body feelings, the movement of breath, thoughts, objectivity about your thoughts, and quietness. The first time you do this, you may experience only the most obvious events – chronic tension in your shoulders; the insistent demand of immediate problems; old, familiar patterns of guilt and regret. But as you become more experienced and sensitive, it becomes easier to identify the different functions of each dimension, and see how experiences are being created. As you do this, you slowly gain greater control over these power functions, and they become more helpful. That means that you have more choices, a greater freedom to act and think.

To help understand each dimension, we can compare them with a sophisticated computer system. Each dimension is analogous to a different function within the system. Remember, however, that this is just an analogy. Even the most powerful computer cannot begin to match the flexibility, power, and wisdom of the human body, mind and spirit.

## The First Dimension: Our Physical Body

The first and most familiar dimension of our personality is the body. The body is analogous to the hardware of the computer system – screen, keyboard, hard disc, logic chips – all the physical elements of a computer. Our health and wellness depend a great deal on how skillfully we care for the body. The relationship between the body and our happiness is simple and direct: when you aren't healthy, you don't enjoy life and you don't function well.

The body is an extremely sensitive barometer to both the mind and the world around us. A valuable source of information and knowledge, it tells us immediately when something is not quite right, both in our environment and within ourselves. If we pay attention to the body's signals, we gain insight into both the environment and our inner reality – the condition of our health, emotional states, and even our instincts and intuition. These physical responses can be quite dramatic, such as a pounding heart when we get up to give a speech, or a tensing of our shoulder muscles as we hear about a new work assignment. But often they are subtle – a feeling of unease in a social situation when there is no obvious reason to be uneasy, or a slight tightening of the tiny muscles around the corners of the mouth when we become angry.

The more sensitive we are to the body's messages, the easier it is for us to stay healthy. The body always lets us know when we are out of balance. The most common signal is muscle tension, but it can just as easily be a change in sleep patterns, the way we breathe, or an elevated blood pressure. These early signals warn us something is wrong, and if we ignore them, we may develop a disease. For example, high blood pressure is most often a clear signal that we are not handling pressure well. If we don't know that we have high blood pressure, it can lead to a disaster, such as a stroke or heart attack. Once aware of the problem, we can easily take steps – deep relaxation, proper breathing, the right kind of exercise, greater emotional control – to correct it.

When we ignore the signs or symptoms of our bodies – or worse, eliminate the symptoms without dealing with the cause – we only create a bigger problem. Taking pain medication for a tension headache relieves the symptom, but it does not change the underlying cause, the chronic tension in our muscles. As a consequence, we end up taking the pills over and over again because we didn't solve the real problem of chronic tension.

## The Anatomy of Self-Mastery

Our goal is self-mastery, the ability to consciously regulate the mind and body to be healthy, happy, and effective. Consequently, we want to understand the mind and body in ways that allow us to achieve a high level of self-mastery. Keeping in mind that we are an open system and not a machine, we can continue with our analogy of the body as a sophisticated biocomputer. The control system for this biocomputer is the brain and nervous system. If we understand how to manage this control system, we have the means to take control of the body. We will need to rely less and less on external resources to control our well-being. Of course, the details of this sophisticated biocomputer are quite complex, but the operating principles are rather simple.

The control center is the brain and its extension, the spinal cord. Together these two are referred to as the central nervous system (CNS). We can think about the brain as the central processing unit (CPU) of the biocomputer where we store information and run programs. All other nerves in the body are part of two powerful nervous systems that carry out the directions of the brain and send information back to the brain for processing.

The first of these two systems is the sensory-motor nervous system, which controls the sense organs and the muscles. This is often called the "voluntary nervous system" because, for the most part, we can easily and consciously choose how we use our sensory mechanisms and our muscles. We can sit or stand, listen to someone speaking to us or tune them out, move with grace or stumble awkwardly as we imitate a drunk. The sensory-motor system also regulates muscle tension and relaxation, allowing us to be active or to relax. The sensory-motor system is also a powerful data collection system. As the key elements of perception, the senses provide us with information about both our inner realities and the world around us. The muscles also respond to this information, providing another feedback mechanism to the conscious mind.

The other system is called the autonomic nervous system and regulates the internal organ systems, such as the cardiovascular system, glands, and the digestive system. The term autonomic derives from the term "autonomy," meaning to act independently. The autonomic system, however, is not completely autonomous or independent. Like every system of the body, it is regulated by the CNS and interacts in complex ways with the sensory-motor system. What the term implies is that this system can act independently of our conscious awareness. The autonomic nervous system can, and does, regulate our internal organ systems without us having to pay attention to it. We don't have to think about beating our heart, or taking a breath, or digesting our food, or making sure the glands are secreting properly.

However, contrary to what we were told by medical science not too long ago, this autonomic system can be consciously regulated. This is particularly important to us because the autonomic system controls the physiological reactions we call stress. As we will see later, if we know how to regulate this powerful system, we can control stress and free ourselves from the diseases and problems created by stress.

## The Balancing Act

The autonomic nervous system is made up of three relatively distinct nervous systems. These are called the sympathetic, parasympathetic, and enteric nervous systems. Together these systems regulate the activities of our organs. The enteric system is just now beginning to be understood. It is a vast system of nerve cells that reside in the wall of the gut. It has just as many transmitters and even more neurons than the spinal cord itself, and is now being called "the second brain." This is the area that is referred to in Chinese martial arts as the *dan tien,* and is considered to be a powerful battery, a generator of enormous physical energy. Although its role is largely unknown, we can be confident that it plays a substantial role in the overall harmony and balance of the system. In tantra yoga and the martial arts, there are specific breathing and physical exercises that stimulate this system directly to energize and/or harmonize the entire system.

Our greatest attention, however, is on the sympathetic and parasympathetic systems. In general, the organs are supplied with nerves from both systems, which is called reciprocal enervation. However, these two systems are structurally independent, and function in very different ways. The sympathetic has a global response in the body and enervates the entire body immediately. The parasympathetic (as well as the enteric) is organ-specific. They do function independently *except* for the heart and the lungs. In these two vital organs, these two systems engage in a very powerful balancing process. Sympathetic stimulation speeds the heart up while parasympathetic stimulation via the vagus nerve slows the heartbeat. At rest, both systems discharge at a low level, and the resting heart-beat represents a balance of the two opposing influences. If we exert ourselves, or if we become anxious, the heart speeds up. This is first accomplished by a decrease in vagal (parasympathetic) activity and then by an increase in sympathetic activity.

More importantly, both systems are involved in the same balancing process in the breathing process. Like the heart, it is a balancing act between the two systems that determines our breathing patterns. As we shall see later, *it is this powerful balancing act in both the heart and the lungs that provides us not only a new conceptual approach to stress, but also a direct way to consciously regulate the autonomic nervous system.*

We can picture all three systems as a complex and sophisticated balancing act to maintain health and vitality. The sympathetic system creates arousal in the body. It does things like speed the heart up and causes the liver to release fuel for the muscles to burn. The parasympathetic does just the opposite. It creates inhibition or rest in the body. It slows the heart down and makes the liver store fuel. The enteric supervises the digestive process, particularly the work of the bowel. When we are healthy, these systems work together like the right and left hand work together to accomplish a task. They harmonize each other, exchanging dominance as the need requires, and maintaining equilibrium (homeostasis) as dominance shifts.

Most of us are familiar with the term "fight or flight." This is the alarm reaction that *supposedly* provides us with the energy and arousal needed to defend against an attack. It is controlled by the sympathetic system, which allows us to have instant arousal throughout the entire body. Whenever something startles us, or we feel under attack, our whole body reacts. On the other hand, the parasympathetic controls each organ or organ system independently from all others. As a result, we can be uptight with too much tension, and still have one or two organ systems dominated by parasympathetic influence.

For instance, ulcers are a parasympathetic disease. But one of the characteristic patterns of people who suffer from ulcers is chronic anger and tension, an expression of sympathetic imbalance. Because the sympathetic and parasympathetic systems are structured and function differently, we have an almost infinite number of possible combinations between arousal and inhibition. This great flexibility in our control system gives the body a variety of ways to respond to the directives coming from the mind.

## The Second Dimension: Energy – The Missing Link

When you turn this page, it feels substantial, a thing you can touch and see, even smell, hear, and taste. That's because you're using your body's senses. From physics, we know that what appears to the senses as a solid object is really not solid at all, but a complex patterning of atomic and sub-atomic energy particles.

As useful as the senses are, they are crude compared to sophisticated micro-scopes. If we put this page under an electron microscope, we would find nothing solid, only patterns of energy. The body is no different than any other physical object. If we could look at our own body beneath an electron microscope, we would only find patterns of energy. This energy sub-structure is the foundation of all material reality, and forms the second dimension of the personality.

The life force is a very subtle form of energy that flows through all living creatures. In our computer analogy, this second dimension represents the electricity that allows the computer to run. The life force sustains the body and its systems. Western science and medicine approach the body on the physical level, as if the only reality is biochemical. When you go to the doctor, she doesn't talk about energy, she prescribes medication to create a biochemical change. Even the physicist whose entire professional career involves studying energy forgets his knowledge when he is sick, and treats his body as if the chemical (physical) level were the only reality. Only very recently has energy medicine been a topic of study, discussion, and practice.

However, this life force has been the focus of intense study in eastern meditative and self-mastery disciplines, such as tantra yoga, zen, and the martial arts. In spite of all the cultural differences between the various traditions, they universally understand energy to be the connecting link between body and mind, and have detailed maps of its channels and various functions. In tantra science, this energy dimension of the personality is referred to as the "pranic sheath." The term "prana" literally means the "first unit of energy," or a subtle form of ener-gy. Just as the body has a vascular system to distribute blood, there are channels to distribute energy throughout the energy dimension. These energy channels are referred to as *nadis*. Chinese psychology and medicine calls this life force *Chi*, and the Japanese call it *Ki*. The Japanese and Chinese refer to the various ener-gy channels as meridians, and use them as the template for acupuncture points.

The various systems also substantially agree on major energy centers that are distributed throughout the energy dimension. These centers, called *chakras*, represent powerful centers of control. The actual chakras exist at the subtle inter-sect of the spiritual and mental dimensions. They are not physical centers, and contrary to what many people think, cannot be located or found anywhere in the body. Chakras are the point through which spiritual energy is transformed into mental energy, and from mental energy into *prana* or *chi*. They are the format-ting templates for the mind and provide the foundation for the physical activities of the body. A genuine yoga master will have complete knowledge of these ener-gy centers, and as a consequence, can demonstrate remarkable controls over both mind and body. A typical representation of the major chakras and their relation-ship to powerful neural plexus, the control centers for the body, are shown in Figure 1.2.

We derive energy from a variety of sources – food, sleep, sunlight. But the most important source of energy is the breath. We can go without food for weeks, without water for days, but we can live only a few moments without breathing. This alone makes breathing the critical power function of this dimension. Because of this critical function, breathing has become so much a part of us that as long as we aren't deprived, we pay little attention to it. We don't realize that the way we breathe plays a critical role in self-mastery.

Figure 1.2
NEURAL PLEXUS AND CHAKRAS

**Diagram of Nerve Plexus**          **Diagram of Chakras**

**Autonomic Nervous System**

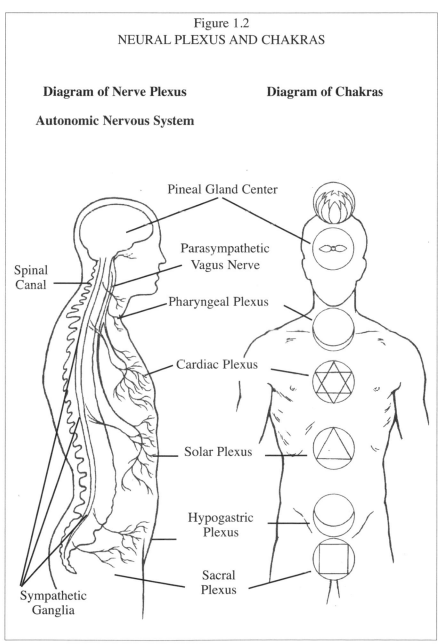

Pineal Gland Center

Parasympathetic
Vagus Nerve

Spinal
Canal

Pharyngeal Plexus

Cardiac Plexus

Solar Plexus

Hypogastric
Plexus

Sacral
Plexus

Sympathetic
Ganglia

All traditions of self-mastery spend significant effort in studying the breath. Each tradition has an extensive repertoire of breathing exercises they use to develop a sophisticated control over the breathing process. Through these sophisticated exercises, they develop a high degree of control over what happens in the body.

Often this control seems miraculous. In *Beyond Biofeedback,* Elmer Green, formerly Director of the Voluntary Controls Laboratory at the Menninger Clinic in Topeka, Kansas, and his wife, Alyce Green, reported on laboratory research on my tantra yoga master, Swami Rama. Under laboratory conditions, he demonstrated remarkable control over his body. In different experiments, he:

• consciously and intentionally stopped his heart from pumping blood by creating arterial fibrillation in which his heart fluttered at 300 beats per minute;

• simultaneously lowered the temperature at one point on his hand five degrees while raising the temperature five degrees at another point on his hand only millimeters away;

• voluntarily controlled the production of different brain waves;

• was fully conscious of what was happening in the room while in deep sleep as evidenced by a slight gentle snoring and steady stream of Delta brain wave rhythms.

These and other experiments demonstrated absolute control of the entire nervous system achieved primarily through control of prana, the energy dimension. Yoga practitioners learn to use this underlying link between body and mind to help maintain a healthy body, as well as to help calm the mind and stabilize emotions. The yoga master uses this knowledge to eliminate cancer from his body, while the martial artist uses it to create such strength in the muscles that blows to her body have no effect.

Whether or not we learn the remarkable controls of this great yoga master is not the point. The critical issue is whether or not we learn how to use our breathing to gain greater self-mastery. While we may not reach the degree of skill demonstrated by Swami Rama, we can certainly learn to use the subtle energy dimension to maintain physical and mental balance regardless of the situations in which we find ourselves. Unfortunately, most of us have a habit of breathing that creates more work for the heart, leads to chronic stress, and often causes hypertension.

In the body, we experience imbalance and disease as physical symptoms. Within the energy dimension, we experience them as unbalanced energy. Too much energy and we become hyper, "bouncing off the walls" and unable to focus. At other times, we feel low on energy, maybe even depressed, and barely able to function. When our energy is balanced, we feel energized, ready and able to take on the world. The more we understand about this level of the personality, the greater our skill and the more useful it becomes. In Chapter 6, we will see that we can balance the nervous systems, take the pressure off the heart, and calm the mind by becoming skilled with breathing.

## From Life Force Energy to Mental Energy

As we move through the energy dimension, we enter the fascinating realm of the mind. Here we find the three most subtle dimensions of the personality. The mind is the instrument that we use to understand the world around us. The mind is also a field of intelligent energy that is modified or altered by its inter-action with the world. We experience these modifications as the thoughts, images, and sensations that constitute our knowledge. Unfortunately, not everything we learn is helpful to us. In fact, some of these modifications are destructive.

Don't confuse the mind with the brain. These are two very different reali-ties. The brain is a physical organ, part of the body, which serves as the control room for the mind. The brain acts as a transducer, changing the subtle energy of the mind into biochemical and neurological events that move the body. Of course, the quality of the mind's expression is greatly influenced by the condi-tion of the brain. If the brain is damaged, the mind's capacity to express itself is diminished. It doesn't matter how sophisticated your software program is – if the circuits are damaged that program will not run properly in your computer. Although the body and energy dimensions influence the mind, the real power lies in the mind.

## The Third Dimension: Sensory Mind: Creating Personal Reality

We call the third dimension of our personality the Sensory Mind because it collects, organizes, and interprets sensory data. This dimension corresponds to the software programs that run the computer. The sensory mind is a busy, noisy place filled with sensory stimulation, emotions, wants and desires, habits and feelings. Its primary job is to interpret the world around us, and to create a personal sense of reality, the matrix through which we view the world. Just like the software program organizes meaningful patterns from data input, the sensory mind makes meaningful patterns of sensory input. It does this through four power functions:

1. Perception      2. Language
3. Emotions      4. Habits

The perceptual process is a reality generator. We collect information through the senses, and organize it into meaningful patterns. A single act of per-ception involves a complex mixture of many different events. Our memory, beliefs, and expectations as well as our constitution, genetic inheritance, state of health, and level of stress all act as filters which shape and color our perceptions, and determine the quality of our experience. More important, in order to struc-ture sensory input, the sensory mind creates our experience of space and time. The sensory mind is also where we experience pain and pleasure. All these fac-tors lead to a unique reality for each individual. Two people sitting in the same room, having the same experience, will see and interpret that experience in high-ly individual ways, and will not always agree as to what really happened.

As we organize sensory stimulation through the perceptual process, language plays a key role. The words we use actually define the personal reality in which we live. A favorite story of mine illustrates this point very clearly. In the clubhouse, three umpires were discussing the pending World Series game. The youngest, proud of being selected to participate in the World Series, bragged to his colleagues: "I never worry about mistakes. I call them as I see them."

The other two umpires laughed, and the middle-aged umpire retorted: "Well, you're still a little wet behind the ears. I call them as they are!"

The old umpire just smiled and looked out the window.

"What are you smiling at?" the middle-aged umpire asked his elder.

"Well," said the old wise one. "It seems as if there are two here who are still a little wet behind the ears. They are what I call them."

Life, too, is what we call it. A particular event in our life can be good or bad, exciting or dull, awful or wonderful. We are not really describing the actual event, but what that event *means* to us. Our personal reality is made up of the meanings we give to things, the values we assign. Language is the tool we use to create meaning. Once we give an interpretation with the words we use, we are stuck with the consequences of our interpretations. Much of the unhappiness that we create for ourselves happens in just this way. We don't realize the impact that our language has, nor do we know how to use language as a tool to help ourselves.

The interpretations we make determine our emotional reactions. In turn, our emotional reactions distort our perceptions, interfere with thinking, lead to conflicts, and create disease. Many of us feel like victims of our emotions, and yet, we alone create them. The problem is a lack of awareness and skill. We aren't aware of our unconscious patterns until after we react. Once we react, it becomes increasingly difficult to redirect all this emotional energy into useful channels.

We need emotional energy to succeed and enjoy life. Our emotions stimulate, challenge, and motivate us to accomplish what we want. We become impassioned and inspired; we persist in difficult tasks until we reach our goal; we focus and become intensely involved – all because of emotional energy. Or we become depressed and withdrawn, anxious and afraid, create misery and unhappiness, and interfere with our own success. It all depends on our level of skill.

Whether we use our emotions to help or hurt ourselves depends a great deal on our habits, the fourth function of the sensory mind. Habits are one of the most deeply-rooted and pervasive functions of the mind. We express our entire personality through habits. They regulate every aspect of our life from the most trivial, such as which part of the body we wash first in a shower, to the most profound, such as the skills of a neurosurgeon.

Habits dominate the three outer levels of the personality – sensory mind, energy, and body. We have driving habits, eating habits, habits of walking and of talking. The way our blood flows and whether or not we tense our muscles are controlled by habit. How we react, feel, even how we think are all regulated by the power of habit. All skills – typing, playing handball, managing, talking, musical skills – are determined and controlled by habit. Sexual activity is controlled by habit. The friends we choose, the work we do, the clothes we wear – all controlled by habit. Of course our actions involve many other factors, such as other power functions of the mind, genetics, and the environment. But habits provide the structure of what we think, what we do, and how we react. Habits allow us to live skillfully and usefully. Habits can also kill us.

Some habits can have serious, even deadly consequences. Taking drugs, driving recklessly, and eating poorly are only a few of the more obvious ones. All of us have habits which result in chronic stress. Knowing that habits may be either useful or damaging is not enough. We must also learn how to bring the power of conditioning under our control and eliminate those habits that create problems for us.

The problem lies in the fact that we didn't consciously choose most of our habits, and many of these are destructive because they feed the three dragons of our mind. However, as we will see later, habits are the power behind our skill. If we take control of this powerful function of the mind, we can build habits that help us create a healthy body and mind instead of chronic conditions of stress, unhappiness, and disease.

The disturbances in our life – the fear, guilt, loneliness, and the consequent stress – create suffering through the power functions of the three outer dimensions of body, energy, and sensory mind. Any time we worry, berate ourselves, or feel lonely, isolated or abandoned, all three dimensions are affected. But these affects are like a storm at sea. When the wind blows, it creates waves and currents that can be dangerous to a ship on the surface of the sea. But below the surface, the water remains calm and undisturbed. The deeper you go, the more quiet and calm it becomes. The body, energy, and sensory mind are like the upper levels and surface of the sea called life. Disturbances are like storms that create all sorts of dangerous conditions. The body, like the surface waves of the sea, is always dramatically affected. The mind is like the great moving currents below the surface that give direction to the waves, and the energy dimension is that exchange between these powerful currents and the surface, which allows waves to form. If we only know how to remain on the surface of the personality, we have no recourse but to weather whatever storms come.

The deeper we go into personality, the greater the calm will be regardless of how stormy the sea of life becomes. The three deepest, most subtle dimensions of our identity are never disturbed no matter how intense our emotional disturbances become. If we access the resources of these dimensions and use them skillfully, we maintain control of ourselves no matter what kind of crisis we face.

### The Fourth Dimension: Discrimination & the Power of Inner Wisdom

Deep within every mind is the capacity to know the truth, to understand reality as it is. This capacity is known as the discriminating mind. At this subtle level, the mind has the power to discern cause/effect relationships, to distinguish between what is real and what seems real. Discrimination is the quiet realization that for all the promises and planning, the project you are working on is not going to get off the ground, or that the contract will be signed even though it appears unlikely now. This is the power of knowledge, the capacity to know the truth, to understand reality as it really is, not as we have learned to think it is. This dimension corresponds to the language dimension of a computer system. Just as computer language determines what the program will be, the power of discrimination determines what reality is.

The discriminating mind allows us to think things out, to analyze situations effectively and make choices. When we don't use it, we act solely on habit. For instance, if we go to a movie every Saturday night, we don't really make a decision, we act out of habit. We use our discrimination only to pick the movie. However, if we make a conscious decision about what to do—visit friends, go dancing, or take in a movie—then we use the power of discrimination. Using discrimination, we make decisions on the basis of information and reasoning rather than from habit.

On a deeper level, discrimination provides us with intuition: insight into the real consequences of our actions. Our inner wisdom allows us to make the right kinds of choices, preventing regret and guilt often created through hasty action. We have all had the experience of doing something that we were convinced was right. But before we did it, a small, quiet voice inside our head said, "Better not do that." We paused for just a moment, but then our desires, wants, wishes, or fears reasserted themselves and told us that, "Of course this is the right thing to do. Haven't we planned it all out? Come on, let's get on with it." We went ahead with our plan, and three days later everything fell apart, and we immediately thought, "I knew I shouldn't have done that." And we did know. We just didn't know how to listen to the discriminating mind.

The emotional disturbances in the mind cannot directly affect the discriminating mind, but they certainly can distract us and prevent us from using it effectively. This dimension of the mind is very subtle and quiet. When the sensory mind is noisy and active, it can easily bury the subtle voice of our wisdom. Distracted by our desires and fears, and locked into our habits, it becomes difficult to access and listen to that still, quiet inner voice. The more disturbances we have, the more difficult it is to think things through, to discern the subtle cause/effect relationships in our choices and actions.

The key to wisdom lies in our ability to create a deeply calm and quiet mind through concentration. In the tantric tradition, as in other traditions of self-mastery, we first learn to bring balance and flexibility to the body, stabilize our energy, and calm the noisy sensory mind. Then the emphasis of the training begins to shift as we learn to develop insight into the nature of things. The discriminating mind is pure intellect, unsullied by the distortions of emotions, and free from the space/time constraints of the sensory mind. In tantra yoga, a variety of techniques and approaches are used to access and develop the power of this pure intellect. As we become more aware of this power of discrimination, and more skilled in its use, we make better decisions and avoid many of the troubles that we would normally create for ourselves.

## The Three States of Knowledge

The power functions of the Sensory Mind and the Discriminating Mind create three different kinds of knowledge: critical thinking (reasoning, analyzing, etc.), instinct, and intuition. Of the three, we are most familiar with and dependent on critical thinking. Our educational system is based on critical thinking and is supposedly designed to enhance it. Whether this happens or not is another question. Critical thinking involves perspective, and is accomplished through a combination of the sensory function and discrimination. Of the three states of knowledge, critical thinking is the most error prone. As a consequence, a variety of logical systems have been designed to minimize error in the thinking process.

The second knowledge state is instinct. Instinct is hard-wired in the perceptual system, and is the mind's ability to tell us immediately what is in our environment that will either help us or hurt us. Since it is based on sensory data, instinct is a recognition process rather than analytic. We don't have to *think* about what is dangerous or helpful, we *recognize* what is dangerous or helpful. Instinct can tell us who to trust and who not to trust, when to move and when to not move. As we will see later, refining perceptual sensitivity enhances our ability to use instinctual knowledge.

The third knowledge state, intuition, is accomplished in an entirely different way than the other two states of knowledge. As we discussed above, intuition arises out of the power of discrimination, or pure intellect. Intuitive knowledge is knowledge through identity. In other words, the mind, through the power function of discrimination, becomes the object or reality it contemplates, and understands this object or reality from the inside out.

Like instinct, intuition is a non-analytical process; unlike instinct, it is not limited to sensory input. The most familiar application of this form of knowledge is the learning we achieve through modeling. As we will see later, intuition is the highest form of knowledge, but often so subtle that it is easily overlooked.

These three states of knowledge are designed to complement each other. Created differently in the mind, they have different purposes, and provide complementary ways of understanding the reality around us. When we only rely on one, we create an incomplete understanding of reality, and are far less effective than we could be.

## The Fifth Dimension: Balance and Confidence

At the center of our mind lies the fifth and most subtle dimension, the balanced state. Here, the mind's energy is in a state of pure harmony and balance, and not yet modified into patterns of thought and knowledge. In this condition of purity, it is beyond the influence of language, emotions and habits, and totally unaffected by any external disturbance. This dimension corresponds to the potential of computer language before it is written into specific instructions.

When we become conscious of this dimension, we experience a profound peace and harmony that has nothing to do with pain or pleasure. We experience complete freedom from any and all conflicts, needs and desires, worry, and anxiety. At this level of our personality, we are at peace with ourselves and the world. This center of tranquility is the source of genuine self-confidence.

Much of the stress that we experience stems from fear and worry. In other words, stress is often the result of a failure of self-confidence. The less confident we are, the more we worry and berate ourselves. The more worry and failure we create, the less confident we feel. We become caught in a vicious circle of negative reinforcement. Yet, each of us has an inner resource of complete self-confidence that lies unaffected by failure and disaster. Every human being is born with this center of confidence and inner strength. However, distracted by the noisy sensory mind, we often don't recognize it, nor do we learn how to tap this enormous resource.

We do experience this pure confidence from time to time. Recall a time when you were out for a walk. You might have been strolling around the neighborhood, or along the beach, or in a forest. More than likely you were by yourself, but not necessarily. All of a sudden, you felt as if "God's in his heaven – All's right with the world," an overwhelming experience of complete contentment. The experience didn't last longer than a few moments, but for that brief time, you were completely free of any worry and self-doubt. You felt absolutely wonderful and content.

Now this didn't happen because you won the lottery, or were taking some kind of drug. In fact, very likely nothing at all had changed in your life. You still had the same job, the same bills, and the same problems to resolve. All of the elements that constantly create stress in your life remained unchanged. But those few moments had a profound impact, and you went home refreshed, ready to tackle the world again.

The magic was all you. You did it by relaxing, quieting the noisy chatter in your mind, and allowing your mind to focus inwardly. You became conscious of your own calm center, which was always there. What if you could access this strength anytime you needed it? What if, right in the middle of a difficult situation, you could simply drop your gaze, focus inwardly for a moment, and experience this inner harmony? How would this ability affect your level of confidence and the amount of stress you experience? The balanced mind, the deepest, most subtle dimension of the mind, provides the inner strength we need to face life without disturbance, with unshakable self-confidence and fearlessness. It is a matter of awareness, access, and skill.

## Ego: Managing The Five Dimensions

The most powerful and pervasive power function of the mind is the individualizing force called Ego. This is not the weak and embattled Freudian ego conceptualized by so much of Western psychology. Here ego is the power function that creates a center of consciousness, an identity that says, "I am this and not that." Ego is the sense of I-ness that permeates the personality. We will focus on the mental function of ego, but it also has implications on the most profound spiritual levels.

The ego's purpose is to establish boundaries, to provide us with a personality center, and to maintain the personality as an integral whole. As manager of the personality system, it must coordinate the different dimensions of the personality, organizing and directing the different power functions of the different dimensions. In so doing, it creates an identity, a sense of ownership and definition that allows us to say that this is mine and that is yours. This is *my* body, these are *my* thoughts, this is *my* spouse, these are *my* children, this is *my* car, *my* house, *my* job, *my* wealth – all relating to me, my, and mine. We will explore the ego, its proper role, and its shenanigans in a later chapter. Suffice it to say here that this function is the most powerful in the structure of mind and body.

## The Sixth Dimension: The Spiritual Center of Control

The owner/operator of a computer is an independent force that decides how the computer is going to be used. The sixth dimension corresponds to the owner/operator of the computer. The human mind and body are complex instruments with a great many resources. But there is a spiritual core beyond the mind and body that we must acknowledge, experience, and learn to use. The mind/body complex has tremendous resources, but the final power lies in the Self, the spiritual force that uses the personality as a tool. Depending on your perspective and beliefs, you may call it the soul, higher power, or center of consciousness. We will simply call this ultimate decision-maker the spiritual Self. Unless we access and experience this indomitable spiritual core, we cannot gain our final freedom from the dragons of the mind nor achieve self-mastery.

In an address to the Congress of the United States, Vaclav Havel, the playwright who became the first president of a democratized Czech Republic, spoke eloquently about the power of the human heart. In speaking of what he learned from his struggles for freedom, Mr. Havel said, "The salvation of this human world lies nowhere else than in the human heart, in the human power to reflect, in human meekness, and in human responsibility."

To paraphrase Mr. Havel, our ability to live without fear, self-hatred, and loneliness ultimately depends on our developing the power of the human spirit, our innate ability to love, to be compassionate, to live fearlessly. This power resides in the spiritual Self. Whether we express this human spirit in religious or philosophical beliefs is a matter of choice. But to truly experience the power of this spiritual core, we need self-knowledge and skill.

When we act in ways that are counter to our human spirit, we create the most subtle and pervasive kind of suffering. We seldom recognize the price we pay when our actions are inconsistent with our values and beliefs. It affects not only the relationship we have with ourselves, but also with others. If we are distrustful, spiteful, egotistical, this not only creates problems in our relationships, but also creates weakness and stress within our own personality. Inner strength depends on personal integrity, the ability to be consistent with our own values. When we stand up for what we believe, not only do we strengthen our will, we also experience self-respect and inner strength. On the other hand, if we act in ways inconsistent with our own humanity and beliefs, we create inconsistencies in the mind that lead to feelings of guilt and weakness.

We all have experiences that allow us to touch in some small way this spiritual core. We often refer to them as "peak experiences." They may happen when we witness the birth of our child, or when we watch a beautiful sunset or sunrise. A surprisingly large number of people have had a "mystical experience," an experience so powerful that it alters the way they look at and experience life. For some, it happens when they have a close brush with death, often referred to as a "near-death experience," and have actually experienced dying and being brought back to life. For others, it happens during a religious retreat after long days of silence and prayer. Still others seem to have them by accident, not knowing what precipitated their experience. Probably the most famous of these is the incident of Saul, the great menace to the early Christian community. As he rode his donkey to Damascus, Saul was struck by lightening (a poetic way of saying he had a profound mystical experience) and became Paul, the great Christian prophet and saint.

Taking a chance with a near-death experience is not a very bright idea, and even if we get on an ass and ride the back roads of Syria, it is highly improbable that we will be hit by lightening and have a mystical experience. Fortunately, the meditative traditions provide the systematic methodology where anyone who makes the effort can develop their capacity for this experience and the knowledge that it brings. The tantric masters know that this powerful experience can be the fulcrum for the achievement of self-mastery. The tantric tradition is dedicated to the personal mastery of this spiritual core. Because it is the highest of all human experiences, there are no simple and quick exercises or techniques on the way to enlightenment.

But as we gain in self-mastery, as we become more balanced, stronger and achieve greater insight, we acquire the capacity to experience this powerful spiritual Self. Because of the necessary preparation it takes, the specific exercises that will ultimately lead to this powerful spiritual experience are given in the final chapters.

## SELF-MASTERY AND THE WHOLE PERSON

We cannot separate ourselves into parts. We come as a complete package. Any action we take involves all dimensions of the personality— physical, mental, and spiritual. Turn back to the beginning of this chapter and go through the Traveling Exercise again. This time, be aware of the different power functions at each level. Don't try to change them, or use them in any particular way. Just pay attention and become more familiar with how they operate within your personality.

As you go through the exercise and become more relaxed and focused, worries, fears, guilt, and other disturbances will disappear. This is because we are most natural when we are relaxed and focused. And unlike the different power functions within each dimension, the disturbances aren't a natural part of the personality. We weren't born fearful, self-critical, or lonely. These are only habits of the mind, not innate functions. When we simply observe the natural dimensions of our personality, destructive disturbances are quieted, and remain hidden in our habits, striking out at the most inconvenient times. Before we can claim self-mastery and take charge of our power, we must find what these disturbances are, and understand how they steal our inner strength. In confronting our habits of fear, guilt, and loneliness, we will see how to take their power away, and use it to create harmony, joy, and love in our lives.

2

# TROUBLE IN PARADISE:
# STRESS AND THE DRAGONS OF THE MIND

*Self-reverence, self-knowledge, self-control,*
*These three alone lead life to sovereign power.*
—Alfred, Lord Tennyson—

With all this inner power, why don't we do better? It seems as if there are a zillion things that can disturb us. There is a child's game in a box that has twelve to sixteen holes in the cover. Suddenly a head pops up out of a hole and you whack it with a club. And then suddenly another head pops up from a different hole for you to whack. Life's difficulties are like that. We solve one problem when another raises its ugly head up to disturb us. No matter how many problems we whack, another one jumps right up, and we must jump from one disturbance to another. There often seems to be no place where we can rest.

Instead of harmony, we have disharmony. We live in a pressure cooker culture, and everywhere we turn, there are problems to solve, dangers to face, and bills to pay. All of which is accompanied by emotional reactions and disturbances. At the end of the day, we collapse into bed, with a racing mind, still trying to solve the day's problems. When we finally get to sleep, we toss and turn, unable to sleep peacefully. The next day, it all begins again. Some days are better than others, but we never really know why, and we certainly don't seem to have much choice about the matter. We are troubled and worried, and endure a variety of physical and emotional ills – headaches, high blood pressure, anxiety, depression, and worry. By external standards we are a very successful culture, but for the most part, we find life unsatisfying, troubling, and unhealthy.

STRESS: THE DIS-EASE OF MODERN LIFE

We all know about stress. At least, we think we do. Since the mid-1970s, "stress" has become a household name. For almost thirty years we have been inundated with information about stress. You would think that we would have solved this problem by now. But for all books, seminars, articles, and experts, we haven't even begun to solve the problem. If anything, life is even more complicated and dangerous, with greater pressures and higher levels of stress. Our ability to reduce these pressures has diminished, not increased. By any measure, we are doing a lousy job of handling stress.

Why haven't we solved this problem? We don't understand what we are dealing with, and much of what we are told about stress is simply not true. Ask the average person what stress is and you usually hear a list of things that "cause stress" – bills, deadlines, coworkers, bosses, teenagers, taxes, government, traffic delays (the list is endless); or they list symptoms – frustration, anger, sleeplessness, headaches, anxiety, high blood pressure (again, the list is almost endless). Almost everyone talks about good stress and bad stress, and a few even mention the fight-or-flight alarm reaction. The consensus is that stress is part of life, and that everyone suffers from it. With all the theories and information, nothing seems to help us very much.

## The Myths About Stress

Part of the problem we face is that what the experts tell us is confusing, misleading, and powerless. The dominant theory about stress involving the fight-or-flight alarm reaction is, at best, only partially true, and riddled with myths and 18th-century thinking. The reality is that stress is uniquely different from what we normally think of as disease. It doesn't have a single source, it's not a germ or virus, and it doesn't have a unique symptom. Stress is literally a dis-ease, an inner systems imbalance that we create and maintain *within* the body and mind. Stress is psychosomatic in the true sense of the word – involving both mind and body. Its source is in the patterns and habits of our lifestyle, a consequence of how we regulate, rather, how we do *not* regulate our mind and body. *We create stress when we mismanage our own inner resources.*

Myth: Stress is something that happens to us.
Truth: Stress is our reaction to the things that happen to us.

When we look for the cause of stress in the world around us, we are looking in the wrong place. The world can be a difficult place, no doubt. There are dragons in the world, and tragedy can strike at any time. But during times of great tragedy, human beings come together, and people show courage, strength, and leadership. During these times we suffer loss, unhappiness and grief, as individuals, as families, and as a community and nation. Even though these are trying times, they are not stress. But if these events leave us fearful, feeling victimized, suffering from unresolved grief and guilt, than we use these events as a source to create stress.

The truth is that stress never happens to us, it is our reaction to the things that happen to or around us that creates stress. Stress happens, or is created, inside of us. The bad news is: *We are the source of our own stress.* We can never point to another person, a situation, some event or "thing" in our environment and say, "That is stress." Contrary to what we may wish to believe about our work, the time pressures we face, or even our spouse, they are not stress. Even tragedies, the great and the small, which all human beings must face, are not stress. They may well be powerful events in our life, but they are not stress. Stress exists in only one place, and that is within ourselves. Many of us don't like to hear that, but only when we understand this do we have any chance to control and eliminate stress.

We cannot control the world around us. Goodness knows, we try. We build armies, make laws, buy insurance, sign contracts, invest, and become union members. But does all this really protect us from stress? No matter how hard we try, we cannot protect ourselves from change, from events, from life itself.

We feel powerless to control the events in life because we often are. No one has that control no matter how much wealth or power they have. Life provides us with endless opportunities to be unhappy, to be fearful, to experience pain. The more secure we try to become by changing the world, the more fear we create, the more insecure we feel, and the more stress we create for ourselves. When we blame outside circumstances for the stress we feel, we deny our own power and become victims.

While we have very little control over what happens to us, we have infinite capacity to develop control over how we react to those events. The good news is: *We are the source of our own stress.* If we have the power to create stress and unhappiness, we also have the power not to create stress and unhappiness. We don't have to become victims – of circumstance, of attack, of change or anything else. We can do something to help ourselves. I may not have the power to stop some deranged human being from taking my life, but no one has the power to make me afraid or feel like a victim. Only I can do that.

We may not have a choice as to *what* we have to deal with, but we always have the choice as to *how* we deal with it. We can either deal with events in ways that strengthen us or we can be fearful victims and suffer constantly. And as long as we look for causes and solutions outside of ourselves, we remain fearful victims, and will never solve this problem called stress.

Myth: There is good stress (Eustress) and bad stress (Distress).
Truth: All stress harms the body and closes down mind resources.

Stress experts talk about good stress and bad stress, yet not a single one can tell you the difference between good stress and bad stress except in terms of the consequences. When we are excited about something, and motivated to accomplish a task, that is called "good stress." When we have a headache, or suffer from an ulcer or a heart attack, then it's called "bad stress." Saying that there is good stress and bad stress is like saying there are good heart attacks and bad heart attacks. Bad heart attacks are fatal, while good heart attacks only damage your heart, giving you the opportunity to have another.

Let's say that you go jogging. You exercise your body, increase your heart rate, and make your muscles work. You come home feeling refreshed and alive. Then someone says to you, "See, you have good stress." The next day you go jogging and suffer a heart attack. While you are lying in the grass, that same person comes up to you and says, "Now you suffer from bad stress."

You have good stress when good things happen, and bad stress when bad things happen. Unfortunately, you can't tell the difference until after the heart attack, the ulcer, the headache, or the consequence of poor decisions. Some people say that it's a matter of too much or too little stress. But how do you distinguish between enough stress and too much? Only after you have the heart attack, or some other symptom of stress.

You end up playing a game of stress roulette. If you win, it's called good stress and you get to play the game again. If you lose, it's called bad stress and you end up in the coronary care unit. Not a very useful way of understanding stress, nor is it valid scientific theory. This approach has no power to predict whether stress is good or bad until after the fact. More importantly, this approach is powerless. It provides absolutely no tools or insight into how to resolve the stress we experience, let alone prevent it. Altogether, this prevalent theory of stress is useless, powerless and of little value to anyone.

The experts rely on laboratory research. But laboratory research is a highly defined, very narrow, and constricted piece of behavior. It isolates variables and ignores the matrix in which every variable must exist. Science is very powerful, but also very limited.

If we limit our understanding to scientific research, we limit our understanding of reality. If we look to our own experience, if we explore our inner reality, we find a very different story: *Whenever we create stress, we have changes in our body that are destructive and lead to disease, we interfere with our ability to think clearly, and we limit our creative abilities. No one ever benefits from stress.*

Myth: The fight-or-flight alarm reaction is designed by nature to
   protect us.
Truth: The fight-or-flight alarm reaction is the body's reaction to fear
   in the mind.

This myth goes hand-in-hand with idea of good and bad stress. The fight-or-flight alarm reaction is the body's reaction to fear in the mind. This reaction is incredibly stressful to the body, closes down the mind, and interferes with action. Depending on how intense the reaction is, the changes in the body may last as long as two or three weeks. Each and every time we worry or become fearful, we create some degree of this stressful reaction. It was never designed by nature to protect us. In fact, it can lead to immobilization and death.

The real protective response provided by nature is a very powerful innate drive called self-preservation. As we shall see later, when self-preservation dominates the mind, the body and mind are in a perfect state of balance. Our sense of time is altered (things appear to be happening in slow-motion), the mind is clear and fully alert, and you know what to do without thinking about it. This is very different from a fight-or-flight alarm reaction.

This confusion about the fight-or-flight mechanism being helpful is the direct consequence of trying to understand human qualities from the outside in, rather than the inside out. Those who make these theories are unaware of their own inner realities, and consequently, speculate from laboratory research that is incomplete and inaccurate to the human condition. The consequence is that we remain powerless to control stress.

Myth: Human beings are born with fear, and fear often protects us.
Truth: Fear is always destructive to the human mind and body.

No human being is born with fear. We are born with the powerful drive called self-preservation, designed by nature to protect us. Fear is nothing more, or less, than a habit. We learn to be fearful. Fear always leads to stress, and when intense, can paralyze us physically and mentally. Fear is the mind-killer. It is a disaster to the human being.

Fear is the most common way we create stress for ourselves. When we believe that fear is a necessary part of being alive, that all human beings are born with fear, we condemn ourselves to a life of stress, disease, and unhappiness. This is totally unnecessary. We have far more power than that.

As we shall see later, it's not difficult to understand the subtle difference between fear and the innate drive called self-preservation. Nor are the tools and techniques we need to free ourselves from this terrible habit difficult to learn or to use. We have the capacity to live without fear; we do need to acquire the self-knowledge and skill to do so.

Myth: We need stress to achieve optimum performance.
Truth: Stress always interferes with performance.

This myth is particularly prevalent among those who wish to control others – governments, religions, supervisors, bosses, and people who feel they must control someone else's behavior. Far too many supervisors, managers, and bosses use fear as a management tool. They think that if they "put the fear of God" in their employees, they get more work from them.

Unfortunately, this myth has some truth to it. You can control people, up to a point, with fear. And if a boss or manager uses fear to motivate employees, they often do work harder. But what happens tomorrow? The vast body of research literature in behavior and productivity leads to the same conclusion. Fear causes an immediate increase in productivity quickly followed by an even greater decrease. Fearful employees soon become hostile, angry, and resentful, all of which damage morale and interfere with productivity. The rapid increase in productivity is short-lived, but hostility, fear, and resentment continue for long periods of time, reducing overall productivity and quality.

It's amazing how many managers, parents, and other authorities have no awareness of the long-term negative consequences of fear. When I hear the boss or manager talk about putting their people under pressure to get better performance, I know that the long-term prospects for their department or business are very bleak. *No one wins through intimidation.*

Fear in a culture inhibits the creative force in that culture. The more fearful people are, the less they reach out to help each other, the less they commit their own resources – intelligence, creativity, problem solving, compassion – to the culture. Simply look at which countries in the world are leading in innovation, in the arts, in any endeavor. These are countries that value freedom of expression, and enjoy personal and political freedom. Those nations led by dictators of any kind are joyless, backwards, and suffering. The real resources of the people are suppressed with fear, rigidity, and suffer from poverty of thought and expression.

Still others think that if they put themselves under pressure, they will do better. They confuse being stressed with being challenged. The arousal or excitement we feel when challenged does not lead to stress. We need challenge in life to excel, to reach heights of performance that we would not normally reach. This is very healthy for us. Without challenges, life becomes rather dull and meaningless. In fact, lack of challenge is a significant source of stress for those who feel regimented in their work.

On the other hand, when we are fearful, which is emotionally and physically different than feeling challenged, the arousal we experience is stressful. Our bodies tense, and our minds become clouded. We don't feel well, or think clearly, and life becomes more and more miserable. The more fearful we are, the more unbalanced we become, and the more stress we experience.

Myth: I don't have stress.
Truth: We all unnecessarily create stress for ourselves.

I never thought I had stress either. I had pressure, I had a few minor health problems, but I didn't have any stress. After all, I have a Ph.D. in psychology. I certainly wouldn't have stress. This way of thinking is all too familiar. Many of us deny any stress because:

1. Real men don't have stress;
2. I am superwoman, I can (have to) do it all;
3. Only weak people can't cope with pressure;
4. We are unconscious of the reality of our life.

There are few people in our society who are genuinely really free from stress. These are individuals with a high degree of self-knowledge and self-discipline. Self-mastery is the path to freedom from stress. It doesn't matter how many degrees you have, or how much money you have, stress is in all probability a significant part of your life. The most dangerous part of stress is that often you don't even know you have it. You become accustomed to a certain level of chronic stress, and it begins to feel normal, a part of everyday life. You even believe that some stress is good for you. In reality, this unconscious and constant level of unrelieved "normal" stress often leads to disease.

## Psychosomatic Disease: Mind/Body Disharmony

The disharmony in our lives reflects the disharmony within ourselves. Medical researchers are finally recognizing the fact that our minds and lifestyles have a great deal to do with whether or not we stay healthy. Consider the following research facts:

• Of those patients who visit a physician with one of the ten most common symptoms, only sixteen percent have symptoms with clear organic causes. That means that over eighty percent are seeing a doctor for psychosocial reasons that medicines and drugs cannot resolve.

• Researchers find that daily small pleasurable events, such as a pleasant family celebration or having friends over, strengthen the immune system for the next one or two days. On the other hand, unpleasant daily experiences, such as work pressures or an argument with your spouse, weaken the immune system on the day of the event.

• When you are unable to let go of your daily grind, your health suffers. Researchers report that men who are incapable of relaxing after work have an increased risk of heart attack nearly three times greater than those who say they can relax and forget about their work. Even for those with slower paced jobs, the inability to relax was associated with increased risk of heart disease.

• Health is grounded in an optimistic, joyful approach to life. Research shows that those who are able to create a strong sense of belonging and connection with others have fewer diseases and less stress. Those who have altruistic beliefs and behavior are more resistant to stress and chronic disease.

Physicians and health-care experts generally agree that a high percentage (perhaps as high as seventy to eighty percent) of our diseases are psychosomatic. The term "psychosomatic" is composed of two terms: *psyche* meaning mind and *soma* meaning body. This does not mean that our symptoms (such as ulcer pain or a headache) are imaginary; they are certainly real enough, and real physiological changes do occur. Nor does it mean that we are neurotic. The term psychosomatic means that emotional, mental, and behavioral habits play a subtle but critical role in determining health. In other words, our personalities and lifestyles lead to actual physiological conditions that can lead to increased health or allow disease to develop.

A new area of research called psychoneuro-immunology, the study of the influence of the mind and emotions through the nervous system on the immune system, is just beginning. Researchers examine how depression inhibits our immune system and opens the way to cancer, and how anger and cynicism play a key role in the development of heart disease.

But then, the opposite is also true. If we become aware of how the mind and body work together, and become skilled in using the mind to direct our emotions, we can heal or minimize many of the diseases we suffer, and even prevent many of them from developing.

My own experience of developing bleeding ulcers by the time I was twenty-five is a classic example. I was highly competitive, tended to worry a lot and found it difficult to openly express my feelings. Added to this psychological mix was the quart of cola I drank every day and a diet rich in fried foods eaten on the run. The stress created by my personality traits and my lifestyle habits resulted in high blood pressure and an ulcer. When I finally took charge of my resources, altered my diet, became skilled in relaxation, breathing, and meditation, my ulcers and high blood pressure disappeared and never returned.

If I hadn't learned to use my own resources properly, medication, a rigid diet, even surgery would have become necessary. And if I had attended to the early symptoms, I could have prevented the ulcer from ever developing. A disease doesn't just happen to us. It is the end result of a series of events that eventually culminate in the disease. But we often overlook the early stages of the disease process. Consequently, the final stage is seen as an entity unto itself, having little relationship to our living habits and patterns. We miss the opportunity to prevent the disease and the suffering and expense that go along with it. This pattern describes the most deadly disease in America.

## An Affair of the Heart

One out of every two deaths in the USA is caused by some form of heart or vascular disease. The costs of this disease in medical and personal terms are enormous.

Heart and vascular disease are classic psychosomatic diseases. We may inherit a genetic weakness, but that inherited weakness does not automatically mean an early death. Whether or not we develop heart disease is most often determined by the choices we consciously and unconsciously make. We have known for years that our personality characteristics (worrying, inability to communicate, hostility, anger, cynicism, impatience) and our lifestyle choices (diet, being a workaholic, or lack of exercise) are the primary causes of heart disease.

In the late 1950s, Mayer Friedman and Ray Rosenman made us aware of the Type A and Type B personalities. In the 1980s, researchers at the National Institutes of Health found that the necessary element for heart disease to develop was "emotional toxicity," or how we react emotionally to the events in our life. More recently, in *Is It Worth Dying For*, Dr. Robert Eliot talks about the "hot reactor," the individual who reacts to stressful situations with extreme cardiovascular actions. Under pressured situations, the hot reactor's body produces large amounts of stress chemicals, which create changes in the cardiovascular system including drastic increases in blood pressure. Eliot estimates that one out of every five people, regardless of whether or not they are a Type A or Type B, is a hot reactor, and most don't know it.

Some commentators take issue with the fact that we are "responsible" for our disease. They confuse the word "responsibility" with "blame." This is clearly not what is meant here, nor is that the message of Eliot or other researchers. People do not knowingly create disease for themselves. The problem is that we do so unknowingly because we are unaware of the subtle consequences of our reactions. We don't pay attention to the subtle pressures, tensions, and feelings that tell us we are out of balance with ourselves, nor do we have the skills to correct those balances and live life without them. The problem is not one of blame, but a lack of self-awareness and skill.

Take hypertension (high blood pressure) for example. This pervasive cardiovascular disease is especially dangerous because ordinarily the warnings are so subtle and slight that we don't notice them. You usually don't realize that you have it unless a doctor checks it for you. Hypertension often leads to tragic consequences – the higher the blood pressure, the higher the risk of developing hardening of the arteries, which in turn leads to heart attacks and strokes. Estimates range from twenty-five to thirty-five percent of the American public suffers from essential hypertension.

In *The Relaxation Response*, Dr. Herb Benson points out that the mechanical or physiological causes for hypertension are few. A constricted artery to the kidney is the cause of two to five percent of high blood pressure problems. Other physical causes can be pregnancy, tumors of the brain or adrenal glands, or a malfunction of the thyroid gland. However, ninety to ninety-five percent of all cases of hypertension are known as "essential hypertension" for which there is no known physiological reason.

High blood pressure is almost always a stress reaction of the vascular system and not caused by an organic disease. Because we don't know how to control our emotional reactions or maintain inner balance, we can't control our blood pressure. The doctor treats us with medication to lower our blood pressure, but that doesn't eliminate the disease or solve the problem, it only manages the symptom. If this is the only course of action you take, you are engaging in a disease maintenance program, not becoming healthy.

## The Chemical Quick-Fix Disaster

Because we don't know how to use our inner resources to solve problems, we depend on external resources. We take aspirins (consuming as much as thirty-two tons a day) to get rid of headaches, tranquilizers (used by eleven percent of the population) to ease anxiety, and alcohol (ten percent of the population is either alcoholic or a problem drinker) to ease stress and psychological pain. Yet, like blood pressure medication, these drugs only manage or alleviate symptoms. Not a single one gives us the power to resolve problems or become a skilled, joyful human being.

The internal biochemistry created by alcohol, tranquilizers or by drugs is not the same biochemistry created by balancing and relaxation exercises. Nor do chemicals provide us with insight, awareness, or skill. Needless to say, the consequences of taking drugs are not the same consequences achieved through self-mastery techniques. Aspirin and other painkillers do not cure a headache, nor do tranquilizers cure chronic anxiety. At best, they provide some relief, a little time to do something to solve your problems. When the medicine wears off, the symptoms eventually return. After all, if taking pills "cures" the disease, then why do we have to take them over and over again? Symptoms are actually warning signs that the system is out of balance. It can be dangerous to make them disappear and not deal with the cause.

It's not the use of medications, or even the glass of wine that is the problem. It is the increasing reliance on drugs to solve problems that leads to abuse and even greater problems. Far more dangerous, they often suppress the awareness and inner strength we need to alter the situations and personal tendencies that cause the problems in the first place. Instead of using drugs carefully as part of an overall program that involves training and education, we turn to drugs as a quick fix to solve every problem that comes along.

We aren't helpless. We simply aren't aware of the power we have within ourselves to be free of disease. What if we didn't react with anger and stress, but instead responded to situations with confidence, calmness, and clarity? What if we became sensitive to how our diet and our exercise (or lack of it) affect us? We can eliminate and prevent high blood pressure, we can live without tension headaches, we can heal our ulcers, and we can even eliminate cancer. And we can certainly live without alcoholism and other drug abuse problems.

An outstanding example of the power of self-mastery to solve medical problems can be found in the cardiac rehabilitation programs of Dr. Dean Ornish. He has proven with research as well as clinical practice that even arteriosclerosis, hardening of the arteries, can be reversed with the proper diet, exercise, and self-management techniques without the use of cholesterol-lowering drugs. By taking control of their own inner resources, developing new habits and new ways to respond instead of react, his patients increase both the quality and the length of their life.

But where is it written that we must wait until we have heart disease or some other problem to help ourselves? Although we might not have learned these skills growing up, no one prevents us from learning them now. Why not teach our children and ourselves how to use the power and resources that we have available to us. Now is the time to become skilled, not after the heart attack.

There is little question that stress is a critical problem, both socially and medically, for all of us. And yet, there is no reason why this should be so. There is a way to understand stress that provides us with the knowledge, tools, and resources we need to free ourselves from this terrible problem.

## STRESS: A SYSTEMS APPROACH TO KNOWLEDGE AND POWER

Our stress reactions are complex events and involve all aspects of life – physical, mental, spiritual as well as our social and environmental realities. To be effective, we must involve all dimensions and functions of who we are. We function as a complete human being, and not some machine made up of parts. In our approach to stress, we will begin with the physical body, and work our way inward. Let's see if we can't find a way to think about stress that not only fits our experience as well as our physiology, but more importantly, gives us the knowledge and power to live without creating stress for ourselves.

We can have all the theories we want about stress, but the real issue is whether or not we have the ability to control it and live without it. We need a way to think about stress that not only accurately describes what happens within us, but also provides us with the knowledge and tools to take control. Only by looking at the whole picture, to see how all dimensions of the human system function – body, mind, and spirit – will we be able to accomplish this.

### Anticipating a Threat

Let's take a time when you very likely experienced stress. Think about the time you were in your automobile and came within inches of having a very serious accident. At that moment you probably felt:
- your heart beat faster;
- dramatic changes in your breathing patterns such as fast breathing or holding your breath;
- perspiration or sweaty palms;
- nausea, possibly spasms in your gastro-intestinal tract;
- trembling or shivers;
- emotional changes such as fear or anger;
- your whole body becoming tense;
- an intense concentration or focus on what was happening.

What you felt during this close call was an intense *fight-or-flight alarm reaction*. We are told that this fight-or-flight reaction is designed by nature to protect you. Supposedly it mobilizes your body's resources to either take action to solve the problem (fight) or by running away (flight). Often the example of the caveman suddenly confronting a tiger is used to explain how the fight-or-flight is activated without thinking to either fight the tiger or run away. Unfortunately, as the theory goes, we still have this activation but no actual tigers to fight. But still, the fight-or-flight alarm reaction is designed by nature to protect us. That's the theory. Not withstanding, of course, that not a single expert has ever talked to a caveman about this.

The key to understanding this event lies in the intense focus occurring in the mind. This psychological event actually determines the kind of physiological events we experience at this time. Whenever we are confronted with danger, this intense focus is created by one of two powerful forces. One is the powerful innate drive called self-preservation. All animals, including the human animal, share four primitive, innate drives – self-preservation, food, sleep, and sex. Food and sleep are in service of self-preservation to protect the individual of the species, while sex serves to protect the species.

If self-preservation dominates the mind, we have a very different kind of experience. Have you ever had a close call in your automobile or faced some other danger or crisis, and suddenly everything began to happen in slow motion? If you recall an instance like this clearly, you will also recall that during the incident while everything was in slow motion, *you did not feel any of the changes cited above as part of the fight-or-flight alarm reaction – at that moment, you weren't fearful or worried at all*. You were relaxed, clear-minded and focused, and you did not suffer a fight-or-flight alarm reaction at that moment.

When self-preservation dominates the mind and directs your response, concentration alters the way the mind organizes sensory input, and you experience everything in slow motion. You are relaxed, alert, and ready for action. You become even more focused, and more aware of your surroundings. This relaxed alertness allows you to see and think more clearly, and to move quickly and gracefully. You are fully prepared to take any necessary action to protect yourself. Your body and mind are completely coordinated, and *there is no stress in the system*. This is self-preservation, which occurs whenever you completely focus on what is happening at the moment. Self-preservation is the mechanism that nature has provided for our protection.

On the other hand, if fear dominates the mind, you have an intense fight-or-flight alarm reaction. Your body becomes tense, less able to move quickly, your blood pressure and heart rate go up, your mind closes down and it becomes harder to think – all the typical reactions of a fight-or-flight alarm reaction. The neurological, biochemical, and psychological changes created by this alarm reaction can be so intense that it's like a big thunderstorm going off in your body. And even if you escape unscathed, the stress hormones released in the body can last as long as three or four weeks and continue to imbalance the system. You can even set the whole reaction off again by remembering the experience.

There is nothing protective about the fight-or-flight alarm reaction. It is the body's reaction to fear. The greater your fear, the more intense the fight-or-flight reaction, the greater the stress on the system, and the less capable you are of responding effectively to the problem. The fight-or-flight alarm reaction is *not* necessary. In fact, it interferes with effective action both physically and mentally, and is counter-productive in any crisis. The fight-or-flight alarm reaction is the consequence of an untrained mind, a mind dominated by fear.

Unfortunately, you don't have to face a crisis to have a fear reaction and engage the fight-or-flight alarm reaction. Every time you worry about something, anytime you feel threatened, you set off some degree of this fear reaction. It may be as innocuous as someone saying something bad about you, it may be deadlines that you face, worries and concerns about your children, even worries about the weather. It doesn't have to be a crisis. Yet, we are so used to being apprehensive that it becomes part of our everyday lives and we are unaware of how much tension we carry.

Often our actions are dominated by self-preservation during the experience – we stay calm, focused, and effective – but after the crisis is over, we suddenly feel weak, our heart races, and we become scared to death as we think about what *might* have happened. If we don't allow our mind to create the fear of "what if," there would be no fight-or-flight. We would remain calm and collected, and continue on with our life. If there is no fear, there can be no fight-or-flight alarm reaction.

## How We Usually Think of Stress

The concept of stress as fight-or-flight originated in the laboratory research of Hans Selye. In the 1950s, Selye, expanding on the work of an earlier psychologist, Walter Cannon, began to explore what happens to living organisms when they maintain a constant state of arousal. Selye was a brilliant researcher, but his thinking was conditioned by the medical and scientific beliefs of his time. One critical belief was that we could not control physiological events in the body, particularly the autonomic nervous system. And yet, we know now that this is simply not true. Unfortunately, today, fifty years later, most experts simply repeat what Selye theorized.

The fight-or-flight alarm reaction originates in our perceptions and thoughts. Whenever we think something or someone is going to harm us in any way – physically, emotionally, socially, or financially – this alarm goes off. It also goes off whenever we think someone or something that we care about is going to be hurt, such as our children, our job, our income, our position in society, even our new car. If we don't see any danger, we don't have a fight-or-flight reaction even if the danger is really there. On the other hand, if we think there is danger, even when there isn't any, we react as if there were. The intensity of our reaction depends on how great we think the danger is. Small threats, such as day-to-day worries, set off a small, limited reaction. Big threats, such as the possibility of being fired or a near-miss in an automobile, set off reactions that involve the endocrine system and last for several days, or even weeks.

The entire fight or flight alarm reaction consists of four stages:

**Alarm Stage**: The Fight-or-Flight Alarm Reaction: When you perceive a threat, your body engages the fight-or-flight alarm reaction and prepares itself for confrontation or flight. Your muscles tense, blood pressure and heart rate increase, breath quickens, and your whole body is ready to do something. Think of the terrific tension you felt after coming close to being in an accident in your car. You can have this same reaction when you see your child in danger, to a lesser degree when you hear that your project is canceled, and to an even smaller degree when you hear someone talking about you in a negative way. It doesn't matter whether or not the threat is real; it only matters if you think it is real.

**Adaptation Stage:** After the intense arousal, the body must adapt to and compensate for all the physiological changes occurring from the alarm. This attempt to return to normal as quickly as possible is called homeostasis. The problem is that you usually don't get quite as balanced or relaxed as you were before the alarm. Even after a threat is resolved, a subtle residual alertness remains in the unconscious mind, keeping the body from becoming completely relaxed. This eventually leads to a chronic level of stress, and you become accustomed to gradually higher levels of arousal and tension in the body.

**Fatigue (Exhaustion) Stage:** If the arousal continues, or if new threats continue to arise, you begin to deplete your body's reserves of fuel. You over-utilize your resources, exhaust yourself, and become fatigued. You have to work harder and harder to get the same amount of work done, and often, you become so tired that all you can do is shuffle papers. The popular term for this is "burnout." At this stage your body begins to break down, setting the stage for disease.

**Termination (Good-bye) Stage:** If there is no relief from the arousal, if you continue to drive yourself, you suffer the consequences: Your health breaks down, you suffer from disease, you can even die. When any organism remains in a state of constant arousal, it literally wears itself out. The resulting stress on the physiological systems leads to breakdown, disease, and death. This is a very accurate description of what causes an executive to have a heart attack at age fifty or even younger.

Most researchers believe that the same physiological arousal that characterizes the fight-or-flight alarm reaction is also necessary for a healthy life. Engaging in any challenging event results in physiological arousal, and it is obvious that these states are very healthy and productive. Hard work and exercise are healthy for both body and mind. Without arousal we could never achieve, gain knowledge, or meet any challenges.

As a consequence, they repeat Selye's mistake and generalize the term "stress" to mean any and all arousal. Selye defined "stress" as "the non-specific response of the body to any demand made upon it." The problem with this definition is that the only time we do not have a non-specific response is when we are dead. For Selye and many others, stress is an unavoidable condition, an unfortunate fact of life. How useful is a theory that tells us that we have no choice, that we will always be a victim of stress?

## Stress as Fight-or-Flight: A Job Half-Done

Laboratory research is too narrow and confining to accurately describe what happens inside a human being. Selye based his theory strictly on his laboratory research on sympathetic arousal, ignoring the less dramatic but equally powerful role of parasympathetic inhibition. The stages of alarm, adaptation, and fatigue are described exclusively in terms of arousal, over-utilization, and depletion of bodily resources. For Selye and most professionals, any arousal is stress. It doesn't matter whether that arousal is generated by exercise, by a challenge, or by an alarm response brought on by fear. But these states are very different from each other physically and psychologically, and have vastly different consequences.

Look to your own experience. Recall a time when you were really excited about a project that you were involved in. You felt confident, ready to take on the challenge, and looking forward to solving the problems and achieving your goal. How did that make you feel? Now compare that experience to the one you had when you were really worried about something, and spent several days thinking about all sorts of negative outcomes. Did that feel the same way? We think differently, feel differently, and act differently when we are challenged than when we are fearful. Calling these very different experiences by the same word "stress" is not only lousy science, it creates a great deal of confusion.

## The Origin of the Myth of Good Stress

Defining stress as arousal (sympathetic dominance) ignores the very real and potentially harmful effects of parasympathetic activity. Consequently, Selye's theory cannot account for the stress created by depression, passivity, or withdrawal. Nor does it account for dietary or environmental stress. For example, the fatigue you feel when you are depressed isn't because of burnout. This low energy state is caused by a lack of activity, not by too much. Depression is extremely stressful, and can easily be as dangerous and as fatal as a prolonged state of fatigue created by too much fight-or-flight arousal.

The confusion of arousal and stress is the source of the myth of good and bad stress. Selye referred to any positive outcome – such as being more productive, having fun, strengthening a muscle group, or success in a task – as

"Eustress." Any negative outcome – a heart attack, a headache, feelings of failure or anxiety, or a bad decision – was called "Distress." In other words, good consequences mean that you had good stress, and bad consequences mean that you had bad stress. As we discussed earlier, Selye's theory has no predictive power, and is essentially useless as scientific theory. More importantly, it does not give you the knowledge you need to control stress. It is useless as a practical guide. Simply creating new terms such as eustress and distress only adds to the confusion. Unfortunately, there is another fatal error to this theory.

## The Possum Reaction: The Other Half of Stress

No one doubts that the fight-or-flight reaction can lead to exhaustion, pathology, and even death. By the same token, though, what happens if there is sustained or intense parasympathetic activity? Does this also lead to difficulties and disease? When we examine human behavior, we find many problems that can only be described as an overreaction of the parasympathetic nervous system. Strangely enough, however, very little attention has been given to this neurological event.

Although the parasympathetic system has not had the same degree of attention as the sympathetic, it's clear that certain illnesses are associated with excessive parasympathetic activity. One is asthma, in which the airways in the lungs constrict abnormally and obstruct the smooth flow of air. Another is the duodenal ulcer, which results from an over secretion of hydrochloric acid in the stomach. Both of these illnesses involve physical changes associated with increased right vagus nerve activity – the major parasympathetic nerve.

Other events also suggest possible negative effect of excessive parasympathetic activity. Fainting from pain or from the sight of blood happens because of a strong right vagus nerve discharge to the heart that slows the pulse so much that the brain does not receive enough blood to maintain alertness. Oddly enough, the initial response to the anticipation of pain (as when you face a dental procedure) often involves the heart rate's slowing down rather than speeding up, indicating increased parasympathetic activity and predominance – even in the face of an overall increase in sympathetic discharge.

It's common knowledge that too much tension leads to very serious disease conditions such as heart disease and high blood pressure. But did you know that too little tension, which is the situation when we feel depressed, could also be deadly? Medical research clearly shows that when you consistently inhibit your internal systems, they begin to lose their capacity to function properly over a period of time. This affects all your internal systems, including the immune system. Medical science also recognizes that a failure of the immune system can lead to cancer. Recent research clearly shows a definite and well-established relationship between depression and certain forms of cancer, as well as a variety of psychosomatic diseases. For instance, those who undergo severe trauma from loss (such as the death of a spouse, or even retirement) may become so depressed that their immune system is severely depleted, and death occurs within a relatively short period of time. The phrase, "He died of a broken heart" may be trite, but it does reflect a general awareness of the impact of grief, loss, and depression on immune functioning and human behavior.

## Turning Off and Tuning Out

It's clear from medical research that if we really want to understand stress, we must account for the power of the parasympathetic nervous system. Our own experience confirms this. When we pay attention to what people actually do, we see another response to threats and danger that does not involve arousal or the fight-or-flight reaction. We've all known people who, when they become afraid, threatened, or worried, go home to bed or become quiet and withdrawn. These behaviors involve completely different neurological, biochemical, and psychological activities, directed by the parasympathetic nervous system instead of the sympathetic nervous system. Although not as dramatic as fear, these emotional reactions create an autonomic reaction that is just as deadly as the fight-or-flight alarm reaction.

We *never* function with just half of the autonomic system. While many of us react with a fight-or-flight alarm reaction, many of us do just the opposite. Just as a possum rolls over and plays dead when threatened, some people, when faced with a threat, exhibit very similar kinds of behavior. Instead of getting uptight, these people react with a "possum reaction." They retreat, become withdrawn and depressed, and often feel tired and worn out. Their reaction to fear is not arousal, but inhibition. We also create the possum reaction when we constantly engage in self-criticism and relive our past mistakes. The more we attack and punish ourselves, the more depressed and withdrawn we become.

In his book, *Helplessness,* Dr. Martin Seligman shows how depression stems from learning the feeling of helplessness, and that this feeling can and often does lead to disease in the body and mind. What is more, it can ultimately result in death. More than likely, the possum reaction is a complex syndrome involving not only constitutional factors and socialization, but also learning. In any event, it is evident that a number of people react to a threat by parasympathetic dominance.

The possum reaction is far too complex and extensive to be explained merely as an extreme state of flight. Just as there are four stages involving the fight or flight reaction, we can differentiate four stages in the possum reaction. These stages are:

**The Alarm Stage – The Possum Reaction:** The body reacts to self-inflicted attacks and external threats by inhibiting vital functions and closing down. It doesn't matter whether it is someone or something attacking us, or we attack ourselves through self-criticism. In the possum reaction, we try to protect ourselves by withdrawing and avoiding confrontation. We feel hopeless, helpless, and out of control of our life. Our physiological reactions include decreased heart rate, decreased muscle tone, and increased mental lassitude.

**The Activation Stage:** Possum reactors turn their systems on low as a way to protect themselves. To re-balance, they need to speed things up, to become more involved in activity, to get their systems back into gear and running up-to-speed. Solving the problems of a possum reaction requires a different approach than for a fight-or-flight reaction. For example, if you have high blood pressure, a symptom of too much tension, part of the treatment process must include deep relaxation in order to reduce the tension and take the pressure off the vascular system. On the other hand, deep relaxation therapy for a "depressed" person can deepen the depression, increasing the potential for suicide. Depression calls for action, such as aerobic exercise and regulated sleep as part of the treatment regime in order to shift the autonomic tone towards a more active state.

**The Atrophication Stage:** Over-activation of the fight-or-flight reaction leads to burnout. But it's difficult to suffer burnout when you sleep ten to twelve hours a day. Possum reactors feel chronic fatigue not because they over-do, but just the opposite. They under-utilize their systems through inhibition, by constantly turning them on low. Eventually, these systems lose their capacity to function. The same thing happens when you break an arm or leg, and wear a cast for six months. Your muscles aren't exercised, so they begin to atrophy. When we don't use our organ systems appropriately, they lose their ability to function. That's why aerobic exercise is so important for the heart muscle. And if you don't make a habit of urinating more than once a day, by the time you are sixty the chances are good that you will lose the voluntary use of your bladder. If you don't use it, you lose it!

**Termination (Good-bye) Stage:** The consequences for the possum reaction are just as deadly as the fight-or-flight response. When we consistently inhibit organ functioning, the end result may well be breakdown, disease, and/or death. Clear examples are an enlarged heart from lack of exercise, and the close relationship between depression and certain forms of cancer, particularly breast cancer. Although some physicians still argue the point, research and clinical evidence points quite compellingly to the conclusion that chronic or severe depression contributes to the onset of cancer.

## The Worst of Both Worlds

We don't limit ourselves to just one alarm reaction or the other. Because the sympathetic and parasympathetic systems are built and function differently (the sympathetic coordinates an overall response while the parasympathetic is organ-specific), we have an infinite variety of internal responses. Because we are capable of mixing our thoughts, we are quite capable of mixing autonomic reactions, and unfortunately, creating problems that involve imbalances in both systems. We

**Table 2.1**

## STRESS REACTION STAGES
## FIGHT-OR-FLIGHT AND THE POSSUM RESPONSE

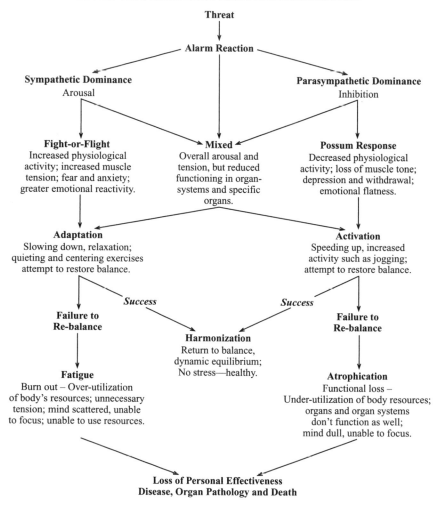

create stress from either a fight or flight reaction, or the possum reaction, or a complicated mix of the two. For example, we can feel both depressed and tense and anxious. This mixture actually characterizes many, if not most diseases, such as asthma, Crohn's Disease, and ulcers.

## Stress: A Question of Balance

Popular, as well as scientific, thinking about stress is too narrowly focused on sympathetic arousal and the fight-or-flight alarm reaction. We are told that being challenged and being under stress is the same thing, although we know that they feel quite different. The great traditions of self-mastery understand that stress is always destructive, and that it involves both the sympathetic fight-or-flight alarm reaction and the parasympathetic possum reaction. The key to understanding stress is not whether or not we get too wound up, or even whether or not we don't get wound up enough. The key is to understand the subtle inner balances of the autonomic system, the subtle processes of harmonization that characterize a living, open system.

We realize that a person can "worry himself to death," or "die of a broken heart," or even "die of boredom." But no one has ever been accused of dying from tranquility or balance. We know that challenges, laughter, and happy surprises are necessary and beneficial to our mental and physical well-being. Yet all of these involve high states of arousal, which, if unbalanced, become stressful and dangerous. It is also obvious that relaxation is not only very pleasant, but necessary and beneficial. Yet too much relaxation, such as in pathological depression, also becomes stressful and dangerous.

With this in mind, we can look at stress from a more comprehensive and more functionally useful viewpoint as shown in Table 2.1. When we take the entire autonomic system into account, along with research and our experience, we can define stress in a very systematic and specific way: *stress is a state of autonomic imbalance, characterized by unrelieved or excessive dominance of either arousal or inhibition, or a complex unbalanced interaction of the two.*

Stress occurs when we are out of harmony within ourselves. And the moment we become unbalanced, we create changes in the body that lead to disease and inhibit the resources of the mind. Our organs and systems are interconnected. If an imbalance occurs within one organ, it will affect the rest of the system. Conversely, if the overall autonomic response is harmonized, individual subsystems will begin to achieve balance.

We can experience two general types of balance. The first is *dynamic* balance, a shifting back and forth between activity (arousal) and rest (inhibition). We can work or play hard for periods of time, and if we balance this with periods of rest and relaxation, we avoid stress. As long as we remain sensitive and responsive to the needs and signals of our body, we can go through the day without creating stress. This kind of balance is like the child's game of teeter-totter.

If both children are about equal in weight, they can teeter back and forth, and have a wonderful time taking turns at going up and down. But if one is too heavy, the game becomes unpleasant, and the purpose is defeated. If we tilt too much to one side, without allowing the other side to have its influence, we become unbalanced, and create stress.

Many of us do this very thing. We like to work hard and play hard, meeting the demands of an active life, but forget that we also need times of quiet and relaxation to clear the mind and recharge our batteries. Or we constantly worry about things, become overly alert, and don't allow our systems to rest. By being action addicts and/or worry-warts, we put too much weight on the sympathetic (arousal) side of the teeter-totter, and create chronic tension and strain for ourselves. On the other hand, some of us become couch potatoes and simply refuse to move, preferring out of choice or habit to stay passive and withdrawn. These individuals have the other side of the teeter-totter down, and don't allow the body and mind to get the action they need to stay healthy and alert. For both, it's a problem of flexibility, of not allowing a dynamic shift to create the proper balance, or harmony.

Internally, dynamic balance is a complex interactive process involving not only the autonomic but also the sensory-motor systems. The autonomic nervous system does not work like a machine where increasing one aspect (such as sympathetic activity) decreases the others. However, as discussed above, there is a direct, reciprocal relationship between the sympathetic and the parasympathetic in both the lungs and the heart. As we will see later, this direct relationship, particularly in the lungs, provides us with the means to consciously create and maintain internal balance by directly regulating the motion of the lungs.

Throughout the rest of the body, inner balance or harmony is determined by a complex interactive process, which involves all three systems of the autonomic nervous systems (sympathetic, parasympathetic, and enteric) as well as the sensory motor system. The enormous flexibility of the autonomic system allows us to be very creative in the ways that we create imbalance and stress. This flexibility can just as effectively be used to create and maintain harmony and balance.

## The Autonomic Nervous System: Sophisticated Energy

The more important form of balance is what we might simply call *harmony* – a dynamic equilibrium between the neural, organ, and others systems of the body. This is the harmonization of an open system that we discussed above. When we achieve this, work seems effortless. A physical example is the resting heart beat, which is in perfect autonomic balance and yet still pumping blood and accomplishing its job, or the example of being so focused on a task that you forget about everything else not relevant to it – even time seems to stop. In this state of concentration, body and mind are coordinated, and work becomes effortless. We work totally relaxed, using only the energy necessary to do the job.

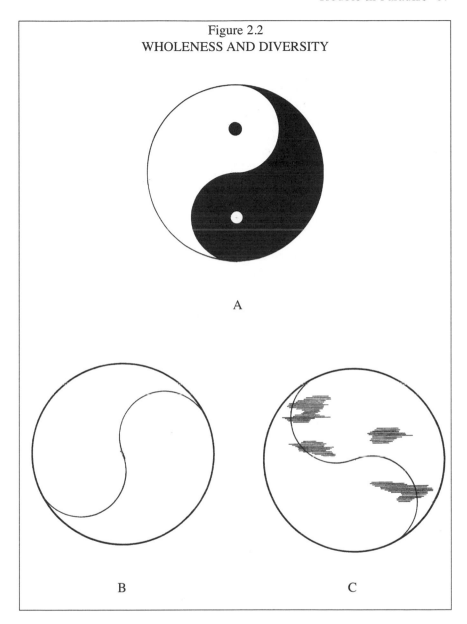

Figure 2.2
WHOLENESS AND DIVERSITY

A

B                              C

The autonomic nervous system is an extremely sophisticated energy system. Its purpose is to direct the organ and other internal systems of the body so we function in an efficient, healthy manner, and maintain balance and harmony. We find a far more accurate portrayal of the principle underlying autonomic function in the diagram in Figure 2.2, the familiar ancient Chinese Taoist symbol of *yin* and *yang* (A) that represents the wholeness, which contains diversity. The complete circle represents the whole, while the interflowing black and white shapes symbolize the fundamental positive and negative forces of the universe. These forces are not in polar opposition but represent complementarity and diversity within wholeness. We can use this symbol to illustrate the sophisticated harmony that characterizes a healthy autonomic nervous system.

Picture the circle as a crystal sphere representing the entire arena of autonomic influence and control. The sphere represents both the sympathetic and parasympathetic (for this example, we include the enteric in with the parasympathetic) systems, separate systems that operate together to form a whole system. When the system is in harmony (B), and there is no stress, the crystal areas are clear. When a disharmony or imbalance occurs somewhere in the system (C), we have a state of stress, represented by a shading within the system. Intense or prolonged imbalance leads to dysfunction and disease. Just how the system breaks down and what diseases any one individual develops depends on a complex variety of factors – constitutional and genetic, psychological, environmental, dietary, and even exercise. The variety of factors and their complex interaction makes it very difficult to predict just how any one individual will be affected. But the critical factor is the underlying systemic imbalance.

While the details are complex, the principle is clear and simple. Think of the harmonics (the energy structure) of a tone. Imagine the tone representing the autonomic system. High tones are sympathetic dominance, low tones represent parasympathetic dominance, and all tones in-between various mixtures of the two. If the harmonics of the tone are balanced, the tone pleases the ear. But if the harmonics of the tone are distorted, the tone grates on the ear, and becomes unpleasant. Now apply this same reasoning to autonomic activity. If the energies and activities of the autonomic system are balanced, the body functions in an integrated, harmonious way. But if the autonomic system is disturbed, distorted, unbalanced – whatever word you wish to use – then there is a "grating" inside the body. Now, depending on all or any of the individual factors – genetics, psychological factors, diet, lack of exercise, environmental pollutants, and so forth – we experience dis-ease (disharmony) in an organ or system which eventually leads to disease.

By defining stress as autonomic imbalance, or disharmony, we eliminate the confusion between "good stress" and "bad stress." Stress is not, and never has been, good for us. The fact that we can have either arousal or inhibition does not, in and of itself, mean that we have stress. *The essential element in determining whether or not we have stress is whether or not the autonomic nervous system is balanced, or harmonized.* The principle is simple and clear. If you maintain neurological balance or harmony, you remain free of stress. On the other hand, anything you do can be stressful if you are out of harmony.

Deep relaxation, diet, and exercise play vital roles in eliminating and preventing stress in the body. These activities also affect all other aspects of our personality. The more relaxed we are, the more creative and insightful we become. Proper diet helps maintain emotional stability and clarity of thought. Exercise not only strengthens the body, but also helps reduce depression and allows us to be more excited about life in general. The more knowledge we have about our body, the more balanced we become, and the better we feel.

But recall that the body is only the first and most primitive of the six dimensions of our identity. The real power lies within the deeper dimensions that constitute the mind, and then spirit. It's clear that any response or reaction in the body is determined by what happens in the mind. Remember, stress is not what happens to us, but rather how we react to the events that happen to and around us. That reaction has its beginnings in our thoughts and emotions, then moves into the body.

The autonomic and other physiological responses are regulated primarily by the limbic system in the brain. The limbic system, in turn, is controlled and influenced by the higher cortical processes, that is, the thinking process. As the neurophysiologist Roger Sperry, succinctly states in *Consciousness and the Brain*, mental events control physical events.

## THE DRAGONS OF THE MIND

Until the advent of biofeedback, the scientific and medical community believed that the autonomic nervous system was really autonomous. We thought we were victims of the nervous system, but we were really victims of our thoughts, emotions, and beliefs. Now we realize what the yoga masters have always known, that the mind exerts absolute control over the autonomic system. The poor body has no choice but to react to every thought we have. Remember, it's not what happens to us that creates stress, it's how we react to what happens to us. It is not what happens to us, but what we say to ourselves about what happens to us that determines whether or not we have stress.

Most of us have very little control over our thoughts and emotions. As a consequence, we have very little control over stress. Like the heads that keep popping up in the child's game, our emotions keep popping up in the mind as we react to one thing after the other. Our emotional disturbances seem endless.

### The Three Dragons: The Displacement of Power

But if we take a close look, we find that most of our emotional disturbances really arise from three destructive habits of the mind. Notice I used the word "habits," and not functions. These three powerful distortions – fear, self-hatred, and loneliness – are the origin of most, if not all, of our emotional disturbances. Importantly, two of these, fear and self-hatred, are closely reflected in the autonomic system that creates stress for us. It is important to understand that these conditions are habits, consequences of how we misuse the innate resources of the mind, and not a natural or integral part of the human mind. They are like fire-breathing dragons that usurp the creative force of the mind and corrupt our resources, creating disease, unhappiness, and suffering. They seem to be so powerful that we feel helpless before them. We don't realize that we ourselves are the source of their power, and that we can take it away from them.

## Fear: The Most Destructive Dragon

The most dramatic consequence of self-mastery is the ability to live without fear. Fear, the most destructive of the three dragons, is the single most important cause of suffering and stress. While we may be familiar with fear, we often don't realize just how pervasive this monster is. Much of our anger and resentment are rooted in fear. Greed most often begins with the fear of not having enough or of not being important. Then when we accumulate wealth, we become obsessed with protecting what we have. Fear drives us to acquire political and military power, feeling that if we can dominate, we will be secure. But this kind of power eventually becomes perverse and feeds the very fears that we are trying to overcome. The more powerful we become, the more we worry about someone else becoming powerful. The old Cold War between America and the Soviet Union is a classic example of how fear drives entire cultures: so much power and intellect dedicated to servicing both individual and national egos leading only to an unending sense of insecurity, of not having enough, of not being "the most powerful."

There are many faces of fear but the most terrible is violence. Whether it is the homelessness and street violence in American cities, the horrors of conflict in Bosnia and Rwanda, sectarian violence in India or Ireland, political murders in Haiti, all have their roots in fear. Terrorists intentionally try to create a culture of fear, and will often stop at nothing to do so. The horrific attack on the World Trade Center is a tragic example. What we cannot do is allow the fear created by violence dictate our decisions and responses to violence. When we do, it simply perpetuates the cycle of violence.

Most of our fears are far less dramatic, but still destructive to us personally. Some people spend their entire life fearful that they will not meet someone else's standards. Even gossip has its roots in fear. If we can make others look small, and by so doing make ourselves look better, we compensate for the fear of being unimportant. Religions, governments, and communities use fear to control others, and parents use fear to control their children.

We usually don't like to think of ourselves as being fearful. We use softer words, such as "worried" and "anxious" which seem a little more acceptable. But worry is a form of fear, and being anxious is how we feel when we succumb to fear. Since we do it often, we get pretty good at it. Most of us become so skilled at worrying that it becomes part of our life-style. And yet, the only thing we accomplish by worrying is misery for ourselves and for others.

What would life be like for you if you lost all your fear? What if you did not worry about what might happen to this or that, or you weren't afraid of what others might think of you, or you didn't have to worry about losing your job or paying your bills? Most of us think that if we were only richer, prettier, stronger, better looking, more charming, safer, taller, slimmer – or if we had a better job, newer car, bigger house, more friends, better looking lovers, more respect (the adjectives are almost endless) – then we wouldn't worry, and we would be happy.

Worry and fear are not created by a lack of things; they are created by how we think. If you have the habit of worrying, it doesn't matter who you are, what you have, or what you do, you will worry because that is the habit of your mind. This useless habit is one of the biggest causes of disease and unhappiness. And yet, it has become so much a part of our lives that we even mistakenly think that a little fear is helpful, and that fear is a natural part of being human.

The truth is very different. Fear is not a natural human condition; it is a habit of the mind. There are people who live life without being afraid. They realize that fear is not a natural part of their being, but rather a product of the mind, a fantasy that grips and destroys, but a fantasy, nonetheless. Through knowledge and practice, they conquer the mind's habit of creating fear. This is one of the first goals of tantra yoga, as well as the martial arts. Tantra yoga masters are called "masters" because they have mastered their own mind and have conquered fear. The same is true of the samurai, the great masters of the martial arts in Japan, or the great Taoist masters of China.

You can do the same. You can live life without the petty fears and worries that dog us from day to day, and without the great fears that every so often rattle our cages. Even the most desperate of situations can be faced without fear. As a young man, my master often walked through the mountains of Northern India. Then, as they still are now, the mountains were rugged, forested, and untamed. Once, while crossing a very narrow footbridge across a deep ravine, a tiger started crossing the same bridge from the other side. The bridge was so small that only one creature could pass at a time. My master knew that if he retreated, the tiger would attack. Instead, he raised his arms, and rushed towards the tiger, giving a powerful shout. The tiger immediately backed off the bridge, turned tail and ran. Through self-mastery, you mobilize the powerful innate drive for self-preservation and create both the energy and the focus to find a solution to any problem. But once you allow fear to paralyze the mind, you lose the ability to make choices and become locked into reaction. The greater our self-mastery, the greater our ability to face any situation without fear and to live our lives without worry.

Because fear seems to be so familiar, we often think that it is a natural part of who we are. But all fears arise out of experience. In yoga science, where reincarnation is a familiar and accepted concept, fears are understood as *sanskaras*, subtle impressions of the mind that come from past experiences in previous lives. Given the right circumstances in the current life, these sanskaras can become active and arise in the mind as full-blown fears. But fear sanskaras are learned, they are not and never have been a natural condition or natural function of the human mind. Whether from past lives, or from the current life, all fears are learned.

The most common mistake is to confuse fear with the powerful innate drive of self-preservation. These two conditions of the mind are very different, and have very different outcomes. Self-preservation, not fear, is the innate protective mechanism for all living creatures. Fear is a distortion, and always destructive, always harmful, and never protects anyone.

## Self-Hatred: The Other Side of Misery

At times it seems that we are masters of creating misery. When we aren't worrying about whether or not something awful is going to happen to us, we remember all the hurts, mistakes and failures in our past. In other words, when we aren't preoccupied with someone or something attacking us, we turn around and attack ourselves. We seldom live up to expectations, we are never quite good enough no matter how good we get, and we keep making the same old mistakes. We suffer from guilt, continually find fault with ourselves, condemn ourselves for not living up to our own, or someone else's, expectations. These are all part of the dragon of self-hatred. After so many failures, mistakes, and broken dreams we begin to give up on ourselves and on life. Some of us become depressed, withdrawn, and passive, accepting whatever life gives as a cruel joke that we must endure. Others, angry with themselves, become angry at the world. They become cranky and hostile, taking out their misery on others.

Like fear, self-hatred is a habit of the mind, an arbitrary way of looking at life and oneself that leads only to further mistakes, poor performance, and unhappiness. When someone else attacks you, at least you might resist your adversary by mobilizing the body's defenses. But when you attack yourself, there is no outcome but defeat. You cannot win in a battle against yourself; you only create conflict and suffering. Instead of mobilizing the body's systems, you become depressed, passive, and withdrawn.

Attacking ourselves is only a habit of the mind, a consequence of the way we learned to see ourselves as we grew up. We can always find reasons to punish ourselves for the mistakes we make and the expectations we fail to realize. Like fear, the dragon of self-hatred feeds on our lack of self-awareness and skill. We strengthen the dragon by constantly reminding ourselves of our weaknesses and mistakes. And as long as we continue to feed this dragon of self-hatred by paying attention to it, it continues to breathe fire and create misery for us.

The secret is to stop feeding the dragon by experiencing your own inner strength and beauty. You can't create self-esteem by constantly telling yourself you are a wonderful person. Self-esteem and self-respect grow out of the experience of committed effort. Whether you succeed or not is not as important to your self-respect as when you know that you tried your best. If you continue to make effort, if you continue to work with resources, you will eventually succeed. Self-respect and self-mastery arise out of effort, the foundation of success.

The tantrics have long known that depression and apathy damage the immune system and lead to serious disease. They also know that when you give up on yourself and become a victim, you deny yourself the power to grow and change. You stay stuck in your own ignorance. That's why the tantrics believe that the only true sin is sloth, the unwillingness to make effort. Mistakes are seen as a necessary part of learning, not reasons for punishment. But without effort, personal power remains undeveloped and unused, and the outcome is self-hatred.

## Loneliness: In Ignorance of Spirit

The third dragon is loneliness, the most subtle of all the dragons. It is the most difficult to defeat in part because it hides in a misunderstanding of its nature. Most of us think of loneliness as being apart from loved ones, having no one to share our feelings, hopes and dreams, our fears and concerns, and our experiences. The less we communicate our inner thoughts and feelings, the more lonely we feel. To solve this problem, we gather loved ones, build friendships, even join clubs and organizations. We think that if we have friends and family, people around us that love and care for us, we will never be lonely.

But it doesn't work. As rewarding as family and friends are, they do not keep us from being lonely, they only distract us from our loneliness. In fact, the more we depend on our loved ones to keep us from being lonely, the more lonely we become. Think about it for a moment. Are you ever lonely for your enemies? Do you miss having unpleasant people around you? No, we are lonely for our friends and family, for those people whom we feel close to. It is the absence of our loved ones that makes us lonely.

We think that loneliness involves our relationship with others, but it really involves our relationship with ourselves. While fear and self-hatred are habits of the mind, loneliness arises directly out of the sense of individuality. Our life experiences seem to confirm that we are truly alone. We are born into this world alone, we die alone. No one feels our pain or our joy, nor do they digest our food, breathe for us, or feel what we feel. Even though we may communicate and share these experiences, it is still "me," the ego-sense of individuality that tells me I am alone. We don't experience any "self" that is connected to, or a part of, any other self. As a consequence, we fail to understand the fundamental connection we have with each other and with the universe at large.

There are times when we experience a sense of wholeness, of completeness, of kinship with the universe at large. It may happen when we look up at the starry heavens, or watch the birth of a child, or participate with others in working through a crisis situation. It doesn't happen because we have expectations or make demands; we simply experience a strong sense of belonging to something greater than ourselves. At this moment, we become free from the ego-sense of self, and experience being part of a greater identity, a greater "Self," and all loneliness vanishes. Unfortunately, these experiences are fleeting, easily lost in the shuffle of our day-to-day distractions, pressures, and reactions.

When we genuinely love, we also break free from the ego-sense of self. But we confuse "loving" with "being loved." Most of us engage in a desperate search for someone to love us, but we confuse the issue by saying that we need someone to love. We say we want someone to share with, someone we can love, but what we are really saying is that we need someone to love us, someone who will make us feel important and keep us from feeling lonely. This is not love, but emotional attachment that leads us into dependency. We believe that we need this person to be happy, to be content, to be fulfilled. So our loving becomes distorted by our emotional needs. When they don't love us back, we feel miserable and unloved. When they aren't around, we feel lonely.

We all have a remarkable, unlimited capacity to love one another. There is a wide range of expression of our love, from brotherly and sisterly love to romantic, sexual love. But as long as we continue to confuse love and emotional attachment, we will continue to be lonely, even when we have someone to love. We can conquer this dragon of loneliness, but we must turn to our deepest resource to do so, our core spiritual Self. The great spiritual sages of all traditions say that loneliness lies in the ignorance of our spirit, the core of our being. When we become aware of this spiritual Self, we experience the mystery of life, the unbroken and unending connection we have with each other and with the universe. We become fully conscious of the universal Spirit that flows within and through us. Picture life like a large oak tree filled with leaves, twigs, and branches. Our ego-sense of self makes us feel like we are a leaf on this tree. When the winds blow, the leaves rub against each other. Sometimes this is a pleasant experience and sometimes it is very unpleasant. As leaves, we feel isolated and apart from each other, even though we can see that we all belong to the same tree. When we become conscious of the spiritual Self, we realize that we are far more than just the expression of a single leaf. We are more than even the branch and the trunk. We are the life force within the tree.

We cannot realize the power of this experience by analyzing it. Intellectual understanding is not the experience of wholeness, nor does it put an end to loneliness. Those experiences of wholeness gained by watching a birth or gazing at the stars are not intellectual events. We must go beyond the intellect and become conscious of the human spirit directly. This is the heart of the meditative traditions of self-mastery: to calm the mind so completely, to be so focused, that we experience the spiritual Self directly. In tantra, it is called *samadhi* while in Western meditative/spiritual traditions it is often referred to as a "mystical experience" because it takes us beyond our thoughts and emotions, beyond even our beliefs.

The mystical experience is powerful and undeniable. In just one experience, our loneliness, our fear, and our self-hatred is diminished by half. As we become more skilled in our ability to have this awareness, we gradually lose all sense of loneliness, all fears are vanquished, and all self-hatred is eliminated. The ego-sense of individuality now becomes an instrument by which we express in our unique way our thoughts, our love, our joy, and our strength. We do not lose our identity, we polish and refine our identity until our spiritual Self shines through like a bright light, and we experience the real joy and freedom that is our true heritage.

These three dragons – fear, self-hatred and loneliness – are not who we are. They are destructive forces within the mind created by our thoughts and ignorance. It is the lack of self-mastery, the misuse of the powerful resources of body, mind, and spirit that create these dragons. They, in turn, lead to the most prevalent and destructive disease of modern life, the dis-ease we call stress.

## Taking Back the Power

The stress myths reflect our ignorance and inability to deal with life from a position of inner strength. Instead of responding effectively and confidently to the pressures and challenges of modern life, we find ourselves playing the role of victim. Chased by one dragon after another, we feel powerless and ineffectual. As soon as we slay one dragon, another appears. Not realizing that these dragons are only reflections of our inner dragons, we become more cynical about ourselves, and our ability to make a real difference in life.

This is a book for dragon slayers. It is for those who are tired of being chased, cornered, and disturbed by the destructive patterns and habits of their own minds. It is a manual for self-mastery. Based on the wisdom path of tantra yoga, it is the way to access inner strength and wisdom and become free of the terrible dragons of fear, self-hatred, and loneliness. And while they only exist in our mind, they are the source of our stress, real enough to create disease and unhappiness for ourselves and for others.

Only through self-mastery can you use the power of your inner resources to create a loving, fearless, and joyful life. You will not find any magic incantations that make the dragons disappear. You won't need them. The dragons of the mind are powerful and persistent, but you are stronger and more powerful. What you will discover is the knowledge and tools of inner strength and wisdom that will give you the confidence to face whatever life brings fearlessly and joyfully, using your own wisdom to make the right decisions.

## AWARENESS AND SKILL: PASSAGEWAY TO FREEDOM

The way to freedom lies in self-awareness and skill. Through our own efforts we can create a life of health and wellness, of joy and love. But just as importantly, we must unlock our inner creative potential and inner strength, which we badly need to solve the tremendous social and economic problems we face. Unless we become skilled in the use of our inner resources and create a bridge between them and our external life, our efforts will be futile. The first step to establish balance and harmony in our society is to establish balance and harmony within ourselves. Like my first lesson from the yoga master; first, we must heal ourselves.

The solutions to our suffering are amazingly simple. This is not to say that they are easy. But they are available. We need to experiment personally and see which ones work for us. We have the map, the dimensions of identity, and we understand the dis-ease, autonomic imbalance, and the dragons of the mind. We need to continue our journey and develop a practical understanding of inner resources. After all, if we are the source of our own unhappiness, we are also the source of our own salvation.

3

# OUR ALL-TOO-HUMAN MIND:
# HOME OF THE DRAGONS

*We have found the enemy and it is us.*
—Pogo—

We don't have to go far to find our dragons. They live inside the mind, we feel them in the body, and they deplete our energy. Whenever we feel attacked, when we worry or become afraid, the poor body reacts with alarm. Our heart begins to beat faster, our blood pressure goes up, our muscles become tense, and we feel knots in our stomach. It doesn't matter what we worry about – finances, someone saying something bad about us, our children – the consequence is the same, we experience an alarm reaction. A little bit of worry or fear creates a small, almost unnoticeable reaction while an intense fear, or sustained worry, creates changes in the body that may last as long as two or more weeks.

When we attack ourselves, remembering all our past mistakes and how we never seem to do anything right, become guilty, or feel like life is out of control, our body reacts by shutting down. Instead of being alert and mindful, we become discouraged, depressed, wearied, and withdrawn.

When loneliness haunts us, our body seems to ache for comfort and touch. It's well known that infants suffer, even die, if they aren't physically held and cuddled. Young children need attention and love from their parents. If it's not forthcoming, it leads to psychological problems that can remain throughout a lifetime. As adults, we don't lose this need for contact comfort. We need to feel close both physically and emotionally. When these needs aren't satisfied, we may compensate with overeating, drug or alcohol abuse, promiscuity, or any number of neurotic symptoms.

It's much easier for our dragons to disturb us if we are physically worn out and unhealthy. When we take care of our body, when we are healthy and balanced, the dragons have a much more difficult time creating problems for us. Part of our power lies in our ability to create a healthy body, resistant to the stress and strain created by fears and worries. In this way, the body becomes a tool we can use to help overcome our fears, worries, and loneliness.

The same is true for the energy dimension. The dragons can over-energize us, filling us with anxious, nervous energy, or they can zap our energy, leaving us feeling tired, worn, and depressed. If we know how to use energy in a positive way, we can use it to weaken the dragons and take control of the mind.

But all the exercise and all the best food cannot compensate for the damage done by these dragons in the mind. No matter how skilled we become with our bodies and energy, as long as we allow the mind to feed the dragons, we will be unhappy, stressed, and unhealthy. We must go the source – the powerful human mind that creates and feeds these dragons.

## MIND AND THE LIMITATIONS OF AWARENESS

No matter what you do, where you go, or who you are, the mind is the one instrument that you always use. In tantra yoga, the mind is known as the *antahkarana*, or inner instrument. It is composed of the three dimensions – Sensory Mind, Discriminating Mind and Balanced Mind – and the various power functions associated with these dimensions, including the key power function of ego. When trained properly and used skillfully, the mind and its functions are an endless source of power, creativity and well-being. But when you don't know how to manage its vast power, the mind creates unhappiness, stress, and disease.

Since the days of Sigmund Freud, most of us are aware that the vast part of the mind is what we call the unconscious mind. Although Freud thought of the unconscious as a cesspool of nasty neuroses and psychoses, this is not the reality at all. The unconscious mind is more like a vast warehouse of processes, knowledge, and resources. Of course, there are patterns that are unhealthy, but they are limited to the sensory dimension of the mind and only have the power to disturb us that we give them.

For practical purposes, it is helpful to understand a few concepts about the mind and the different degrees of awareness that we bring to the mind. Figure 3.1 illustrates the interaction of consciousness and the mind. The smallest part of the mind is called the conscious mind. The conscious mind includes everything that we are aware of at the moment. This changes from moment to moment as our attention moves from one thing to the next. We may be aware of several things at once, as happens when we are driving in traffic, or we may be lost in a thought, and unaware of anything around us at that moment – as others seem to be when we are driving in traffic. The conscious mind really only has one power, the ability to direct attention. Everything else is basically decided and done in the

Figure 3.1
AWARENESS DIMENSIONS AND CAPACITIES OF THE MIND

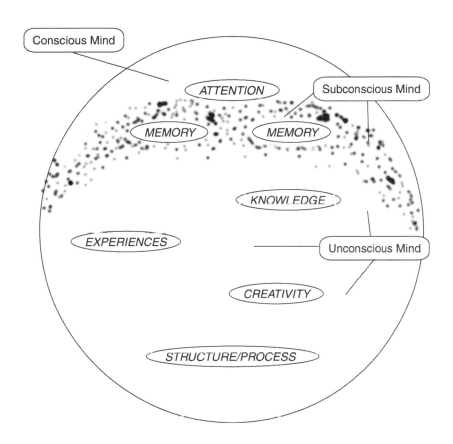

**Conscious Mind:** The capacity to focus attention; the ability to direct and focus the power of the mind.

**Subconscious Mind:** Awareness penetration into the unconscious mind, long and short-term memory.

**Unconscious Mind:** Seat of all experiences and knowledge; organizer and creative problem solver, location of all power functions.

unconscious part of the mind. But as we shall see later, this one capacity of the conscious mind is the necessary tool for self-mastery.

The vast unconscious mind is where all the mind's processes perform their functions – such as perception, habits, regulating the body, structuring information, and basically, creating and managing our personal sense of reality. The term "unconscious" refers specifically to the degree of our awareness of these processes and content. For instance, any single act of perception is an incredibly complex event involving the ego, sensory input, memory, language, emotions – to name just a few. Yet, we are typically not aware of any of this, only the interpretation, the final thought or picture in our mind. The unconscious mind is also a vast storehouse of knowledge and past experiences. Whatever we experienced or learned that meant something to us, good or bad, is stored in the unconscious mind. From the tantric point of view, it also includes the experiences and knowledge from past lives.

The unconscious mind is incredibly responsive to its environment, and in a very profound way, more engaged in the world than the conscious mind. It is constantly integrating sensory information at levels beyond our awareness as well as what we are conscious of. The power of the mind resides in the unconscious level, beyond our normal awareness. For example, problem solving is done primarily in the unconscious. Think about the last major problem or task you had to solve, one you had to really spend some time thinking about. You probably think that you solved the problem by thinking about it, and in a way you did. But the key was the attention you put to the issue, and the subsequent involvement of the unconscious mind. When you were thinking about the problem, did you review all your past experiences and education, sort out what was relevant and what was not, prioritize all the information, and then select what was significant out of what was not? Of course not, but your unconscious mind did. Then add the creativity, the organization and structuring of all that information, along with all the other things you are doing at the same time that are regulated by habit, and you begin to get some idea of just how much work the unconscious part of the mind performs on a moment-to-moment basis.

The truth is that you know far more, and have far greater resources and power than you can even imagine. The problem is that you simply aren't aware of this power and knowledge. That doesn't mean that these resources must remain unconscious. We can expand our awareness into this aspect of mind, and as we do so, we create what is called the sub-conscious mind. These are the activities and content of the mind that we aren't aware of at the moment, but can easily access when we direct attention to them. For example, our short- and long-term memories are part of the sub-conscious mind. But it also includes any function, resource or content of the mind that we can become aware of. For example, at this moment your attention is on this page. What does the bottom of your left foot feel like right now? The moment you pay attention, you are aware of the sensations of your left foot. This experience was always there, but it was part of the sub-conscious mind. Or you recall something that you did yesterday that seemed very important. Today, this activity was not even in your thoughts, but you can recall it fairly easily from the subconscious level.

However, if I asked you how your blood pressure is at this moment, you probably can't feel that. This experience is still part of the unconscious level of the mind. With a little training in internal focusing, you can become aware of your blood pressure, and then the experience would become part of the subconscious mind rather than the unconscious mind. This awareness would allow you to monitor and regulate the blood pressure, giving you the information you need to take any necessary corrective action to prevent a disease from developing. Self-mastery is a process of expanding awareness into the unconscious mind, accessing the powerful resources, and making them part of the subconscious mind. For example, instinct is a powerful form of knowledge that we only occasionally access. What if we could bring instinctual knowledge totally into the sub-conscious arena and have access to this powerful tool whenever we choose?

More importantly to our purpose, the dragons in the mind, the fear, self-hatred, and loneliness have their source in the unconscious mind. They are either powerful habits in the sensory dimension (fear and self-hatred) or a lack of awareness of the spiritual Self (loneliness).

Only by expanding our awareness, dragging these dragons out of their lair in the unconscious mind, will we be able to take control of stress. Fortunately, the very same tools that allow us to eliminate the dragons also open the powerful resources of the mind and body for our conscious use.

## Awareness and Control

We must begin with what is available to us. No one can simply drop into the unconscious part of mind and change a lifetime of habits. All too often we expect ourselves to handle problems when we haven't the knowledge or the skill necessary to do so. How can we expect to deal with stress effectively when we don't understand how the mind created it? We "know" we shouldn't worry, but we do so everyday. We "know" we should respect ourselves, but we constantly criticize and berate ourselves. This kind of "knowing" is useless.

Mark Twain said, "I am an old man with many troubles. Most of which never happened." Most of the time, the things we worry about never take place. But even knowing that doesn't stop us from worrying and creating problems for ourselves.

Even when our past experience tells us that everything will eventually work out, we spin our wheels, stress our bodies, and become irritable with our friends and family. All for very little reason.

But while you were worrying, it didn't seem like it was inappropriate. In fact, it probably seemed as if all hell was going to break loose and you were going to really have problems. Who was telling you to be frightened? Who was telling you that you wouldn't be able to handle whatever is coming at you? You don't have to go far to discover the culprit.

## THE CHATTERING MIND

Pay attention to what is happening inside your head at this moment. Notice how you are constantly talking to yourself. We call this mental activity "thinking," but that's a very generous term. Most of what goes on inside your head isn't very "thoughtful" at all, just one idea setting off another, one image leading to another. This inner dialogue, or chatter, can become quite remarkable. Not only do you talk to yourself, you also answer yourself. You even talk to others, and they answer you. You can even have complete conversations going on inside your head.

Mind chatter can be thoughtful, creative, and productive. We can use it to solve problems with critical thinking, direct our emotional energy for motivation and determination, and express our creativity and self-confidence. But left unmanaged, it can become an endless source of unhappiness, stress, and disease. How does this happen?Remember that the purpose of the sensory mind is to create sense out of the world around us. Through its power functions of perception, language, habit, and emotions, it provides us with a personal interpretation of reality. Since this part of the mind creates our experience of space and time, it is not limited only to the present. In fact, one of the first things you will notice is that your mind moves easily in time and space. You can think about what you are going to do next week, or what you did last week, or pay attention to what you are doing now. You can imagine yourself in one place or another.

Close your eyes and imagine your favorite vacation. Where would you be? What would you do? How would you dress? Who would be with you? After a few moments, open your eyes. Notice that your body, including your brain, hasn't gone anywhere. Only your mind traveled. It has the freedom to play in time and space, but your brain (and the rest of your body) only functions in the present. The brain's job is to take the subtle movements of mind energy that we experience as thoughts, images or sensations, and translate them into biochemical and neurological events so the body takes the action involved in the thoughts or images.

The brain doesn't discriminate between thoughts or images about the past, the present or the future. To the brain, every thought happens only in the present. Nor does it differentiate between thoughts about something actually real or fantasies. To the brain, every thought, every image, is as real as the next one. So *every* thought is immediately translated into the body for action. When the mind anticipates the future or dwells on the past, the body responds as if the event were happening in the present. Mind and body are no longer coordinated, creating a state of imbalance.

This lack of coordination is insignificant if our thoughts are emotionally neutral. Let's say your attention wanders while you are reading this book, and you think about the quart of milk you must pick up before dinner tonight. The moment you have that thought, your body is being programmed to literally pick up the quart of milk. If you were hooked up to sensitive medical instruments, such as an EEG (electroencephalograph) to read your brain waves, and EKG (electrocardiograph) to measure your heart rate, and a GSR (Galvanic Skin Response) instrument (such as a lie detector) to read electrical changes on the surface of your skin, we could record subtle changes in your body as it responds to the thought.

Since you probably aren't emotionally involved in picking up a quart of milk, you invest very little energy in that programming. The changes in the body are so subtle and slight that you will not even feel them. When your mind chatter does not have an emotional charge, it has very little impact on the body.

If, on the other hand, you started thinking about losing your job or being in an accident, the emotional energy of these threatening thoughts would dramatically increase and set off the fight-or-flight alarm reaction inside your body. Not only would we measure rather dramatic changes going on inside your body but you would feel your shoulder or jaw muscles tighten, your stomach begin to churn, and even hear tension in your voice. The greater the threat seems to you, the more intense the emotional response and the more dramatic are the changes in the body.

### Fear: Imagination Run Amok

Like stress, fear is not something that happens to us, we create it all by ourselves through our imagination. Even though the danger may be real (and it may not, we may only think it is real), fear always arises from a fantasy in the mind. When we have to deal with something we think is dangerous, we allow the mind to imagine all sorts of harm. We anticipate something awful happening to us, or our loved ones, even if we aren't exactly sure what that awful thing will be. Whether we are fearful of being in a plane crash or of someone criticizing us, the process is the same. The only difference is in the degree of the threat. Our mind is in the future, but our body is still in the present. This anticipation of harm stimulates the fight-or-flight alarm reaction and energizes the disconnection between mind and body. The greater the threat seems to us, the more intense our reaction becomes, the greater the imbalance between mind and body, and the greater our stress.

Look carefully where fear appears. We create fear when we speculate about the future. We never fear what is happening, we only fear or worry about what *might* happen. Fear is a consequence of "what if." Even if someone points a gun to your head, you are fearful about "what if" he pulls the trigger. "What if" the terrorists attack again? "What if" we have an accident? "What if" we have depression? "What if" my boss doesn't like my work? In every case we are dealing with a fantasy, an expectation of some future terrible event, not something that is happening at the moment. The mind perceives possible future harm; the body *acts* as if it is happening now; and voila! we have a fear reaction.

Because of the intense emotional reaction, the process of anticipating harm quickly becomes a habit. Every time we worry about something, we reinforce the habit of worrying, of creating fear. We are literally practicing worrying, and we get very good at it.

This habit of worrying and being fearful not only creates stress, it literally creates real dangers for us. The more we fear, the more energy and attention we direct toward these possible events – and the more we unconsciously create the conditions that bring about exactly what we wish to avoid. By worrying, we literally practice for disaster. A good example is what happens to many of us when we have to give a talk to a large audience. The mind begins to worry: What if I forget? What if I stumble when I walk up on the stage? What if I confuse my words and sound stupid?

The more we imagine all these terrible possibilities, the more we are actually rehearsing them. By the time we begin our talk, we are so unnerved that we actually commit these very mistakes.

Look closely at the language of fear. Our thoughts are based on *what if*, and we create all sorts of terrible descriptions and images of what might happen to us. People skilled in manipulating others often use our own imagination to control us. Instead of threatening us directly, they trick us into threatening ourselves. If we plan something they disapprove of, they tell us. "You better not do that. You *know* what will happen if you do." Of course, we have no idea what will happen, but our mind quickly begins to tell us about all the awful things that might happen if we don't toe the line. These sneaky people don't have to threaten us. They know that our own minds will do a much better job of it.

Fear is the most dramatic dragon. Nothing is more dangerous, more destructive and more useless than fear. Fear also closes down our mind – it colors our perceptions, limits our creativity, and distorts our thinking. Fear can destroy us as individuals as well as our families and neighborhoods, even our nation. The more fear we have as a nation, for instance, the more police powers people will want the government to have, the less freedom we will have, and the more fearful we will become. Taking actions based on fear leads to more fear and less freedom.

And yet, *fear is nothing more than a fantasy of the mind.* Born in the uncontrolled chatter of the sensory mind, fear is the creative force of our mind run amok, a powerful habit that grows deep roots in the mind. We can be harmed in many ways – by nature, by accident, by attack – but only we can create fear for ourselves. It has become so much a part of our life that we have come to believe that it is necessary and helpful, that it somehow protects us. *Nothing is further from the truth.*

## A Matter of Focus

What if we did not allow our mind to fantasize about the future when we are confronted with a threat or a dangerous situation? If we focus on the reality of "what is" instead of anticipating "what if," the natural biological drive for self-preservation dominates the mind. In fact, we probably have no mind chatter at all at this moment, we are totally focused on what is happening. By staying focused on the present, mind and body are coordinated, resulting in a relaxed alertness, clarity of mind, flexibility and balance, *and no fear!* You cannot be focused on the moment, attentive to the perceptual reality, and be fearful at the same time.

This is the key to all martial arts training. You never anticipate an attack; you focus on the attack that is real at the moment. In this way, the mind is free from any fear or worry; consequently it is clear, responsive and creative. When the mind is clear and focused, you perceive the intent of the attacker before his body can carry out that intent. The body is free from the fight-or-flight alarm reaction, and so it remains relaxed, movements are flexible, and coordinated, and reflexes are quick and accurate.

Self-preservation is exactly what is needed to deal with any crisis. If I don't allow my mind chatter to fantasize about the future, I can focus on the problem and deal effectively with what is before me. Just think for a moment. How many times did you worry about something that never happened? And how often have you missed the obvious because you were worried about the future? Do you solve problems by anticipating harm and worrying, or do you solve problems by taking whatever steps you can do now? What seems most effective to you?

## Confidence and the Future

This is not an issue about thinking or planning for the future. We have a marvelous capacity to prepare for future events – plan meetings, anticipate problems, prepare for important evens – without creating stress. The key is whether or not we anticipate harm in some way, either to ourselves or to someone or some thing that is important to us. In the deeper sense, underlying the habits of the mind, fear is actually the consequence of a failure of self-confidence. Just think for a moment. If you were genuinely self-confident, what would you ever worry about?

Fear always involves an anticipated threat to the ego, our personal sense of identity, which expands to include the people and things that we emotionally identify with. Instead of simply having a problem to solve, we have a problem that potentially will harm "me." Often, this happens so subtly that we don't even notice that we have just trapped ourselves. Suppose you get assigned a project at work. If you see the assignment as a challenge and feel confident about yourself, you focus on the problems to be solved, make decisions, take necessary steps, and evaluate your outcomes. If you make mistakes along the way, you take corrective actions until you achieve your goal. But if you perceive this assignment as a threat, and worry about what your boss or someone else thinks about the quality of your work, you set off the fight-or-flight alarm reaction. Your mind begins to play in the future, anticipating what might happen if you fail. The resulting fear and worry upsets your balance, your body becomes stressed, and your mind too disturbed to focus properly. You inhibit your creative and intuitive abilities, and end up with a headache or stomach pain. All of this makes it increasingly difficult to do the job creatively and successfully, and life becomes difficult and unpleasant.

Listen to and compare the language of someone who worries about a certain event and someone who faces the same event with confidence. Along with pessimistic references to the future, the worrier will also have a number of self-references, all reflecting some kind of pending tragedy or harm that he will suffer. The individual with confidence will speak about the problem that must be solved, and will probably already be planning some action. Her ego is not on the line in any negative way.

We train ourselves to fail by the worries and fears we imagine. The greater the imagined threat, the more energy goes into the imbalance between mind and body, and the more dis-eased we become. Even a small worry brings about some activation of the fight-or-flight alarm reaction and inhibits mental resources. Whenever we create fear, we harm ourselves at all levels. Fear has no value other than to create stress and misery, cloud the intellect, inhibit memory, and close off access to intuitive and instinctual knowledge.

Remember Chicken Little, the storybook character who made a career of worrying? Like Chicken Little, the worrier lives from one crisis to the next, and every little thing seems to upset him. Much of his mental activity is useless – consisting of endless speculations on future events and reconstruction of past events. The impact on his body is very apparent. He is always tense and his movements are uncoordinated and jerky. He probably complains about headaches, and his breathing quickly becomes rapid and shallow. There is very little focus on the here and now, just a lot of "what if" kinds of statements. When we constantly program ourselves with this fantasy called fear, our poor bodies have no choice but to respond with tension and stress.

## Self-Hatred: The Destructive Power of Selective History

Human beings are amazing. When no one is attacking us, we turn around and attack ourselves. These self-attacks from self-hatred, though not as dramatic as fear, are just as deadly. And like fear, self-hatred is not a natural condition of the human mind. We weren't born with self-hatred; it is something we learn. It becomes a habit of the mind. Self-attack takes many different forms and patterns, ranging from guilt and inferiority complexes to conscious self-hatred and suicidal thoughts – all of which bring on the possum response.

It isn't difficult to create a chronic pattern of failure and misery. All you have to do is constantly remind yourself of how awful, weak, or incompetent you are, and brood on your past mistakes, hurts and failures. Just as unmanaged chatter about the future creates fear, unmanaged chatter about the past creates self-hatred. But instead of the fight-or-flight reaction you have when you are fearful or worried, your body responds with a possum reaction, becomes passive, and goes into retreat. Again, you lose touch with the present, and cannot deal with it effectively and joyfully. The consequences are that you become withdrawn, weaken the immune system, make more mistakes, and feel even weaker and more incompetent.

One of the most common ways we punish ourselves is unforgiving self-criticism that eventually leads to self-hatred. Let's say that you are out for dinner with someone you really want to impress. As you reach across the table for the saltshaker, you accidentally knock over a glass of red wine that spills onto her lap. Out of embarrassment, you probably judge yourself harshly, and you feel the consequences. How long do you continue to mentally berate yourself for that incident?

The reality was that you spilled the wine. If you quickly forget the incident, the impact of the possum response is negligible. But if you continue to remind yourself about what a stupid act that was, the greater is the impact on your self-respect and on the body. The anger or shame or other feelings were the consequences of your interpretation; they were not part of the event itself. Your interpretation, however, led directly to a possum reaction and your unhappiness.

Chronic self-criticism leads to chronic feelings of inferiority. Nearly everyone suffers from believing that at some time they are just not good enough. Sometimes we use negative self-talk to motivate ourselves to succeed, but we never seem to achieve enough success to overcome our nagging self-doubt. We try to prove our self-worth over and over. No matter how much we have or how much we achieve, we still feel like second-rate or that we've failed. And to complicate things, we constantly worry that others will find us out. We end up paying a very high (and unnecessary) price for our success.

Another common destructive expression of self-hatred is guilt. Guilt is double-edged misery. Not only do we create strongly negative feelings about ourselves, we reinforce the very behavior that led to the guilt. When we feel guilty, we become preoccupied with the behavior that makes us feel guilty. The more attention we give it, the greater the probability that it will happen again. Guilt leads directly to conflict and resentment, which interfere with our ability to act. The guiltier we feel, the less competent we become, the more we beat ourselves up, and the more miserable we feel.

As we will see later, guilt has nothing to do with our genuine conscience. When we react with guilt, we simply repeat the condemnations we learn from others. Our natural, or real conscience lies in the more subtle discriminating mind, the next dimension of the personality. The real conscience is not punitive.

Nor does it make judgments, so it doesn't activate the possum response. It quietly tells us what is helpful and what isn't, what will benefit us and what will not. Discrimination provides us with the opportunity to recognize mistakes, learn from them, and make more effective choices.

Just as we weren't born fearful, we weren't born guilty. Like other types of self-hatred, we learn to be guilty through our interactions with parents, teachers, preachers, and other members of society. Instead of using the power of discrimination to discern cause/effect relationships and learn from our mistakes, we use guilt to call names, make value judgments and, most of all, punish ourselves.

The language of self-hatred is just as destructive as the language of fear, and much more varied. In *The Quiet Mind*, Dr. John Harvey identifies several different categories of destructive inner chatter that feed the dragon of self-hatred:

**1. Demands on others, on ourselves, and on life:** Frequent use of words like should, must, and have to, as in, "You should do this," "I have to have this position," and "She must have a certain dress."

**2. Denial:** Using words to avoid facing reality, or the truth of our own actions. There is frequent use of phrases like "I can't believe," or "I don't understand," or "How could this happen?"

**3. Overreaction:** We often overreact to disappointments and to things that go wrong, using language that only adds to our troubles. We often refer to this kind of talk as "terriblizing" or "horriblizing." It includes words such as "terrible, horrible, awful," and "miserable," and such familiar phrases as, "I can't stand it," "This is awful," and "It tears me up."

**4. Always/never:** This is language that helps us live our negative history. We project our past failures onto the future and refuse to believe that any change is possible. Language becomes prophetic (and pathetic) in such phrases as "Things will never change," "It will always be like this," "I'll never get . . .," and "She always does this." These are words of a victim.

**5. All/nothing:** We generalize faults and mistakes into global realities. By not achieving perfection, we become a complete failure, good-for-nothing, an utter jerk; or, we have totally destroyed our careers.

**6. Mind reading:** When we think little of ourselves, we project these judgments onto others, and assume we know how they perceive and evaluate us. It includes words and phrases such as, "They know I'm a failure," or, "She thinks that I'm unattractive," or "They know what a fraud I am."

## Mind Chatter: The Power of Thought

Words and images are powerful. They inspire, create insight, solve problems, hurt, and even destroy. In the sensory mind, words and images define our personal sense of reality. As the wise old umpire knew, our reality is what we call it. Not only do our words have an impact on others, they have an impact on us.

The words we use to describe our experiences and to interpret our perceptions also determine our feelings and emotional reactions. Whether we are happy, sad, angry, depressed, challenged or fearful depends on the language and images we use. If I describe a situation as very difficult, and the people involved as hard-nosed and judgmental, I will probably feel insecure and not very comfortable. If I describe the same situation as a challenge, and the people as interesting and discriminating, my attitude towards the situation will be quite different.

Our mind chatter is actually the expression of our creative force. We can't escape thinking, nor should we. This creative force can be a powerful tool for us if we have the skill to choose words that are free of destructive emotional connections. Unfortunately, we don't always choose our words with care. In fact, most of the time the words we use are determined by our habits. Because we aren't sensitive to how these words affect us, we are stuck with the emotional reactions that they create. This emotional connection to the words we use is a large part of the dragons' power.

Take a moment to become aware of your chatter. Don't get involved with it, just be a witness and watch the different thoughts, images and sensations that arise in your mind.

Now, try this short exercise in mind/body awareness. Read through the exercise first, and then close your eyes and go through the four steps.

Which was most comfortable: watching the thoughts pass through, letting the thoughts pile up, or having just the image of the empty room? How did it feel when you let the thoughts pile up in the room? Isn't that very similar to how you feel on a busy, rushed day?

## MIND/BODY AWARENESS

1. Close your eyes and visualize your mind like a room, with thoughts and images coming in one door, passing through the room and going out the other door. Notice how one thought leads to another in a seemingly endless progression of thoughts, images and sensations. As you do this, be aware of how your body feels.

2. Close the door the thoughts are going out, and let the thoughts pile up in the room for a few moments. Then pay attention to your body. What differences do you notice?

3. Now open the door and let the thoughts clear the room. How does your body react as the thoughts depart the room?

4. Then close both doors, and picture an empty room. What do you notice now in your body?

## Thoughts and Images: Mind Magic

Until we begin to pay attention, we don't realize that every thought we have has an impact on our body. Mostly these changes are very subtle, far below our level of awareness. They may be as gentle as the slightly increased blood pressure and heart rate that take place when we think about engaging in exercise, or the increase of saliva in the mouth as we think about dinner or smell food cooking. More dramatic are the changes in physiology induced through hypnotic suggestion. Even more spectacular are the occasional reports of someone performing a dramatic physical feat during a crisis. Recently, the media reported on a man in his late fifties or early sixties who saw a young girl pinned beneath a large concrete pipe. He had just recently recovered from a heart attack and was avoiding any strenuous activity, particularly lifting. But when he saw the little girl pinned beneath the pipe, he didn't waste a second. He ran over, and single-handedly lifted the pipe off her, allowing others to pull her out. Later, he and his two grown sons tried to lift the pipe again and were unable to budge it. He figured the pipe must have weighed around 700 pounds. The actual weight of the pipe was over 2,000 pounds. This incident demonstrates the power of the mind and brain to initiate, direct and alter physiological events through thoughts and images. The more emotional energy we tap and direct, the more powerful the impact.

## The Powerful Butterfly

To demonstrate it for yourself, try this small experiment. Put your thumb and forefinger together, forming a circle. Have a very strong friend put his two forefingers through the circle of your thumb and forefinger, hooking his fingers around yours. Then ask him to try to pull your thumb and finger apart slowly, and without suddenly yanking your fingers. At the same time, try as hard as you can to keep him from pulling your thumb and finger apart. Of course, your friend will succeed.

Relax your hand a minute or two and try the experiment again. This time, close your eyes and picture as clearly as you can, a large, beautiful monarch butterfly that you are holding between your thumb and forefinger. If you hold the butterfly too tightly, you will crush its wings and kill it. If you don't hold it tight enough, the butterfly will flutter away. Keep your arm, wrist and hand very relaxed, with just a slight separation between the thumb and forefinger. When the image is very clear, nod your head and have your friend again try to separate your thumb and finger, doing so slowly and without yanking the fingers apart quickly. No matter what happens, concentrate on holding the butterfly. Don't let go of it. If you maintain the image clearly in your mind, you will find that your friend will not be able to open your fingers. It will help if another friend stands there and keeps saying, "Hold the butterfly, hold the butterfly!" This suggestion helps maintain and strengthen the image in your mind.

Think for a moment of the images and suggestions that you keep in your mind on a day-to-day basis. Be particularly aware of those which have a significant amount of emotional power. What happens inside the brain is complex. We don't have to know the details, but we must realize that every thought we think has an impact on our body. The greater the emotional content, the stronger the impact on the body. We often talk as if thoughts and feelings were separate, but the truth is that they are both part of whatever we experience. Every thought has an emotional component, even though many of them are so slight that we don't feel the emotion in the thought.

## THE DRAGONS' LAIR

Now you can see why you felt a little tense when you let the thoughts pile up inside the room of your mind. Each and every thought has some direct impact on our body. This is where the dragons of fear and self-hatred live – in the uncontrolled thoughts and images of the sensory mind. Most of us pay little attention to our mind chatter even though it easily dictates our happiness or unhappiness, whether or not we feel challenged or afraid, whether or not we experience joy or get locked into depression. We get caught up in our mind chatter and forget to be a witness. When we lose awareness of this creative force, we lose our ability to exercise choice and control over what we think.

If you have a fearful or self-critical thought, and then let it go, your reaction is usually very slight. But how often do you keep fretting about the same thing? The first reaction we have often comes right from the unconscious part of mind. Something happens, not necessarily even to us, and we get our buttons pushed. Then anger, or fear, or worry, or self-doubt pops right up. If we stopped at that first reaction, there would be no problem. But we don't. We let our mind chatter continue down a track that ends in disaster. Think about something that really worries you. Notice that your mind chatter doesn't stop with that first disturbing thought. Instead, it immediately creates one imaginary unpleasant scenario after the other. Don't you ever wonder why doesn't it create pleasant scenarios? What happens to your confidence when your mind does this?

Most often it is not that first conscious concern that creates the emotional disturbance, but what you do next. You take that first thought that pops into the mind, "Oh my gosh, this is terrible!" and build a house with it in the mind by thinking about all the other terrible things that might happen. Then you build a village around the house by adding all the other awful things that happened related to this one incident. That, in turn, reminds you of the awful people who were involved. This now takes you into your history with some of those awful people and you build an entire city with skyscrapers in your mind. The problem is that now you have to pay rent on all this real estate in the form of emotional disturbance and stress. All of this just feeds the dragons and make them stronger.

If you don't have the skill to take command of your mind chatter, you are helpless to defend yourself. The dragons become stronger and stronger, and after a while, they seem to be a permanent part of your mind and personality. Even the body begins to change as chronic tension and disease reflect your inner conflicts. This in turn further weakens your will and a vicious cycle develops as your destructive thoughts lead to further destructive thoughts.

You can do something about this. You don't have to be a victim to the dragons in the mind. Let's confront the dragons and see just how they distort the creative force of the sensory mind.

## The Misleading Mind

We may not have the power to change our situations, but we certainly have the freedom to change how we define them. Often, it only takes changing a word or two to get a different perspective and see new opportunities. But as long as we use the kinds of words and phrases described above, we can't avoid the emotional states these words stimulate in the unconscious. It is our language and the consequent emotional states that reinforce fear and self-hatred and make them stronger. The words we use rob us of our strength and give it to the two dragons.

The first mistake that we make over and over again is to accept whatever the mind tells us as "the truth" instead of calmly evaluating the usefulness of our mind chatter. The sensory mind was never designed to tell us truth, but to provide us with a perspective, a consistent way to interpret perceptions. Its function is to collect and present sensory data, all of which is organized by the unconscious habits that control perceiving and thinking. These unconscious emotional habits can create many disturbing and unproductive lines of thought that have little to do with reality.

You've seen this happen to your friends many times. They become emotionally upset, and base their interpretation of the events going on around them on their emotional reactions. Remaining outside the fray, you can easily see how their emotions have misled them. For example, how many times have you been riding with someone in a car who reacts to an incident as if the other driver had intentionally created a problem for him?

The truth is that most of the time, the other driver doesn't even know that someone else is on the road. But this isn't how your friend interprets the situation. You can easily see how your friend reacted in a way that was totally out of line to the reality of the situation. Unfortunately, these interpretations often lead to real problems, particularly on the highway.

But when your emotions are involved, it's a different story. You know what is happening. You know that these people are intentionally giving you a hard time. Have you ever stopped to wonder how your friends' minds can fool them so easily and so often, and yet your mind always tells you the gospel truth?

Our emotions aren't the only source of misleading information. Our mind can offer us completely arbitrary thoughts, images, and sensations that seem very real.

Try this exercise:

### THE GREEN FROG EXERCISE

Sit back, close your eyes and relax. Focus on an even, smooth breath, and clear your mind as best as you can. Let your facial muscles relax, and follow that relaxation down to your toes, relaxing the whole body. Now imagine yourself as a great green bull-frog, sitting on a lily pad in the middle of a beautiful, small, clear pool. Over on one side you can see cattails and reeds, and a red-winged blackbird building a nest. Picture a blue sky with puffy white clouds.

It's about ten o'clock in the morning of a beautiful August day. The sun is shining and you feel the heat of the sun on your back. The sunshine feels very warm on your back. Now jump off the pad into the water. Kerploosh! Ahh, the water feels cool and nice on your warm skin. Swim down under the lily pad. You see the stem coming up from the bottom, attached to the lily pad. As you look up to the surface of the water, you see the sunshine filtering through the water. Beautiful sight! Now come to the surface, swim over to the lily pad and climb back on. Feel the pad moving underneath you as you climb on. Now the sun feels really good on your cool, wet skin. Life is wonderful!

Now open your eyes. Do you really believe that you are a large, green bullfrog? If you do, then you need more help than this book can give you. Most of us distinguish easily between our imagination and what is real...or do we? Consider this: What makes the thoughts, images, and sensations of being a bullfrog any less real than the others that your mind chatter presents? They are all nothing more than mind forms. You determine which ones you'll believe and accept, and which you won't.

You may not be able to stop the mind from telling you things, but no one says you have to believe them! You don't have to accept as gospel everything your mind chatter says. Take self-criticism, for instance. You probably have some particularly troublesome thought that keeps gnawing at you. You may not feel smart enough, or pretty enough, or you may always feel that what you accomplish is second rate, or worry that someone will find out just how incompetent you really are.

We spend an enormous amount of time and effort proving to ourselves that these thoughts aren't really true, and the very next day, we have to prove it all over again. The same thoughts pop into our mind day after day, no matter how much we succeed, how many degrees we earn, or how much money we make. Every time we have to prove ourselves, we reinforce the underlying negative thought by paying attention to it. This is the second mistake, trying to use language to control the consequences of language.

## The Strengths and Limits of Positive Thinking

Recognizing the power of language and changing it to create a more satisfying emotional state allows us to make more effective choices. In neuro-linguistics, consciously choosing words and images that are more helpful is called "reframing," a term used by Richard Bandler and John Grinder in their 1982 book called *Reframing*. Long before this, Norman Vincent Peale popularized this same message in his book *The Power Of Positive Thinking*. Centuries earlier, Shakespeare wrote, "There is no right or wrong but what thinking makes it so." And in Proverbs we find, "As he thinketh in his heart, so is he."

As we will see later, we can use language as a conscious tool to help us minimize the damage done by the dragons. We have long recognized the power of language, and yet, we continue to struggle. Even with reframing and positive thinking, we still create emotional stress for ourselves. The problem lies in that language, as a power function of the sensory mind, has limitations. If we don't understand these limitations, we remain trapped by them, and actually reinforce the very habits we are trying to change. We can begin the process of eliminating fear and self-hatred by using language as a tool, but we can't complete the job by working only with our thoughts and emotions. You cannot control the sensory mind, the seat of language, as well as perception, emotions and habits, by using only the sensory mind.

The sensory mind collects, organizes and interprets data; it does not discriminate. At times of stress, confusion, or anger, if we ask the mind to give us an answer, it will find one for us. How helpful these answers actually may be is highly questionable. Like any organization, the mind will protect its own structural integrity, and tell you whatever it needs to in order to maintain its internal consistency. These defense mechanisms, such as suppression, repression, projection, and denial, are designed to keep unacceptable parts of the personality hidden. Even when you do understand the reasons for what you do, turning to the sensory mind doesn't necessarily give you the skill or power to change anything.

There is a powerful characteristic of the sensory mind that makes changing habits difficult. The sensory mind builds on opposites. In other words, there must be an "up" to have "down," and "good" to have "bad." If things are easy, then somewhere things are hard. If we think positively, than somewhere in the mind, we have negative thinking. As long as we deal in opposites, we cannot eliminate just one side. When we stand in front of the mirror, smile and say, "Today is going to a wonderful day in every way" what is the mind saying on an unconscious level? Probably something very much like, "Wanna bet?" or, "Yesterday sure was lousy."

When we deal only with positive statements, we force our negative feelings into the unconscious mind. In fact, the very motivation to think positively comes from a negative condition. Why would you need to think positively unless you had already created a negative state? If you didn't create any negative feelings about yourself, you wouldn't have to think positively. Your mind would be free to focus on problem solving. No matter how many times you repeat positive affirmations, they only subtly reinforce the negative, and you never gain freedom.

When we focus only on positive thinking, we create a false identity, a mask that is inconsistent with our real feelings. This inconsistency creates a subtle form of stress that weakens both the body and our will. This insincerity prevents us from dealing with the truth of who we are, and from dealing accurately and adequately with our problems. Gradually this mask that we create begins to crack, and we find that we have no idea of who we really are.

An all too common example of this is the person who always has to be "nice." No matter what happens, this person always looks at the bright side of things, or no matter how badly he is mistreated, he always blames himself and tries to be nice. This type of denial leads to superficiality as it isolates us from the power of our emotions. Not only do we seem insincere to others, but we also become more and more rigid as we struggle to stay safe.

Positive thinking, rephrasing language, or reframing interpretations are all helpful to a degree. They are necessary steps on the path to freedom, particularly if you have been negative about yourself. They open new possibilities, provide fresh insights, and allow us to create a greater degree of balance and harmony. But they are only a step, not the final goal. If we don't know how to transcend the sensory mind and its power function of language, we remain caught in its subtle traps. We must go beyond language, beyond thought, beyond our emotions, to finally free ourselves from the problems created by these functions of the sensory mind. As we shall see later on, we can access the deeper levels of the mind and neutralize the power of our emotional and language habits. When we eliminate the need to be positive, we will find that we already are.

## Mix and Match: The Dragon Twins

Once we understand the power of language, it is easy to see why most of us are quite skilled in finding ways to disturb ourselves. When we aren't worrying about what others think of us, we spend our time thinking badly of ourselves. The two dragons of fear and self-hatred not only come from the same source – uncontrolled mind chatter – but they support and feed off each other. The more fearful we are, the less self-respect we have for ourselves. The less self-respect we have, the weaker we feel, and the more we worry about things.

The difficulty is that we are ignorant of what we are doing in our mind. We aren't sensitive to the organizing faculty of the sensory mind that acts as a filter mechanism, and we seldom, if ever, receive the training necessary to be aware of and to take control of this process.

For example, take a deck of cards on which the spades are red and the hearts are black. If each card was flashed in front of us, we would probably see red hearts and black spades because many of us can't change our conditioned mental categories and don't see what is really there. The same principle can also be observed at just about any sports event. The two groups of fans, one for each team, will generally have two differing views of events.

In a controversy, each will be absolutely sure of what they saw! Another example of preconditioning is when we believe that our colleague at the office is actively competing with us, when, in fact, he isn't. We tend to ignore those actions that are inconsistent with our beliefs and prejudices and interpret all other actions as proof of them.

What if our colleague really is competing with us? Do we feel threatened, or insecure? Do we give it any importance at all? If we are secure and confident, we may be excited by it – or we may choose not to concern ourselves at all. On the other hand, if we interpret his actions as a possible threat, then we react with anger, aggression or fear. It is not what he does that matters; it is how and what we think about it. It is never what someone does or says that disturbs us; it is what we tell ourselves that creates the disturbance.

What goes through your mind when someone criticizes your work, or gives you a deadline that "must" be met? Are you really aware of the thoughts that pass through your mind and sensitive to the emotional consequences of those thoughts? Most of us feel that we are usually pretty cool under pressure and fairly mature in our emotional responses. Sadly, we are often unaware of how the mind is shaping our reactions – unaware of how much time the mind spends in creating problems for us. The fears and punishments from which we suffer are usually not from life-threatening events, but rather from the petty disturbances that we create on a day-to-day basis.

It would be impossible to catalog all the fears from which we suffer. Fear of failure, of rejection, of being "found out" are only the tip of the iceberg. Fears from financial pressures, time pressure, and deadlines are dangers of a more immediate kind. There are also fears of what others think about us, our work, or our family. The fear of others' opinions is probably the greatest threat that we create for ourselves – with negative self-judgments running a close second. These thoughts are so pervasive and so subtle that we fail to recognize the tremendous pressures they create. Mistakes too often turn into convenient "whipping posts" for self-flagellation, and we lose the benefit of the learning that always takes place when mistakes are made. The fact that we are insensitive to the pressures created by these negative thoughts does not eliminate or negate them; it only allows them to operate unconsciously.

## Out of Three – All the Others

Of course, we have emotional disturbances other than fear, self-hatred, and loneliness. We suffer from jealousy (envy), greed, pride – the list varies depending on how you want to approach it. We feel a lot of different emotions; they differ in intensity and focus, and it seems like we resolve one only to be confronted by another. But if we analyze closely, we find that the three dragons of fear, self-hatred and loneliness lie at the root of all these other emotions. They are subtle combinations of these three powerful dragons. Of the three, fear and self-hatred play a more active, energizing role in forming the other emotions. For instance, greed, a destructive force throughout the world, may have its roots in a fear of not having enough, a fear of the future, or a need to be important. More often it is a combination of many different fears and feelings of inadequacy. Jealousy and envy also have roots in fear and self-hatred.

No one is jealous of another unless he thinks that what the other person has is somehow better, meaning that what he already has (goods, talents, ideas, a mate, etc.) is not good enough. Arrogance certainly has its roots in self-hatred. Those with self-respect and a healthy, strong ego have no need to show how important they are. But when there is self-hatred in the subtle levels of the mind, pride turns to arrogance to compensate for the lack of genuine self-respect.

There is no doubt that these other emotions do become powerful disruptive forces on their own. Once they are established as habits, they are as ugly and destructive as fear and self-hatred. But without fear and self-hatred, they have no energy and become powerless. We can chase every emotion, but that would be fruitless. Like the heads popping up in the child's game, we would whack one only to have another raise its ugly head. But if we attack the source, if we slay the two dragons of fear and self-hatred, we significantly weaken all other emotional disturbances. And as we will see later, when we resolve loneliness, even fear and self-hatred, along with all other emotional disturbances, fall away like ripe fruit off a tree.

## A Habit of Dragons

In order to become free of these two dragons, we must first realize that fear and self-hatred are nothing more than patterns of thought in the mind. They are habits in the form of beliefs and fantasies that we accept as true. The problem is not that we are weak and fearful, but only that we have learned to see ourselves as weak and fearful. Once these fantasies become habits, a part of our self-concept, we lose touch with our powerful inner resources.

Mind chatter follows the pattern of our habits. Most of us pay little attention to the flow of thoughts, and we often aren't aware that our mind chatter is taking us down a track that will create misery for us. *We suffer from fear and self-hatred because we are insensitive to the mental and physical habits that create them.* Only when our discomfort has reached the pain threshold do most of us even begin to pay attention. By then, however, it is too late to prevent the consequences. If you are sensitive to a particular emotional process before it becomes overwhelming, however, you have the opportunity to redirect the energy into more helpful and satisfying patterns.

Remember when you were a child running down a long hill? Remember how the momentum carried you along and how, at a certain point, it was almost impossible to stop? I remember such a hill in an open field when I was a young lad. About two-thirds of the way down, there was a ditch that you could not see from the top because of the long grass. In fact, you could not see the ditch at all until you were just a few feet from a drop-off into a large muddy area.

We used to take friends from a different neighborhood to the top of the hill and shout, "Let's run down the hill! Last one down is a chicken!" With that, we would take off. By the time we were two feet from the ditch we were going pretty fast, and only then would the poor fellow from the other neighborhood see it right in front of him. What was his reaction? Emotional conflict! He didn't want to run off the cliff into the muck, but he couldn't stop his body's momentum. Of course, since we knew where the ditch was, we could consciously direct the flow of our energy. We would run right alongside of him and then veer off at the last minute – while he sailed off into the ditch.

This is analogous to what happens in our minds. We don't want to be angry, or fearful, but in some situations our emotions are strong, and by the time we recognize them, we are out of control. The emotional response is too strong to direct. At best we can stifle it – and then pay another price.

We know the power of our emotional habits to create suffering, but how many of us have the awareness and the skill to free ourselves from their grasp? Becoming more aware of these habits leads naturally to a greater degree of choice and control. If we can see the ditch from the top of the hill, we can easily direct our energy so that there will be no conflict.

Analyzing our fears and negative mind chatter is useful, but of limited benefit. If thinking were all that we needed, none of us would be disturbed. After all, don't we already *know* what to do? Our intellect cannot resolve our fear. The tools of intellect – logic, information, reasoning, and beliefs – are powerless in the face of fear and self-hatred. The effectiveness of the intellect is hampered by our emotions, attitudes, and experiences. What, and even how we think is determined by *all* the elements of the mind, not just the intellect. When we ignore these elements, they remain as traps in our unconscious, creating fears and weakness.

Our beliefs are useful tools as they determine the structure and substance of our reality. But even beliefs become impotent in the face of the powerful, unthinking emotions of fear and self-hatred. Our intelligence, logic, and beliefs have not conquered fear. How often do we know we have nothing to worry about, but still we worry? We often have great insights about our personality, but our emotions prevent us from acting on them. When we depend only on our intellect and our beliefs, and ignore the other dimensions and functions of the personality, we remain unaware of our inner strength. We allow the ego to become unbalanced and fail to develop the other powerful innate resources of the mind such as our emotional power, intuition, and innate self-confidence.

## LONELINESS: THE FINAL DRAGON

While fear and self-hatred arise out of uncontrolled mind chatter, loneliness has a different source that is far more subtle. We can do much to eliminate fear and self-hatred by taking control of our mind chatter. But to overcome loneliness, we must become aware of the deepest dimension of our being, the spiritual Self, and take back the power that we have given to the ego.

We need a healthy, strong ego in order to have a healthy strong personality. The problem arises when the ego begins to act as if it is actually the owner, the master of the personality, instead of manager and caretaker. Under the influence of the ego, we lose track of the spiritual Self. *We forget that we are really spiritual beings here to have human experiences, and come to believe that we are only human beings trying to have spiritual experiences.* Once we identify ourselves as only the personality consisting of mind and body, we are stuck with all the limitations of this personality.

When we identify with the ego instead of the spiritual Self, we become egocentric, and the ego becomes unbalanced. We can easily see the destructiveness of an unbalanced ego if we look at the extremes of an overinflated ego and an underinflated or fragile ego. Our society is full of so-called famous people – the Elvis Presleys and Marilyn Monroes – who work desperately hard to get attention but end up so isolated and alone they destroy themselves with drugs or commit suicide. When the ego is over inflated, the world exists to satisfy the ego's needs, and even people become objects to be used. The more power the ego gets, the more demanding it becomes, and the less strength we have as a person. Inflated egos look at the world as a feeding trough. Everything and everyone exists only to serve the needs and desires of the individual ego. We become infatuated with power, with position, with being number one. We continually have to prove how much better we are than others. But even if we get to the top of the heap, we still feel isolated. The more inflated the ego, the more isolated we become, and the more loneliness we feel.

On the other extreme are the fragile egos that are easily intimidated and find threats at every turn. They become the victims, the blamers who find fault with everyone, including themselves. Some suffer quietly, afraid to make changes or confront themselves and the issues around them. Insecure about other people's opinions, they are afraid to express themselves or to rock the boat. Others join groups and find safety in numbers. They see the world in divisive terms, "us" against "them," the "good guys" against the "bad guys," "my religion is better than your religion." Instead of celebrating diversity, they use it as a focus for hate. And no matter how many other people they get to join with them, they still feel insecure, alienated from the rest of humanity, and suffer a great deal of fear and anxiety.

Most of us don't reach these ego extremes. But at one time or the other, all of us suffer from letting our egos become the center of power. You don't have to drive long in heavy traffic before seeing some ego expressing itself, or perhaps feeling your own ego taking over: "You can't cut in front of ME like that!" In many ways, our ego gets in the way. We may "blow up" at some poor clerk, or we gossip and prove that we are better than someone else, or we don't speak up when we should. The need to be right all the time, the fear of admitting mistakes, an inability to form lasting, committed relationships, the unwillingness to share resources, having to have it "my way" – these are common ego-driven attitudes that we all experience from time to time. When the ego takes center-stage, the capacity to love, to be open to and share with others, to live in harmony with each other, is diminished.

When our experience of self is limited to the mind and body, then the ego becomes owner and we mistakenly think that all we are is the mind and body. In the tantric tradition, as well as other spiritual traditions, this mistaken identity is called ignorance, and is considered to be the single, greatest source of suffering. Ignorance doesn't mean that we don't have enough academic degrees or that we aren't smart enough. Ignorance means to lack awareness, to be "unaware of." At the most profound level, what we ignore is the spiritual Self, the core of our identity. Many of us will even talk about having a soul, and it may be something that we firmly believe. But if we only have belief and faith, we remain ignorant and without power. If we do not experience that soul, if we do not have a conscious awareness of that spiritual reality, we do not have the strength to wrest control from the ego. When experience and identity is locked to the ego, we experience life as an individual leaf instead of a unique expression of the life force within the tree.

The personality is designed to be a unique expression of the spiritual Self. No one can be like another, nor should we even try. Part of the purpose in life is to express the unique talents, views and beauty of our individual personality. But that expression must include all of who we are, not just part. When we ignore the spiritual Self, the personality remains limited. We are unable to see the larger picture, and how we are an integral part of something much greater than ourselves. Isolated, we are unable to draw upon the powerful resources of this larger reality.

We now know that the environment is a complex ecosystem, and that everything great or small within the environment plays a role in maintaining the integrity of the ecosystem. When we ignore the inter-connections of the various subsystems, we create problems that are very harmful. The same is true for society. When we ignore the elements that create a healthy community – sufficient income and jobs, education, loving and supportive families, a sense of community, an equitable distribution of wealth, respect for self and others, clean air and water – we create ghettos of crime, disease, and violence. When we treat the symptoms by building more prisons, we create even greater problems, even more harsh realities.

The personality is no different than any other complex organization. When we ignore painful parts of the personality, we create distortions within it which foster emotional problems and disease. When we ignore the spiritual core dimension, we become trapped by the habits of the mind, and remain locked into our fears, our self-hatred and our loneliness.

The function of the ego is to maintain a sense of separateness, a boundary between what is "me" and what is "not me." If I identify with the ego instead of the spiritual Self, I also experience separateness, an uncrossable boundary between myself and others. To protect what is "mine," I create barriers, isolating myself from the rest of humanity. The more separate I feel, the more isolated I become, and the greater my loneliness. Unfortunately, the more isolated I feel, the greater will be my need to protect myself from others. This can lead to a vicious cycle of even greater weakness, loss of self-respect and further isolation, all of which only increase my fears and loneliness. But the most damaging aspect of being ego-centered is that it diminishes our capacity to love. As we will see in the final chapter, the more self-centered we are the less capacity we have to give to others, the less able we are to love and to experience love. When we are ego-centered, we love in order to get love. It becomes a trade-off, a position of bargaining. "I will love you if..." then we give our conditions. This often takes the form of expectations. This isn't love; it's emotional blackmail. And the more we do this, the more we find that what we call love is a bittersweet experience.

The love we experience from the spiritual Self is unconditional. That doesn't mean that any and all behavior is acceptable. It means that I love you even though I may have to protect myself from your behavior. And I love you no matter where you are or even if you don't love me back. This doesn't make me a sucker, it makes me strong and free of disturbance. Unconditional love isn't foolish or weak, it can only come from strength, and this strength comes from the spiritual core.

As we experience the selfless love that characterizes the spiritual Self, loneliness comes to an end. We are never lonely when we love. This is what is meant by the word yoga. The word yoga comes from the root *yuj* meaning to join together or unite. When we unite our personal awareness with the spiritual Self, we no longer feel isolated or alone. The greater our awareness of the spiritual Self, the more we overcome any loneliness.

## Taking Power Back From the Dragons

The dragons exist only because we do not have the knowledge, strength, and skill to take back the power that we gave them long ago. They have no power to exist on their own. No one else makes us afraid. If someone points a loaded gun at your head, they have the power to take your life, but they have no power to make you afraid. Only you can do that. Fear exists only at our invitation. If we stop using the creative force of the mind to create fear and worry, we no longer suffer from them. If we have the ability to draw upon our inner strength whenever we need it, fear is no longer a part of our life.

The same is true of self-hatred. Even if we experience the condemnation of others, it has no power unless we join in and condemn ourselves. We will always be judged by external standards. There will always be expectations to meet. But so what? Even if we fail to meet these expectations, that doesn't mean that we must abuse ourselves. Failure, like fear, only exists at our invitation. It doesn't matter how many condemn us or how many praise us, the key is how we respond. If we have control of our mind chatter, if we experience the unlimited spiritual Self, self-hatred, like fear, becomes a thing of the past.

Likewise, no one else compels us to suffer from loneliness, to live our lives as a small, self-centered people. The great sages throughout history have repeatedly told us that we are more than what we see, hear and feel. But even if we are sparks of the Divine Light, it has little power in our life unless we experience it. Loneliness, isolation, self-centeredness – all exist only because of ignorance. When we quiet the mind, when we go to the center of our being and experience the power of the spiritual Self, we are free.

We know what the dragons are, and we know how these dragons are created and sustained. We also have a map of the different dimensions of our identity, and at least know on an intellectual level, the powerful resources of the mind. But this is only the necessary first step. Self-knowledge has power, but without skill, that power is empty. Unless we know how to use that power, unless we become skilled human beings, we have nothing. We must turn now to the other side of the equation of self-mastery, self-discipline, the skill to use the power of human nature.

4

# SKILL: TAKING CHARGE OF THE POWER

*Habit rules the unreflecting herd.*
—William Wordsworth—

Like Mickey Mouse in Disney's version of Paul Dukas's *The Magician's Apprentice,* we bumble around with our power and create problems for ourselves instead of helping ourselves. The trick is to respond to the world with a calm, clear mind rather than allow our reactions to create dragons for us. We can seldom choose what happens in the world around us, but we sure can do a much better job in choosing how we respond to that world. In other words, we must become skillful people. To accomplish this, we must come to grips with the other half of self-mastery – skill, the conscious ability to use our inner resources without creating problems for ourselves. We create skills through our natural capacity for self-discipline.

Self-discipline doesn't mean self-punishment. Self-discipline is about accessing our inner strength and developing the ability to do whatever we choose to do. We already have everything we need to become skillful human beings. Now we must bring that power under our conscious control so we can use it in creative and useful ways for ourselves and others.

## OUR HABITS: CHANNELING THE POWER

The same power functions that create and sustain the dragons in the busy and noisy sensory mind also contain the secret of self-discipline and skill. Here we find the power function of habit formation, the conserving force of the mind and one of its most powerful and pervasive tools. The ability to form habits allows the mind to conserve effort and energy. In and of itself, the habit function is neither good nor bad, but like other power functions of the sensory mind – perception, language and emotions – we can use it to help ourselves (good driving habits, healthy eating habits), or to harm ourselves (smoking, poor posture, chronic worrying). It all depends on whether we take control of this function, or unconsciously and automatically follow whatever habits happen to be developed.

A habit is like a groove that channels the energy of the mind in a certain direction. The more often the mind's energy travels down that channel, the deeper the channel, and the stronger the habit becomes. We form these grooves, or habits, through a process called conditioning, repeating behaviors that give us pleasure and avoiding behaviors that give us pain. Sometimes the consequences of our actions are immediate, such as eating a delicious piece of cherry pie. The next time we get hungry, we will think about that cherry pie and try to figure out how to get more. Soon we develop the habit of eating cherry pie whenever we have the opportunity. We probably won't think about how we feel four hours later. The immediate taste of sweetness reinforces the desire to have that particular dish. On the other hand, we may eat something that tastes awful, and if so, we probably will never try it again.

We also build habits through association. The cause and effect may not be related to each other, but occur close enough in time that we make a connection. A friend of mine had stomach flu just after eating sushi fifteen years ago. Even though she knows intellectually that the sushi was not the cause of her illness, the unpleasantness of the illness is so strongly associated with the sushi that she cannot force herself to eat it again. This process of association is how we become superstitious. If a baseball pitcher wins a couple of games, and notices that before each of these wins, he ate mashed potatoes and wore a red hat to the game, he may make sure he eats mashed potatoes and wears that same red hat on the day of an important game. After all, it can't hurt!

But the real key to forming habits is to do the same behavior over and over again. It doesn't matter what we do – walking, talking, sitting, clenching jaw muscles, tightening our shoulder muscles, reacting to someone else's behavior, worrying – only that we repeat the same action, same thought, or same emotional reaction. For instance, we don't always worry about the same thing, but we always worry. It is the act of worrying that builds the habit, not the specific thing we worry about.

When habits are practiced and refined, they are called skills. If we do something well or easily, it is because we have the habits for that particular behavior. When something is difficult, it means we don't have the habits to support the behavior. We become skilled drivers, skilled tennis players or skilled accountants because we practice the actions over and over again. We become skilled at brushing our teeth, having good posture, or developing healthy sleeping patterns. We also become skilled at worrying, self-criticism, self-doubt, and poor health habits because we practice them. Every time we worry, we are practicing worrying. No wonder we become so skilled at worrying.

The most powerful and subtle habits are those learned in the first five or six years of our lives. But we don't choose these habits. They develop unconsciously as a result of our interactions with our parents and society. Once these early habits are established, they shape our personalities and influence everything we do for the rest of our lives. If we grow up as Americans, we look at the world with the perspective of an American. If we grow up believing that we aren't important or very smart, it becomes difficult in later life to experience ourselves as important or smart. And we will probably spend a great deal of effort trying to prove that we really are important and smart. As long as we remain unaware of these built-in biases, we don't have any effective way to counteract them.

These habits have only an accidental relationship to "the truth." They are not true or false; they are simply habits. But if they are part of the personality, they seem like "the truth" to us because they are such an integral part of our personality. As we age, it becomes increasingly difficult to think in some other way. The myth that fear is a natural part of being human is a classic example of how a habit comes to be seen as "the truth," something other than what it actually is. The same can be said for all the negative and critical thoughts we have about ourselves. These are nothing more than habits masquerading as "the truth."

## Bad Habits Bring Bad Outcomes

This is how we use our own power against ourselves. Many of our habits are certainly not ones that we would choose for ourselves, but they still control us. The most powerful are the mental, emotional, and perceptual habits that determine who we are, how we think, and what we do. These habits allow me to be me, and you to be you. How I understand my world, how I feel about myself, even how I communicate all depend on these subtle mental habits. But they may also create stress, neuroses, and unhappiness. If I develop a habit of self-rejection or an inferiority complex, then I experience myself as inferior and suffer the emotional trauma that this brings.

We are all too familiar with those habits that create emotional reactions for us. Sooner or later, we all get "our buttons pushed," or we occasionally blow up over a trivial incident. Let's say that you walk into a crowded room and see two people together. One is a stranger, the other is someone you know but don't like or trust. Your eyes meet with this "enemy," and you experience a moment of mutual recognition. Then this person smiles and drops his gaze. You see him whisper into the ear of the person sitting next to him. The next moment the stranger looks in your direction, smiles and quickly looks away. Now, what does your mind do with this? Are they talking about you? No doubt! Are they saying what a wonderful person you are? Very doubtful! And what is your emotional reaction? Does the term "paranoia" fit?

Did you make a conscious decision to be upset? Highly unlikely! You walked into a situation and unconsciously interpreted actions along the lines of your past experience (habits). The consequence was an emotional reaction made in the unconscious part of the mind, not a conscious, thoughtful choice. Very few of us consciously choose to be disturbed!

You might recall what you felt when you went through this experience. More than likely, your shoulder muscles tensed, perhaps your jaw muscles tensed, and you might have even felt a little nauseated. You felt self-conscious, were hesitant to talk to others and stood off by yourself trying to look occupied. That singular emotional reaction impacted both your body and your behavior.

Over time, our emotional habits, along with all the other habits and patterns of our personality and lifestyle, impact our health. In time, we may develop asthma because of a subtle lack of self-confidence, ulcers because we have a habit of not expressing our anger, migraine headaches because we have a habit of denying negative feelings, or even cancer because we have learned to feel hopeless and helpless about life. Rarely does a single habit create harm, although individual habits can have a significant impact, such as smoking. Like stress, what counts is the whole picture – lifestyle, physical, mental-emotional, even spiritual habits. The way we conduct our life reflects the condition of our emotional health. Healthy habits lead to a healthy body and appropriate behavior. But destructive emotional habits always leave their mark on the body and our behavior.

Stress is an obvious consequence of habits. The most troubling habits are the ones that lead to the dragons of fear and self-hatred. Self-critical beliefs that we developed during early childhood years, such as feeling that we aren't smart enough, or pretty enough, or lovable enough, are often unexpressed and unrecognized. But they have a powerful impact on our attitudes and perceptions. We may lack confidence in our work, feel insecure in social gatherings, be hesitant about taking risks and accepting new challenges. Or we may become a raging Type A personality, driven by inner voices to prove that we aren't second-rate. If these early childhood patterns are pathological, we can become very judgmental, constantly fearful of other's opinions, depressed or neurotic, even psychotic. This is definitely not the kind of magic that we really want.

## The Unconscious Power

We have this unimaginably powerful instrument we call the mind, but we don't know how to control it. Instead, it controls us, and the consequences are not pretty. The first step to self-control is to take charge of our habits. Regardless of how they develop, all habits share one critical aspect – they only operate in, and because of, the unconscious mind. We consciously create habits when we practice playing a piano or proper breathing and relaxation techniques. The purpose of the practice is to develop a habit a certain behavior or skill that we don't have to think about, i.e., a habit. Not a single habit functions as part of the conscious mind.

Many social scientists and philosophers believe that while habits exist in the unconscious, they are really controlled by events in the external environment. These external events provide the reinforcement – the pain or pleasure – that build and strengthen the habit, and stimulate it to action or inaction. According to the late B.F. Skinner, the "Grandfather of Behaviorism," we are products of our environment, and the environment controls us. If someone knows how to push our buttons, there is little we can do. In other words, we are slaves to our habits, habitual automatons with no real freedom of choice. Whatever stimulates and reinforces those habits in the environment controls our behavior. (A more modern version of scientific determinism tells us that it is our genetics that control us.)

For example, let's say you have acquired a deep-seated habit of feeling incompetent. Learned in childhood, this attitude lies in the unconscious, where you are not fully aware of its power. However, whenever anyone questions your judgment, you react with anger, and aggressively overwhelm your questioner with intense, logical argument. The intensity of your response indicates that one of your buttons (your old habit of believing yourself to be incompetent) was pushed, and you react to this threat with the fight-or-flight alarm reaction. When your inquisitor backs down, both the effectiveness of your reaction and the old habit of feeling incompetent are reinforced. More than likely, you rationalize your reaction without ever being aware of the real reason behind your actions.

Eating habits are another example where being unaware of what we are doing allows a habit to control what we do. Many of us gobble our food in record time, meal after meal. The food is there, and the setting has become a stimulus for the habit of eating fast – even when there is no time pressure. When you sit down to eat, where is your attention? Are you really paying attention to eating, or are you conversing with family or friends, having a working lunch, or reading the paper? Most of us are hardly aware of eating. We allow our habits to take over while we are busy being aware of something else – socializing, working or thinking about something. Consequently, even though we may know that eating fast is unhealthy, we gobble our food because that is our habit.

The unconscious aspect of habits makes them difficult to change. It is also one of the factors that make the unconscious mind so powerful. As we learned in Chapter 3, the unconscious mind is a reservoir of great power. The conscious mind serves mostly as an excuse maker for what is determined by the habits in the unconscious part of mind. We rationalize with the conscious mind what has really been determined in the unconscious mind. For instance, we can all think of very good reasons why we chose the person we did to live with, particularly if we recently made that decision. Research, however, tells us that one of the most critical factors, if not the most important, for this choice is individual's similarity or dissimilarity to our opposite-sexed parent. I can assure you that my wife's similarity to my mother was definitely not on my mind when I asked her to marry me. However, after 25 years of marriage, the similarity of my wife's strengths to those of my mother is very striking.

## AWARENESS – TAKING POWER AWAY FROM THE DRAGONS

What Skinner and other behaviorists never realized is that the laws and principles that govern habits only apply as long as the habit remains on the unconscious level of the mind. The moment that we become conscious of a habit, it no longer has the power to control the behavior. We now have the opportunity to do something different. For instance, most of us eat far too fast. However, if we are conscious of eating, and not paying attention to something else, we can choose to eat slowly. We don't need an expert to tell us how to eat slowly and chew more completely. We have the power to chew slowly, to put the fork down between bites, to really taste the food rather than just swallow it. But if we are distracted, we lose the opportunity to choose, and our habit of eating takes over.

We all know how hard it is to change a habit. Someone looks at us in a "funny way" and we react. We know that our reaction isn't helpful, we may even know why we do it, but we still find ourselves doing what we don't want to do. The problem is that we are only *partially aware* of the entire pattern of the habit, most of which still lies hidden in the unconscious mind. Partial awareness only gives us partial control, and this almost always leads to conflict. We have decided to do one thing with the conscious mind but the unconscious has programmed a different behavior. Whichever has the highest emotional charge is the one that usually determines the course of action. As long as we must struggle to control a habit, it means that we still aren't fully aware of the habit.

Intellectual understanding has little power to control unconscious habits. We know, for instance, just how unhealthy smoking is. Yet, quitting smoking is one of the most difficult habits to change. We can know about our habits, but that doesn't mean we are aware of the habit pattern itself. Awareness is not "knowing about" a habit; it is direct experience of the habit itself. Intellectual understanding is thinking about food, where awareness is tasting it.

I remember trying to quit smoking. Of course, I knew that smoking was bad for me, but I was not very conscious of the pain my body felt when I smoked. Like most smokers, I quit several times, but my habit was too strong, so I would start again. One day, after a particularly intense practice of meditation, I lit a cigarette. I was so aware of my inner feelings that I felt the impact of the smoke in my lungs and the depressing effect that the carbon monoxide and other gases had on my body. My enhanced sensitivity to the subtle pain killed all my desire to smoke, and I was able to quit immediately and forever without any difficulty.

Most of the time we won't be aware of the reasons behind a habit, or even why a habit becomes active. In fact, it is difficult to be aware of the roots of our most troubling habits. The more aware we are, of course, the greater our ability to choose a different response rather than react in the same old way. Fortunately, however, we don't have to have the awareness of a yoga master in order to control our habits. We do have the capacity to interrupt a pattern, to act, think and feel differently, even if we aren't completely aware of all its unconscious roots, or the reasons the habit was established in the first place.

One of the most common symptoms of chronic stress is neck and shoulder pain. Unconsciously we tense our neck and shoulder muscles in response to some pressure, or responsibility, or perhaps as a way to protect ourselves. Very often, the original reason for the behavior has long since disappeared. For instance, as we began our career we may have been somewhat overwhelmed with the responsibilities we faced. Our reaction was to "carry the weight of the world" on our shoulders, resulting in chronic tension in our shoulder muscles. Fairly quickly, this tension becomes a habitual reaction in the shoulder muscles to any pressure in the environment. Consequently, we suffer terrible neck and shoulder pains from the unrelieved tension.

Every time that there is an increase (or a decrease) in muscle tension, a message in the form of neural feedback is sent from the muscle to the brain telling the mind, "I'm starting to get tense here." Unfortunately, no one is home. You are too busy paying attention to something else to be aware of this signal of the body. Finally, the poor muscle sends a strong message called pain, yelling at the mind to pay attention to this problem. Now you do something – take an aspirin, get a message, do a stretching exercise – but only after the pain grabs your attention. If you are sensitive to the change in muscle tension before it becomes painful, you easily relax the muscles and avoid the painful symptom. A little bit of awareness gives you the opportunity to stop the neck and shoulder pain, or tension headache, or high blood pressure, before the body is harmed.

When a compulsive eater, for example, becomes overly stressed, he will start snacking. He thinks that he is hungry, but his "hunger" is not really for food; it is a habitual reaction to a high level of inner tension which eating temporarily reduces. Unfortunately, eating never resolves the underlying problem. Eating is an action that satisfies the stimulus of real hunger or nutrient deprivation. Compulsive eating is an emotional pattern that has its source in some other emotional need. Let's suppose, for example, that his compulsive eating is really due to repressed sexual urges. No matter how much he eats, this complex is never resolved. The associated guilt, desires and anything else that is a part of the emotional complex continue to create a disturbance – and, of course, a constant level of stress.

Let's say that our compulsive eater gains some awareness of his compulsive behavior and realizes that he is eating mostly as a way to relieve stress. He recognizes intellectually that his behavior is not healthy for him. What then follows is a constant battle between his good intentions and will power on the one hand and his habits of snacking driven by suppressed sexual feelings on the other.

The compulsive eater has taken an important step – but it is only a beginning. He even may have stopped his compulsive eating, but it hasn't reduced the pressures caused by his suppressed sexuality. In fact, he may feel even more stressed since he is no longer acting on his habit and getting whatever relief that it provided. He will continue to have conflicts until he takes the next step in dealing with his repressed sexual feelings directly.

We all have personal histories that include enough unconscious conflicts to cause a lot of unhappiness. Sadly, few of us develop the inner sensitivity and self-knowledge necessary to resolve these conflicts. Instead of working with our habits, we try to control the events and conditions in the external world that stimulate and reinforce these habits. We may only keep a few cigarettes with us at any time. But then, we find ourselves "bumming" them off another smoker. Or we insist that coworkers behave a certain way so we can be comfortable. As we all know, controlling external circumstances or other people is an impossible and frustrating task. Even partial success will leave us feeling like victims of circumstance. However, we do have infinite possibilities of doing something different ourselves. We can create options for ourselves.

The compulsive eater who eats when he is tense has several options. He can continue his habit and then suffer the consequences – or he can substitute an alternative behavior. He may decide to eat only at certain times. Instead of eating between meals when he feels the urge, he practices a relaxation or breathing exercise. The more relaxed he is, the easier it is to deal with the compulsion to eat. In this way he not only controls his compulsive behavior, he also avoids the negative consequences of inappropriate eating. The more sensitive he is to the first stirring of compulsive feelings, the quicker he can act with an alternative response, and the weaker the compulsion becomes. The more skilled he is at relaxing, the more sensitive he is to the thoughts and feelings that drive the compulsion. This gives him even greater insight into the real reasons behind the urge to eat, allowing time to resolve the real reasons for the compulsive behavior. While he must learn and practice new and more effective behaviors, the first step was to pay attention, to begin to act with conscious intent. The more awareness, the greater the opportunity for choice, and the more control he exerts.

Becoming aware of unconscious patterns is not an exercise in counting symptoms. It means that you become more sensitive to the thoughts and feelings that accompany and even precede your actions. If you watch television while you exercise on your stationary bike, you gain very little benefit from the exercise. On the other hand, if you pay attention to your body as you exercise, becoming more aware of your heart's behavior, which muscles are moving, the changes in your breathing, you become more sensitive to what actually is happening in your body. As you become more aware of your internal states, you begin to experience and understand the cause/effect relationships between thoughts and behavior. The more aware you are, the more able you are to choose a different behavior as well as choose different ways of thinking.

## Biofeedback: Using Technology to Enhance Awareness

Biofeedback is a fascinating combination of modern technology and awareness. A biofeedback instrument monitors a physiological process, such as skin temperature (which indicates whether or not blood vessels are constricted or dilated), or electrical activity in the muscles (which determines muscle tension). For example, an electromyograph (EMG) biofeedback instrument tells you when the neurons in your muscle are firing and when they are not. This tells you exactly what is happening in the muscle at the moment. The more electrical activity, the more tension in the muscle.

The biofeedback instrument doesn't do anything to you; it only indicates what is happening inside your body. With its help, you become aware of subtle physiological events, like nerves firing, or blood flow, that you weren't aware of before. By paying attention to the different thoughts and feelings associated with the changes going on inside your body, you soon learn how to direct these thoughts and feelings to change the nerve activity or the blood flow. Instead of letting your body continue with old patterns, you consciously alter the response, and create a new, more helpful and healthy habit pattern. With a little training, you can control blood flow, increase or decrease pulse rate, change brain waves, or reduce muscle tension.

Proper training with biofeedback produces astonishing results: people who suffer from tension headaches for ten and fifteen years quickly learn to relax their muscles and eliminate their tension headaches; patients with migraine headaches change blood flow patterns by consciously learning to increase blood flow to their hands, and in so doing, reduce the frequency and intensity of the migraine; people suffering from paralysis caused by spinal injury or stroke have regained use of their limbs. To suggest 40 years ago that this kind of control was possible would have brought derisive laughter from the medical and scientific community. Yet the tantra yoga masters have demonstrated this kind of control for thousands of years. And they do it without any help from biofeedback machines.

As the biofeedback experience shows, you don't have to be a yoga master to control your body. The people who accomplish this day in and day out in biofeedback clinics are ordinary people, with no special training other than the breathing, focusing and relaxation exercises learned in the program. Nor is the awareness limited to just physical problems. In fact, becoming aware of underlying emotional habits is the key to resolving the physical symptoms.

One client, a middle-aged woman suffering from migraine headaches, came to a biofeedback program seeking relief. After several weeks of training and several biofeedback sessions, it was obvious that she was becoming quite skilled at relaxing, at least during the biofeedback sessions. But something was missing because there was no change in her headaches. The director talked with her at some length about possible conflicts, but she kept insisting that everything in her life was just wonderful. Her only problem was these awful headaches.

The director decided to use the next biofeedback session to explore her emotional reactions. After hooking her up to an EMG instrument, he asked her to focus on relaxation and breathing. After only a few moments, the signal from the biofeedback instrument became very slow and steady, indicating a state of relaxation. He asked her if she had any problems or difficulty at work. She answered, "No." There was no change in her level of relaxation. He next questioned if she had difficulties with her children. Again, the answer was no, and the instrument maintained a slow, steady signal. Then he asked if she had any conflicts with her husband. She quickly answered, "No," but the biofeedback instrument took off like a rocket.

She was stunned. She couldn't believe that this question could create so much tension. Although she was skilled at relaxing, she was even more skilled at denying conflict between herself and her husband. Using the biofeedback instrument allowed her to be aware of a conflict that she had unconsciously suppressed. Once she became aware of the problem and was willing to face it, her headaches disappeared within a few weeks, and she and her husband were dealing more openly and honestly with their conflicts.

The biofeedback instrument didn't change her headaches. It was her enhanced awareness that allowed her to recognize and take control of her headaches and hidden conflicts. Once she used the biofeedback signal as a mirror to reflect her own internal processes and to develop awareness, she quickly began to deal with the problem. As she became skilled in introspection, she found that the biofeedback equipment wasn't even necessary. In fact, in many cases, the instrument interferes with inner concentration and awareness. And unless the individual practices the various breathing, relaxation and focusing exercises at home, the biofeedback machine is not very helpful. The key to any success with biofeedback is the skill developed through practicing the proper exercises when you are not using the biofeedback instrument.

Biofeedback doesn't teach us how to control the body. It allows us to become conscious of the controls we already have. Once we are aware of these controls, we use them to create a healthier process. By becoming skilled in the use of sophisticated internal tools, such as hatha yoga, breathing, and meditation practices, we become sensitive to our own internal biofeedback systems and we change our unconscious misery-producing habits to more useful ones.

The belief that we cannot, and do not, control our body, our thoughts or our emotions, is false. The truth is that we have absolute control over everything in our personality. The crucial factor is whether we are conscious or unconscious. When we are unconscious, our habits are in control – when we are conscious, we have the power to choose!

We have a far greater ability for self-control and self-discipline than most of us realize or have experienced. Our bodies and minds have extremely sophisticated internal sensory mechanisms and control systems. We use these mechanisms when we learn how to control blood flow or to fire a single muscle neuron, whether through biofeedback or through an intensive program of inner development. The body/mind complex is the most sophisticated biofeedback instrument you can find. The greater our self-awareness, the more choices we have, and the less we disturb ourselves. Often, the awareness itself is all that is needed to correct a problem.

An excellent example of this can be seen in a technique used to help clients eliminate a typical tension headache problem that occurs in both temples at the same time. This is caused by chronic muscle tension in the masseter muscles in the jaw. The source of this tension is an unconscious habit of clenching the teeth when angry. The technique is extremely simple. Individuals are instructed to carry a small notebook, and every time they find themselves clenching their teeth, they relax their jaw and make a small mark in the notebook.

All of this, of course, counteracts the tension and weakens the habit of clenching. Usually the number of marks they make in the first two or three weeks far exceeds the marks in the next two or three months. Typically within three or four weeks, if not sooner, their headaches begin to disappear. They often find that they are also no longer grinding their teeth at night.

Of course, relaxation training to lower chronic tension levels and other balancing techniques are part of the program, but the essential key was simply becoming aware of when they were clenching their jaw, and stop doing it.

### Focused Attention: The Secret Power of the Conscious Mind

In a recent seminar, one of the participants was a jogger. He told the group that while jogging with a colleague, he had developed the habit of discussing work problems. Over a period of time he noticed that he did not enjoy the jogging as much. He was running more slowly and could not maintain his speed. During the seminar, he realized that his habit of thinking about work problems while jogging had unconsciously created stress and reduced his efficiency. The very next day, he re-focused his attention on running, and did not allow his mind to follow the habit of going over work problems. Immediately, he began running as fast as his best time. His joy of running returned, and he felt better than he had for months.

The jogger took charge of his thoughts. He chose different thoughts, altered the pattern, and improved his efficiency in running. He tapped the secret power of his conscious mind. This power is the ability to focus attention, to focus the energy of the mind. It is secret because we seldom acknowledge the power of attention. We are told to pay attention in school, but no one shows us how. We learn all sorts of facts and methods, but we seldom learn how to use the mind. As a consequence, we don't know how to systematically expand our awareness into the subconscious and unconscious areas of our mind.

Many scientists, psychiatrists and psychologists speak appropriately of the hidden power of the unconscious mind and the power of habit. Most believe that we can only have indirect communication with the unconscious mind through symbolic representation such as dreams and ink blot tests. Psychoanalysts believe that we can become aware of the unconscious only after years of analysis, and only with the help and guidance of an analyst. The myth that we cannot directly

## MIND/BODY AWARENESS EXERCISE

Try it for yourself. If you pay attention, you don't need a biofeedback machine to tell you when your muscles are tense and when they are relaxed. Sit quietly for a moment, and pay attention to the muscles in your face – the jaws, around the eyes, and the forehead. What do you feel? Be aware of the muscles in the back of your neck and your shoulders. What do you feel here?

Think about the last conflict you got involved with at work. Go over the situation clearly in your mind as if you were reliving it. What is happening to your muscles? Now picture these muscles as being very relaxed and loose. Imagine yourself sitting in your favorite vacation place, relaxing in the sun. Pay attention to what happens to the muscles in your face, neck and shoulders. Notice how your thoughts about your favorite spot relax these muscles.

Which thoughts and feeling would you rather have? Which condition would you choose for your muscles? Your awareness gives you the opportunity to make a choice.

Becoming aware of the unconscious mind and its contents is not impossible. We only need to train the power of attention. By learning to concentrate and focus attention inwardly with detachment, we create a state of neutral observation. As we become more skilled in our ability to be an observer, we become more aware of the patterns and movements of the mind and we have a greater opportunity to choose the patterns and behaviors we want.

confront our own unconscious has been the basis for much of Western psychology and psychiatry, particularly behaviorism. As a result, Westerners don't have a systematic approach to introspection and self-awareness. Nor do we have a science of self-mastery.

My scientific, academic education taught me that conscious control over my body and my emotions was not possible. My tantric master showed me that it was not only possible, but that I could do it myself, and do it well. The key was not my unconscious, but my ability to focus the conscious mind. The conscious mind has a single powerful ability – the ability to direct attention. With the right approach and the right tools, we can refine our ability to pay attention and direct the entire mind and body and all of their resources – knowledge, creativity, will, emotional energy, even habits. By refining our attention and expanding our awareness, we expand our capacity for choice, and take the power back from the dragons.

The unconscious mind is not some alien reality; it is that part of our own mind that we simply are not aware of. Why shouldn't we have the capacity to know our own mind? As we will see later, there are specific methods to expand awareness that also lead to very sophisticated emotional controls. By knowing how to pay attention, we become more sensitive to the unconscious mind, take control of stress, and learn more about how the mind works.

## THE SECRET OF SELF-DISCIPLINE

No one consciously chooses to be afraid, hate herself, or feel isolated and alone. But unconsciously, our habits create and feed these dragons and make our lives miserable. As long as we remain insensitive, ignoring our unconscious habits, B.F. Skinner was right. We don't really have any freedom. Instead of experiencing our power as human beings, we are enslaved by the habits and patterns of the mind. We learn to see ourselves as weak, ineffectual, unlovable, stupid – all the negative judgments we learned growing up.

In tantra psychology, the source of all suffering is considered to be ignorance (*avidya* in Sanskrit). Ignorance doesn't refer to our level of intelligence, or how many degrees we do or do not earn. It means exactly what it says – to ignore, to be unconscious of. On the most mundane level, habits control our actions because we are unaware, or ignorant. The consequence of ignorance is constant fear, self-hatred, and loneliness, a denial of the true strength and joy of the spiritual Self.

But we don't have to suffer because we don't have to remain ignorant. These habits are not who we are, they are only habits, grooves in the mind that we unconsciously developed at some point in our lives. Once we understand the power of habits, we see that self-discipline is nothing more than consciously choosing and practicing habits that help us grow and be joyful. We can take charge of this powerful function in the sensory mind and create the habits that we want.

On the most profound level, ignorance means to be unconscious or unaware of the spiritual Self. This truth of attention and awareness is known in all great spiritual traditions. John's declaration in the Gospels, 8:32, "The truth shall make you free" doesn't refer to some secret "truth" hidden in a musty book on some forgotten shelf. It is about awareness – at a spiritual level as well as a mundane level.

When you become conscious, when you become aware of the truth inside yourself, you are free  – to choose your responses, to live without fear, self-hatred, and loneliness, and to experience joy, tranquility, and love.

### Choice, Not Struggle

The emphasis must be on choosing the habits we want to build, not struggling to eliminate the old habits. Most of us think of self-discipline as making ourselves do something we don't want to do. If this is the case, very few of us will ever succeed. We can successfully learn self-discipline if we remember three key points:

**1. Inspiration is ninety percent of the success for self-discipline.** Work on building habits that you really want to have. Don't waste energy and effort struggling against already established habits. As we will see later, that only leads to conflict and strengthens these habits. Instead, focus your efforts on the habits you want to build, the patterns you are interested in having.

**2. Practice makes perfect.** Once you decide on the habit or pattern of behavior, or thinking that you want, practice that behavior or thinking pattern every day. You won't create change by wishing something will happen, or by imagery alone. You must act on your choices in order for the choices to become deeply grooved in the mind.

**3. Determination and persistence will always lead to success.** There is no failure, only premature stopping. A habit takes time to establish itself in the mind. Once you decide on a particular behavior that you want to build, allow at least three months to begin to groove the habit into your mind.

## Above All, Balance

To be successful, self-discipline must be tempered with balance. We don't grow much as human beings if we become over-developed in one area and remain retarded in everything else. We may become highly skilled in our careers or professions, but this should not be at the sacrifice of the other elements of our humanity.

Genuine balance is not a static condition, but a dynamic process, constantly evolving as we grow and evolve. When we are balanced, we are spontaneous instead of programmed, relaxed instead of tense, responsive instead of reactive, and in tune with the world around us. Balance involves the integration of all dimensions of our personality. On a physical level, balance is regulated primarily through the autonomic nervous system that controls our organ systems. When the physical systems are out of balance, we suffer from the symptoms of stress. Knowing how to control this powerful control mechanism is a key factor in our ability to live in this pressure cooker society of ours and remain relaxed, calm and effective.

But physical balance must involve emotional balance. Even the best food becomes toxic and our exercise becomes just another pressure if we don't know how to balance our emotions. Emotional balance requires practice, just as physical balance requires practice. If we become fanatical in our practice, we lose perspective, reinforce our fears, and create greater problems for ourselves. Balance is characterized by both persistence and patience. Emotional balance requires that we build our relationships with others with the same care that we build the relationship with ourselves.

Both emotional and social balance emerge naturally from our increasing spiritual awareness. If we become zealots in our religious or philosophical beliefs, if we think that our way is the only way to live, and our beliefs are the only true beliefs, we only increase our fear and loneliness, and become small and egocentric. As we grow in our capacity to experience ourselves as the life force within the tree, as a part of the universal Spirit, our respect, compassion and regard for others evolves naturally and completely. We must always remember that there are as many ways to understand reality as there are individuals. I recall the phrase used by my great and enlightened friend, Rabbi Gelberman, "In addition to…." In addition to my way, there is your way, and his way, and her way, and all the ways of seeing and living life.

The same tools and techniques that give us control of ourselves also help us to become balanced human beings. But along the way, we must allow ourselves and others the freedom to think in different and unusual ways and to make mistakes. We need only be patient with ourselves and with others. The practice of patience is just as much a part of our own self-mastery as anything else we may do. Like other skills, patience takes sincere practice and effort.

## Laziness: The Path to Nowhere

Like any organization, our personality resists change. This resistance comes from our habits. Once we build a habit of worry in the mind, the body builds the habit of the fight-or-flight alarm reaction. When we build the habits of self-hatred, the body also builds the habits of the possum reaction. All these habits resist change. If we allow resistance to limit our choices and actions, we have little chance to take control of our magic. Laziness is one of the most pervasive ways in which we experience this resistance. The mind says, "Why bother?" It's easier to take an aspirin for a headache, a drink to relax, and to watch television to dull my mind than to spend fifteen minutes a day doing an exercise.

It's all too easy to feel a little miserable than create a change. Our fast food mentality constantly hunts for the easiest, quickest way out, whether it's a lottery, a shorter work week for more pay, or drugs and alcohol. We don't realize that we are shortchanging ourselves. The less effort we invest, the less we gain, and the more damage we do our personality and sense of self-esteem.

It's easy to rationalize laziness. It often takes the form of not having enough time. In our society, everyone is busy. We are "action oriented" but with a heavy dose of couch potatoism. The most common complaint is, "I don't have the time to do the relaxation exercise (or anything else)." Yet we find the time to watch an average of three hours of television a day, the time to waste in idle chatter, the time to "hoist a few cold ones." We find time to clean our bodies, our cars, our homes, but we don't take the time to clean our minds.

The great danger of laziness is that it turns us into victims. Once we become victims we are guaranteed lives of misery. If we are unwilling to make the effort necessary to take control of our inner resources, or our inner chatter, there is no way we can take the power away from the dragons or solve the problems of stress.

## LIVING WITH STRENGTH: PRACTICAL APPLICATIONS OF MASTERY

Self-mastery is not an empty promise, but the consequence of the systematic development of our inner resources. It is, in essence, the unleashing of our inner strength, joy, and love. The culmination of self-mastery is freedom from the dragons of the mind and the mystical experience of spiritual Self-realization. We don't accomplish this by trying to change ourselves, but by consciously developing our inner awareness and strengths.

Instead of change we create transformation, becoming all of what we truly are – an expression of light, love, and power. As we progress in this transformation, our minds become more and more free of disturbance and we become more effective, joyful, and loving human beings. Instead of using the creative force of the mind to create fears and worries, we use it to solve problems and create harmony and beauty.

As we experience our inner strength and confidence, we become more flexible in both mind and body. We think more clearly, and our instincts and intuition become sharp and clear. As we lose our self-hatred, we discover an unlimited self-confidence, will, and decisiveness, and begin to use them as *conscious skills*. In other words, we become skilled human beings.

### Developing the Whole Person

But we won't be successful if we work with just part of the mind. Remember, we function on a number of different dimensions at the same time. We are a whole person, and we must work with all our resources if we want to become skilled human beings. The power of habit formation is a tool that we must learn to use, but we must also use the other tools that we have – our physical tools and controls, insight, strength and courage, sensitivity and creativity – in order to be successful.

The tantric masters are very practical. They have researched and studied all the dimensions of human life because they realize that we live in all dimensions. They use the resources of the mind and body in a systematic way. Like professional athletes, they know that in order to become skillful, you must approach skill building in a very systematic way. The masters teach about food and exercise as well as about spiritual truths. They teach about breathing as well as concentration exercises. Many of us only want to learn about spirituality, but we can't think clearly if our body is troubled or our emotions are clouded. Systematically, the great masters lead us through all the dimensions, providing us with a strong foundation to build upon.

We will do the same here. In the second part of the book, we will explore each of the dimensions of the personality, and discover the most practical techniques to use in order to build useful habits and develop conscious skills. You see, our goal isn't only to get rid of the dragons or to become healthy. Certainly we will do that. But the real purpose is to become a master ourselves, to free ourselves from self-imposed limitations and unlock the power and beauty of the body, mind, and spirit.

As we discover the strength and wisdom within ourselves, others begin to discover the strength and wisdom within themselves. The way we relate to others – our close personal relationships, our sense of community, our capacity to give, to belong and to relate to other human beings – depends on who we are as individuals. If we teach ourselves and our children how to live without fear, we create a culture free from violence. If we teach ourselves and our children how to love and respect ourselves and others, we create a culture free from hatred and condemnation.

We cannot have a society free of fear, violence, and hatred until we have a citizenry free of fear, violence, and hatred. The key is education and training in self-mastery, not slogans, guns, and prisons. It begins with us.

## A Culture of Mastery

The quality of our entire life is dictated by our state of mind, yet most of us spend incredibly little time enhancing, or even maintaining, sound mental health. In fact, very little effort is made in modern society toward training the whole mind. Reflecting this deep-felt need, many are turning to religion, self-help books and pop psychology to find some relief to the mental dissatisfaction so prevalent in our society.

But what is it we are looking for? Are we really searching for knowledge and mastery, or is it just another search for an easy, quick answer – a psychic pill, a magic crystal, a new religion to lead us into the "Promised Land" and remove all our unhappiness, and leave us free from loneliness and disease?

If we invest in self-mastery we can create a different culture. Our hospitals will become health-learning centers, and teach the basic skills of diet, exercise, and stress management as well as practice the healing arts. Prevention will be the primary thrust instead of disease maintenance as it is now.

With the proper focus in education, our children will learn early in life how to use their internal controls to maintain balance and direct their emotional energy. They will have the self-respect as well as the self-discipline to resist drugs and teen pregnancies. Then we won't need to spend fourteen percent of our gross national product on health care, or build more and more prisons. Our cities will become true cultural centers rather than ghettos of violence, drugs, and hopelessness.

We don't need more money or external resources. We need to refocus our energies. What would be the consequences, for instance, if we turned on the TV, and instead of someone hawking the latest drug or diet gimmick, there was a celebrity saying, "Don't forget to practice your relaxation tonight. Don't forget to work with your mind tonight. Don't forget to tell someone you love them.

Most of all, don't forget that you have all the strength and resources you need to be happy and healthy."

What if we started to sell self-mastery instead of drugs, providing insights and simple techniques that people could practice? What if we made stories showing self-confidence, compassion, and common sense the focus of our television shows instead of infantile greed, petty jealousies, and violence?

## SELF-MASTERY – REACHING FOR OUR BIRTHRIGHT

Would you rather dance with life or be dragged through it? This is what self-mastery is really about. It isn't about self-therapy, it is about self-transformation. We often become so focused on what is wrong with us that our troubles and weaknesses become all-consuming issues that devour our energy and life.

It's time to end this self-defeating behavior. We are far more than our failures, we are much greater than our pettiness, and we are more powerful than our technology. Self-mastery means knowing ourselves for what we really are, a unique spark of the Divine, the life force within the tree. But unless we come to know and master that force, unless we become skilled human beings, we limit ourselves to the ego, and become the pawns and slaves of our own habits.

The power does not lie anywhere outside of yourself. You can wear crystals but that piece of mineral rock, no matter how polished and refined, is nothing compared to the power of your mind. You can use technology to alter your brain waves, and you can have highs with drugs. But what will you do when the batteries are dead and the drugs have created side effects?

### Self-Training: Taking Steps to Freedom

It is up to each of us to make the choices necessary to be free. No one can be aware for another, and no one else can slay our dragons. When we blame others or ourselves for our behavior, we end up with even greater weakness and fear. Our habits are ultimately our own responsibility. If we choose to ignore them, no therapist, doctor, friend, spouse, teacher, or even God, can help us. We alone choose to be unaware, we alone allow our habits to remain in power, and we alone suffer the consequences.

The path to self-mastery and freedom lies in our conscious decision to use our own power to create and sustain balance, to develop and use our inner resources. Everything we need is sitting right here within us, hidden only by our ignorance. Take the next step. No one asks that you believe, only that you experiment, practice, and become strong. We can take back the power. We can become masters.

PART II


# THE
# SKILLS
# OF
# SELF-MASTERY

We begin our journey with self-knowledge, but we complete it with self-discipline. We do not realize the power of our human spirit simply by believing in it. Inspiration is very helpful, but without perspiration, it only ends in disappointment. Faith and belief are powerful tools, but without direct experience and skill, they are impotent and ineffective. How many times have you heard someone give an inspiring talk only to have a feeling of futility and sadness a few days later when you realize that nothing really has changed?

There are no "easy" answers – a magic crystal, the right book, a powerful teacher – that will solve all our problems and make life beautiful. Only we have the power to do that for ourselves. This is our freedom: to know and to do for ourselves. It is only when we become skilled, when we can "walk our talk" that we gain freedom from the dragons of the mind and open the power and strength of our personality and spirit.

In Part II, we explore specific techniques used by the great masters to develop self-mastery. You will learn a number of different exercises and techniques that will help you take command of your inner resources. Of course, you won't use every exercise or technique. And you will very probably find other techniques that might work as well for you. But you will find a complete approach to working with all dimensions of yourself, and this is essential.

As you read through the next five chapters, try the different exercises to get a sense of what they do and how they feel when you do them. Don't try to become an expert at any of them at this point, and don't worry about which ones to focus on. In the Addendum following Chapter 9, we will explore how to design a self-training program that will meet your own unique needs.

The great traditions of self-mastery are very systematic, taking care to build the foundation so strong that it can support any height that we can achieve. They also know that we must begin to master all dimensions – physical, mental/emotional, and spiritual – if we want to become skilled human beings.

You will do the same here. You begin with your physical foundation, the knowledge and skills you need to make the body healthy, strong, and flexible. In Chapter 5 we explore some basic knowledge, skills, and techniques about relaxation, diet, and flexibility training. You will learn about the different levels of relaxation you can achieve through different exercises. By making a few simple changes in how you approach diet, you can put an end to many of the problems created by poor eating habits. You will also learn an integrated stretching exercise that has been used by yogis for thousands of years to keep the body flexible, to build strength and to increase energy.

Then we turn to the more subtle dimension of energy. In Chapter 6 you learn how to use the breath to bring balance and harmony to the body and mind, and to create a healthy cardiovascular system. You will see how what is regarded as "normal" breathing leads to heart disease and discover how to return to your natural breathing motion. This chapter provides the foundation that is *absolutely essential* if you want to be free of stress.

Once you know how to minimize stress and create a relaxed, balanced foundation, it is time to confront the dragons of fear and self-hatred found in the sensory mind. In Chapter 7 we explore the techniques that give you the ability to take command of the creative force of the mind. With these techniques you reclaim your power from these two dragons, and create a calm, clear mind.

Once you gain the upper hand over the dragons, you learn how to increase the power of the mind and use it to gain access to inner strength and wisdom. In Chapter 8 we explore how to enhance the power of concentration and then refine that power through meditation techniques.

Finally, in Chapter 9, you learn how to use the power of the mind to access the spiritual Self and put an end to the dragon of loneliness. Once you have this foundation, you have access to unlimited inner strength and confidence that you can use in day-to-day life. In this chapter you will discover how to fully resolve emotional disturbances through the power of selfless love and other positive emotions.

Learning and doing these exercises is not meant to be work, but the engagement of intention, effort, and joy. Learn to play, to experiment, to see what you discover as you systematically explore your capacities with the exercises. It is time to dance, so turn the page and begin.

5

# BODY SKILLS:
# RELAXATION, DIET AND EXERCISE

*If anything is sacred, the human body is sacred.*
—Walt Whitman—

The great masters know that the body is a powerful and useful instrument. The body is a sophisticated biocomputer that not only serves as our mobile home, taking us here and there, but also simultaneously provides us with an enormous amount of information both about the world around us and about our own inner states of knowledge. It lets us know when we are in danger, what kind of food is healthy for us, it even signals when we are making a wrong choice. Depending on how we train the body, we can use it as a weapon to defend ourselves, or as a tool to enhance the lives of ourselves and others. Because of its power and usefulness, the body is seen as a sacred temple by all spiritual traditions. Many of the most powerful traditions, such as tantra yoga, have gained a profound knowledge on how to keep the body healthy and use its power.

Yet most of us hardly know how to treat the body or use the power we have. We seldom think of the body as an instrument, a tool to develop and use. Instead, we let our bodies suffer from stress and disease and they become obstacles instead of tools. Not only do we suffer pain and discomfort, but our mental resources are inhibited, our relationships suffer, and we waste incredible amounts of money on drugs that may relieve the symptoms but do nothing to change the cause.

My tantric master was raised from the age of three in a cave monastery at 10,000 feet in the Himalayan Mountains. Needless to say, there were no doctors, drug stores, health spas, or personal trainers. Yogis such as he rely on themselves to maintain a healthy body. Of course, they have extensive knowledge about healing, using herbs and plants, and other natural products. But the emphasis has always been on prevention, making the body so healthy and strong that it is naturally resistant to disease.

The exercises and techniques they developed to make the body healthy and strong are highly refined and very sophisticated. Hatha yoga, for instance, is designed to bring balance to body and mind through stimulation of critical neural and glandular centers as well as creating flexibility throughout the body. Martial arts such as karate, taijiquan, and kung fu are recognized as powerful and sophisticated systems of self-defense and combat. But, what is not commonly known is that they began as a way to keep the monks of the Shao Lin Temple healthy. Da Mo, a Buddhist yoga master from the Himalayas came to the temple and taught the monks self-defense in order to help them protect themselves and to restore their health.

Naturally, the different approaches to physical health emphasize different aspects. But there are three key elements that are found in every sophisticated system, whether it is hatha yoga, taijiquan or karate. These are the heart of physical health, and are essential to the magic of self-mastery. These three are relaxation, diet and flexibility.

## RELAXATION: A CRITICAL FOUNDATION

We *must* master two skills if we want to be free of stress and develop our inner resources: relaxation and diaphragmatic breathing. These two crucial skills provide the foundation for self-mastery and personal development. Unless we know how to maintain a relaxed mind and body, and breathe properly, there is no way we can eliminate stress, or develop the power of our inner resources effectively. (In fact, breathing is so critical to self-mastery that we will spend the entire next chapter on it.)

Deep relaxation is much more than a stress management technique. It opens the gateway to your inner resources. When you are relaxed, you work more efficiently, think more clearly, solve problems more creatively, and feel better physically and emotionally.

When we think of being relaxed, however, most of us think about deep relaxation. We see ourselves as completely limp and lethargic, unable or unwilling to move. While this may characterize the first level of deep relaxation, being relaxed does not mean being limp and lethargic. The term "relaxation" simply means no *excess* tension, a condition of physical and mental balance and efficiency. To be relaxed at work (or anywhere else) doesn't mean you walk around like a cooked noodle, but rather that you work without tense shoulder muscles, a clenched jaw, or a hectic mind.

Unnecessary tension interferes with physical actions. The martial arts, for instance, demand a relaxed mind and body for effective, balanced, quick movement. When students begin martial arts training, they are always too tense in their movements. This slows their reflexes, interferes with perception, and creates awkwardness. All martial arts, both the "hard" and "soft" styles, are a combination of relaxation and tension, of softness and hardness. The skilled martial artist is completely relaxed, moves in a relaxed, balanced way, and uses tension only at a point of contact, and then moves quickly back into a relaxed stance. The ability to be relaxed and use tension is a key element in almost everything we do.

You become skilled at deep relaxation by practicing systematic exercises that eliminate all tension from the body. Practicing deep relaxation quiets the organ systems, eliminates chronic tension, strengthens the immune system, and helps you stay calm and focused during daily activities. As with any skill, relaxation requires a consistent practice of systematic techniques. The more skilled you become, the less time it takes. When you become skilled at deep relaxation, what once took fifteen minutes can be done in a few breaths.

## The Three Levels of Deep Relaxation

The depth of your relaxation depends on two things: your degree of skill and the particular technique you use. Each level has its own purpose, and each provides us with certain benefits.

**Level 1: Structural or Muscular Relaxation.** The most common techniques achieve deep relaxation through the release of muscle tension. Two major forms are used: tense-release exercises and imagery (auto-hypnosis) exercises. In tense-release exercises, individual muscles or groups of muscles are tensed and then relaxed. For those who don't know what it means to relax, this is an excellent way to experience the difference between a relaxed muscle and a tense one. Imagery techniques use imagery (such as picturing your muscles as very warm and loose, or picturing yourself lying in the warm sunshine on a secluded beach) or auto-suggestion (such as repeating phrases such as, "My arms are very warm, my arms are very heavy") in order to create a state of muscular relaxation.

These exercises require no previous experience or skill at relaxing. They are excellent beginning exercises and result in a light to moderate level of deep relaxation. When done effectively, they leave the body feeling very heavy and warm, as if it were encased in lead. Your mind is lethargic, and you feel reluctant to work or make any effort. These exercises effectively reduce chronic stress and muscle tension and reduce or even eliminate a variety of symptomatic problems related to muscle tension, such as tension headaches, back problems, and neck and shoulder pain. Detailed instructions for a systematic muscle relaxation exercise are given in Appendix B.

**Level II: Autonomic Relaxation.** A deeper, more complete level of relaxation is achieved by directly influencing the autonomic nervous system. You should recall that this powerful nervous system controls the fight-or-flight alarm reaction and the possum response in the body. By consciously and systematically altering the motion of the lungs, you can change the dominance pattern within the autonomic nervous system. By changing the motion and rhythm of the breath, you increase parasympathetic activity and achieve a deeper state of rest in the body. Instead of feeling heavy and lethargic, your body feels light, and your mind becomes clear and alert. As we shall see in the next chapter, breathing is an excellent way to maintain balance and create the conditions for effective problem solving. There are a number of different breathing techniques, each one leading to progressively deeper states of relaxation.

**Level III: Concentration.** We create the most profound states of relaxation through concentration. The more focused, or concentrated, the mind, the deeper the relaxation and rest in the body. Any concentration exercise calms the body, but the "61 Points" exercise given in Chapter 8 is extremely effective because it reaches the deepest systems of the body. While muscle-relaxation exercises are helpful for muscle-related problems, they are not so effective for more complex problems such as essential hypertension. Because of the depth of the relaxation it creates, 61 Points is particularly helpful in treating and preventing high blood pressure.

## Becoming Skilled At Relaxation

The most effective way to practice deep relaxation is to use the Relaxation Posture, which is called the Corpse Posture in Hatha Yoga. This posture allows every muscle in the body to achieve a deep state of relaxation. Any other position creates muscle tension to sustain the position, or at least will allow some muscles to remain tense. We use this posture to practice the breathing techniques given in Chapter 6, and to develop skills in deep relaxation.

The best time to practice deep relaxation is when no one will disturb you for at least fifteen minutes. At the end of a work day, go to a quiet room, and take fifteen minutes to clear your mind and body of all stress, tension, and all the

**Relaxation Posture**

This basic posture should be used for all relaxation exercises. Lie on your back on a carpeted floor, and gently close your eyes. Place your feet a comfortable distance apart, about twelve to eighteen inches, and your arms and hands slightly away from the body, palms facing up, and fingers gently curled. Use a small pillow or a folded blanket under your head to support the curve of your neck. Do not lie haphazardly or place the limbs too far apart. Lie in a symmetrical position. In this posture the body lies still and relaxed. It is important to avoid drowsiness; keep the mind alert and focused on the flow of the breath. (If you suffer from low back problems, and have difficulty lying flat, place a large pillow under the knees so the feet are flat on the floor. This will take the pressure off your back muscles and the pillow will allow the leg muscles to relax.)

pressures from work. At first, it may be difficult to take this time when your family wants your attention. But if you persist, you will find that you feel more refreshed and calm, and your interaction with your family and friends will be much better. In fact, after a few weeks your family will probably insist that you take this time. Obviously, the more you practice, the more skillful you become. Start with fifteen minutes a day. As you gain skill, the time required shortens dramatically. After you have built your skill, never spend more than five minutes doing relaxation. The rest of your time is better spent making your mind stronger with concentration and meditation exercises, developing your creativity, or working with your intuition.

You will soon realize that the harder you try to relax, the more tense you become. Relaxation is like floating. Simply lie back and allow it to happen. This is called passive volition, or effortless effort. The best way to learn a relaxation exercise is from an audio-cassette tape or CD until you memorize the exercise. They allow you to listen and follow directions without getting actively involved.

You can purchase tapes and discs commercially or make your own. Detailed instructions for the three major relaxation exercises are given in Appendices B, C, and D. First, read through the exercises and make sure you understand the systematic approach. Then slowly read the instructions while recording them. The periods between the sentences indicate a pause for a few seconds. After you have taped the exercise, lie down in the relaxation posture and listen to it.

People often tell me that their most favored relaxation technique is to listen to music. Others listen to whale sounds, the sound of waves on a beach, or "white noise." Obviously, certain kinds of music and sounds will help you relax. There are, just as obviously, certain kinds of music and sounds that irritate. But listening to music or whales communicating with each other does not teach you the skill of deep relaxation, nor will the relaxation be as complete or as deep. Also, you won't always have the opportunity to turn on your stereo, or plug in your earphones. If you have the skill, you can relax at any time, in any situation.

**Figure 5.1**

## DIET: FUEL FOR SELF-MASTERY

As a source of stress, diet is second only to emotional disturbances. Given the disastrous dietary habits of the average person, and that we eat several times a day, we have ample opportunity to create problems. We don't pay attention to the quality of the food we eat, and we allow junk food to dominate our diet. We don't prepare or cook our food properly. Instead of being relaxed and enjoying food, we are often tense, under pressure and eat too fast. Now add to this the gradual depletion of vital nutrients in our food from leached soil, the alteration of foods through biochemical additives and genetic changes, the proliferation of additives and chemicals in our foods to "enhance" storage, quantity, flavor, color, and you begin to realize the dangers we create with our diet. The stress that all this creates is evident in the high and increasing incidence of "digestive diseases" such as Crohn's Disease, ulcers, and diverticulitus, and the high incidence of obesity. Also evident is the impact that diet has on cardiovascular disease, and the American Cancer Society estimates that at least one-third of all cancers are due to poor diet. What is not known are the possible long-term consequences to the immune system and genetic structures, dangers that exist more for our children and their children than for ourselves.

One of the difficulties we face is the confusion and contradictory advice we hear about diet and nutrition. Much of what we hear is designed to sell us something. The primary focus of the food industry is *not* our health; its purpose is to earn profits. There is enormous pressure from advertising for us to accept what the food industry wants to sell. Furthermore, much of the scientific research on the impact of foods is paid for by the food industry and is consciously or unconsciously designed to bolster their claims. We should be alert to the biases and intentions of those who are trying to sell us products, and not believe everything we see or hear. Remember, advertising has only one purpose: to get you to buy.

The controversy about aspartame, an artificial sweetener made by Monsanto, a chemical company, is a case in point. There are many studies that indicate that aspartame is completely harmless, and many more studies that show that this is a very dangerous chemical to put in the body. The most interesting study was done by Dr. Ralph Walton, MD, Chairman of the Center for Behavioral Medicine and Professor of Clinical Psychiatry, Northeastern Ohio University College of Medicine. Instead of studying aspartame, Dr. Walton analyzed the peer reviewed medical literature about aspartame. Using MEDLINE and other databases, Dr. Walton isolated 166 studies which had relevance to human safety questions. His purpose was to see if there was any difference between the studies conducted by researchers sponsored by the aspartame industry, and those studies conducted by independent researchers.

The outcome is more than startling. All seventy-four (100%) of the industry-sponsored aspartame studies claimed that no problems were found with aspartame. On the other hand, eighty three out of ninety (92%) of the independent studies identified at least one or more problems with aspartame. More significantly, the FDA, the government agency responsible for ensuring food safety, conducted six of the seven supposedly independent studies that did not find a problem.

A very troubling aspect of this was that a number of FDA officials went to work for the aspartame industry immediately following approval (including the FDA commissioner). One might reasonably suspect that the studies conducted by the FDA were not truly independent. How much faith do you think we should put into these industry-sponsored studies? And, perhaps a more important question is how much faith should we put in the FDA to give us accurate and unbiased information about the food we ingest?

There is a significant methodological bias in all of scientific research, particularly when dealing with human activity of any kind, such as our diet. Recall that human beings are complex, whole, living systems. Science cannot deal adequately with living, multi-dimensional, multi-variable realities, such as the integrated human system. Scientific methodology is to isolate and study the impact or interaction of single variables.

For instance, broccoli is well-known to be a good anti-cancer food. However, scientific logic would likely tell us to isolate the specific active anti-cancer agent in broccoli, and then we can reproduce that agent and give people a pill. But when we do that, we lose the matrix in which that "specific agent" works, the living plant we use for food, and we create a different reality. Consequently, scientific findings concerning nutrition are limited, often contradictory, and when used by any industry interested in making money, very often misleading.

## Genetic Engineering: Dangerous Scientific Arrogance

We must be extremely skeptical when a scientist tells us that they know that their experiments with food are safe. In a recent article titled "Unraveling the DNA myth – the spurious foundation of genetic engineering" (*Harpers* magazine, February 2002), Barry Commoner, a senior scientist and director of the Critical Genetics Project at Queens College, points out that the theory put forth by Crick and Watson (the scientists who discovered the DNA double helix) that DNA is the exclusive agent of inheritance in all living things has been proven absolutely false. "Known to molecular biologists as the central dogma the premise assumes that an organism's genome – its total complement of DNA genes – should fully account for its characteristic assemblage of inherited traits. The premise, unhappily, is false."

As Commoner goes on to point out, the findings of the Genome Project showed that there are far too few genes to account for the complexity of inherited traits, and that this finding ... "destroyed the scientific foundation of genetic engineering, and the validity of the biotechnology industry's widely advertised claim that its methods of genetically modifying food crops are 'specific, precise and predictable,' and therefore safe." In other words, the biotech industry has no idea what the outcome of their genetic modification will be! When the scientists tell us that they can absolutely control the outcome of genetically modified soybeans, corn, tomatoes, or anything, they are telling us a great, big lie!

The article goes into detail about how inherited traits are not controlled by DNA, but are based on a number of different mechanisms that go far beyond the DNA. He states that, "Biological replication does include the precise duplication of DNA, but this is accomplished by the living cell, not by the DNA molecule alone … genetic information arises not from DNA alone but through its essential collaboration with protein enzymes – a contradiction of the central dogma's precept that inheritance is uniquely governed by the self-replication of the DNA double helix. …The net outcome is that no single DNA gene is the sole source of a given protein's genetic information and therefore of the inherited."

The crucial point of Commoner's article is, "The fact that one gene can give rise to multiple proteins also destroys the theoretical foundation of a multibillion-dollar industry, the genetic engineering of food crops. Most alarming is the recent evidence that in a widely grown genetically modified food crop – soybeans containing an alien gene for herbicidal resistance – the transgenic host plant's genome has itself been unwittingly altered. … The likelihood in genetically engineered crops of even exceedingly rare, disruptive effects of gene transfer is greatly amplified by the billions of individual transgenic plants already being grown annually in the United States."

The food industry is experimenting with the very safety of our food supply. Thanks to biotechnology, we face grave dangers from unknown, long-term consequences of the genetic manipulation of our basic foods. Science has not, and cannot, provide us with accurate information about the long-term impact of much of what has been done to our food by the food industry. That research would take generations, and will never be found by those interested in the economic benefit of selling genetically modified food. Are you willing to experiment with your family, your children, your grandchildren on speculation, which almost always has a profit motive?

That doesn't mean we should ignore or discount scientific findings. The better information we have, the better decisions we can make. For example, Dr. Dean Ornish's research and clinical programs demonstrate, with a high degree of consistency, that a combination of low-fat diet, exercise, meditation and social support will actually reverse arterial disease and improve the efficiency of the heart. We must take into account the motivations of the researcher, particularly those that violate the scientific principles of independence, disinterest, and objectivity.

We don't need to be experts on nutrition and diet in order to make sound decisions about our diet. But we do need to look at the entire pattern of our diet, and understand a few principles that can guide our decisions about what we eat.

Science is only one source of information. Another more important source is to look at what has worked well for others throughout history. Again, the traditions of self-mastery provide us with some very useful guidelines.

The diets of the great masters of self-mastery vary as widely as the cultures and climates in which they live. Many are vegetarian, but not all. But regardless of the differences, the diets of these great masters share some important similarities. First of all, these masters all eat simple diets and avoid rich, complex foods. They know the negative impact that rich food has on the mind as well as the body. Secondly, attention is always given to individual needs. The great masters avoid fanaticism in their diet as in all aspects of life. They approach their diet like they approach life: with attention, experimentation, and flexibility. Third, the attitude that masters have toward food is amazingly similar. They consider food an offering, and eating as an act of worship. Great respect and attention are given to the freshness and quality of the food, its preparation, and the eating of it. And while diets vary from tradition to tradition, we find that the key elements in all traditions are simplicity, balance, and a respectful attitude.

Unfortunately, in our culture many of our eating habits can only be called abusive. Although we have become much more sophisticated about diet and nutrition, our knowledge and practices are primitive and our attitudes disrespectful. We forget that our diet is the foundation for our physical health and has a profound impact on our emotional health. Even though many may repeat prayers before eating, few, if any, consider eating food a spiritual experience.

We can do a great deal to create a healthy diet with a little understanding and a few simple practices. The digestive process is a complex balance of many factors, but it basically involves two complementary processes: nourishing and cleansing. If we don't build the proper dietary habits, the body gradually builds up toxins that lead to mental and physical diseases. If we take the principles that guide the dietary habits of the great masters, we can create a healthy diet and build a healthy system. These principles – simplicity, balance, and attitude – are reflected in the quality of the food we eat, what we eat, and how we eat. If we manage these, we will have a healthy diet.

## Simplicity – Quality and Naturalness

The food qualities most suitable for our health are fresh, simple, and nutritious. Unfortunately, for many of us, these qualities are not consistently found in our diet. An important guiding principle is to eat food that is natural, both in its structure as well as to our food chain. Listen to advertising, and the term "natural" apparently means anything that appears on the face of the earth. Some years ago when high fiber diets were faddish, a bread was marketed called Fresh Horizons. Touted as natural, high fiber bread, the bread was actually made with processed wood cellulose. I suspect that most of us would not break a limb off a tree and chew on it. Fortunately, this brand had a short life span. Unfortunately, there are far more dangerous things that we put in our food supply.

For instance, Americans yearly consume an estimated five pounds of chemicals that do not occur naturally in the food chain. Did you know that over 2,000 additives are commonly used by the food industry? The basic research on how these additives affect us *has not been done*. No one can tell us what happens when we combine additives (which we do when we eat different foods together) and subject them to the refining process of digestion. Add to this combination the herbicides and pesticides which enter the food chain, and we are looking at chemical mixtures that are potentially dangerous.

Recently, scientists have discovered that chemical pollutants in the environment have had an impact on the sexual development of men and women as well as animals. Since 1938, sperm counts of men in the United States and twenty other countries have dropped by an average of fifty percent. As one researcher told a Congressional panel, "Every man in this room is half the man his grandfather was." The problem of decreased sperm count seems to be caused by estrogen and pollutants that mimic estrogen's structure. More research is needed, but it is clear that both animals and humans have undergone dramatic changes in sexual development that indicate increasing fertility problems.

Long-term effects over generations on such delicate mechanisms as genetic structures and reproductive capacities are largely unknown. As we might suspect, industry sponsored research tells us that the minute quantities that we ingest of any one chemical are not going to create a problem for us. But, as the authors of *Our Stolen Future* point out, for the estrogen-like substances found in the chemicals in our environment, it is the minute quantities that are most dangerous. Again, by researching a single chemical, the overall picture is ignored. We ingest minute quantities of a broad range of chemicals, not just one, and over a long period of time. What is the cumulative effect over several years of this broad intake? To assume that it is safe to take all these chemicals into our bodies is more than naive; it borders on insanity. Chemicals that do not occur naturally in the food chain are not useful to the body. It is absurd to think that they have no impact on the body or mind.

Here again, it is the pattern that is most disturbing. Any single additive to a food substance is probably not going to create harm for anyone. But what is the cumulative effect on our immune, digestive and hormonal systems of:
- food additives (flavor enhancers, synthetic vitamins, preservatives, waxes);
- fertilizers, insecticides, herbicides used in the growing process;
- hormones, antibiotics, and other chemicals given to the animals we eat;
- chemicals in the water we drink;
- pollutants in the air we breathe;
- thousands of industrial chemicals in the environment in which we live?

We are a long way from natural, simple, nutritious, and healthy food. We have also radically altered the way we have traditionally prepared food. As a population, we are participants in a grand social experiment with at least three potentially dangerous variables that have long-range consequences to our physical, mental, and genetic health. These three are genetically modified foods, microwave cooking, and food irradiation. The overriding purpose of this experiment is not the health of the individual, not the protection of the nation's food supply, *but to make money!*

As mentioned above, we really don't know the long-term effects of genetically modified foods, referred to as GMOs, or genetically modified organisms. Some argue that genetic modification is no different than hybridization, in which plants are changed through selective breeding. Wrong! Hybridization is a development within the same species, while genetic modification involves the introduction of genetic material from entirely different species. This is not found in nature. Tomato plants do not mate with fish, nor do soybeans consume herbicides. This is a different reality that we are creating. Are you confident that the food industry is more knowledgeable than nature?

The second variable is microwave cooking. We know little of the effects of this approach on the subtle energy levels of food. Recent research has shown that in microwave cooking, about half the L (levo) isomers switch to D (dextro) isomers, and D to L. Our enzymes are designed to fit as mirror images to these isomers in order to break down and access the nutrients in the food. When the isomers are switched, these enzymes cannot fit, and so the nutrition is unavailable. The longer the food is microwaved, the more switching that occurs. It appears that up to half the nutritional value of the food can be lost in microwave cooking. If this research is accurate, then we are creating even bigger problems with our diet.

The third variable, irradiation, is a process which involves exposing food to cobalt-60 which bombards the food with gamma rays. Gamma rays are extremely energetic electromagnetic waves. Like an X-ray passes through your body, gamma rays pass through the food. However, enough are intercepted to provide the energy to kill pathogens – bacteria, fungi and parasites – by destroying their DNA.

This does not make the food radioactive. It is a process that has been used for many years to sterilize medical equipment. Endorsed by over forty countries and many professional organizations, irradiation has long been approved for fruits, vegetables, poultry, and pork, and more recently for red meat. Irradiation has been shown to be effective for destroying E. coli as well as salmonella, campylobacter and shigella, together responsible for about 9,000 deaths annually.

Irradiation is not widespread as yet, and is used primarily to expand the shelf life of fruits and vegetables. For example, by irradiating strawberries and killing the bacteria and fungus on the berries, you can extend the shelf life of an irradiated strawberry to twelve weeks. The economic benefits are obvious. The possibilities for food safety regarding pathogens are also obvious.

What is not obvious is the change in the energy dimension of irradiated foods. We saw in Chapter 1 that the second dimension of the human personality is the energy dimension. The foundation for the physical body is the energy body. At the most basic physical level, we are not biochemical, neurological beings, but energy beings. What is the impact of irradiation – extremely energetic rays – on the energy structures of the food we eat? Are they still compatible to our human needs?

This question has not been addressed, as the scientific community does not research this subtle level of reality, unless, of course, you are a physicist. Irradiation may change fundamental structures within the energy patterns of the food. We don't know the answer to this. And yet, we are asked to endorse this process by an industry that stands to profit from this process.

We do need reliable scientific data, research that is done by independent, objective researchers, not influenced by financial and commercial interests. We need long-term studies on humans, not generations of lab rats bred to exhibit a certain trait and die early. Until we have this information about the physical as well as the energy levels, it may be wise to stay with a diet that is founded on what is natural and appropriate to our food chain. No matter what the food industry may claim, the FDA may endorse, or the ads may tell us, fresh, natural, unadulterated food, prepared in a traditional and simple way, is still the healthiest diet.

## Balance – Diet and Inner Harmony

Amazingly, sixty to seventy percent of the average American diet is of suboptimal nutritional value. That means we are using the body's resources to process food that is not very helpful to the body. This is not because there isn't enough to eat, but because much of what we eat is adulterated and/or of little or no nutritional value. Refined sugar, which has no nutrients, can make up as much as twenty-five percent of the diet. Add a high percentage of fats, as much as forty-five percent, and you have a diet that is not only nutritionally deficient, but takes nutrients away from the body in order to process the sugar and fats.

Sugar is an excellent example of how we create stress through diet. Blood sugar, which is called glucose, is one of the essential elements of the body. It plays a key role in metabolism, in brain chemistry so we think clearly, and in our moods. As Dr. O'Brien states in *The Wellness Tree,* the "...body's chemical makeup is so precisely balanced that whatever we put into the body has the potential to drastically alter the balance. In terms of emotions and energy, the amount of glucose in the blood must balance with the amount of blood oxygen for maximum efficiency. Our adrenal glands maintain this balance with fine precision."

We find glucose along with other types of sugars in our vegetables and fruits, which are part of a natural human diet. But today, the sugar we ingest most is sucrose, which is refined from sugar cane and sugar beets. Refined sugar (sucrose) acts very differently in the body from naturally occurring sugars, such

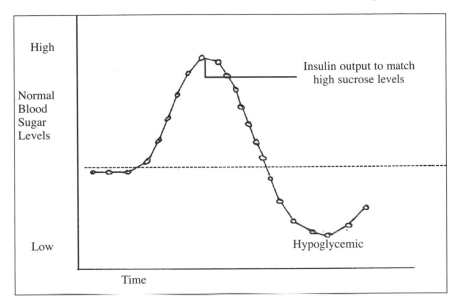

**Figure 5.2 — Blood Sugar Reaction Levels with Refined Sugar**

as found in fruit. First of all, the body doesn't need to digest refined sugar in order to absorb it into the blood stream. The sugar is immediately absorbed leading to a quick increase in blood sugar levels. This quickly upsets the balance of blood sugar, leading to what is an emergency to the adrenal glands and the pancreas that releases a large amount of insulin necessary to breakdown the sucrose into useable glucose. This emergency reaction, like most emergency reactions, leads to an opposite effect of too much of a decrease in blood sugar levels and the bottom drops out. This leads to further adrenal and pancreatic activity.

If, for instance, you eat a candy bar on an empty stomach, you feel a surge of energy for about a half-hour created by elevated blood sugar levels. But then, your energy drops below normal levels and you feel tired, nervy, shaky, and can't focus easily. These are the symptoms of low blood sugar. Since we don't like to feel that way, we take another sugar hit, creating the same blood sugar spiking and over-production of insulin as before. The figure shows this drastic impact of refined sugar on blood sugar levels.

The precipitous rise and decline in blood sugar often leads to a strain on the liver, which has to clean the insulin from the blood stream as well as imbalances in insulin production. This in turn can lead to hypoglycemia and diabetes. A more serious consequence is the danger posed to the nervous system – such as a diabetic coma. Low blood sugar can also intensify emotional problems, anxiety, and restlessness as well as tiredness and depression. Physical problems related to high sugar intake include kidney irregularity, fluctuations in blood pressure, and adrenal imbalances.

If, instead, we eat an apple that has to be digested before the sugar is available, we have a very different process occurring. First, the sugar in an apple consists of both sucrose and fructose. You don't need insulin to process fructose inside the body as you do with sucrose. Secondly, you must take the apple through a digestive process to get to the sucrose. The level of sucrose is not only smaller, but released over a period of time as you digest the apple. This keys a much smaller insulin production, creating less work for the liver. Unlike the candy bar with its refined sugar, an apple satisfies your nutritional needs without stressing your systems.

**Figure 5.3**
**Blood Sugar Reaction Levels with Naturally Occurring Sugar**

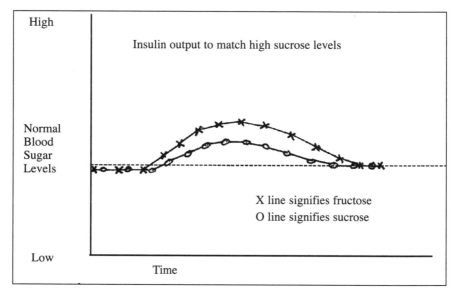

Blood sugar is the major fuel for our cells, but we can usually get enough naturally occurring sugar in fresh fruits, vegetables, and grains. Sugar in any form is a stimulant and leads to heightened arousal; refined sugar is too much of a stimulant for the body to be able to handle comfortably. When we add caffeine to the refined sugar, we double the stimulants. There is a rush of sympathetic activity, which we feel as a new burst of energy. Unfortunately, the end result is autonomic imbalance (stress), which leads to even more fatigue – particularly in those who suffer from low blood sugar. The "relaxing" coffee break is actually a stress producer!

When we need a break, a relaxation and/or breathing exercise would be far more helpful. These reduce stress, clear our minds, and leave us feeling wonderfully refreshed. Instead of being over-stimulated from refined sugar or caffeine, our energy would be appropriate to the task, and the mind would be focused.

Releasing tension would leave us more flexible both mentally and physically. We also avoid the withdrawal problems associated with stimulants.

Unless you have a clinical problem, there's no reason to eliminate all refined sugar from your diet. But you should know how to use it intelligently. An average yearly consumption of over 100 pounds per person, or twenty-five percent of the diet, is certainly not intelligent. Epidemiological studies clearly show that countries with a high consumption of refined sugar have a high incidence of blood sugar diseases. In countries where naturally occurring sugars are ingested, there is a low incidence of blood sugar diseases.

By being sensitive to the impact of refined sugar on our bodies, we make better choices. Eating a piece of pie on an empty stomach has quite a different effect than eating it after a full meal. When treats become the rule instead of the exception, we aren't using sugar intelligently.

While we have become more sensitive to fats in our diet, fats still make up as much as forty-five percent of our diet. These are also "empty" calories with no nutritional value. While a certain amount of fat is necessary, the American Heart Association recommends not more than thirty percent However, Dr. Dean Ornish recommends ten percent or less if the purpose is to reverse arterial disease. Medical authorities agree that a high-fat diet is associated with heart disease as well as certain forms of cancer, such as cancer of the colon and prostate.

## The Unhealthy Convenience

Since World War II the consumption of soft drinks has gone up by eighty percent, pastries by seventy percent and potato chips by eighty-five percent. On the other hand, consumption of dairy products has decreased by twenty-one percent, vegetables by twenty-three percent and fruits by twenty-five percent. Recent statistics show an alarming pattern:

1. We consume an average of 221 cans per person of soft drinks per year. This translates roughly into twenty-two gallons of carbonated sugar.
2. Soft-drink consumption exceeds milk consumption.
3. Americans spend forty-six percent of their food expenditures on restaurant meals.
4. One-third of all adults are overweight to the extent that it impairs their health. (Only two percent of this can be attributed to a glandular problem).
5. The top ten television shows are supported by ninety-one commercials for fast-food restaurants.

The main ingredients found in snack foods are sugar, refined flour, salt, and chemical additives that enhance flavor and color – and extend shelf life. How can anyone doubt that this adversely affects our health! The nature of even the "nutritious" food that we consume has been adversely altered in the past twenty years.

"Convenience," or processed, foods are notoriously lacking in both nutritional value and fiber. We pay an enormous price in our health and well-being in order to have "fast food." The term "fast" also describes how we now eat our food.

## To Chew or Not To Chew

How we eat is just as important as what we eat. Unfortunately, most of us are in too much of a hurry to take the time to really chew and taste our food. After two, three, or four quick chews, we swallow, expecting the rest of our over-worked system to break it down further. But neither the stomach nor the liver has teeth. Neither can adequately break down food that has been reduced in size just enough to be swallowed.

There are several important consequences of gulping down food. First, the digestive process is incomplete. Gulping food prevents the proper mixture of digestive enzymes with the food and interferes with the absorption of nutrients that is supposed to occur in the mouth. This creates stress within the entire system. And when gulping food becomes a consistent habit, the stress becomes chronic.

Furthermore, when we gulp our food, we don't really get an opportunity to taste it. We only experience a few strong flavors – sweetness, saltiness and sourness. The more subtle flavors (which require a more complete breakdown of the food as it mixes with the digestive juices) are not tasted. Thus, we don't allow our taste buds to tell us what is good for us and what is not.

Most processed food, and in particular, snack or junk food is intentionally designed to appeal to the obvious tastes – sweet, salty, and/or sour. These products contain either sugar and/or salt as a major ingredient, and eating quickly will leave this taste in the mouth. Their real appearance, odor and flavor are disguised by a variety of chemicals. The words "enhanced" or "imitation" on the label usually indicate the addition of chemicals.

While artificial colorings can fool the eyes, it is much more difficult to fool the nose – and even more difficult to fool the taste buds. Our taste habits are primarily conditioned by a few strong flavors, and gulping food reinforces our dependency upon them. But if our olfactory and taste capacities are given a chance to do their work, it is very difficult to hide or "enhance" the real flavor or smell of what is going into your mouth.

Here is an experiment that will give you an opportunity to discover your potential for tasting food. You will need two pieces of bread. One should be the fluffy white kind made from highly refined, enriched white flour, complete with all sorts of artificial additives. The other should be a piece of fresh, whole-grain flour bread made without any additives or preservatives. Rinse your mouth with water. Then take the white fluffy bread, hold it to your nose and sniff several times to get a good smell. Put it into your mouth and chew until it becomes liquid. Spit it out, rinse your mouth, and repeat the same process with the whole grain flour bread. Do your sense of taste and smell tell you anything about which bread you should be eating?

This same experiment should be tried comparing a piece of snack food (such as a packaged chocolate cupcake) with a piece of fresh fruit. Make sure you chew each until there is nothing but liquid in the mouth. Give your taste buds a chance to work, then decide what you want to put into your system.

Another reason not to gulp food is that when we chew completely, we generally eat about a third less than if we "wolf" it down. Approximately one-third of digestion is supposed to take place in the mouth. When we bypass it by only chewing two or three times, we also bypass about a third of the nutritional value in our food. Consequently, we will eat about a third more than what we really need. When we thoroughly chew each bite, digestion takes place more efficiently, hunger is satisfied more quickly and thoroughly, and we require less intake.

Compulsive eaters, or overeaters, rarely, if ever, really chew their food. If this is a problem for you, taking the time to chew your food will be very helpful. If you are on a weight-loss diet, take particular care to chew thoroughly. A participant in one of my seminars reported that he lost ten pounds in two weeks simply by chewing his food more thoroughly.

Eating when you are calm and quiet is also helpful. The emotional disturbances of anger, sadness, and fear create an "impossible" internal environment for the digestive process. Even the most perfect food creates serious digestive difficulties when eaten under these conditions. When you pause for a moment of silence before meals, it gives you time to clear your mind of disturbing emotions – and thus calm your body – before you eat. Silent prayer cultivates an attitude of thankfulness and prepares the mind and body to receive grace in the form of food. It allows you to focus on positive, joyful emotions. This, of course, leads to a restful condition and the proper neurological balance required for efficient digestion.

In the growing pressure and hurry of our lives, we have lost track of this simple wisdom. Instead of being the center of peace, the dinner table is all too often a battleground, or we eat when we are under pressure. The price we pay for this is reflected in the epidemic of digestive tract diseases we suffer from today.

## The Hurry to Indigestion

While this is somewhat oversimplified, it is essentially correct to say that the more hurried we are, the less we are able to digest food properly and the greater the stress we created for the system. The pervasive habit of "grabbing a bite to eat" or "eating on the run" almost guarantees digestive misery. The more frequently we do this, the more likely it will lead to ill health. Yet how many times do we approach our meals with any degree of calm?

Eating at the wrong time leads to more problems. Constantly snacking (which forces the digestive process to continually work), eating before bedtime, or eating right before engaging in strenuous mental or physical activity all tax the digestive system. Asking the body to perform two neurologically opposing tasks invites misery. For example, wining, dining, and then lovemaking is the romantic ideal, but its real consequence is decreased digestive efficiency, decreased sexual capacity, and increased stress. More practical and far less stressful for your body's systems is to first make love and then wine and dine. This way you are not asking your body to perform two conflicting activities at the same time. If performed in proper order, all activities – the functioning of your nervous system, digestion, and lovemaking – are enhanced.

It isn't difficult to slow down. Before you eat, simply take two minutes to focus on the breathing exercises you will learn in the next few chapters. You may reflect on a silent prayer or focus on your breathing. When you feel calm and relaxed, you will notice that you have more saliva in your mouth, indicating that your body is prepared to digest food. Once you have the habit of doing this at every meal, you'll notice that you feel better after you have eaten, but you will also find greater enjoyment in the activity.

## Respect: The Missing Ingredient

The third principle of the great spiritual masters – respect – is the key to creating a healthy, satisfying diet as well as a healthy, satisfying life. These masters respect the life force as the creative expression of the divine. There is a point of view that one should not eat animal flesh because it is wrong to kill. This logic has been extended by the animal rights organizations to include any abuse to animals. This point of abuse is well taken regarding any life form. But, the real issue is not whether or not we eat animal flesh, but whether or not we respect life, including our own.

When we don't respect life, we treat each other, the environment, and food as commodities. People, animals, food, and the environment simply become "things" to manipulate, to take as much value as one can from the commodity and then discard it. It is this lack of respect for the life force, the creative expression of the Divine, that lies at the heart of greed, the willingness to poison the environment, adulterate food, and focus on money, convenience, and pleasure rather than health. It is a lack of respect that allows the scientist to arrogantly think that he knows better than nature how to genetically structure food. It is a lack of respect that allows us to put convenience before quality, eat poor quality food, and abuse our digestive system. We take our diet for granted, and when we do, we take our health for granted.

What does it mean to respect life? It means to pay attention to the value of life. We do that by paying attention to our food, respecting its life-sustaining quality. Instead of gulping our food, we should prepare our bodies to receive it by spending a few moments in silence and relaxing. We respect food when we lovingly prepare it for others, ensuring that the others are receiving the very best we can give them. We respect food when we ensure that the soil in which it grows is rich in natural nutrients and free of unnecessary chemicals. We respect food when we ensure its freshness in the best possible way, not the most convenient, or in a way that brings us the greatest profit. We respect food when we honor the animal we have killed in order to sustain our own life. We respect food when we select the proper food for our own digestive system rather than gulp fast-food down because we are in a hurry. We respect food when we pay attention to eating rather than eating absent-mindedly while we are working on some project.

The list could go on and on, but the point is attention and honoring the power of food to sustain life. If we cultivate this awareness, then our diet begins to change. There is no one diet for everyone. Within general guidelines – simple, fresh nutritious food natural to the food chain, balance in our diet, eating in an atmosphere of serenity, healthy eating patterns such as proper chewing, and respect for the life force – each of us is unique in our nutritional needs. We can discover what we need by paying attention to how food makes us feel not just immediately, but four hours after we eat it. Again, the key is relaxed awareness. The more sensitive we become, the better choices we make, and the fewer problems we create for ourselves.

The following are some specific guidelines to help you stay within the three principles of simplicity, balance and respect. Some of these are taken from *The Wellness Tree* by Dr. Justin O'Brien.

• **Buy and eat only the best food:** Choose food that is as close to its fresh, natural state as possible. The less food is processed, the more nutrition it retains. Prepare your own food as much as possible. The longer food remains in containers, the less vitality it holds for you. The same goes for cooked food that you store. As much as possible, avoid eating any genetically modified foods.

• **Avoid as many chemicals as possible:** Eat food that is natural to your food needs. Chemical additives will not only reduce nutrients in food, but can be very dangerous. Minimize your intake of chemical additives. Avoid food that contains aspartame, such as diet sodas and candies.

• **Substitute natural sugars for refined sugar:** Use natural forms of sweetness like fresh fruit, dried fruit, raisins, even raw carrots. Whenever you do have sugar, make sure it is with meals. Eliminate refined carbohydrates as much as possible. Use artificial sweeteners only if medically necessary. You are generally better off with refined sugar than chemical substitutes.

• **Reduce your fat intake:** Go easy on dairy products, using skim or low-fat instead of whole whenever you can. Remember that cottage cheese, like yogurt, has virtually no fat. However, butter is better for your body than the chemicals of margarine. Anytime you need to be critical and alert, avoid large meals of fried or roasted foods, especially meat.

• **Watch your protein:** In our sedentary society, we consume an excess of protein. This can lead to calcium imbalances and produces excessive uric acid, inviting a host of intestinal problems. In terms of quantity, meat is the least important item in your diet. The older you get, the less red meat and pork you should eat.

• **Snack on raw fruits, veggies, and nuts:** Keep your snacks healthy and fat-free. Roasted, toasted foods are hard on the digestive process, particularly the kidneys, liver, and gall bladder. Let nuts and fruits appease your hunger.

• **Drink lots of water:** You need fresh, unpolluted water – not canned drinks, tea or coffee – for proper neural activity (including brain activity) and for cleansing the body. You should drink at least two quarts a day, enough so that your urine runs clear at least once a day. Avoid fluids, even water, during a meal. Fluids, even water, do not aid digestion but merely dilute digestive fluids.

• **Create a pleasant lighthearted atmosphere when eating:** Even the best food becomes toxic when you are emotionally disturbed. If you are upset about something, postpone any eating.

• **Exercise regularly:** Exercise vigorously for half an hour at least three or four times per week. This will improve your overall metabolism and aid your digestive capacities.

• **Be creative, and discover your own unique needs:** Diet is highly individual. Experiment with selections and amounts of food. Your metabolism is personalized – adjustable, but highly individualized. Your nutritional needs have a certain universality about them, but the forms and combinations of food from which you supply these needs is entirely yours to figure out.

## EXERCISE: CREATING FLEXIBILITY AND AWARENESS

Research leaves no room for doubt: Those who exercise consistently will be healthier, have fewer coronary-vascular diseases and less diabetes, fewer frustrations, a more active sex life, and generally have greater satisfaction in life than those who do not. They also have fewer medical expenses and ingest smaller quantities of drugs. This is true regardless of age or sex. In his book, *Ageless Body, Timeless Mind,* Deepak Chopra reports on a program conducted by gerontologists from Tufts University in which a group of the frailest residents from a nursing home were selected for a weight-training program. "Within eight weeks, wasted muscles had come back by 300 percent, coordination and balance improved, and overall a sense of active life returned. Some of the subjects who had not been able to walk unaided could now get up and go to the bathroom in the middle of the night by themselves, an act of reclaimed dignity that is by no means trivial. What makes this accomplishment truly wondrous, however, is that the youngest subject in the group was eighty-seven and the oldest ninety-six."

No one seriously disputes the fact that exercise is necessary to maintain a healthy body. But little is said about the impact of exercise on the mind. Most people exercise to build muscular strength, cardiovascular endurance, flexibility and physical balance. These are important and necessary for our health. There is a great deal of good information available about aerobic exercise and weight lifting, so we don't need to focus on these here. Instead, our focus will be to use exercise to increase inner awareness as well as to enhance flexibility. The simple exercises that follow will strengthen both body and mind, build balance and coordination as well as strength, and enhance concentration and confidence.

If you exercise regularly, you will recognize that there are times when your exercise program doesn't seem very helpful. Jogging wasn't enjoyable, you did not feel invigorated after your handball game or martial arts session, or you felt low after your walk in the park. It isn't the fault of the exercise program – your mind was not properly engaged. Whenever the body is exercising but the mind is not involved, the exercise yields fewer benefits. In fact, if you merely exercise your body without paying attention, it can be harmful.

A classic example of this is the "screaming" Type A personality who has been told by his doctor to start jogging every day. In true Type A form, he compulsively sets up a jogging schedule in which he attempts to achieve certain goals as quickly as possible. After all, if he is going to run, then by God, he will be "the best damn runner on the block." He runs against the clock just as he works against the clock. The result is that he adds another strain to his day rather than a beneficial play for his body. Working or jogging, his mental attitude creates his stress. What happens to his body is determined by what happens in his mind.

*If we want to use exercise as a tool to increase our self-mastery, we must pay attention to how our exercise affects the body and mind.* We must coordinate mind, body, and action, and this takes attention. This is the key to successful exercise.

Like the Type A jogger, we create stress and other problems when we allow our mind to think about future threats or past mistakes and hurts, instead of focusing on what we are doing. This is why competitive sports can be very stressful, particularly when there are heavy emotional attachments (such as financial or self-esteem considerations) involved with winning or losing.

Both professional and amateur athletes now recognize that the mind plays a key role in performance. Early books on the subject, such as Timothy Galway's *The Inner Game of Tennis,* point out how concentration and mental imagery (performing the actions perfectly in the mind before performing with the body) enhance performance. Now sports psychologists work in all fields of professional and amateur sports, using imagery to develop performance skills. However, the focus is still on performance at the physical level.

Western physical fitness programs are just beginning to use exercise as a way to sharpen the mind and increase inner awareness. In Eastern systems, on the other hand, the focus has always been to perfect control of the mind over the body. We don't have to become yogis or martial artists to use exercise to increase our conscious control over the body/mind interaction. We can easily bring balance to our physical fitness regimens and enhance control over both our mind and body.

## Exercise for Mind/Body Coordination

The interdependent relationship between mind and body is very complex. The mind has ultimate control, but events in the body deeply affect the mind. If you don't believe this, simply spend a few hours hunched over and see how you feel. When the body becomes rigid and inflexible, it means that there is rigidity and inflexibility somewhere in the mind. If we make the body more flexible, we also make the mind more flexible.

The most common symptoms of rigidity are stiff muscles, backaches and painful joints. We create and sustain inflexibility through muscle tension. This problem is exacerbated when the tendons become short and rigid, allowing for little flexibility and leading to sprains, torn ligaments and muscles, and dislocated joints. More serious, and also stress-related, is arthritis, the crippling joint disease.

We know that we must loosen up before playing handball or tennis, and that exercises which systematically stretch muscles and tendons are very important. So what do we do to warm up? A few jumping jacks, a shrug of the shoulders, a few quick deep-knee bends, running in place, or other quick, short and choppy movements – definitely the wrong way to stretch muscles!

To relieve tension, to stretch and loosen tight muscles and tendons, requires slow, sustained movement together with holding the stretched posture. Pumping muscles with quick movements does not stretch them out; it builds more tension within them. These movements energize muscles, but don't necessarily release tension.

A wide variety of simple stretching exercises are available (at the end of this chapter you will find several which are excellent for increasing flexibility). But there is one important secret to doing stretches – coordinate your breathing with the movement. This dramatically improves your capacity to stretch. If you pay close attention to both the movement and your breath, you can determine whether that movement should be done on an exhalation or an inhalation. A general rule is to exhale whenever you stretch down, or bend over, and inhale whenever returning to the original position or stretching the body up or back. This coordinates the mind with the movement. Breath coordination also ensures that the movements will not be too fast.

Breathing is also an important variable in holding the stretch. For example, when you stretch down to touch your toes, don't bounce up and down as if you were bobbing for apples. Rather, bend down to touch your toes, and then stay bent as far as you comfortably can. Do not bend until you feel pain. You are exercising, not taking a course in pain control!

Do not hold your breath. This only increases tension. After a few moments, concentrate on relaxing the point in the body at which you feel the most tension. Then, on an exhalation, bend a little bit more, and hold the stretch. Concentrating on the flow of the breath, relax into this posture as much as possible. Then, after a few moments, rise slowly and relax standing up. The longer you comfortably hold the stretch, the more benefit you gain from it. Slowly increase your capacity to hold or remain in the stretch posture. Work within your limits and your limits will certainly increase. Go beyond them and you will certainly suffer.

With concentration and comfortable breathing, you will be able to stretch much farther than you thought. However, use the exhalation and bending technique only once or twice after the initial bend. Otherwise you may extend yourself too far, and you will feel the consequences for the next few days. By moving gently and relaxing into the posture (holding the limit of the stretch) you begin to develop the most important skill that comes from exercising. By paying close attention to the internal feelings and movements, you become conscious of the subtle feedback cues of the muscles and systems involved. This increased sensitivity leads to a greater conscious control over these muscles and systems.

You are learning how to use your own innate biofeedback machine. You must develop this sensitivity if you ever want to have control over the body, and be able to use the mind to keep your body healthy and free of stress and disease. The more skilled you become, the greater your power.

Most people are not sensitive to the tension in the shoulders and neck until they feel soreness or pain or even a headache. The muscles use pain as a final signal in order to grab your attention. The problem isn't your shoulders. These poor muscles are only following instructions, and all along they have been sending signals back to the brain with every change or increase in tension. The problem is that no one was paying attention to the feedback signals! The muscle was forced to remain tense. Finally, the muscle sends a pain message, and you begin to pay attention.

Why wait until the tension becomes so chronic and extreme as to cause pain? By becoming aware of your internal messages and controls, you hear the messages of the body and do something much earlier to prevent a problem from developing. While exercising, if you think about how wonderful you look while stretching, or how far you bend in comparison to others, or about your job, or anything else, you have wasted your time. You have missed the most important elements of the exercise: developing awareness of your changing internal physical and mental states. Even just five minutes of stretching done consistently with intense concentration develops your internal awareness. You actually need very little time to become aware of and develop control over your muscles. You can do it with all the muscles, as well as your heartbeat, blood pressure, and just about any system in the body. The deeper the system, of course, the more time and attention it takes.

## Body, Mind, and Consciousness

Hatha yoga is a sophisticated, practical exercise system that consists of a series of postures designed to bring balance and flexibility to both mind and body by stimulating neural and glandular systems. Hatha yoga is very precise and effective in correcting physical problems. Research in England has shown that hatha yoga is more effective for healing back problems than any other exercise system, and far more effective than surgery.

Several of my clients and associates have used hatha yoga as a therapeutic system, both for problems stemming from accidents as well as from congenital defects. One classic example is an elderly gentleman by the name of Bua Swami from a small farming village in India. I met Bua Swami about thirty years ago and attended several of his classes. At the time we met, he was around seventy-three years old and was capable of bending his body like a pretzel, accomplishing the most difficult of yoga exercises. What was most fascinating was that he was born a cripple. Early in his life, he was sent to study hatha yoga with an accomplished yoga master. Through his training, he was able to completely overcome his disability, and went on to teach hatha yoga all over the world. He is now over a century in age and still teaching and doing postures.

On the physical level, hatha yoga strengthens organ, glandular, and neurological systems. In addition, it reduces physical tension by slowly stretching the muscles and tendons and eliminating the physical habits that sustain stress. It consists of stretches and held postures, alternated with relaxation, all of which work synergistically to coordinate mind and body. Hatha yoga also includes practices that cleanse the body of accumulated toxins and waste products. But its ultimate goal is to bring perfect balance and harmony into the body/mind/spirit relationship and eliminate conditions of "dis-ease."

In the West, hatha yoga is taught primarily as a physical cult to keep oneself young and healthy. The real purpose of hatha yoga, however, is not only to strengthen and balance the body, but to calm the mind, increase concentration skills and expand inner awareness. It isn't by accident that the postures are centered around the spine and central nervous system. Through proper manipulation, exercise, and concentration, the postures benefit particular glandular, structural, and organic systems. In this way our physiological systems achieve harmony and balance, which allows us to sustain deep concentration and a one-pointed mind, the key tools for self-mastery. This, in turn, leads to emotional equilibrium and a powerful mind – building blocks for a healthy life.

Beginning exercises, such as the joints and glands exercises and some of the stretches, can, and should be practiced on your own, and several of the more immediately helpful ones are described at the end of this chapter. The ideal, however, is to find a competent instructor and learn the postures. Then develop a routine that fits your nature and needs.

When selecting a teacher, remember that the ultimate purpose of the system is to work with the mind and internal concentration skills. The competent teacher knows her subject well and practices what she teaches. One critical point is breathing, a necessary part of hatha yoga. If the teacher is not knowledgeable about the breath, including the neurophysiology of breathing, this teacher is not competent. Certification by this group or that group is no guarantee of competency.

You can usually find a variety of classes in hatha yoga and martial arts in your community. Sample the classes, study the teacher and his methods, and choose wisely. There are many fine traditions and excellent teachers. It is simply a matter of taking the time to check out your resources, finding what best fits your temperament and needs, and then committing yourself to a consistent practice.

Hatha yoga does not replace sports or aerobic exercises. You need balance in your exercise program just as you need balance in the other areas of your life. A short daily period of hatha yoga postures that will prevent many physical and mental problems can (and should) supplement your regular exercise routine.

## Stretching Exercises for Flexibility and Balance

The following are a series of exercises that anyone can do easily and quickly. The first consists of desk exercises, simple stretching exercises for the face, neck, and shoulders, designed to increase circulation and decrease tension in the various muscle, joint and glandular areas of the body. You can do these easily while sitting at a desk (and at any time during the day). If used often, they provide immediate and effective stress reduction.

The second set of exercises are simple cross-pattern movements that coordinate left and right brain hemispheres. They are part of Brain Gym, a system of educational kinesiology developed by Dr. Paul Dennison that uses simple movements to enhance learning abilities. These are useful morning exercises to help balance and coordinate mind and body.

The third set of exercises and stretches are more involved and require some time and space to perform. Integrated with relaxation, they offer a practical series of beginning stretching exercises.

When you exercise, there are a few points to bear in mind:

• **Be consistent.** Set a specific time each day for your practice, and practice at least a little each day. Don't rush; take the time you need to do them properly. Consistency builds very helpful habits.

• **Morning and evening are the best times to practice.** Morning exercise helps you remain calm and alert during the day. In the evening, the exercises help relieve the day's tensions so that you can enjoy a peaceful night's sleep.

• **Do the exercises in a clean, quiet, and well-ventilated room.** Wear loose, comfortable clothing.

• **Always practice on an empty stomach.**

• **Women should not practice strenuous exercises during menstruation.** However, all the exercises given below can be done. Just remember to relax and work gently with the body.

• **Do not become discouraged if your body does not respond the same way each day.** Just practice regularly, and don't compete with others or yourself.

- **Study your body and its movements.** Be aware of your capacity and learn not to go beyond it. Your capacity will increase with practice.
- **Let body movements flow evenly and gently with the breath.** Do not hold your breath at any time unless specifically instructed to do so.
- **Follow any exertion with relaxation.** However, do not allow the mind to drift toward sleep while you relax.

Remember, the purpose of all the stretches is to relieve tension, increase flexibility, and increase internal awareness and control of bodily processes. Concentrate on what you are doing. Keep the breath even, steady and coordinated with the movement. Most importantly, enjoy the exercises.

## Desk Exercises

*Shoulders:* Do these simple exercises several times during the day. Be sure to coordinate the breathing with the movement, and pay attention to what you feel. This will not only stretch the muscles but also increase your awareness of these muscles. This will increase your control and reduce the chronic tension in the muscles.

Stand or sit with the arms hanging loosely at the sides. Begin to rotate the left shoulder in a complete circle, first moving it forward and in toward the center of the chest, exhaling as you do. Then move it up toward the ear and back while inhaling, trying to touch the shoulder blade to the spine, and then down back into the starting position. Rotate three times in this direction and then reverse and rotate three times in the opposite direction. Do the same for the right shoulder, and then do both shoulders together. Relax.

*Neck:* These exercises are very good for relieving accumulated tension in the back neck muscles. If you have tension headaches or are bothered by a stiff neck and shoulders, these will be very helpful, and can be practiced several times daily without any difficulty.

*Forward and backward bend:* Exhale slowly, bringing the head forward and taking the chin towards the chest. Feel the stretch of the muscles in the back of the neck. Inhale slowly, lifting the head up and back, stretching the muscles of the front of the neck. With an exhalation, slowly return to the forward position.

*Chin over shoulder:* With an exhalation, turn the head as far to the left as possible and try to bring the chin in line with the shoulder. Inhale and bring the head back to the forward position. Repeat in the same manner on the right side.

*Ear over shoulder:* With an exhalation, bring the left ear towards the left shoulder. Inhale and come back to the center. Exhale and bring the right ear towards the right shoulder. Again inhale, come back to the center and relax. Only the head and neck should move. The shoulder should not be raised to meet the ear.

*Neck tilts:* Lower the chin to the chest and slowly begin to tilt the head in a clockwise direction. Inhale as you tilt the head to one side and then to the back. When you reach the back point, reverse direction and exhale as you tilt the head

**Figure 5.4**

counter-clockwise to the side and then forward. Continue the counter-clockwise direction, inhaling as you tilt to the other side and then to the back. When you reach the back, again reverse direction, inhaling back to the side and to the forward, chin-down position. Remember to tilt the head, bringing your ear to your shoulder, and not to turn the head. Your chin should always face the front. The head, neck and body should be relaxed, allowing the head to tilt and rotate freely and loosely. Neck tilts can be safely done if you move slowly and methodically. If you feel any slight dizziness, or if there is any pain when tilting the head back, simply do not allow the head to tilt as far back, avoiding any pain or discomfort.

*Forehead and Sinus Massage:* Sit in a comfortable posture with the head, neck, and trunk straight. Using your fingers or the heels of your palms, begin to massage the forehead by working up and out with a stroking motion. Follow the bony structure around the eyes and continue out across the temples. Next, massage just below the eyes and next to the nose. Make the same motions, moving outward across the face and temples.Using the thumbs and your forefingers, gently slide across the upper rim of the eye sockets toward the temples. Put pressure on the bony ridge, but don't put any pressure on the eye itself.

On the lower ridge of the eye sockets close to the bone, use your fingers to press down gently, and then release. Don't rub, just press. Then move your fingers over, and press again. Continue to move and press until the entire bony ridge has been massaged. Don't put any pressure on the eye.

Massage around your mouth and up the jaw line to the temples. Ease up on the pressure whenever you come to the temple area. All of these movements begin at the center of the face and move outward. This pushes all the tension off the face, forehead, and temples, and smoothes away any wrinkles on the forehead or crows-feet at the eye edges.

Rub the palms of your hands quickly together until the hands become very hot. Then gently lay the palms of the hands on your closed eyelids, without pressing, allowing the heat from the skin to permeate the eyelids. Visualize the warmth moving from your hands and penetrating all the way to the back of your eyes. Feel your eyes relaxing in the warmth. This is called palming, and is very useful, particularly if you work with a computer.

## Balancing Exercises

These simple movements help balance brain hemispheres. They are adapted from Paul Dennison's book *Switching On*. Cross-motor Patterning or Cross-crawling "is any rhythmic, balanced movement which requires the individual to dynamically relate the right side of his body to the left side, while being aware of the top half of his body and the lower half.

"Cross-crawling requires precise switching on and off of the muscles by the brain at exactly the right time, and requires feedback from and to the muscles to maintain the exercise. Infants learn this highly intricate bilateral integration during the creeping and crawling stages before walking. It is the same type of cooperation of the cerebral hemispheres that is required for reading and writing."

These exercises begin with simple cross-pattern, touching the inside of the knee with the opposite-side hand, and moving to more complex patterns of touching the inside of the knee with the opposite-side elbow. These movements coordinate left/right, top/bottom and back/front areas of the brain and body simultaneously, leading to better coordination and balance. Start these exercises slowly and rhythmically. Slowly increase your speed as you feel more coordinated. Most people (myself included) who do these simple exercises in the morning feel more coordinated throughout the day.

*Hand to knee cross pattern:* (Figure 5.5) Lift your right knee upwards and bring your left hand down to touch the knee. Then lift your left knee, bringing

**Figure 5.5**

Hand-to-knee
Cross-pattern

**Figures 5.6**

Elbow-to-knee
Cross-pattern

**Figure 5.7**

Elbow-to-knee
Cross-pattern
Front-to-back

your right hand down to touch your knee. Alternate between the two until you have at least ten repetitions on each side.

*Elbow to knee cross pattern:* (Figure 5.6) This is similar to the above exercise except that you extend the arm and opposite leg in opposite directions and form an X to complete the movement. Lift your right knee, touching your left elbow, and then stretching the right leg out to the right and the left arm out to the left. Then lift your left knee, touching the knee with your right elbow, and then stretching the left leg out to the left and the right arm out to the right. This creates an X pattern with the arms and legs. Do at least ten repetitions on each side.

*Elbow to knee cross pattern front to back:* (Figure 5.7) This exercise is the same as the above except instead of stretching arms and legs to the side, the arms are stretched to the front and the legs to the back. Lift your left knee and touch your right elbow to the knee. Then stretch your right arm forward as if reaching in front of you, and simultaneously, stretch your left leg out behind you. Then lift your right knee and touch your left elbow to the right knee. Then stretch your left arm forward as if reaching in front of you, and simultaneously, stretch your right leg out behind you. Do a minimum of ten repetitions on each side.

## Stretches

Before doing the following stretches, lie in the Relaxation Posture (See Figure 5.1). This centers the mind and prepares it for focusing on the body. It helps you to relax the skeletal muscles, enabling you to go further into the stretches while reducing the likelihood of injuries. Relaxing between stretches helps prepare the mind for the next exercise in the sequence. After each posture, lie in the Relaxation Posture until respiration and heartbeat return to normal. However, beginners should not remain in this position for more than ten minutes. After finishing your stretches, complete your exercise period by lying on your back, breathing from the diaphragm and concentrating on the breath for five minutes. This is an excellent time to practice 2:1 Breathing as described in Chapter 6.

*Side stretch* (Figure 5.8): Assume a simple standing posture with feet about shoulder width apart and legs and knees relaxed. Movements should be made slowly as if you are standing in water and moving your arms or legs through the water. Begin inhaling, and slowly raise the right arm out to the side with the palm facing downward. When the arm reaches shoulder level, turn the palm upward. Continue inhaling and raise the arm until it is next to the ear. Still continuing to inhale and keeping the feet firmly on the floor, stretch the entire right side of the body upward. Then, without allowing the body to bend forward or backward, or the right arm to bend, begin exhaling and slowly bend at the waist, sliding the left hand down the left leg.

Breathe evenly for three complete breaths. Inhaling, slowly bring the body back to an upright position. Exhaling, slowly lower the arm to shoulder level, turn the palm downward, and return to the simple standing posture. Concentrate

Figure 5.8
Side Stretch

Figure 5.9
Simple Back Stretch

Angle Pose

Figure 5.10
Angle 1st Position

Figure 5.11
Angle 2nd Position

Figure 5.12
Angle 3rd Position

Figure 5.13 — Torso Twist

1st Position

2nd Position

on the breath until the body relaxes completely. Repeat the side stretch in the opposite direction. When you first begin to stretch, hold the stretch for at least three breaths each side. As you become more flexible, you can hold the posture for as long as you are comfortable, but make sure that you hold each side for the same length of time. Note: For a more intense stretch repeat this posture standing with the legs together.

*Simple back stretch:* (Figure 5.9) Assume the standing posture. With the fingers facing downward, place the heels of the hands on either side of the spine just above the buttocks. Exhaling, gently push the hips forward, slowly letting the head, neck and trunk bend backward as far as comfortable without straining. Inhaling, return to the standing pose, keeping the hands in the same position. Keeping the entire body relaxed, slowly bend the body forward from the hips as far as possible. Hold this position until all the muscles of the back relax completely. Note: The forward bend balances the effects of the backward bend.

### Angle Posture

*First position* (Figure 5.10): Assume a simple standing posture with the feet two to three feet apart. Placing the arms behind the back, grasp the right wrist with the left hand. Keep the heels in line and place the right foot at a ninety-degree angle from the left. (Beginning students may turn the left foot slightly inward – to the right – if it is more comfortable.) Inhaling, turn the body toward the right foot. Exhaling, bend forward from the hips and bring the head as close to the knee as comfortable. Breathe evenly; hold this position for five counts. Inhaling, slowly raise the body; exhaling, turn to the front. Turn the right foot so that it faces forward. Repeat the exercise on the left.

*Second position* (Figure 5.11): Keeping the arms straight, interlace the fingers behind the back. With the right foot at a ninety-degree angle from the left, turn the body and bend forward from the hips, bringing the head toward the right knee. Raise the hands overhead as far as comfortable. Breathe evenly; hold this position for five counts. Inhaling, slowly raise the body and turn to the front. Repeat the exercise on the left side.

*Third position* (Figure 5.12): With the arms straight, interlace the fingers behind the back and press the palms together. Exhaling, raise the arms and bend forward as far as comfortable. Breathe evenly and hold for five counts. Inhaling, push the hands toward the floor and bend the head, neck and trunk back as far as comfortable without straining. Breathe evenly; hold for five counts. Slowly return to a standing position and relax.

### Torso Twist

*First Position* (Fig. 5.13): Assume a simple standing posture with the feet two to three feet apart. Raise the arms overhead; interlace the fingers. Keeping the arms next to the ears and stretching the body from the rib cage upward, rotate the upper torso, arms, and hands in a clockwise direction. The waist, hips, and legs remain stationary. Inhale as the body leans to the right and to the back; exhale as the body leans to the left and to the front. Repeat three times clockwise and three times counterclockwise. Continue by moving into the second position.

*Second position:* Keeping the hips stationary and bending from the waist, repeat the above exercise three times clockwise and three times counterclockwise. Continue by moving into the third position. (Remember to breathe as described in the first position.)

*Third position:* Keeping the legs stationary and bending from the hips as far as comfortable, rotate and twist the entire upper part of the body in a large circle. Repeat three times clockwise and three times counterclockwise. (Remember to breathe as described in the first position.) Relax. Concentrate on the breath.

## The Sun Salutation: An Integrated Stretching Exercise

This is an integrated exercise that stretches and limbers the spine as well as all of the limbs and joints. It is a series of twelve positions, each one flowing into the next in one graceful, continuous movement (Figure 5.14). First become familiar with the movements, and then coordinate your breathing with them. You will find, as you progress from doing two or three every morning to doing seven or eight or more, that you will feel the difference on the days you do not do them. If you feel like you only have the time to do one exercise in the morning, this is the one to do. (This is the author's favorite wake-up exercise.) The benefits are innumerable.

During sleep the body is very inactive. Our metabolic rate decreases, the circulation of body fluids slows and all of the body's functions are reduced. When we wake up, we must make a transition from an inactive condition to an active one. By not stretching properly, the body isn't prepared to function adequately, and this can lead to problems, including strained and pulled muscles.

The sun salutation is excellent for the transition between sleep and activity. The exercise massages and stimulates the glands, organs, muscles and nerves of the body. The breath rate increases, bringing more oxygen into the lungs, and the heart rate speeds up. This in turn causes more blood to pass through the lungs, which picks up more oxygen, providing a greater supply of oxygenated blood throughout the body.

It's a wonderful exercise. Try it for a month, gradually increasing the number of salutations you do each morning until you are doing at least eight to twelve. The first one you do will be difficult as the body is not used to stretching. The second one will not be as difficult, and by the third or fourth salutation, you will feel as if your body has been oiled at the joints, and your internal energy is beginning to flow. You will notice the difference in how you feel for the rest of the day.

*Position 1* (Exhale during movement): Stand firmly with the head, neck and trunk in a straight line. Beginners can stand with the feet slightly apart. With palms together in a prayer position, place the hands at the heart level and gently close the eyes. Standing silently, concentrate on the breath.

*Position 2* (Iinhale during movement): Inhaling, slightly lower and stretch the hands and arms forward with the palms facing downward. Raise the arms overhead until they are next to the ears. Keeping the legs straight and the head between the arms, arch the spine and bend backward as far as possible without straining.

*Position 3* (Exhale during movement): Exhaling, bend forward from the hips, keeping the back straight and the arms next to the ears. Continue bending; place the palms next to the feet, aligning the fingers with the toes. Bring the head to the knees keeping the legs straight. Note: If you cannot place the hands on the floor without bending the legs, then lower the upper body only as far as comfortable without straining.

*Position 4* (Inhale during movement): In this position bend the knees if necessary in order to place the hands on the floor. Inhaling, stretch the right leg back, rest the right knee and the top of the right foot on the floor, and extend the toes. The left foot remains between the hands; the hands remain firmly on the floor. Arch the back, look up, and stretch the head back as far as comfortable. The line from the head to the tip of the right foot should form a smooth and graceful curve.

*Position 5* (Retain the breath; this is the only position in which the breath is held): While retaining the breath, curl the toes of the right foot, extend the left leg, placing it next to the right. The arms remain straight but not locked and the body forms an inclined plane from the head to the feet. This position resembles a starting push-up position.

*Position 6* (Exhale during movement): Exhaling, drop first the knees, and then the chest to the floor, keeping the tips of the fingers in line with the breasts. Tuck in the chin and place the forehead on the floor. In this position only the toes, knees, hands, chest, and forehead touch the floor. The nose does not touch the floor and the elbows remain close to the body.

*Position 7* (Inhale during movement): Without moving the hands and the forehead, relax the legs and extend the feet so that the body rests flat on the floor. Inhaling, slowly raise the head. First, touch the nose and then chin to the floor; then stretch the head forward and upward. Without using the strength of the arms or hands, slowly raise the shoulders and chest; look up and bend back as far as comfortable. In this posture the navel remains on the floor. To lift the thorax, use the muscles of the back only. Do not use the arms and hands to push the body off the floor, but to balance the body. Keep the feet and legs together and relaxed.

*Position 8* (Eexhale during movement): Without repositioning the feet and hands, exhale, straighten the arms and push the buttocks high in the air. Bring the head between the arms and try to gently press the heels to the floor.

*Position 9* (inhale during movement): Inhaling, bend the right knee and

## Figure 5.14
## The Sun Salutation

place the right foot between the hands. Align the toes with the fingers. Rest the left knee and the top of the foot on the floor and extend the toes. Arch the back, look up, and bend back as far as comfortable.

*Position 10* (Exhale during movement): Exhaling, place the left foot beside the right keeping the palms on the floor. Straighten the legs and bring the head to the knees.

*Position 11* (Inhale during movement): Inhaling, slowly raise the body, stretching the arms out, up, and back. Remember to keep the arms next to the ears and to keep the legs straight as you arch the spine and bend backward as far as possible.

*Position 12* (Exhale): Exhaling, return to an erect standing position. Slowly lower the arms and bring the hands to the chest in prayer position.

Repeat the sun salutation, but alternate the leg movements by extending the opposite leg in positions four and nine. After completing the number of sun salutations you desire, relax in the Corpse Posture and practice a few minutes of even diaphragmatic breathing.

# THE BREATH OF LIFE

*If you know the breath, you will know everything.*
—Tantra Yoga Master Swami Rama—

Once there was a great gathering of all the active and passive senses of man for the purpose of deciding which of them was to be king. They each dressed in their finest, most impressive clothing, and each was busily trying to impress the others with his importance and power. The sense of sight was dressed in shimmering, brilliant colors and spoke movingly of the utility and beauty of his power. The sense of sound, garbed in subtle clothing that moved and sounded like a gentle wind in the trees, and wearing jewelry that tinkled like tiny, clear silver bells, argued just as movingly for his power. All the others, beautifully robed, were equally as insistent, each attempting to outshine the others.

Finally, breath, unnoticed in his common and ordinary clothing, grew tired of the useless noise and senseless argument, and announced in a strong voice that the decision was already made. He, the breath, was the most vital, and thus king of all. There was a stunned silence, and then a clamoring of denial and argument as each sense pointed out its own beauty and power. Having heard enough, and somewhat irritated by all the hubbub and foolishness, breath decided to leave, and quietly slipped out the door. Within a few moments, all the other senses began to dim, and their power and beauty began to fade. Finally realizing the power of breath, all the other senses called after him and begged his return, paying full respect to his sovereignty.

This ancient tantric parable is as relevant today as it was 2,000 years ago. In our fast-paced, exciting, technologically driven society, we are charmed and hypnotized by the sensory experiences of life. We become addicted to the changes, sensory stimulation, and distractions that are so characteristic of modern culture. The more dependent we become on our technology, the more we lose touch with the fundamental realities within ourselves and the more insensitive we are to our inner harmony and strength. As a consequence, we become victims to the whims of our senses and the unconscious play of our habits. Even our relaxation is often done with music and soft lights, or to the accompaniment of the various tones, beeps, and lights of sophisticated biofeedback equipment.

Like the senses in the story, we don't pay much attention to the breath until it isn't there. Yet the breath is the most powerful tool we have for achieving self-mastery. Because of its unique relationship to the autonomic nervous system, the powerful nervous system that controls our organ systems, *breathing plays the critical role in determining whether or not we suffer from stress*. Breathing is part of both the voluntary, or sensory-motor nervous system, and the involuntary, or autonomic nervous system. We can either consciously control the way we breathe, or we can let it run on automatic. This dual connection allows us to use the breath as a doorway to the autonomic nervous system, giving us the control we need to regulate autonomic balance and eliminate stress.

Western sciences study breathing from the perspective of ventilation perfusion and blood gases. The great traditions of self-mastery, from yoga science to Taoism to the martial arts, have gone far beyond this limited view, and have also studied the impact of breathing on the nervous system. For thousands of years, yoga science has researched, experimented, and verified methods of breathing that lead to direct control over the autonomic nervous system. Through yoga science, we know that changes in neurological functioning are related to changes in breathing patterns. This is critical information if we are to achieve self-mastery.

Let's explore the relationship between breathing and the autonomic system. Take your fingers and find a place where you can feel your own pulse, either on the inside of your wrists, or in your neck. Pay attention to your pulse for a few moments. Notice that your pulse doesn't tick like a clock. Instead, it fluctuates slightly. There is a slight slowing and speeding up of your pulse. This gentle rhythm is related to another process going on in your body.

As you keep track of your pulse, pay attention to your breath. As you inhale, notice how your pulse begins to speed up, and as you exhale, your pulse begins to slow down. This is called sinus arrhythmia, and is a healthy and natural rhythm or fluctuation in your pulse. Western medical science has known about it for hundreds of years, yet scant attention is paid to its implications. The pulse is controlled by the autonomic nervous system, the control system that controls our organ systems. The sympathetic arm of the autonomic system, which creates arousal in the body, speeds up the heart rate. The parasympathetic arm, which creates rest for the body, slows the heart rate. Recall from Chapter 2 that the sympathetic system controls the fight or flight alarm reaction, the physical reaction created by the dragon of fear, while the parasympathetic system controls the possum response, the physical reaction created by the dragon of self-hatred.

The fluctuation in the pulse reflects the influence of the breath on the autonomic nervous system. Inhalation reflects and stimulates sympathetic activity, in turn speeding up the heart beat, while exhalation reflects and stimulates parasympathetic activity that, in turn, slows the heart beat. This influence is so strong that you can use your breath to regulate autonomic balance. Taking charge of your breath is the crucial "first step" to self-mastery. If you know the secrets of breathing, you learn the secret to controlling the physical reactions to fear and self-hatred. Not only do you now have control of your stress reactions, but you also have a powerful tool to begin to take control of your emotional reactions and the two dragons of fear and self-hatred.

## BREATH AND ENERGY: THE VITAL LINK

All traditions of self-mastery see the breath as the major vehicle for the second dimension of the personality, the subtle life force that connects mind and body. They use a variety of breathing techniques to develop inner balance, strength, and self-control. These traditions are extremely sophisticated, such as the yogic science of *Swar Swarodayam,* a vast and intricate science that details the relationship between breathing rhythms and states of consciousness. The great masters of the martial arts use breathing to develop their ability to use their energy to throw their opponent several yards without any effort. However, the practical aspects of these subtle sciences are very accessible, and provide powerful tools for self-mastery.

For instance, when you are angry, you can calm yourself by simply slowing down the flow of the breath and making sure that you don't hold it at any time. Panic disorders are intimately linked with bad breathing habits. By taking control of the breath, you can often resolve this difficult and common anxiety reaction. Even insomnia can be resolved by a particular breathing exercise, the Sleep Exercise, given later in this chapter. All of this is possible because of the connection between breathing and the autonomic nervous system.

We generally ignore the breath except when we have a severe problem such as asthma or emphysema. As a consequence, we develop unconscious breathing habits that often create stress and reinforce the dragons in the mind. These habits can also prevent us from taking control of the mind and body no matter how many stretching and relaxation exercises we may do.

If we understand the basic and simple principles about how and why we breathe, we can take control of our inner resources. We can use our knowledge and skill to create a healthy body free of the problems of stress and develop the power of the mind. There are three key points about breathing:

1. **Efficiency:** The primary purpose of breathing is to provide oxygen to the blood stream. The diaphragm is the breathing mechanism designed by nature to utilize the natural efficiency of our respiratory system. Proper diaphragmatic breathing will minimize pressure on the cardiovascular system and prevent essential hypertension.

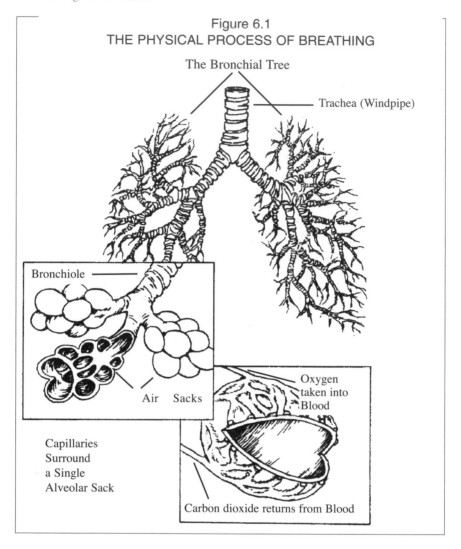

Figure 6.1
THE PHYSICAL PROCESS OF BREATHING

The Bronchial Tree

Trachea (Windpipe)

Bronchiole

Air   Sacks

Oxygen taken into Blood

Capillaries
Surround
a Single
Alveolar Sack

Carbon dioxide returns from Blood

2. **Neural Connections:** The direct relationship between breathing, the autonomic nervous system, and our emotions gives us a mechanism to control both stress in the body and emotional reactions in the mind. By taking control of the way we breathe, the physical motion of our lungs, we take control of the autonomic nervous system. This gives us the power to control the fight-or-flight and possum alarm reactions.

3. **Nose Breathing:** The nose serves as a switchboard for the entire nervous system. Breathing through the mouth alters neural patterning and can lead to greater physical weakness and dangerous health conditions.

## The Physical Process of Breathing

Obviously, we must breathe to stay alive. The primary function of the lungs is to enrich the blood with oxygen and remove the waste product of carbon dioxide from the blood. This entire process is called ventilation perfusion. The respiratory process is a complex process involving a great many factors. For our purposes here, we will focus on a few key principles of the breathing process, particularly those that are important in the development of self-mastery. For a more detailed description of the respiratory process, see the *Anatomy of Hatha Yoga* by Dr. H. David Coulter.

When we breathe, we take air into the lungs. This consists, roughly, of twenty-one percent oxygen, seventy-eight percent nitrogen, nine-tenths percent argon and other gases including carbon dioxide. As we bring air in, it is dispersed to the smallest functional part of the lung – a small air pocket called an alveolus, which is surrounded by microscopic blood vessels as shown in Figure 6.1. The lung is literally shaped like a tree. The windpipe (trachea) is the main trunk that divides many times into smaller and smaller branches; the alveolus corresponds to the leaf. Just as a tree breathes from its leaves, so too do we breathe at the alveoli. In the alveolus there is a constant exchange going on. When oxygen enters into the alveolus, it diffuses into the blood stream. At the same time, carbon dioxide diffuses from the blood back into the alveolus.

As the oxygen enters the blood stream, it turns the blood a bright red color. This energized blood is pumped by the heart to every cell in the body. Body nutrients, which provide energy fuel to the body, need to burn oxygen. This burning produces carbon dioxide and water as waste products, which are eliminated from the body through the lungs and kidneys, respectively. If a cell doesn't get oxygen, it dies. This is what happens when a stroke occurs. The brain cells are deprived of blood and oxygen, and they die. The consequence is loss of speech, paralysis or death, depending on which brain cells are affected.

The upper part of the torso is designed to ensure that enough air gets into the lungs. Imagine the torso as a somewhat flattened cylinder divided into an upper chamber (the chest cavity), and a lower chamber (the abdominal cavity). The chest cavity is defined structurally by the rib cage that provides rigidity. The widest part of the chest cylinder is the lower area where the ribs have their greatest length of curvature, and most of the space in this cylinder is filled by the lungs.

When the cylinder expands, it creates a suction, which pulls air into the lungs, and we inhale. We exhale when counter pressures (primarily from the elasticity of the lung, but also from the external, rigid structure of the chest cavity in combination with the intercostal muscles, the specialized muscles which surround and are sandwiched between the ribs) force the entire structure back to its original position.

Respiration is so crucial that we have three primary ways to bring air into our lungs. The first is very minor, and used only for emergency breathing. This happens when we lift our shoulder blades, create a vacuum and pull air into the upper part of our lungs. This is the kind of breathing we do when someone sneaks up behind us and startles us. Try lifting your shoulders quickly. Notice how there is a small natural intake of breath. What if you had to walk around breathing like this all day? You would use more energy than what you get from your breathing. We use this mechanism only in emergencies, or when we want to completely fill our lungs with air, such as in the complete breath in yoga.

The second breathing mechanism is thoracic breathing, commonly called chest breathing. Using it, we use the intercostal muscles to expand and contract our chest. When we inhale, the external intercostal muscles pivot the ribs upward and forward, increase the diameter of the chest, and pull air primarily into the upper two thirds of the lungs. The internal intercostals then perform the opposite function for the exhalation – pulling the ribs downward, reducing lung volume, and forcing air out of the lungs. Place your hands on your upper chest and fill your lungs with air. You will feel your upper chest expand. Now as you exhale, you will feel your upper chest contract. Notice that you can get a lot of air into the lungs this way, certainly much more than when you lift your shoulders to breathe.

The third mechanism we use for breathing is the diaphragm, with help from the abdominal muscles. As you see in Figure 6.2, the diaphragm is a large, dome-shaped sheet of muscle and tendon that forms the floor of the chest cavity, separating it from the abdominal cavity. Depending on whether you are lying down, or sitting and standing, the diaphragm plays the key role in different ways to expand the lungs. When you inhale, the diaphragm contracts and flattens, pulling the chest cavity down, and expanding the lungs. This creates a vacuum that pulls air into the lower two thirds of the lungs. When the diaphragm flattens, it pushes against the abdominal organs, and they, in turn, push out against the abdominal wall. Instead of the upper chest going up and down as happens when you chest breathe, the lower chest cavity expands slightly outward.

When you exhale, the diaphragm relaxes. When you sit or stand, the abdominal muscles, acting as an "antagonist," contract slightly, and push the organs back and up. This forces the relaxed diaphragm into its original dome-shaped position and reduces chest cavity volume, pushing the air out. This action is a significant part of exhalation. When you lie down, gravity serves as the "antagonist" to the diaphragm, pulling the raised belly down and forcing the flexible abdominal organs up. This also pushes the diaphragm back into its dome-shaped original position, creating an exhalation. This is pure diaphragmatic breathing.

Sit back, place your hands on your upper stomach, right below the chest, and breathe as if you are filling a small balloon in your stomach. When you inhale, your stomach will rise gently; when you exhale, your stomach will fall gently. Your upper chest shouldn't move at all. You might find this a bit difficult to do at first, particularly if you have a very strong habit of chest breathing. But after a few moments, you will notice that it seems to take less effort to breathe

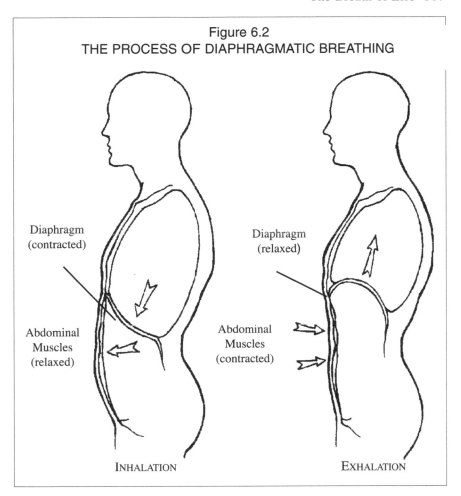

Figure 6.2
THE PROCESS OF DIAPHRAGMATIC BREATHING

Diaphragm
(contracted)

Diaphragm
(relaxed)

Abdominal
Muscles
(relaxed)

Abdominal
Muscles
(contracted)

INHALATION

EXHALATION

with the diaphragm than with the chest.

Diaphragmatic breathing gently massages the internal organs, pushing them back and forth. This contributes to proper blood perfusion in these organs and is one of the driving forces behind the normal digestive movement of the intestines. This massaging action doesn't happen during chest breathing. Deep diaphragmatic breathing also stimulates the adrenal glands, which are situated right above each kidney below the diaphragm. But more importantly, diaphragmatic breathing plays a crucial role in creating inner balance. It makes three necessary contributions to healthy and relaxed functioning. These are:

• Increased efficiency of the cardio-pulmonary system;

• Maintaining autonomic balance, creating a balanced relaxed state, and countering the fight or flight alarm reaction which occurs during chest breathing;

• Regulating the motion of the lungs, the actual flow of breath in and out of the body.

## Cardio-Pulmonary Efficiency: Taking the Work Out of Breathing

Obviously, the heart and lungs are intimately connected to each other. Blood is pumped from the heart directly to the alveoli where fresh oxygen molecules are exchanged in the blood stream for carbon dioxide molecules. The first of the freshly oxygenated blood goes directly to the heart itself, keeping that muscle supplied with lifesaving oxygen. Most heart attacks happen because clogged arteries prevent enough oxygen-rich blood from getting to the heart. When this happens, our heart muscle cells die. We may have warning signs such as severe chest pain (angina pectoris), a signal that our heart is being starved of oxygen and that the cells are beginning to die. But many times we won't feel any symptoms. When enough cells die, it interferes with the electrical activity of the heart, which stops pumping. Then we have a heart attack.

How does diaphragmatic breathing relate to this? Doesn't chest breathing supply oxygen to the blood? Yes, it does, but not efficiently. Figure 6.3a shows the distribution of blood in the lungs. Because of gravity, most of the blood distribution for gas exchange takes place primarily in the lower half of the lungs. When we breathe with the chest, the expansion pulls air into the top two thirds of the lungs, as shown in Figure 6.3b. The gas exchange is inefficient, making the heart and lungs work harder to accomplish the proper amount of oxygenation.

When we breathe with the diaphragm, it pulls air all the way down into the blood-rich lower lobes illustrated in Figure 6.3c. This increases the efficiency of the gas exchange, requiring less effort. There is no difference between chest and diaphragmatic breathing in the amount of air entering the body, nor in the oxygen consumed by the body. But there is a vast difference in how efficiently oxygen is taken up in the blood stream. By breathing with our diaphragm instead of the chest, we reduce the workload of our heart and lungs by as much as fifty percent.

We can easily see the difference simply by counting the number of times we breathe per minute. Chest breathers will average sixteen to twenty breaths per minute. It may go as low as twelve breaths per minute when sitting quietly, or be as high as twenty-four breaths per minute. On the other hand, diaphragmatic breathers average only six to ten breaths per minute. In one twenty-four hour period, a chest breather will take 22,000 to 25,000 breaths, while the person who breathes with their diaphragm will take only 10,000 to 14,000. Chest breathing demands double the effort to accomplish the same task of ventilation perfusion.

## When Normal Means Stressed

Let's take a quick test to determine your breathing habit. All you have to do is count the number of times you breathe in one minute. An inhalation and an exhalation together count as one breath. If you have a normal pattern, you will breathe somewhere between sixteen to twenty a minute. If you are sitting quietly, it may go as low as twelve. You may also notice that your breathing slows down slightly when you pay attention to it. Your actual moment-to-moment breathing rate will probably be a little higher than your count in this test. It can be as high as twenty-four times a minute, and still be considered normal.

Chances are you breathe normally. So-called "normal" breathing is done with the chest. However, the term "normal" does not mean "healthy." It is a statistical term meaning "most cases." And most people breathe with their chest. If you are a "normal" breather, then it's absolutely certain that you suffer from chronic stress!

We believe that chest breathing is natural for us when it's really a bad habit we developed over the years. The best example of natural breathing is the breathing done by a healthy infant. If you observe the infant closely, you will see little or no movement of the chest when he breathes – only the stomach goes up and down indicating diaphragmatic breathing. Even under stress, a newborn infant still breathes with the diaphragm. It's only later that we develop the capacity to breathe with the chest.

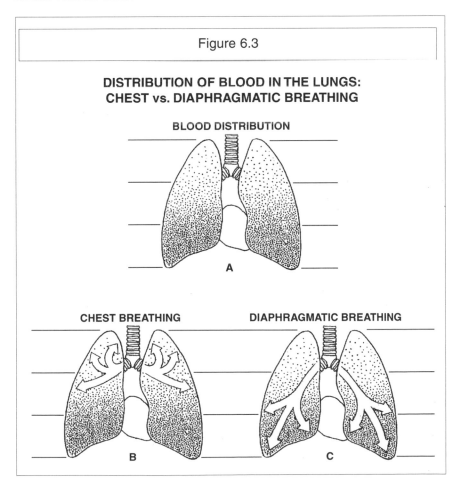

Figure 6.3

**DISTRIBUTION OF BLOOD IN THE LUNGS:**
**CHEST vs. DIAPHRAGMATIC BREATHING**

**BLOOD DISTRIBUTION**

A

**CHEST BREATHING**                **DIAPHRAGMATIC BREATHING**

B                                    C

As we grow, we develop unhealthy habits that interfere with natural innate breathing patterns. Eventually the habit of chest breathing becomes so strong that we no longer use the diaphragm in normal, day-to-day resting breathing pattern. In fact, in many people the diaphragm becomes "frozen," showing little to absolutely no movement at all. They hold it rigidly in place and breathe totally with the chest muscles. There are any number of reasons why we develop poor breathing habits. Social and cultural conventions play a significant role. We are told that flat stomachs are attractive, and we learn to hold in the stomach. By tensing the abdominal muscles, the internal organs are prevented from moving out of the way in order for the diaphragm to flatten. This freezes the diaphragm, forcing us to rely on chest breathing. Any kind of tight clothing around the waist also hinders the natural expansion of the abdominal cavity and interferes with diaphragmatic breathing.

Men, particularly, often puff their chests out, in the classic macho pose. Watch what happens to a young man walking casually down the street when he suddenly meets a couple of young girls. What does he do with his chest? The exaggerated expansion of his chest interferes with diaphragmatic breathing and forces reliance upon chest breathing. This lifting of the chest is actually part of military training. The military want their soldiers to stay very alert, in a constant fight-or-flight reaction. They think that this makes better soldiers. It certainly makes for more tense soldiers. For normal day-to-day, moment-to-moment breathing, a "macho" chest is dysfunctional – it creates stress as well as extra pressure on the coronary-vascular system.

Psychological trauma is the most important reason we become chest breathers. If you watch children when their parents or other authority figures are scolding them, you will see their stomach muscles tighten, forcing them into chest breathing. You will see how fear literally tightens the stomach muscles, preventing diaphragmatic movement. We all experience traumas as we grow up – and they have a powerful affect on our breathing patterns.

Posture also affects the way we breathe. Most people do not sit properly, with their head, neck, and trunk straight. Instead, they slouch or slump, with the spine curved out and a slight bend in the abdominal cavity. This prevents the diaphragm from moving, forcing us to rely on chest breathing. In addition, poor posture interferes with the proper function of the sympathetic and parasympathetic nerves, which affects the entire system.

As you can see, a number of powerful influences lead to chest breathing and the inefficient use of the lungs and heart. We learn to be "normal" breathers. On the other hand, natural diaphragmatic breathing reduces pressure on the heart and vascular system, and the entire system operates in a more balanced, relaxed way. When we feel the symptoms of heart disease such as angina, diaphragmatic breathing is the one immediate step we can take to ease the strain on our over-worked heart. But why wait until you have heart trouble?

## Relearning Diaphragmatic Breathing

If you do no other exercise, be sure to practice this one.* Everything else you do to develop self-mastery depends on your ability to breathe with the diaphragm. Fortunately, it takes very little effort to re-establish diaphragmatic breathing as your moment-to-moment breathing habit. To replace your old habit of chest breathing, you should lie down and practice diaphragmatic breathing at least twice a day for ten to fifteen minutes each time. Since you are already lying down twice a day, when you go to bed and when you wake up, this exercise is easy to practice. Gradually, the easy rhythmic motion of diaphragmatic breathing will replace the strained, unnatural chest breathing of the old habit. You can speed the process by being aware of your breathing pattern as much as possible during the day. The more aware of it you become, the more often you correct it, the faster you will replace your old habit of chest breathing with diaphragmatic breathing.

## Even Breathing

When you practice diaphragmatic breathing, concentrate on making the breath very smooth and even. The inhalation and exhalation should be of the same length and have the same pressure. Do not exhale all the breath at the beginning of the exhalation. Concentrate on keeping an even flow pressure throughout the entire cycle. Eliminate all pauses, stops, and shakiness in the breath, including the pause between inhalation and exhalation. Imagine that the breath is like a large wheel moving through the body without any pauses or stops. It is often helpful to picture the breath flow as a completely smooth, even sine wave (see Figure 6.5).

Don't worry if it feels like you aren't getting enough air and you feel like you have to take a deep breath after a few minutes of diaphragmatic breathing. This sometimes happens when you first change from chest breathing to diaphragmatic breathing. You are getting plenty of oxygen into your system, but your mind isn't comfortable with the change. Your mind is used to the old habit of chest breathing, and when you change breathing patterns, it isn't sure you are breathing properly. Go ahead and take a deep breath. After a few weeks of practice, this feeling will disappear as your mind registers the beginning of a new habit.

*Benefits:* The practice of even, diaphragmatic breathing leads to autonomic balance and a relaxed state. After some weeks, depending on your particular habits, you will begin to notice subtle and gradual changes in your daily breathing pattern. Its movement will be more relaxed and rhythmic.

---

* The breathing exercises presented in this book can be safely and easily practiced on your own. However, since breathing is so intimately connected with neurological functioning, it is highly advisable that you do not engage in advanced or rigorous breathing practices except under the guidance of a competent teacher. Do not practice breath retention under any circumstances unless you are being given expert instruction.

### DIAPHRAGMATIC BREATHING

To Practice: Lie in the relaxation posture and practice diaphragmatic breathing for a minimum of ten to fifteen minutes twice a day. (Again, the easiest time to practice is when you go to bed and when you first wake up in the morning. Doing it before you go to sleep will help you have a restful sleep.) In the Relaxation Posture, place your right hand on your stomach, your little finger over the navel, and the other fingers stretching up towards your chest. Place your left hand on the upper part of your chest, with the little finger between the two breasts.

When the diaphragm contracts, it flattens out and pushes against the internal organs in the abdominal cavity. Instead of the chest going up and down, the stomach moves out and in as if there were a small balloon inside.

Now breathe as if you are filling this small balloon in your stomach. Your stomach and right hand will rise with the inhalation and fall with the exhalation. This should be very gentle, no effort or work required.

Don't try to completely fill or empty your lungs. Let your body decide how much air it needs. There should be no movement at all in the left hand. You should feel a slight motion in the lower portion of the chest cavity, but the upper portion should remain still.

Within a few moments you will become more rested and quiet. Do not try to force the breath. Allow the motion to be gentle and effortless. Notice how easy it is to breathe deeply and easily, without any effort. Practice being an observer, or witness, allowing the body to do the breathing for you. The evenness and balance of the breath will balance the nervous system.

To build a quicker and stronger diaphragmatic response, place an eight to ten pound pliable weight, such as wrist or ankle weights, a sand bag, or a sack of beans or rice, across the upper abdomen when you practice. This weight lifting strengthens the diaphragm, and establishes diaphragmatic breathing more quickly as your moment-to-moment breathing response.

When you change from the habit of chest breathing to diaphragmatic breathing, you will notice that you aren't so tired at the end of the day. By using the natural efficiency of the lungs, you reduce the body's workload, and use less energy. Moreover, when you feel under stress, you will be able to regulate your breathing. After a few moments of even, rhythmic diaphragmatic breathing, the feelings of pressure disappear and you will feel balanced and calm. Diaphragmatic breathing will allow you to breathe more efficiently and to achieve balance in the autonomic nervous system.

## BREATH AND AUTONOMIC BALANCE

There is a very close connection between the way you breathe and your emotions. Whenever you become emotional, your breathing patterns become disturbed. When you are tense, frightened, angry, or intently focused, you often unconsciously hold your breath, or have pauses of different lengths between your breaths. Similarly, if you are depressed, your breathing will be very shallow with frequent sighs. Shallow, jerky breathing in itself disturbs the mind. And when the mind is disturbed, it affects the biochemistry of the body. If you want a calm, steady mind, your breath must be calm and steady, without any noise, jerkiness, shallowness, or prolonged pauses.

The key to this relationship between mind and breath is the autonomic nervous system and its control center in the brain, the limbic center. The way we breathe directly influences two key neural systems. The first, the tenth cranial nerve, called the vagus nerve, separates into two paths and passes through the left and right chest cavity. The vagus nerves account for nearly eighty percent of the parasympathetic system. The way that we breathe creates a certain pressure on the left and right vagus nerves, causing them to either increase or decrease their activity. The second key neural system, the Herring-Breuer reflex, consists of nerve receptors scattered throughout the lungs. These receptors send signals directly back to the limbic system in the brain indicating the exact motion of the lungs.

When we breathe with our chest, we send a signal to both the limbic system and the autonomic system that says, "Get ready! There is danger. Take protective action!" *Chest breathing is the body's emergency breathing system.* Chest breathing activates the subtle beginnings of the fight-or-flight alarm reaction. It doesn't matter whether or not there is actually any danger, once we use the chest mechanism the body responds as if we really are in danger. Of course, when we are in danger, we need to be fully alert, but we do not have to be stressed. Depending on the circumstances, it may be appropriate to use a greater capacity of the lungs, bringing into action all the mechanisms at our disposal. However, when we are skilled in self-mastery, we take command of these resources and respond with self-preservation, which provides clarity, balance, and alertness, instead of reacting out of a habit of fear and unleashing a full fight-or-flight alarm reaction.

Rarely do we face life-threatening emergencies, and we seldom need to put ourselves on emergency status. If you chest breathe while reading this book, you may think you are calm and relaxed, but your breathing is sending an alarm message to the brain and into the autonomic system. The message may be very subtle, but it is still an alarm, and it is constant. Like water dripping on a rock, any one drop is insignificant, but over time, it has an enormous effect. Any one "emergency" breath is insignificant in its impact, but over a period of time it wears and tears at the system. Your "normal" habit of chest breathing maintains a chronic stress in both the body and mind, and you can never completely relax. The longer you continue to utilize this emergency capacity without any need for it, the more ingrained becomes your imbalance.

On the other hand, the motion created by diaphragmatic breathing sends a message that says, "Everything is calm … stay relaxed … all is well … you are in control." *Smooth, even diaphragmatic breathing is the key for regulating the autonomic nervous system, and taking control of inner resources.*

Figure 6.4 illustrates the relationship between breathing and the autonomic nervous system. Inhalation directly but subtly reflects and stimulates sympathetic discharge, while exhalation directly but subtly reflects and stimulates parasympathetic discharge. What is fascinating about this relationship is that we already know it. We simply never paid attention. Earlier we saw that if we pay attention to our pulse, we find that it increases slightly as we inhale, and slows slightly as we exhale. Medical scientists, laboring under the illusion that we could not control the autonomic nervous system, attributed this phenomenon to mechanical pressure, ignoring the role of the vagus nerves and the Herring-Breuer reflex.

Even the language we use indicates that we unconsciously understand this relationship between breathing and the autonomic nervous system. We have all heard someone say, "Let's take a breather." Why did they use that term? Why not, "Let's take a liver," or even, "Let's take a bladder." At least we could justify

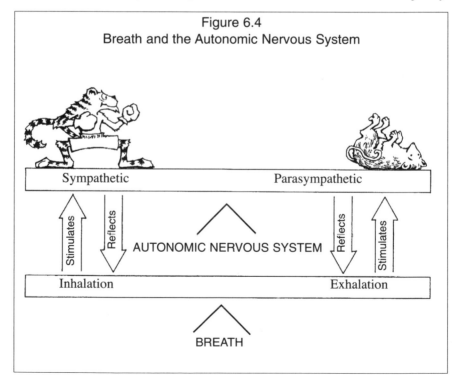

Figure 6.4
Breath and the Autonomic Nervous System

the latter expression. Even more dramatic is what happens when we experience a sharp invasive attack to our body. Let's say that you were right in the middle of an exhalation, and at that moment, you received a sharp slap on the face. Internally, this slap results in an immediate and strong sympathetic discharge, an instant arousal reaction as your body prepares to defend itself. But what happens to your breathing? Your exhalation stops as you quickly gasp (quick inhalation) for breath. We've all heard of a "gasp of pain," reflecting the relationship of inhalation to sympathetic discharge.

We find different expressions when we speak of periods of relief or strong parasympathetic states such as depression. Have you ever heard anyone use the expression "a gasp of depression" or a "gasp of relief?" Instead, we hear about "sighs of relief" or "sighs of depression," reflecting the strong relationship of the exhalation to parasympathetic dominance.

Any emotional state, such as anxiety or anger, also disrupts our breathing patterns. When we are angry, we inhale and hold our breath, and the moment we do, we become a little angrier. When we are depressed, we sigh, and then there is a long pause before we breathe in, and we become a little more depressed. Whenever we pause or hold our breath, it intensifies our emotional state. Because of the direct relationship between inhalation and sympathetic activity, and exhalation and parasympathetic activity, uneven, arrhythmic breathing leads to uneven stimulation of sympathetic and parasympathetic discharge – in other words, autonomic imbalance, or stress.

Yoga science sees the breath as the flywheel mechanism in the autonomic system. If the flywheel becomes unbalanced, it unbalances the entire system. So it is with our breathing and the autonomic system. The evidence for this relationship between the autonomic system and the breath is extensive. An increasing number of scientific studies show that changes in respiratory patterns accompany changes in a wide variety of emotional states and mental and physical activities. Breathing techniques are used to solve a variety of problems, ranging from stress and anxiety management to post-surgical care and treatment of stuttering.

The best evidence, however, is your own experience. The next time you feel pressure, or you are beginning to get tense, sit back and take two minutes to practice diaphragmatic breathing. Focus on your breath becoming very even and steady. Watch what happens to the pressure you feel. The situation will not have changed – deadlines are still there, people are still making demands, problems still need your attention – but the pressure you felt will have dissipated. Whenever you feel stressed or under pressure, you can use the breath to restore inner balance. The more you do this, the more skilled you become, and the greater benefit you gain.

When we understand this relationship between breathing and the autonomic nervous system, we can skillfully use it to relax or create more energy. One of the easiest ways to stay relaxed is 2:1 breathing in which you exhale twice as long as you inhale. The extended exhalation provides a greater stimulus to parasympathetic discharge, leading to a deep and balanced relaxation. This is the reason for the common practice of focusing on exhalation as a technique for inducing relaxation. But this should be done skillfully, and you should not exceed your personal limits. You should always be comfortable when doing breathing exercises, working within your natural capacity. Practice will naturally extend your capacity, giving you increased capability without creating any difficulties.

## 2:1 Breathing: A Restful Pattern

During the practice of diaphragmatic breathing, when your breathing is balanced and even, and has become very smooth with no jerkiness, stops or pauses, gently slow the rate of exhalation until you are breathing out about twice as long as you are inhaling. (It might be necessary to shorten the length of inhalation very slightly.) You are simply changing the rhythm of the breath, not trying to fill the lungs completely nor empty them completely. The purpose is to alter the motion of the lungs in a very systematic way. You may count six on the exhalation and three on the inhalation, or eight on the exhalation and four on the inhalation or whatever is most comfortable for you. Then, after you have established this gentle rhythm, stop the mental counting and focus on the smoothness and evenness of the breath flow. Eliminate all jerks and pauses. Maintain 2:1 diaphragmatic breathing for as long as you wish. Pay attention to what happens to your heart rate and any other changes in your body.

*Benefits:* The exhalation stimulates the parasympathetic system twice as long as the inhalation stimulates the sympathetic system. This rhythm greatly reduces tension and creates a deeper state of rest for the heart and vascular system. Once you become skilled with 2:1 breathing, you can use it anytime during the day or night. Several of my clients who are joggers use the 2:1 pattern while they jog, coordinating their stride with their breathing. This allows them to go further with less effort, and provides a more stable and complete conditioning for the heart.

Do not reverse the rhythm, however, and inhale twice as long as you exhale. This reversed pattern can make you tense and nervous. Also do not practice 2:1 breathing if you suffer from chronic depression. In chronic depression, the parasympathetic system is already too dominant, and you don't want to emphasize its dominance with long exhalations. For depression and low energy states, the Alternate-Nostril Breathing Exercise given below is much more appropriate.

## The Importance of Motion

As you might gather from the above discussion of 2:1 breathing, it is important to control the motion of the lungs skillfully. While the intercostal muscles can control the movement of the chest cavity, they cannot adequately control the smoothness and evenness of the breath itself. Only the diaphragm, in coordination with the abdominal muscles, is large enough to really control breathing motion and depth.

The flow of the breath (the smoothness and evenness of lung motion) can be measured on an instrument called the Cottle rhinomanometer. As you breathe into the nosepiece of the instrument, it records a wave motion on a strip chart. The exhalation is measured above the base line, the inhalation below it. Each of us has a unique pattern of breathing, just as we each have unique fingerprints. The ideal breathing motion looks like a perfect sine wave – an even, smooth wave that indicates an even, uninterrupted flow of breath (Figure 6.5).

Researchers find very few people who can even begin to approach this type of breath flow pattern without proper training. Most people have patterns that differ dramatically from this ideal.

Chronic emotional states also seem to have characteristic wave patterns. For instance, a person who is constantly angry often has a distinctive type of mid-cycle pause just after the inhalation and before the exhalation (Figure 6.6)

The effects of irregular breath-flow patterns are very subtle and often go unnoticed. However, if you pay close attention to your own breath and the thoughts, feelings, and sensations that go along with it, you will begin to notice these patterns. If you observe carefully, you will see that when your breath is uneven and unstable it is impossible to concentrate. Take a few moments to

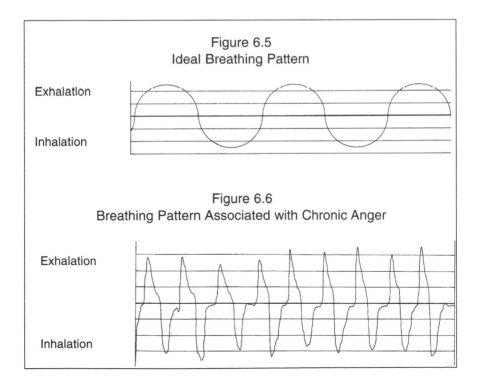

Figure 6.5
Ideal Breathing Pattern

Exhalation

Inhalation

Figure 6.6
Breathing Pattern Associated with Chronic Anger

Exhalation

Inhalation

observe your breathing patterns closely. Do you breathe with your chest muscles? Are there any pauses or stops in your breath? Is your breath uneven? Do you sigh a lot? Do you hold your breath and not breathe for periods of time? Through simple observation you will quickly determine the kind of breathing habits you have.

As an experiment, simply concentrate on diaphragmatic breathing, making the inhalation and exhalation as smooth and even as possible. Picture in your mind the breath flowing exactly like the ideal waveform shown in Figure 6.5 – no bumps, no pauses, and no shakiness. Do this for five minutes, paying close attention to the flow of breath in and out of the nostrils. Then see how you feel both physically and mentally.

Also experiment during the day. The next time you are in a situation in which you are becoming angry or upset, concentrate a few moments on breathing. Breathe with the diaphragm, keeping the breath very even and steady. Then observe what happens to your feelings.

You will notice that your ability to remain calm in the face of adversity is vastly improved. And the one who remains calm is able to think and act more creatively in any situation. Similarly, when you are feeling depressed or sad, observe how shallow your breathing has become. Then concentrate on diaphragmatic breathing and observe what happens to your mood.

## Alternate Nostril Breathing: An Exercise For Control

One of the most important breathing exercises you can do is Alternate-Nostril Breathing. It increases the capacity of the lungs as well as your control over the breathing process and the autonomic system. It is also very useful in developing concentration. It should be practiced three times daily, and it only takes a few minutes to do. There are several ways to do this exercise. The following is the most simple.

You should begin the exercise with whichever nostril is active, or most open. The entire exercise consists simply of exhaling and inhaling through the active nostril and then through the passive nostril and repeating this procedure two more times. There are only six complete breaths in the exercise, three on each side. Notice that you begin the exercise with an exhalation, not an inhalation.

Begin with a count that is comfortable and concentrate on making the breath smooth and even at this length. It is the smoothness of the flow that is important here, not how long you can make your breath. Maintain the same count until you can breathe comfortably and effortlessly without any bumps, jerks or pauses. Make sure the flow of air is evenly distributed throughout the entire cycle. When you are very sure of your control, increase the length of the breath (for example, go from a count of six to a count of eight). The length of the breath will gradually increase as your control increases.

After completing the exercise, resume your normal breathing for two breaths, and then repeat the exercise, starting with the opposite nostril. After completing this second set, resume normal breathing for two breaths, and then repeat the exercise, starting with the original nostril. After finishing three sets of the exercise, resume natural diaphragmatic breathing.

Focus as much attention as possible to the flow of the breath during the exercise. As you develop your ability to concentrate, gradually learn to direct the flow of breath by using only your mind and not your fingers. This enhances the power of concentration.

*Benefits:* With this exercise, you learn to control the motion of the lungs, and gradually take control over the autonomic nervous system. It also strengthens the autonomic nervous system and leads to increased lung capacity. This allows you to maintain balance, control emotional reactions, and enhance your power of concentration. Alternate-Nostril Breathing practice also corrects unhealthy breathing patterns and is a subtle but helpful exercise for resolving depression. The benefits of doing this exercise are usually not dramatic, but over

---

### ALTERNATE NOSTRIL BREATHING

Close your eyes and sit comfortably, with your head, neck, and trunk in alignment (the back should be straight but allow for the natural S curve of the spine). Rest the index and middle fingers of the right hand on the space between the two eyebrows. Determine which nostril is active. (The active nostril is the one in which the air is flowing freely. The passive nostril is the nostril in which there is some natural blockage due to the natural cyclic swelling of the mucosa.)

1. If the right nostril is active, press your ring finger gently against the left nostril, closing it, and gently exhale through the right nostril, counting to six (or about six seconds) mentally as you exhale. Then inhale immediately through the same nostril for a count of six.

2. Now press the thumb gently against the right nostril, closing it off, and at the same time release the pressure on the left nostril. Exhale for a count of six, and then inhale for a count of six through the left nostril.

3. Now press the ring finger gently against the left nostril, closing off the flow, and at the same time release the pressure from the thumb on the right nostril. Exhale for a count of six, and inhale for a count of six through the right nostril.

4. Close the right nostril and open the left. Exhale and inhale for a count of six in the left nostril.

5. Close the left nostril and open the right. Exhale and inhale to counts of six in the right nostril.

6. Close the right nostril and open the left. Exhale and inhale for counts of six through the left nostril. You have just done three rounds. This completes the exercise.

a period of time, it calms the mind and stabilizes the emotions. The tantric masters become so skilled using this exercise that they gain complete conscious control over the autonomic nervous system.

## The Pause That Kills

It's not only our emotional states that are affected by irregular breathing. Preliminary research indicates that the wave patterns can reflect severe pathological states. For example, research by the late Dr. Maurice Cottle, an ear, nose, and throat specialist who practiced in Chicago, shows a distinctive wave pattern associated with heart attacks. This pattern, too, is characterized by a mid-cycle rest, or pause, but in a slightly different way than that associated with chronic anger.

As you can see in the simulated pattern in Figure 6.7, the mid-cycle rest is a constant pause in the breathing pattern after the exhalation and before the inhalation. This is a form of apnea, and may reflect a very dangerous condition. The longer the pause, the greater the danger. When this pause occurs during sleep, it is called sleep apnea, and is characterized by loud, open-mouthed snoring with periodic silences between the snores. Sleep apnea is considered a central nervous system disease, and is a major reason why people suffer heart attacks at night.

It's the focus of much joking, but if you have heart disease, snoring is no longer very humorous. There are two kinds of snoring. If you snore with the mouth closed, the sound is created by the vibration of the uvula and is harmless. If, on the other hand, the mouth is open, the snoring sound is created by the collapsing of the larynx (caused by a total relaxation of the muscles) that temporarily closes the air passageway. The breath flow is blocked, and breathing may pause for relatively long periods of time.

Dr. Alan Hymes, a thoracic surgeon who researched sleep apnea and its relationship to heart attacks and mouth breathing, points out that when we stop breathing we create oxygen imbalances in the blood gases. This creates a strain on the heart. More importantly, as we discuss below, this pause may destabilize the electrical system of the heart, creating arrythmia. While a variety of treatment modalities have been tried, particularly drugs, there has been little success in

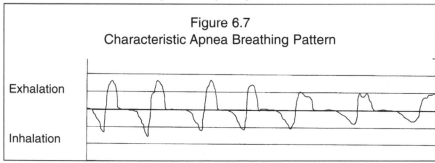

Figure 6.7
Characteristic Apnea Breathing Pattern

Exhalation

Inhalation

treating this potentially life-threatening condition. In extreme cases, individuals must wear a mask at night in order to sleep. The instrument is called a C-Pap, and blows a small puff of air into the nostrils to prevent sleep apnea.

Dr. Hymes reports, however, that simply closing the mouth of the person who is snoring (thus forcing nasal breathing), corrects the sleep apnea – the snoring stops, the breath becomes even and steady, and chest breathing appears to change into diaphragmatic breathing. The patient's respiratory efficiency is increased, and the strain is off the heart. The stimulation of the nerve endings in the nasal mucosa appears to restore respiratory balance and lead to diaphragmatic breathing. Unfortunately, most people with apnea do not have a nurse present while they are sleeping to perform this function for them.

Preliminary studies by Dr. Hymes have shown that over seventy-five percent of those who have heart attacks breathe through their mouth instead of through their nose. What is more, nearly all of those who habitually breathe through their mouth also snore; and of those who snore, eighty-four percent showed patterns of sleep and waking apnea lasting for periods of six to thirty seconds or longer. *On the other hand, the patients who breathe through their nose exhibit little or no apnea.*

Dr. Hymes suggests that it may be possible to minimize or even eliminate the apnea by retraining ourselves to breathe diaphragmatically and through the nose. This not only relieves a very serious breathing problem, it also ensures restful sleep. We revitalize the body, relieve stress and create balance in the most natural way there is. By practicing the proper breathing exercises, we can bring about deep, restful sleep without sleeping pills.

## BREATHING AND THE HEART

Several years ago I had a meeting with a lieutenant general (three stars) to talk about a stress management program for his staff. The appointment was actually engineered by the general's sister who was concerned about his health. A hard-driving individual, the general was taking medication for high blood pressure. Typical of any busy executive, the general started the interview by saying how over-scheduled he was, and that he could only spare thirty minutes. In the process of the interview, the general mentioned his high blood pressure and asked if I thought stress had anything to do with it. We discussed this for a few moments, and then I pointed out that he was breathing with his chest, which could affect his blood pressure. I could see that the general wasn't exactly convinced. Like most people, he simply accepted the fact that he had the problem. He was fairly sure that, other than taking medication, there was little he, or anyone else, could do.

Fortunately, I had a blood pressure monitor with me, and I asked if we could try a little experiment. Out of politeness, he agreed. We took his blood pressure. It was 147/95. I then had him lie on the carpet in the relaxation posture,

BEHAVIORAL TRAINING FOR ESSENTIAL HYPERTENSION

1. Ten to fifteen minutes of Diaphragmatic Breathing on the bed or floor before going to sleep and before getting up in the morning (chapter 6, page 188).
    A. Place an eight to ten pound pliable weight (such as a sandbag, a bag of rice or beans, or ankle weights) on the upper part of the abdominal cavity below the rib cage. This weight strengthens the diaphragm.
    B. Begin with Even Breathing (page 187), then after the breath is even and steady, shift to 2:1 Breathing (page 192), exhaling twice as long as you inhale.
2. "61 Points" Exercise once daily (Chapter 8, page 135).
    A. Lie on a firm surface (not a bed) in the Relaxation Posture (Chapter 5, page135)
    B. Begin by concentrating on Even or 2:1 Breathing for five minutes.
    C. Do the 61 Points using a blue star or a blue flame at each of the 61 points.
3. Emotional control: Anger, worry and other emotions can underlie and aggravate essential hypertension. The following techniques help regulate emotional energy.
    A. A two-minute period of Breath Awareness (Chapter 7, pages 186) every hour will help clear the mind and calm the body.'
    B. Use a ten-minute relaxation break in the morning and in the afternoon.
    C. Try not to identify with any of the problems you must solve on a day-to-day basis. Use Breath Awareness and focus on the problem at hand, not one that might happen in the future.
4. Diet: Adopt a prudent approach to diet; don't overeat, and reduce the amount of red meat, caffeine, and sugar in your daily diet. Follow a sensible low-cholesterol, low-fat, and low-salt diet.
5. Aerobic exercise: A minimum of twenty minutes three times weekly with an appropriate level of aerobic exercise such as jogging, walking, bicycling, swimming, active sports.
6. Stretching exercises (Chapter 5, page 160): five minutes of stretching in the morning, five to fifteen minutes of stretching in the evening.
Morning stretches free energy, stimulate vital neural and glandular functioning, and make you feel alert and alive. Evening stretches will increase flexibility, remove structural tension, and allow for a more peaceful sleep.

and instructed him in even diaphragmatic breathing and 2:1 breathing. After four minutes of focused, diaphragmatic breathing, I had him sit up and we measured his blood pressure again. To the general's great surprise, his blood pressure had dropped twenty-seven points systolic and twelve points diastolic. Our interview went on to last for over an hour and a half. Since then, I have been a trainer for several agencies within the Defense Department.

It's not coincidence that we call chest breathing "normal" and we suffer a high rate of coronary-vascular disease. According to University of Chicago Cardiologist, Dr. D.S. Gupta, when we breathe with the chest, we can create problems for the heart in at least four ways:

• **Heart Rhythm:** The heart creates its own electrical impulse through a sodium chloride/potassium chloride ion exchange in the pacemaker cells of the heart. This ion exchange is regulated by the autonomic nervous system. If autonomic balance is disturbed by sleep apnea, it can lead to severe rhythmic dysfunctions in the heartbeat, such as atrial fibrillation, and then ventricular fibrillation. Once ventricular fibrillation begins, survival becomes problematic. For those already suffering heart damage, sleep apnea is a grave danger.

• **Chronic Arousal:** Chest breathing, the emergency breathing mechanism, stimulates sympathetic arousal. As part of the arousal response, the peripheral blood vessels constrict, sending more blood to the center of the body. This constriction can contribute to higher blood pressure levels.

• **Coronary Effort:** Chest breathing exerts pressure on the heart cavity that increases the amount of blood that enters the heart, which is called *preload*. The more blood that enters the heart, the harder the heart muscle must work to pump the blood out. This effort is called *afterload*. Higher levels of preload and afterload lead to higher levels of blood pressure.

• **Carbon Dioxide Cleansing:** Carbon dioxide is a waste product eliminated through exhalation. During chest breathing, the lower lobes of the lungs are not properly cleansed, resulting in a build-up of carbon dioxide. This carbon dioxide re-enters the blood stream, and elevates the level of carbonic acid in the blood. This can change the acid/base balance of the body and may eventually disturb the inner linings of the blood vessels, which can lead to hardening of the arteries. It may also influence the reactivity of the blood vessels that, in turn, can affect blood pressure. (Carbon dioxide is an essential part of the blood gases mixture, and a certain level must be maintained for proper respiration. When we blow-off too much carbon dioxide, we hyperventilate. It is very difficult to hyperventilate when doing diaphragmatic breathing. This is a problem for chest breathers.)

Both Dr. Hymes and Dr. Gupta point out that essential hypertension is a disease of chest breathers, and that diaphragmatic breathers rarely suffer this disease. It's clear that chest breathing increases your risk of high blood pressure in several important ways. On the other hand, if you breathe with the diaphragm, your chances of getting essential hypertension are very slight.

By breathing with the diaphragm, you maintain internal balance and reduce pressure on the vascular system, which helps prevent high blood pressure. The lesson here is very clear and simple: *If you don't want to suffer from essential hypertension, then don't become a chest breather.* The six-point list of Behavioral Training for Essential Hypertension (page 182) is a self-training program to help resolve and prevent this disease.

There is a great deal that we can do to help ourselves. Breathing is a tool that we always have with us. If you become skilled in its use, you become skilled at living without stress. It only requires practice. Diaphragmatic breathing is just the beginning.

At the end of this chapter are several more simple exercises. One will energize you, another will take you to the second level of relaxation, and the third you can use to eliminate insomnia and train yourself to have a very restful sleep. But first, there is one more facet of breathing that we must understand.

## THE NOSE: A SOPHISTICATED NEUROLOGICAL ORGAN

The nose, surprisingly enough, is an extremely important organ. It is not simply twin exhaust pipes for the lungs. While we may worry about its size and how it looks, we seldom think about what happens inside the nose until we get congested or have a sinus headache. In fact, many of us breathe through the mouth and don't properly use the nostrils at all. This is a serious mistake. The nose is a switchboard for the entire nervous system. When we don't breathe through the nose properly, it can affect every system in the body, as well as the mind.

As you can see in Figure 6.8, the nasal passages occupy a unique position. The roof of the mouth forms the floor of the nasal cavity, and the roof of the nasal cavity forms part of the floor of the brain. Thus the nose is in a strategic position, for it is very near the nervous system and the pituitary gland. The mucosa (the inside lining of the nose) is saturated with nerve endings that connect with all major neural systems. The most important are the olfactory bulbs, which are part of the limbic system, the brain's emotional center. The olfactory bulbs, which provide our sense of smell, are the only part of the limbic system that has direct contact with the outside world. All other input to the limbic center is mediated through other parts of the brain. The mucosa also contains nerve endings from both the sensory motor and the autonomic nervous systems.

The passageways in the nose are not straight channels where air flows directly into the lungs. A series of structures within the nasal cavity guide and direct the air as it flows in and out of the nostrils. The most important are three seashell-like bulges called turbinates. They serve to baffle the air, to stir it up. They force the air moving through the nostrils to go through a series of winding, bending, looping, and convoluting passageways. This creates a great deal of turbulence.

Check the airflow of your nostrils by closing off one nostril and then the other. You will very likely find that the airflow is not even. The nasal passages are lined with erectile tissue that can engorge with blood and swell dramatically. The only other place you find erectile tissue in the body is in the sexual organs and the nipples. As blood flow shifts within the nose, different nasal passages alternately swell or shrink. This continuous shrinking and engorging of the nostrils creates an infinite variety of flow patterns. It constantly alters the direction and reshapes the flow of air through the nasal passages in a cyclic process. In a healthy person this change of airflow shifts the breath from one nostril to the other over regular periods of time.

The narrowness of the passageways compresses the air, increasing its force as it passes through the nose. Even when you are sitting quietly, the wind speed in the narrow nasal passageways is approximately twenty miles an hour. If you decide to really exert yourself and run up and down the steps, you will create wind velocities up to two hundred miles an hour inside the nose. And this flow is all turbulence. Can you imagine what would happen to the community you live in if it was subject to turbulent wind speeds of two hundred miles an hour? And yet, you can do this easily inside your nose with some good aerobic exercise.

There is a definite purpose to all this speed and turbulence. When we breathe, the turbulent air flowing through the nostrils stimulates the various nerve endings. This creates a switchboard effect for the entire nervous system. If you alter this neural stimulation, you create changes elsewhere in the body. You can verify this yourself. The next time you have indigestion, check which nostril is open, and is allowing the air to move freely. Almost every time, you will find that the left nostril will be the dominant, or open nostril, and the right will be

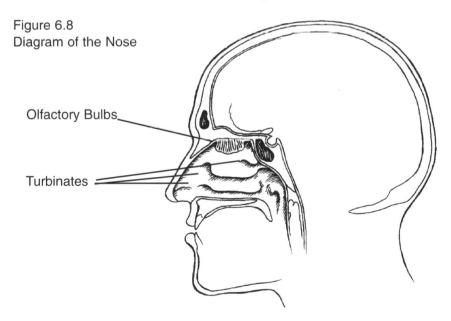

Figure 6.8
Diagram of the Nose

Olfactory Bulbs

Turbinates

mostly closed. Instead of taking an Alka-Seltzer, lie down on your left side. Gravity will force the flow of blood from the swollen right nostril over to the left. In a matter of a few minutes, the mucosa in your left nostril will begin to swell. The mucosa in the right nostril will shrink, and air will begin to flow freely through the right nostril. When you can breathe freely through the right nostril, you will find that your indigestion has disappeared. Why spend money on an antacid that only relieves the symptom when you can alter the underlying condition yourself for free?

This isn't the only affect of nose breathing you can notice. You will find that when you breathe through your mouth, you tend to lose approximately ten to fifteen percent of your physical strength. If your muscles can be so weakened, what about the more sensitive systems of your body, such as the immune and endocrine system? More critically, *only mouth breathers develop sleep apnea.* Those who breathe through the nose, even when they have heart disease, seldom, if ever, develop sleep apnea.

Even Sigmund Freud found a connection between what happens in the nose and certain systems in the body. He and Wilhelm Fliess, an ear, nose, and throat specialist, found that menstrual cramps were often related to an inflammation and discoloration of specific areas in the lining of the nose. When these were anesthetized, the menstrual pains disappeared until the effects of the anesthetic wore off. They then decided to do a surgical removal of this part of the nose. This radical move led to so many problems that they quickly stopped doing it. There are instances where cosmetic nasal surgery becomes so invasive that it impinges on the neural centers in the nose. This can lead to personality changes that are totally unpredictable, and not always beneficial.

Breathing through the nose is a critical process, yet Western science still does not recognize the neurological role of nose breathing. In fact, almost all respiratory research is done on mouth breathing. There is very little attention being paid to the nose and its role.

According to yoga science the physiological effects associated with the airflow through the two nostrils are quite different. Interestingly enough, when research was conducted on discharge from the two nostrils, it was found that the electrical potential of the discharge was different for each nostril. While this puzzled the researchers, who clearly did not understand its implications, it confirms the experience of yoga science. Modern research is also finding that emotional states appear to be related to an over-dominance of either right or left nostril activity. For example, preliminary research indicates that some forms of depression are related to over activity in the left nostril, while excessive air flow in the right nostril has been found to be associated with hyperactivity. This doesn't necessarily mean that a constantly overactive left nostril causes depression, or that an overactive right nostril leads to hyperactivity. What it does show is the connection between the way we breathe, certain neural conditions, and physical and emotional states.

Yoga science states that when you are doing active work, the right nostril should be open and dominant. When you are quiet and reserved, the left nostril should be dominant. Consciously working with the breath in this way gradually allows you to establish control over your breathing with your mind. The goal is to be able to establish sushumna, the ability to willfully direct both nostrils to be open equally at the same time. According to yoga science, this creates a calm mind, and balance in both the autonomic nervous system and between the two hemispheres of the brain. The application of sushumna allows the mind to be deeply concentrated without effort. To practice meditation, you must apply it in order to reach the deepest states of meditation. One of the most important techniques for developing this control is the Alternate Nostril Breathing exercise given on page 179 of this chapter.

## The Nasal Wash

For healthy nasal passages, a daily nasal wash with saline solution is extremely helpful. The most difficult part of this technique is our attitude. Whenever I present the nasal wash in a seminar, many of the participants roll their eyes. You can tell by the look on their faces that they think that washing out the inside of the nose is disgusting. What is disgusting is that we walk around with all that excess mucus inside our nose and sinus cavities. We carry it around like a national treasure.

This simple, easy wash is one of the most beneficial techniques we can do, particularly if we have sinus problems, such as allergies or sinus headaches. A daily nasal wash keeps the lining of the nose healthy and free from excess mucus. It helps drain the sinuses, reduce allergies and prevent colds. You can pay $50 or so to have the same procedure, called a nasal irrigation, done at a doctor's office or follow the simple procedure outlined below for less than the cost of a teaspoon of sea salt.

One of the most consistent messages I hear from past participants in my seminars is how helpful the nasal wash has been for them. Sometimes the relief is immediate, and for others, it happens over a period of time. The benefits most often reported are easier breathing, elimination of sinus headaches, reduction in allergy symptoms, increased clarity of thought, more energy, even the elimination for the need for surgery. Everyone who really uses the wash reports some benefit from doing it.

## TAKING CONTROL: BREATH AS KEY TO HEALTH AND FREEDOM

Breathing is a very powerful tool for controlling stress. The basic exercises are not at all difficult, and take very little time. All you need is a little consistent practice. The easiest way to eliminate an unhealthy breathing (or any) habit is to replace it with a healthy one. We can use our breath to create and maintain

## THE NASAL WASH

As a part of your morning wash, fill a regular kitchen glass (eight ounces) with lukewarm tap water. Add approximately one-eighth teaspoon of either kosher salt or sea salt. (Commercial salt has chemicals added to it that create a slight burning sensation in the nose.) The water should be about as salty as tears. The salt acts as a drawing agent, helping to cleanse the nose. You will be able to tell if the solution is too salty – it will sting slightly. If it isn't salty enough, it may create an unpleasant pressure inside the nose.

Bring the glass up to the nostrils, slightly tilting the head back. Relax your throat, mouth and jaw, and pour just enough to fill the nasal passage. As you tilt the glass, inhale just enough to help pull water into your nasal passages. Then drop your head, exhale with a gentle force through both nostrils and let the water drain back out.

A little water may trickle down into your throat as you first begin, causing you to cough or slightly choke. Don't worry; you will quickly learn how to close off your throat.

After a little practice you will be able to tilt your head back and to one side. Then bring the water in through the upper nostril and let it drain out the lower. This cleans and rejuvenates the mucus membrane lining the inside of the nostrils. After a little more practice, you will be able to take the water through both nostrils, down into the throat and out the mouth. This cleans the entire passageway.

Benefits: This wash cleans and rejuvenates the mucous membrane, alleviating congestion and helping to prevent infections in the sinus area. It helps eliminate the problem and pain of sinus headaches, reduce the symptoms of allergies, as well as prevents colds and other minor infections of the mucous membrane. This can also be a very important exercise in helping to eliminate open-mouth snoring. Open-mouth breathing often occurs because a slight sinus infection partially blocks nostril passages. Doing the nasal wash before going to sleep helps clear the nasal passages, allowing you to breath more easily through the nose.

balance, to minimize the pressure on the heart and vascular system, and to stay relaxed throughout the day. We can also become skilled at deeper states of relaxation, control energy, and learn how to sleep peacefully. To energize use the breathing technique called a complete breath. This technique utilizes all three breathing mechanisms – collarbones, ribs and diaphragm – to completely fill the lungs with air. Read through the exercise completely before trying it.

## Deep-State Breath Relaxation: The Second Level of Relaxation

We achieve the second level of relaxation, autonomic relaxation, by using the breath to shift the balance in the autonomic nervous system. Systematically changing the motion and rhythm of our breath increases parasympathetic activity and creates a deeper state of rest in the body. Autonomic relaxation provides a different kind of experience than muscle relaxation. Instead of feeling heavy and lethargic, our body feels light, and our mind becomes clear and alert.

We can breathe in a number of different ways to create progressively deeper states of relaxation. The simplest is the 2:1 breathing discussed on page 176 of this chapter. Another simple but extremely effective relaxation exercise is called the Sweeping Breath. This exercise is very direct and easy to use. A few minutes of concentration on the sweeping breath brings on a deep, restful state. Use this exercise as a preliminary exercise for the "61 Points" concentration exercise in Chapter 8, or as a finishing exercise to other relaxation techniques.

More complex is the Deep-State Breath Relaxation. Detailed instructions are provided in Appendix C. In this exercise, you systematically alter the motion of the lungs, moving from very deep and slow breathing to very shallow, rapid breathing, and then returning to very deep, slow breathing. The effectiveness of this exercise lies in the systematic and gradual change in the motion of the lungs. The impact on the autonomic system creates a profound state of rest for the body. Yoga masters claim that this specific exercise will provide a complete metabolic rest. As your breathing becomes more shallow, it naturally becomes more rapid. Breathe as quickly as you need to feel comfortable. But you shouldn't have to pant. All breathing should be done effortlessly and without any sense of struggle or panic.

This exercise is very sophisticated and takes practice. Any disruption of the rhythm, such as a yawn, makes it somewhat less effective. Don't let this discourage you; even if you do it imperfectly, you will be more relaxed than if you do the muscle relaxation exercise in Chapter 5 (page 128). Like that exercise, this

## SWEEPING BREATH EXERCISE

Begin by lying in the Relaxation Posture. Breathe with the diaphragm, allowing your breath to become very even and smooth.

Now visualize the body as a hollow reed. Then breathe in as if inhaling through the toes and filling the body with breath to the crown of the head. Exhale as if you are breathing back down the body and out the toes. Breathe easily and gently, without any effort. Do not try to force your breathing; let your body decide how much air you need.

Focus your concentration on feeling the entire body breathe, and imagine every cell and pore in your body breathing in and out. It's as if you are feeling your entire body expanding on the inhalation and contracting on the exhalation.

After a few moments, visualize the breath as a wave washing upon the shore on the inhalation and receding back into the sea on the exhalation. Maintain this imagery as long as you wish.

## THE COMPLETE BREATH

In this exercise all three mechanisms for breathing—diaphragm, chest, and collarbones—are brought into use. When you first practice this exercise, place your right hand on your upper stomach area and your left hand on your upper chest. When you breathe with the diaphragm, the right hand will rise on the inhalation and fall on the exhalation. The left hand will rise when you inhale with the chest mechanism. Once you are sure of the proper movement of the diaphragm, chest, and clavicles, you can do the breathing without using your hands.

Inhale first, using the diaphragm and expanding the belly; then continue the inhalation by expanding the chest; then let the inhalation continue to the very top of the lungs at which point a slight upward movement of the clavicles may be experienced. The exhalation is done in reverse motion, letting the clavicles drop slightly, then letting the chest wall collapse slightly and the belly collapse as the diaphragm moves upward, pushing the air out of the lungs. The breath should be slow and smooth, without any pauses or jerks.

The complete breath is a useful technique to use when you are sitting at your desk and feel a tension in your shoulders. A few minutes of practice will be very helpful in reducing not only muscle tension but also mental fatigue. It is an energizer and can be used when you feel mentally dull, or need to be more alert. For instance, when you have been driving for some time and are beginning to feel a little tired, you can energize yourself by taking six or seven complete breaths.

one is easier to do if you first read through the exercise, and record it on a cassette tape. Then lie in the Relaxation Posture and listen to the cassette.

## The Two-Minute Breath Break

During the day, every hour on the hour, or as often as you can remember, take a two-minute breath break. Close your eyes and concentrate on either Even Diaphragmatic Breathing or 2:1 Breathing for two minutes. This important practice clears your mind and breaks the daily tension habits that can lead to headaches and high blood pressure. Make sure to breathe through your nose and not your mouth.

You can easily check to see if you are breathing properly with your diaphragm while sitting or standing by using a wide belt or piece of cloth. Put the belt around your lower rib cage. When you inhale, the lower rib cage and upper abdominal area should expand, using more of the belt to encircle you. When you exhale, the lower rib cage and upper abdominal area contract, and the belt can be tightened. Remember, don't try to fill the lungs completely, or exhale

SLEEP EXERCISE

- • All breathing is 2:1. Exhale for twice as long as you inhale.
- • Use a comfortable count such as 6:3 or 8:4. You are not trying to completely empty or fill the lungs. The 2/1 ratio should be effortless.
- • Pay close attention to your breath. There should be no stops, pauses, or shakiness during either the inhalation or the exhalation. Minimize the pause between inhalation and exhalation. The exercise goes as follows:

      8 breaths lying on your back
      16 breaths lying on your right side
      32 breaths lying on your left side

completely. Your breath should be effortless, rhythmic and diaphragmatic, with no movement in the upper chest.

## Sleep Exercise

Many of us struggle with chronic fatigue due to sleep deprivation. We usually have enough time; we just don't know how to get restful sleep. We don't usually think about sleeping as a skill. However, it isn't any different than any other kind of behavior. It all depends on our habits. With a little practice, we can train ourselves to sleep peacefully. This is also an excellent exercise to teach children who suffer from night terrors or sleepwalking.

We can also use the 2:1 pattern of breathing as an effective sleep exercise to minimize and eliminate insomnia, a common and difficult stress symptom. Whether the problem is falling asleep or waking up in the middle of the night and not getting back asleep, insomnia is most often caused by an agitated mind. You can remedy this problem with a little training. These exercises don't depend on anything but your own willingness to practice.

The ancient yogic sleep exercise takes advantage of the relationship of breathing and the autonomic nervous system, the impact of posture, and our ability to focus attention. Follow these steps closely. If you don't fall asleep the first time, repeat the exercise. After two times, simply focus on 2:1 diaphragmatic breathing and don't worry. The exercise is very effective, but it might take some practice. Practice every night until you can fall asleep easily and stay asleep all night.

## FROM BODY TO BREATH TO MIND

The breathing exercises presented above establish the necessary foundation for self-mastery. But they are just the beginning. In all self-mastery disciplines there are more sophisticated exercises that are used to develop the power of the body, mind, and spirit. For example, there are breathing techniques to energize the system, such as *bhastrika, kapalabhati,* and *khumbaka* in yoga, and Taoist breathing and the various breathing practices to coordinate breath and chi such as Small and Grand Circulation in Tai Chi Chuan. The more advanced the technique, the more powerful they are, but the more knowledge and skill are required to do the exercises. Advanced breathing practices should always be learned under the guidance of a competent teacher.

You must take control of your breath if you want to achieve self-mastery. Once you start practicing the exercises and consciously working with your breath, you will have a powerful tool that you can use at any moment to relieve pressure and tension, and prevent stress. With breathing and relaxation skills, you now have a strong foundation for freedom. We are ready to take the next step. We must now turn to our creative mind and learn how to take our power back from the dragons, and use it to create a life of joy and fulfillment.

# MIND AND MASTERY:
# TAKING ON THE DRAGONS

*Untwisting all the chains that tie the hidden soul of harmony.*
—Milton—

Breathing and relaxation skills provide the foundation for self-mastery. If these skills were all we needed, slaying the dragons would indeed be easy. Powerful as it is, breathing reflects only what goes on in the mind. Watch someone become angry, and you will see her inhale and hold her breath. Watch someone who is depressed, and you will see him exhale, and then hold his breath for a few moments. Someone who is anxious will be breathing very quickly and very high in the chest.

It's apparent that the real power and control lies within the mind, not the body. It's time to face the real source of our misery, the dragons of the mind. If we don't take control of the creative force we call the sensory mind, all the breathing and relaxation in the world won't keep the dragons from breathing fire and creating unhappiness. In Chapter 3 we saw how the dragons of fear and self-hatred disturb the coordination between mind and body, which leads to stress. The greatest cause of stress is fear. It sets off the fight-or-flight alarm reaction, and we worry ourselves to death. When we identify with all the hurts, mistakes, and disasters of the past, we react with the possum reaction, and suffer from depression, negativity, and guilt. This is the second greatest cause of stress. Many of us are quite capable of doing both at the same time. Because we aren't skilled in using our inner resources, our habits dominate the mind and we become victims of our own misdirected creative force.

We also saw in Chapter 3 that we alone are the source of fear, of self-hatred, and stress. Remember, it's not what happens to us that creates stress, it's what we say to ourselves about what happens to us. The truth is that we have very little control over what happens around or to us. We seldom get to choose the diffi-culties and dangers we face. But we do have great capacity to control how we respond to those dangers. Our power lies not in controlling the world, but in choosing our response to the world. If we don't make ourselves fearful, no one else can do so. At any one moment, someone may hold the power of life and death over us, but we alone hold the power to create fear for ourselves. This power lies in our ability to direct mind chatter, the creative flow of the mind.

When we use the sensory mind skillfully, we solve problems, create new possibilities, tap instinctual knowledge, and bring balance and harmony into our lives. But left unmanaged, this creative force is disrupted by emotions, made rigid by habits, and limited through beliefs. Instead of visualizing solutions, we fantasize harm and failure.

We all know someone like Sharon, a middle-aged, attractive, and intelligent woman, whom I met at one of my seminars. She spends a great deal of emotion-al effort just trying to cope – not with the world, but with her own fears of rejec-tion and thoughts about how stupid and unlovable she is. Sadly, like many oth-ers, Sharon had a difficult childhood. Her father was rejecting and cold, and her mother incapable of providing the love and security every child needs. It's easy to see how these early patterns of rejection create such strong feelings of fear and self-hatred. Sharon understands this, but this intellectual understanding doesn't change the habits of her mind. She still accepts these early judgments that con-tinue to play in her mind as her identity. Even though she practices relaxation and breathing exercises, she still feels fearful and unloved. Sharon must and can learn to distance herself from these habits locked into her sensory mind. If she learns how to quiet the mind and take control of her inner chatter, she can free herself from these old habits.

This is the first and critical step when working with the mind: We must con-trol the creative force of the mind. We can conquer the dragons of fear and self-hatred if we master four steps:

• First, take control of our mind chatter and not allow it to create fear and self-hatred. In this way, we cut the circuits to our past emotional reactions and redirect our emotional energies.

• Second, begin to carefully choose the words and images we use to create the realities we want and not waste time and energy on unproductive thinking and emotional reactions.

• Third, develop effective strategies to eliminate fear and self-hatred. With the right techniques and practice, we can overcome fears, minimize negative self-criticism, and maintain a calm, clear mind even in the face of conflict and attack.

• Fourth, refine perceptual sensitivity and develop instincts to provide us with the knowledge and timing to make more effective decisions.

## TAKING CONTROL OF MIND CHATTER

It should be fairly obvious by now that even on our best days mind chatter can be difficult to deal with. And when fear and self-hatred raise their ugly heads, it seems impossible. The harder we try to control this chatter, the more it fills our mind. Try not to think for fifteen seconds. Don't think about not thinking, as this is still thinking. You will quickly find how difficult it is. The mind is a field of intelligent energy in constant motion. Like a crazed monkey jumping around in a tree, the mind hops from one thing to another, often making unexpected and undesirable leaps.

We try all sorts of things to control the mind – positive thinking, sleep, and drugs. Unfortunately, many of the things not only don't work, they create even bigger problems for us. And the harder we try, the more thoughts we think. We just can't seem to turn that monkey mind off! Our inability to control the chattering monkey mind is exceeded only by the frustration and suffering it creates for us.

There are times, though, when the mind behaves perfectly, and seems to be under almost complete control. Remember when you became so focused on your work that even time seemed to disappear? Psychologists call this "task absorption," or a "flow experience." It often leads to a "peak experience," a time of great personal fulfillment and expression. During this time, the body and mind are completely coordinated. The mind is free of worry and unconcerned with past failures, and all of your attention is concentrated on the task at hand.

When you are totally focused, you do your best work, find creative solutions to vexing problems, and apply them effortlessly. When you are finished, you feel wonderfully alive, alert, and very relaxed. You feel positive about yourself as well as others. Even if the work was physically exhausting, you aren't irritable or stressed. Instead, you feel the satisfaction of a job well done, and a rest well earned.

Now contrast this experience with the time when you had a lot of work to do, but sat around and worried. How did you feel after several hours of working like this? More than likely, you couldn't concentrate, your mind and body were out of sync, and you felt frazzled, tense, and irritable. Unfortunately, we have far more of these experiences than the peak experiences of task absorption. Work, relationships, and leisure activities don't always fascinate us to the point that we become completely focused on them. We need some way to control mind chatter when we aren't absorbed in the task before us, which is most of the time.

What if you had a simple, effective technique to control your mind chatter, one that could be used anywhere, anytime, and was effective the moment you used it? And what if this technique, when refined to a high degree of skill, would provide you with absolute control over your emotional reactions? Furthermore, what if this same technique would allow you to think more clearly, listen more effectively, and even improve your memory? Would you practice until you became very skilled in its use?

Get ready to practice! There is a technique that will provide all of this and more. The key lies in understanding the two basic operations of the mind. In its task to create and understand the reality around it, the mind engages in two primary operations that permeate both the conscious and unconscious levels of the mind. The mind thinks (talks to itself, analyzes, contemplates) and the mind perceives. But, the conscious mind does not do both at the same time. And whether we are thinking or perceiving, the whole mind is engaged. The mind always functions as the single reality that it is. We talk about the different aspects of the mind – intuition, instincts, habits, dimensions, and levels – as if these were separate realities, but this is only for our convenience. Whatever the mind is doing at the moment, the whole mind is engaged.

Many of us like to think that we are skilled at multi-tasking, doing more than one thing at a time. But the truth is that this is not humanly possible. The conscious mind never does more than one thing at a time. However, we can shift between modes of operation, between thinking and perceiving, so quickly that we are unaware of the shift. Yoga science claims that this shift occurs within $1/525^{th}$ of a syllabic second, the amount of time it takes to utter a single syllable. So while it appears to us that we are listening and thinking at the same time, this does not actually happen. We are simply shifting very quickly from one mode of operation to another. And, as many of us well know, when we do this we don't really listen very well.

It's not necessary to be aware of this shift between thinking and perceiving, only that we understand that this is what happens. This subtle fact of the conscious mind provides the opening for a powerful technique that gives us control of our thinking, or mind chatter. When our thinking is running amok, feeding the dragons in the mind, we can shift the operation from thinking to perceiving, and in so doing, take control of our mind chatter. This technique is called Breath Awareness, and it is one of the most powerful self-management tools that you will ever use.

## Breath Awareness – Reining in the Monkey Mind

Watch your mind think for a few minutes. Don't get involved in the thoughts; just observe them as if you were watching a train go by. Now, focus your attention on the *feeling* of the breath as it moves in and out of your nostrils. When you inhale you will feel a slight touch of coolness right at the opening of your nostrils. When you exhale, you will feel a very subtle touch of warmth. You may have a little difficulty feeling warmth, but you will feel the air as it moves through the opening of the nostrils.

*Don't think* about the breath, concentrate on *feeling* it as it enters and leaves the nostrils. Whenever you find your mind wandering off into thought, bring your attention back to the feeling of the breath. At the same time, be aware of how you feel, and what happens in your mind. But keep your attention focused on the coolness of the inhalation and warmth of the exhalation.

What happens to your thoughts? Does your breathing change? Do you feel anything different in your body when you focus your attention on feeling your breath? Four things immediately happen when you focus on feeling your breath:

1. The mind chatter stops and your mind becomes clear and calm;

2. Your breathing slows and becomes more stable, creating balance in the autonomic nervous system;

3. You feel a slight release as your body relaxes because there are no longer any demands being made by your mind chatter. The body's natural state is one of relaxation. The more focused, calm, and quiet your mind, the more relaxed your body.

4. You become perceptually more sensitive to the environment around you; you hear more clearly, you are more sensitive to emotional currents, and you are more aware of the total picture.

By focusing on the feeling of the breath, you shift the mind's operation from thinking to perceiving. Instead of imagining what *might* happen, you are fully attentive to what *is* happening. You are no longer living in the future or the past, but fully in the present. At this moment, you cannot be fearful or negative, and you are more capable of dealing with the present. Even if danger is present, instead of a fight-or-flight alarm, self-preservation takes control, and you deal effectively with the danger. Your mind is calm, clear, and focused. You are no longer disturbing yourself, and if you don't disturb yourself, no one else can!

Think about the last time that someone started screaming at you. What was your initial reaction? If you are like most people, you reacted in one of several ways. You might have thought, "You can't talk to me like that!" and went on the attack, probably even screaming back. You might have ridiculed this person either mentally or verbally. Or, you might have been overwhelmed, and began thinking something like, "Oh my gosh, this is awful!" Intimidated, you back-stepped and tried to find a way to retreat. You may have completely tuned the other person out, and not even heard what was said. In either case, your ego was engaged and you reacted to the attack.

But what if, instead of thinking, you looked the screamer right in the eye and simply focused your attention on feeling your breath? By doing this, you maintain a calm, collected mind, and prevent an emotional reaction from forming. When you do this, you can usually count on one of two things happening:

1. The person attacking you becomes frustrated because you aren't reacting to his emotional attack. He may become even more intense. This is a clear sign that he is trying to intimidate or manipulate you with an emotional outburst. His frustration stems from the fact that it isn't working. Don't worry, just stay calm and focused. Sooner or later, he will calm down and probably end up feeling rather foolish for overreacting. When you don't react, the screamer often backs off and gains respect for you because he can't manipulate you. At the very least, he learns he can't manipulate you in this way.

2. The person calms down because you aren't fueling his emotional reaction with your own. Usually, this person has overreacted, and isn't trying to manipulate. They are often grateful that you remained calm.

In either case, by controlling your mind chatter, you stay in control of your emotions and respond more effectively to the situation. Your mind remains clear and focused, and you solve the problems presented more effectively and efficiently without giving yourself high blood pressure or an ulcer. By remaining calm and focused, you stabilize the entire event.

Let's take another common example. We're all familiar with traffic stress. For many of us, it's a daily event, and it's all too easy to become tense and angry. Your shoulders tighten, you begin to feel desperate about arriving on time, and your jaws clench in anger. Instead of a calm, relaxed ride to the office, you are riding with a monster, and it turns out to be you! By the time you reach your destination, you are in no shape to be productive or to lend a helping hand.

You don't have to create this frustration, tension, and stress. The next time you are in traffic and feel the pressure starting to build, practice Breath Awareness. (Of course, don't close your eyes to do this!) Watch what happens to your frustration and tension. You can't do anything about the traffic, but you can do a great deal about the kind of company you keep for yourself. If you don't disturb yourself, all the idiots in the world have no power to disturb you.

For moment-to-moment control over emotional reactions, nothing is more powerful than Breath Awareness. If you don't let mind chatter create a disturbance for you, you don't have a disturbance to deal with. All it takes is a little practice. We have endless opportunities to practice Breath Awareness: at meetings, in social situations when someone else is talking, even when going for a walk by yourself. Whenever you focus on Breath Awareness, you are immediately more attentive to what is happening at the moment. You hear more clearly, see things you never noticed before, even remember things better. These all depend on your ability to focus your attention. Think about it. What is going on when you don't hear clearly what someone is saying to you? Isn't it always because you are distracted by your own thoughts? You are so busy talking to yourself that you don't pay attention to what he or she is saying to you.

Breath Awareness even impacts memory. Memory is based on attention. Where is it when we aren't paying attention to the things going on around us? When we are busy talking to ourselves. For example, how often do you remember the name of someone you met at a party? Where was your attention when the host introduced this person to you? More than likely, you were busy thinking about the impression you might be making, or the person you really wanted to meet, or the thousand different things that are in your thoughts. In other words, you weren't really focused on listening to the introduction; you were busy talking to yourself. Consequently, the name of the person you just met simply didn't register with enough impact to stay in your memory.

The first few times you practice Breath Awareness, it will seem like all of your attention is on the feeling of the breath, and you aren't aware of anything else. That's because this is a new experience for the mind. After a few days practice, you will find that you are aware of the breath, but you are also much more aware of the reality around you, whether it is traffic, another person talking to you, or the dynamics of a meeting that you are attending. The more often you practice, the more skill you acquire, and the more benefits you experience.

## Damage Control: Regaining Clarity and Balance

But what about the times when you lose control? There will be many times when you get your buttons pushed and react before you can remember to do Breath Awareness. The habits of fear, worry, and self-criticism often lie hidden in the unconscious, waiting for the right time to emerge as a conscious thought. For example, remember the last time you started screaming at someone who obviously deserved it? More than likely, it was over some trivial thing, but that final straw "broke the camel's back." Your anger welled up and you exploded. Afterwards, you probably felt upset for several hours, maybe even days or weeks, as you kept thinking about what happened, or couldn't resolve the difficulty to your satisfaction. You continued to upset yourself long after the disturbing event.

Even when we don't react so dramatically, we can still do a good job of disturbing ourselves. We get strong emotional surges, and don't know how to take effective damage control to stabilize our thoughts and feelings. We dwell on anger and hurts long after the initial event has passed. This is where Breath Awareness can play a powerful role by preventing the secondary effects of emotional reactions.

Remember the example from Chapter 3 about walking into a room and seeing a person we dislike apparently talking about us? Your emotional habits usually have a field day with this one. You often can't prevent that first emotional rush that leaves you feeling paranoid, defensive and hurt. But that first surge has only a limited impact. It's what you do next that really keeps you miserable. After the initial emotional reaction, your mind chatter takes off. You review your history with that person, justify your behavior, go over past arguments, and past hurts and injustices. We build houses, villages, and cities in our mind, and then have to pay rent on all of it. That rent, of course, is not only a spoiled evening, it includes the emotional disturbance and stress that we continue to create long after the initial incident.

Instead of allowing your mind to react and build all those scenarios and recall all those memories, what if you quickly refocus your attention on Breath Awareness to clear your mind? Then, once you rebalance, you can easily redirect your attention to something more useful and enjoyable. Remember, the solution is simple: If you don't allow your mind chatter to create a disturbance, you don't have a disturbance to contend with. It doesn't matter what the other person does or says, it only matters what you say to yourself about what they say or do. By taking control of your mind chatter, you can refocus your attention on a more useful, creative, and productive train of thought. You end up in a very different place, and without the misery and unhappiness that your old habits would have created.

This is not suppressing your feelings, nor is it repression. It is not necessary, or healthy, to deny that first emotional reaction. But nothing, except our own habits, makes us continue that initial reaction and build a house, or village or city with it. With Breath Awareness we override these habits and consciously choose not to continue to disturb ourselves. As we will see in a later chapter, through meditation we access our inner strength and gain so much self-confidence that even these initial emotional reactions disappear. But first we need to take control of our mind chatter, and not build on that initial disturbance from the unconscious.

No one learned this better than Marge. She was a participant in a four-week stress management training program sponsored by an agency of the Defense Department. As office manager, she was responsible for supervising seven people. She came to the seminar to learn how to relax, but what she really wanted was to find a way to avoid the stress she felt around her immediate supervisor, a difficult and demanding individual. By the end of the four weeks, Marge was able to tolerate her supervisor as long as she remembered to do Breath Awareness whenever he walked into the office. To help her, she kept a little card on her desk that had "Breath Awareness" printed on it. Every time she looked at that part of her desk, the card reminded her to practice. This early success made quite an impression on her, and she faithfully practiced many of the techniques she learned in the seminar. After several months, Marge became fairly skilled at using Breath Awareness, and at staying relaxed. This had a calming effect on the entire office, and led to an unexpected outcome. The supervisor signed up for the next stress management seminar, and after participating, sent every one of his staff to the next seminar. The last I heard from Marge was that she was being promoted on her supervisor's recommendation, and both were sorry to have their working relationship change. She still keeps that little card on her new desk just as a reminder.

Our emotional reactions follow our perceptions and thoughts. This process usually begins in the emotional habits in the unconscious. By the time we experience these reactions, we are already out of balance. Remember running down the hill? The stronger our reactions are, the more difficult it is to rebalance the system. But with Breath Awareness, we stem the tide of emotional energy and prevent the reaction from occurring in the first place. Of course, the more difficult the situation, the more skill it requires. It's usually easier to remain calm with strangers than with family members. The closer the emotional ties, the more practice it takes to maintain a calm, steady mind.

### Conflict Control: Taking Out the Opposition

The more skilled we become with Breath Awareness, the more opportunities we find to use it. Just think of all the times you wish that you would have been more in control of your emotional reactions, such as the times when you get involved in a conflict situation, an argument with your boss or coworker, or with a member of your family. How differently would you have behaved if you had remained calm? Would that have changed the outcome? Using Breath Awareness, you can confront the issues without creating even more disturbance by overreacting.

In fact, you now have the tools you need to deal with any conflict situation without being disturbed. Let's put the elements together. The key element in any conflict is opposition. We may disagree and have different viewpoints, but unless we oppose each other, we don't have conflict. Opposition, whether it involves another person, a different ideology, or differing wants and desires in our own minds, creates all conflicts. If we understand this key element, we very quickly see that once we remove opposition and resistance, conflict cannot exist. This does *not* mean that we avoid conflict or become passive. Avoiding conflict is a sure way to lose self-respect and become a victim. Rather, it means that we take charge of the mind and direct the flow of energy instead of opposing it.

The most sophisticated martial artist knows that she doesn't need to meet force with force. The key is to use the opponent's force and energy rather than trying to oppose that force with a greater force. With calmness and clarity, the martial artist joins with the attack and redirects the flow of energy, channeling the power into the direction she chooses. The opponent has no choice and is actually controlled by his own redirected power. This requires sensitivity by the martial artist as well as control over her mind and actions.

There are four key steps to effectively manage conflict and take control of any situation. They maximize your ability to resolve difficulties or problems by helping you maintain a calm and clear mind. This is called the RARE model of conflict management:

1. Relax
2. Accept
3. Restrain
4. Explore/Express

**Step 1: Relax**

One of the hardest things to do when you are under attack is to relax. Conflict generates tension very quickly. The more emotional the situation, the greater the possibility of tension. When we engage in conflict, the ego sees it as a battle. As part of the fight-or-flight alarm reaction, tension is the body's armor against physical attack. However, as any skilled martial artist knows, tension slows the body's reflexes, interferes with movement, and makes the mind more rigid and less perceptive. In interpersonal conflict, tension is a signal to the other person's unconscious that a battle has been engaged. In turn, his unconscious mind reacts by increasing tension, and the emotional intensity builds. Instead of protecting us, tension actually intensifies conflict and disturbance and interferes with our effectiveness.

The first step, consequently, is to maintain a state of relaxed calm. This can be very hard to do if you are not skilled in deep relaxation. Of course, if you are only fighting yourself, you can relax anytime. But when you are face-to-face with an angry person who is emotionally out of control, it's a bit difficult to say, "Excuse me. I must go and practice my relaxation tape now."

If you are already skilled in deep relaxation, you can effectively use a technique called Scanning anywhere, at any time. After Scanning, you stay relaxed by focusing on your breath and maintaining a subtle awareness of your body. Your relaxation signals to the other person's unconscious that you are not trying to give him a hard time or create any resistance to his communication. More importantly, by staying relaxed, you remain calm and your mind is clear, flexible and creative, and more able to find solutions to the problem in front of you.

### SCANNING EXERCISE

To scan, mentally go from the top of your head to your toes, and then back up, and quickly relax any tension you find. You can do this in just a few seconds. Practice this now. Start at your forehead, and then mentally go down through your face, your neck and shoulders, your torso, and then down your legs to your toes. Relax any tension you find. Then come back to the top of your head. Periodically check your habitual tension points, for example your jaws, shoulders, stomach, lower back, and relax any tension you find. Scanning is a very useful technique to use when you go to the dentist. At the dentist's office, you can really notice the effect of tension. When you sit in the dentist chair, your body touches the chair in only three places: the back of your head, your buttocks and your heels. Everything else is suspended by tension! All this tension guarantees that you will experience pain. Pain is intimately connected with tension. The more relaxed you are, the less pain you experience. When you first sit down in the chair, begin to systematically scan and relax every muscle from the top of your head to your toes. By the time you have relaxed every muscle, the dentist will be finished, and you will have felt very little pain. Of course, the more skilled you are at relaxing, the greater control you will have over your pain.

## Step 2: Accept

When you reject a part of your personality or repress certain feelings or patterns of thought, you create inner conflict. When you struggle with unwanted habits, feelings and thoughts, trying to push them from your mind, the struggle itself is often more destructive than the "unacceptable" thoughts or feelings. Your mind has become a battlefield, and no matter which side wins, you have already lost.

To accept something doesn't mean that you approve of or agree with it. When we accept our inner thoughts and feelings, that doesn't mean that we believe them to be true or helpful. You immediately eliminate inner conflict by simply accepting negative thoughts or feelings that come to your mind as *only* thoughts and feelings, not truth. As we learned before, you can't fight with your thoughts and win. You don't have to, nor can you, prove anything to your mind. It is this struggle to prove something isn't true that creates inner conflict and weakens our will. Instead, be an observer and just accept the thought as a thought. Don't invest it with any importance by adding more mind chatter to the thought and creating a house. By doing this, you rob it of its power to affect you. It can no longer create conflict or make you feel bad.

This same principle operates on an interpersonal level. Remember a time when you had something very important you really wanted to ask of a friend or family member. As you were halfway through your first sentence, your friend looked at you and started shaking their head, "No." How did that make you feel? Most of us get very angry when this happens. If you want to really anger someone, and create intense opposition, just refuse to listen. We do not get nearly as angry when someone disagrees with us as we do when we feel they don't listen.

If our goal is to eliminate opposition, we must facilitate communication, not block it. We can do this very easily in any conversation by nodding our head up and down, and saying. "Yes," or "OK." This does not mean that we agree with what is being said, only that we are acknowledging the other person's communication. Nodding your head up and down indicates acceptance and encourages the other person to talk.

When the other person is finished talking, you can disagree all you want. In fact, by not creating any resistance to the communication, you disarm the other person's resistance to your communication. Now whatever you want to say back will be heard, whether your listener likes your response or not. Some people may take your nodding and saying, "Yes" as an agreement to what they are saying. This doesn't have to be a problem. In fact, in a conflict situation, this is an advantage to you. It often disconcerts the other person and blunts his aggressiveness.

## Step 3: Restrain

This is where skill in Breath Awareness pays great dividends. In order to take control of a situation, you must keep your ego under control by restraining your emotional reactions. If you want to be effective and solve problems, you cannot allow emotional reactions to distort your perceptions and cloud your thinking.

In a conflict, the focus can very quickly shift from the problem at hand to the issue of personalities – particularly when the other person is reacting emotionally. The first thing they do is reach out and try to grab you by the ego. This often takes the form of blaming and personal attack. Some people intentionally attack on a personal level as a manipulative technique. They try to control the situation by provoking an emotional reaction in you.

You can remain calm if you do only one thing: stop your mind chatter with Breath Awareness. By utilizing Breath Awareness while the other person is speaking, you listen more effectively, perceive more clearly, control emotional reactions, and remain relaxed and calm. This allows you the clarity and flexibility to take Step 4.

**Step 4: Explore**

Emotional reactions in conflict situations make solutions very difficult to come by. The more disturbed you become, the more difficult it is to solve problems, and the easier it is to become embroiled in further conflict. But if you stay relaxed, facilitate and accept the communication by nodding your head, and utilize Breath Awareness to keep your mind calm and clear, conflict situations can be productive. The emotional energy involved in a conflict situation can be redirected into an exploration of alternative viewpoints and solutions, creating mental flexibility instead of rigidity. The emotional energy now enhances the creative force of the mind instead of distorting it. By remaining open and accepting, we create an atmosphere that also allows the other person to be more flexible, to explore, and accept alternatives. But, we only gain this benefit when we remain in control of ourselves and allow our creativity to flow in a productive, non-fearful way.

When the mind is calm and clear, we are far more effective in conflict situations. People respect strength. They do not respect emotional reactions and over-the-edge force. When we demonstrate self-control and inner strength, our words are more powerful and command greater respect. If we overreact, the more likely we damage the relationship and create even greater problems. By staying calm, we have the flexibility to adapt to changing circumstances easily and quickly, and find effective ways to solve any problem.

## Language: The Power to Create

Once we take command of the creative force and stabilize our emotional reactions through Breath Awareness, we can take the next step and learn to use the powerful function of language. We have already seen that words define our personal sense of reality, and they trigger emotional reactions. We can use our thoughts to starve fear and self-hatred.

When we are sensitive to the words we use, we can choose words that create positive, stress-free moods and attitudes. Toshi is a young woman who has always shown an uncanny ability for self-control and inner strength. I have never heard her use the word "failure." She will talk about mistakes, and the lessons that she has learned, but failure isn't part of her lexicon. Once she and one of her friends were working on a class project. Towards the end of the time allotted for the project, they suddenly realized that they had mistakenly done the wrong assignment. The other girl was in tears, saying over and over again how she couldn't believe that they had made such a stupid mistake. After about fifteen minutes, Toshi told her to go on home and that she would try to find a way to fix the problem. After she left, Toshi calmly sat back and thought about what they had done, and the assignment they were supposed to do. After a few minutes, she made a few changes in their project and was able to present their project as a novel approach to the assignment. Later she told me that she asked her friend to leave because she couldn't think clearly while this girl was talking about how awful the problem was. By taking control of her thoughts and imagery, she was not only able to salvage her work, but also earned high marks for her creativity and ingenuity.

Here again, the key is self-awareness. Often we aren't very sensitive to what we are saying and how our own words affect us. My master was skilled in making me aware of the consequences of my own words. On one occasion he called me and another psychologist into his room and started teasing us. After a few minutes of small talk, he suddenly said, "You people (meaning psychologists) talk funny." And he began to imitate the way I spoke – the professional jargon I used, the tonal qualities, even the facial expressions were perfect imitations of my own speech patterns. As he spoke, I saw myself in his words, and could feel how those words affected me. The entire event didn't last longer than a few minutes, and I was laughing so hard that I had tears in my eyes. But I remember clearly how those words felt. Since then, I have been much more selective about which words I use and more aware of how they create emotions and reinforce habits.

It isn't difficult to take charge of this powerful function. As we learned with the Green Frog exercise in Chapter 3, the first step is to stop believing what your mind says. The next time that voice says, "You are really second-rate," follow it immediately with another thought that says, "OK, someone has to be. What's next?" Then clear your mind with Breath Awareness and refocus your attention on something more useful. You have the power to determine your emotional states by *consciously choosing* what to attend to, how to describe or talk about it, and what to dismiss as an unproductive line of thought.

The language we use can interfere with our ability to understand what is going on. There is an ancient Chinese proverb that warns us of the deceptiveness of words:

If you wish to see the truth, then hold no opinion for or against anything.
To set up what you like against what you dislike is a disease of the mind.

Practice using non-judgmental words. Instead of "good" or "bad," use words that have less emotional charge, such as "helpful" and "not helpful." Play with your language. Use different words to see what kind of changes they create. Instead of saying, "That is awful," use the phrase "That's an interesting development." Instead of telling yourself you can't do something, say, "Let's see what I can do." By stepping back and experimenting with the words and phrases we use, we learn how to use language as a tool rather than be abused by it.

By using Breath Awareness and being mindful of the language we use, we take power back from the dragons and redirect it into far more useful and productive channels. With these two skills as the foundation, we are ready to directly confront the dragons. We can now directly attack the two dragons – fear and self-hatred – and dramatically minimize their impact. We won't win each battle. There will be many times that the dragons are more powerful and far sneakier than what we anticipated. But it doesn't matter. Each time we become worried and afraid, every time we abuse ourselves with self-contempt or guilt, we have an opportunity to practice our techniques and become a little stronger. In this way, we use the dragons to make ourselves stronger. Instead of obstacles to self-mastery, they become our means.

## CONFRONTING FEAR: STEPS TO A LIFE OF FREEDOM

We are now ready to develop effective strategies to eliminate fear and self-hatred. We should *never* accept these dragons as an inevitable part of life. We have the resources we need to be so strong that fear and self-hatred play no role whatsoever in our life. This is evident in times of crisis when suddenly we call on inner resources we never realized we had. The problem is that these resources – inner strength, creativity, will, insight, even wisdom – seem to disappear when the crisis is over. The issue is not one of lack, but one of access. As we will experience in the next chapter, these resources are always part of our identity. But first we have to confront and tame our dragons. We must prevent the sensory mind from creating these destructive beasts of fear and self-hatred, and distracting us from our strength and joy.

We begin with the fantasy we call fear. The next time you begin to worry, step back and examine your thoughts, images, and feelings. Pay close attention. Is what you are worrying about *actually* happening to you, or is it something that you think *might* happen to you? Is it an actual event, or just a picture in your mind? Then pay attention to how you deal with an actual dangerous or potentially harmful situation. What are your feelings and thoughts when you are actually taking action? You will notice that when you are attentive and involved, you do not feel fearful.

This is the essence of martial arts training. In martial arts, you don't anticipate an attack, you are fully attentive to the moment. You become so focused that you are sensitive to the subtle thoughts and movements of your opponent. In karate, this advanced state is called *mu shin* or *mu no kokoro,* the "empty mind" or "the mind of nothingness." It indicates a mind so free of conceptual thought, worry, or concern that it accurately reflects the perceptual reality around it. It is an active, all-embracing state of mind in total harmony. By focusing on the present, you prevent the mind from anticipating the future, and you remain free from fear. Your body is relaxed, your mind responsive to its environment, and your movements are quick, coordinated, and graceful.

Even if you don't practice martial arts, you can eliminate fear. You can practice confronting your fears and living in the moment. To do this, we need a simple strategy to follow. The following has been very helpful to many people. Why not give it a try?

## Strategies to Control Fear

**1. Take control of your mind chatter.** Use Breath Awareness to clear your mind of everyday fears and worries. Don't allow the mind to build a city of disturbance where you are forced to pay the rent. It doesn't matter if you have to clear the mind a thousand times to get past a worrisome situation. Each time you do so, the habit of Breath Awareness gets a little stronger. The more you use Breath Awareness, the more control you have over your mind chatter, and the less fear it can produce.

Having control of mind chatter doesn't mean that you don't think; it means that you skillfully direct your thinking. Make sure that the words you use help you remain strong, and don't create weakness or fear for you. Reframe (reinterpret) a worrisome situation, using words that are descriptive rather than judgmental, that offer options rather than only one way of doing things. For instance, any difficulty can be defined as a "disaster," a "problem," even an "opportunity." Which do you think would be more useful? When you find yourself starting to worry, take a few moments to clear your mind, then redefine the situation using different words.

Whenever you face a problem that includes a personal threat, depersonalize it so you can maintain mental clarity. Focus on the problem to solve, and avoid being part of it by imagining all the terrible things that will happen to you. In Chapter 8 you will learn centering techniques that will clear your mind deeply, give you the opportunity to refocus your attention, and allow the unconscious mind to present you with a creative alternative.

**2. Be present-centered, focus on your strengths, and take action.** Once you clear your mind of chatter, focus your attention on the problems that you face now, not what might happen in the future. Remember, fear doesn't exist in the present; it only exists in relationship to a future event. If we pay attention to what is happening now, we prevent the mind from creating fear and we are more aware of the choices and opportunities that are already available. To paraphrase a famous advertising slogan for wine, make sure that you, "Solve no problems before their time."

You must take action to solve any problem. You solve problems by what you do, not by what you can't do. Focus your mind, energy, and effort on the strengths and the resources you have available to you and on the actions you can take. Every time you act on your strengths, you are literally practicing to be strong. This reinforces both your strengths as well as the habit of using them. On the other hand, every time you act out of weakness, you are practicing weakness and become weaker.

Action also completes the circuit between mind and body. By taking focused action, by doing something, you coordinate body and mind and prevent fear from forming. Many people resist taking action because they are afraid of making mistakes. Doing nothing reinforces this fear and builds barriers to success. This loss of confidence leads to even greater fear. Mistakes provide the opportunity to make adjustments and corrections that eventually lead to a solution or resolution of the problem. If you keep a clear, calm mind, you learn from your mistakes and avoid making the same mistake twice. But if you sit and worry, nothing is resolved, nothing is learned. The only result is that you become more skilled at worrying.

**3. Face your fears directly.** When fear, worry, or anxiety grip the mind, most of us engage in avoidance behavior: we find friends to console or reinforce us, we sleep, go shopping, we eat or drink. Avoidance behaviors distract us, but they also prevent us from understanding or resolving our fear. Instead of trying to get rid of the fear, sit quietly and examine it as if you were a court reporter. Where do you feel the fear? What color and shape is it? Then completely examine the assumptions your mind makes. Follow through with each consequence, and don't allow your mind to stop until you've reached the very end. Bring everything out in the open for your observation: If this happens, my boss will be mad at me. What then? ... Well, she will chew me out. What then ... I'll lose her respect, and feel bad and stupid. What then? ... I may get fired, not be able to make my mortgage payments and lose my house. What then? ... Oh, I probably wouldn't lose my house, I'd just have to find another job ... might be tough going for a while, but I'd get through it. What then? ...

As you follow each of these thoughts and force them to a conclusion, watch what happens to your fears. Then use the other strategies to maintain a calm and steady mind.

Fear, as powerful as it is, is only a habit of the mind. But habits are persistent. They don't go away very easily or quickly. To be strong and courageous doesn't mean that you don't have fears; it means that you confront them, and do not allow them to make decisions for you. Being skilled in the strategies that eliminate fear takes time and practice. They do work, but only if you do the work.

With practice and skill, you will free your mind of petty fears, worry, and anxieties. Of course, the stronger and deeper these habits, the more effort and training it takes. But as you work with your mind, you gain an added benefit. The same methods that eventually free your mind from fear also free your mind of the habits and patterns of self-hatred.

## LETTING GO OF HISTORY: FACING THE SELF-HATRED DRAGON

In Richard Bach's book *Illusions:Confessions of a Reluctant Messiah,* there is a phrase in the Handbook For Messiahs that states, "Argue for your limitations, and sure enough, they are yours." Many of us do this. We constantly remind ourselves of our mistakes, our weaknesses, and our shortcomings. No wonder depression is so prevalent in our society.

Every human being makes mistakes, feels rejected, and experiences hurt and failure. Childhood experiences often leave scars that are deep and painful. We develop self-destructive patterns in the mind that become a false identity, ones that lead to self-hatred, guilt, and hopelessness. We seldom experience the power and beauty of our personalities because we spend so much of our time looking only at the pain and negativity. This, of course, creates enormous unhappiness and stress for us.

A dangerous condition comes from self-hatred – feeling hopeless and helpless, that nothing you do will ever make a difference, and that you are completely out of control of your life. A large body of evidence clearly shows that people who feel hopeless, helpless, and victimized slowly but surely destroy their immune systems. Animal research by C. P. Richter in the late 1950s, and Martin Seligman and Bruce Overmeir in the late 1960s, showed conclusively that animals do learn helplessness. When this happens, the animals lose motivation, stop making effort, and even die. The clinical research in cancer by O. C. Simonton and Lawrence LeShan in the late 1970s showed that a sense of helplessness in people is a consistent pattern prior to the development of cancer. Current research in psycho-neuroimmunology all point to one and the same conclusion: Depression, hopelessness and helplessness depress immunity functioning and lead to serious disease states such as cancer, as well as to premature death.

Clearly, when you spend a lifetime arguing for your limitations, it can cost your health, your happiness, and even your life. We can, and must, put an end to this self-inflicted disaster. We start by no longer allowing ourselves to be a victim of our own emotional habits and mind chatter. Medication may be necessary and helpful for various forms of depression. But in the end, we still must help ourselves. We must take charge of the mind and find ways to access our inner strength. We begin at the level of sensory mind by taking these four steps:

**1. Develop response-ability by giving up the role of victim and taking back our power.** When we blame ourselves and/or others for our circumstances, our feelings, or anything else, we deny our inner strength and power. We can never be free of self-hatred as long as we don't take full response-ability (remember, the word responsibility is really best understood as two words, "response" and "ability") for our thoughts, feelings and actions. Others may harm us, but they cannot make us feel a certain way. Just like fear, no one else can make us feel bad about ourselves. You may condemn me, but you do not have the power to make me condemn myself. Only I have the power to do these things.

One of the problems we face is that we aren't aware of the emotional impact of words on ourselves. We are so focused on how others react that we don't pay attention to our inner reactions. Every thought we have or say has some internal emotional impact. Often this is subtle, and we aren't aware of the damage we inflict on ourselves. But we will feel this damage if we pay attention. For example, say aloud the following sentence three times as if you were really angry with someone. Pay attention to how you feel as you say this sentence. "You make me very angry when you do that!" How does that feel inside to say this with intensity?

Now say this next sentence three times as if you were really angry with someone, and pay attention to how this sentence makes you feel. "I get very angry when you do that!" Does this feel differently? Don't think about the sentences or words; focus on the different feelings of each sentence. Which one feels heavier? Which feels more tense? Which is more uncomfortable?

We can analyze the sentence structure, but the relevant factor is how we felt by using different words. For most of us, the first sentence will feel heavier, more tense, and leave us feeling somehow uncomfortable and dissatisfied. Obviously, in the first sentence we are blaming the other person for how we feel while in the second, we take responsibility for our own feelings. When we blame others for what we feel, good or bad, we deny our power and become a victim of the other person's behavior. Whenever we become a victim, we lose self-respect and strengthen the dragon of self-hatred. The heaviness and discomfort we feel is a consequence of this self-inflicted damage.

The truth is that we are fully responsible (remember, this means response-ability, not blame) for our feelings. We don't always make the best choices about which feelings we create, but we are still the ones who choose. It is our unconscious habits that make us react, not someone else's. No one has the power to manipulate our glandular responses or our neural synapses. When we deny our power by blaming others or ourselves, we become victims, lose self-respect, and begin to feel hopeless and helpless. At that point, we damage our immune systems. As long as we continue to deny our own choices and power, we continue to create stress and disease.

When we take responsibility, and use language that reflects this responsibility, we may not like what we feel, but we maintain personal integrity and self-respect, and we maintain personal power. Taking responsibility for our feelings facilitates communication and understanding. Other people can hear our complaint more easily, and are often more willing to accommodate us. This all has a positive impact on our self-confidence. On the other hand, when we blame others, not only do we damage ourselves, the other person often becomes defensive, and we end up with conflict and a damaged relationship.

Those who are successful and in command of their lives generate self-respect. They don't begin with any more control over their circumstances than those who feel hopeless and helpless. They simply do not allow themselves to feel victimized by their circumstances. Successful entrepreneurs must believe in themselves, or they can never take the risks necessary to build a business, or a career. A close friend of mind, Oded Lurie, president of Gray Matter Inc., is a good example of perseverance. He had a successful career as a senior executive for several major corporations. He decided to begin his own consulting firm, using technology and information to help small companies compete more effectively. For several years, it seem as if every move he made ran headlong into poor economic conditions. After several years of financial hardships, during which he even had to give up his home, the tide began to change. Today, he has a thriving consulting firm and has developed a unique computer program that promises to revolutionize management decisions. Oded trusts his strengths, and doesn't depend on fate to create opportunities for him. People like Oded hold firm to the conviction that whatever happens, they can learn from it, and use it for growth and benefit. They carefully build this attitude through constant practice of taking full response ability. In so doing, they actually gain control of their lives, while those who live their life as a victim lose it.

**2. Practice forgiveness (patience and acceptance).** An important step in developing full response-ability is to free ourselves of guilt. Guilt is entirely useless. It enslaves the mind and reinforces the very behavior we wish to avoid. The simplest way to free ourselves from guilt is to practice forgiveness. Forgiveness consists of two elements: patience and acceptance. We learn to be patient with ourselves and others if we don't judge ourselves or others. Acceptance is the ability to separate the behavior from the individual. We may think the behavior is wrong, even destructive, but we can still hold on to the value of the individual. Forgiveness is one of our greatest virtues, but we must begin by forgiving ourselves. Once you develop forgiveness, it becomes easy to recognize and learn from mistakes, so you don't keep repeating them.

I remember one incident that taught me a great lesson. I was involved in helping stage a large international congress. On the opening day, I was running around taking care of final details. In typical Type A fashion, I was busy directing and giving orders. As I walked into a large room, I saw an old friend whom I hadn't seen in years. He cheerfully greeted me and extended his hand. Instead of returning his greeting, I (again in typical Type A fashion) said, "Oh, Larry, quick, go into the front office and do such and such." Without another word, I continued on my busy way. About forty-five minutes later, Larry caught up with me and confronted me. He said that he was very angry and didn't like the way I had treated him.

I had no idea what he was talking about. As he explained his anger about the abrupt and off-hand way in which I had greeted him, I realized that he was absolutely correct. I quickly and sincerely apologized. He was surprised that I was willing to admit my mistakes so easily and very quickly forgave me, and our friendship continued to grow and deepen. I recognized my mistake, corrected it, and moved on without any guilt. Because it was such a clear lesson for me, I am more careful about letting my Type A qualities override my love for my friends. When you accept yourself, it's easy to apologize for, and correct the mistakes you make.

One of the best ways to practice forgiveness is to let go of the need to be perfect. It's amazing how much disappointment we create for ourselves because we never measure up to some fantasy. Create psychological space to grow by giving yourself permission to be you. By constantly wishing you were different, you create a continual rejection and depression in the mind. You don't have to puff up your ego, simply stop telling yourself what a jerk you are. If you don't create the negative, you don't have to compensate by creating the positive.

**3. Focus on the here and now.** It's not hard to banish the negative when we use Breath Awareness to clear the mind. Like any other mind chatter, we can quickly eliminate self-negation if we focus on the here and now. Be on full alert with your mind chatter. As soon as old habits surface telling you that you are a terrible person, that you will never change, or whatever your mind does to punish and blame you, go immediately to Breath Awareness and clear the mind. Then redirect your attention to the task in front of you. It doesn't matter if you have to use Breath Awareness a thousand times a day. That just means more opportunities to become skilled. Never give up on yourself, and never give up on Breath Awareness. It has taken your entire life to build the habits you have now and it will take some time to replace them.

**4. Use language carefully.** Avoid language that involves blame and self-pity. For instance, the punitive or blaming use of the word "should" strongly reinforces guilt feelings. We keep repeating, "I should (not) have done …" or, "You should (not) have done …" over and over until we have ingrained the pain of failure into our or someone else's mind. When we make a mistake, it's appropriate to recognize what we should or should not have done. But the second or third time we repeat the phrase, we aren't recognizing a mistake, but beating up on ourselves (or someone else). This damaging habit leads to a great deal of stress, resentment, and unhappiness.

The next time you find yourself repeating a "should have" statement, try this should-stopper exercise. After the third repetition, walk over to a window and look up into the sky. If you do not see the hand of God writing in indelible gold letters, "You should not have done that!" then you can figure that what you did or didn't do was okay. If God doesn't personally punish you, why do it to yourself? Accept the mistake, learn from it, and move on.

The physical action of walking to the window, along with the mental action, helps weaken the neural synapses in the brain that structure the habit. About the third or fourth time you do this exercise, you will find that the habit of "shoulding" yourself has weakened. Now you can successfully replace it with a more productive pattern of behavior, such as paying attention to the task in front of you.

Fear and self-hatred slowly but surely destroy the capacity to freely express ourselves and experience the self-respect and feelings of power and confidence that this engenders. We avoid the challenges of life and become indecisive and weak. We lose self-respect, leading to even more self-negation. It becomes a vicious cycle, and the only outcome is stress, unhappiness, and disease.

## PERCEPTION: THE BASIS OF KNOWLEDGE

There is far more to Breath Awareness than just controlling emotional reactions. It is also the most effective way to develop our perceptual sensitivity, to become more aware of the world around us. By keeping the mind clear and calm, we become more sensitive to the subtle cues in our environment. We begin to notice things that we hadn't paid attention to before. Now we begin to master the fourth step, refining perceptual sensitivity, and to use the power of the sensory mind in a more useful and effective way.

Remember, the conscious mind only does two things: It either thinks (chatters) or perceives, but it doesn't do both at the same time. We don't realize that perception, not thinking, is the primary process of knowledge formation. This means that most of the time we base our knowledge on sensory information. The collection, organization, interpretation and presentation of sensory data are perceptual processes, not analytic ones. Thinking is an abstraction, a secondary process based on perceptions. If we are busy thinking, we aren't doing a very good job of perceiving. There are times when we want to tune out the world, and focus only on our thoughts. But all too often we get lost in our thoughts when what we really need to do is pay attention to our perceptions. When we want to know what is happening in the world around us, when we want to see the whole picture and not just analyze its parts, we depend on perceptual sensitivity.

Just as we stop perceiving by focusing on thinking, we can also stop thinking by focusing attention on the perceptual process, e.g., Breath Awareness. Instead of reacting, we use even more information and make better decisions for ourselves. Now we use the creative force of the sensory mind to help us rather than create dragons.

### Creativity: Changing the Rules

Free from the dragon's influence, the mind becomes naturally creative. Perception and thought combine in a joyful dance to create new possibilities, patterns, and behaviors. We see things in a new light, hear things in a different way, and feel the joy of novelty and fresh expression. Sadly, many of us don't feel very creative, and we miss out on this joyful dance. We think that creativity is something that only a lucky few are born with. We don't realize that creativity is a natural function of every human mind. The mind is busy at every moment creating our personal reality and making sense of the world. It is the sensory mind's natural ability to organize perceptual data into meaningful categories. Unfortunately, if we aren't aware of this organizing function of the mind, we never learn how to take conscious control and use this creative force as a conscious skill. As a result, our creativity is constricted by habits, and we get locked into seeing things in the same old way.

These habits are like rules. When we always follow the rules, we never have the opportunity to develop new perspectives. Admiral Kirk made one of the most succinct statements of creativity in the Star Trek movie, *Star Trek II: The Wrath of Kahn*. Kirk was approached by a cadet commander about a training simulation that was contrived so that no matter what the trainee would do, she would always lose. Angered by the impossibility of the simulation, the cadet had been told by Spock that the only person to beat the simulation was Admiral Kirk. Asked how he beat the simulation, Kirk responded, "I changed the rules." Creativity is all about changing the rules. When we aren't sensitive to the mind's creative force, it becomes difficult to change the rules and express our natural creativity.

If we feel we aren't creative, it isn't because we lack creative capacity. It's because we unconsciously limit the inherent and spontaneous creative power of the sensory mind through fears and habits, or because we narrowly restrict the input to the mind. These limits or rules on creativity are entirely self-imposed. Our environment may reinforce or inhibit our creative expression, but our environment has no power to limit the creative nature of the mind. Only we can do that.

We engage the creative force in every moment as we continue to bring new meanings, interpretations, and reactions into existence. Our personal reality is a product of the fertile and imaginative mind that constantly creates, sustains, and destroys a vast number of interpretations, realities, behaviors, and events. The entire dance of the sensory mind is one continuous creative movement that either reflects spontaneity, or becomes restricted by rigid repetitive behaviors.

It isn't hard to experience this creative movement. It simply takes a little reflection and attention to your mind chatter. You can easily watch the creative process if you step outside of it and become a witness. Try the exercise in creative thought. First read through the exercise, then close your eyes, do the exercise, and watch your mind work.

Throughout the exercise, your mind created images, thoughts, and feelings. Some lead to action while others interfere with taking action. Your habits structured some of the images, thoughts, and feelings that arose, while others were spontaneous, leading to feelings of anticipation and joy. The problem is not can you be creative, but rather, how you use your creative force. Through self-mastery, you consciously direct the creative force, and use it to your benefit instead of allowing old habits to choose for you.

If you consciously direct the mind to create scenarios, you stay more relaxed, feel more in control, and become more sensitive to all the possibilities that your mind offers. Remember, the tendency of the sensory mind is to follow its habits. If you simply react to a problem, the mind takes the path of least resistance provided by old habits and you lose touch with the creative process. These old habits are the rules of the mind. Automatic reactions diminish both your creative capacity and effectiveness at solving problems. By maintaining a calm and reflective attitude, your mind can play, and the creative force will work for you. Like Admiral Kirk, you can change the rules.

## Listening With the Whole Mind

When we use breath awareness to calm the mind, we become more sensitive to all of our sensory input. We don't just hear a conversation with our ears, we also see the person's face more clearly, and feel his emotional energies more clearly.

In our seminars and classes, we often have participants pair up and practice listening to each other. While one partner talks about a problem he or she is

### A BRIEF EXERCISE IN CREATIVE THOUGHT

Sit back in your chair, get very comfortable, and close your eyes. For a few moments, focus your attention on Breath Awareness, clearing your mind of extraneous and unnecessary thoughts ... As you do this, you will feel yourself relax, and your attention will direct itself inward. Next, visualize yourself in your ideal vacation setting ... Imagine as clearly as you can what it feels like to be there ... what you are wearing ... the weather ... be as complete as you can ... Enjoy this vision for a few moments ... You have always wanted to live and work in this setting, now is your chance. What must you do to transfer your job and your family here? ... Mentally go through all the steps it will take to do this ... What does your office or work station look like? Surely, it's quite different than what you have now ... How will you go about conducting your affairs?... What will you need to do to bring about this ideal setting and work conditions? ... Observe your feelings as you allow your mind to create possibilities for you ...Now, think of all the reasons why you can't possibly do this, why it wouldn't work ... the company won't move, you can't earn a living, your family doesn't want to move ... Let your mind create all the reasons why it won't work ... Be aware of your feelings as you allow your mind to create obstacles for you ... Then open your eyes.

involved in at work, the other must listen without responding, using Breath Awareness to keep their mind clear of inner chatter. One of the most typical reactions is for the person listening to say, "This is uncomfortable. I want to respond back, and help my partner solve their problem." It's very difficult to listen with full attention. We are too practiced in talking to ourselves. Often, the person who does the talking responds with, "I didn't want you to solve the problem, I just wanted you to listen. By talking to you, I get a chance to be more objective as I listen to myself, and that gives me my own insights into how to solve the problem." If we constantly solve other people's problems, we rob them of an opportunity to develop their own creative insights. The most important thing we can do is simply listen, but with the whole mind.

After a few minutes of conversation, I ask the one who is listening to focus on what she feels as she listens, what thoughts pop up into her mind, even to name their partner's favorite color. It's often quite shocking for the listener to find out that she knows far more about her partner than what she heard in the words. When we listen with the whole mind and body, we experience the emotional states – the doubts, worries, happiness – that the other person is experiencing as he talks. This information is the basis for real understanding. It allows us to make better decisions, avoid unnecessary conflicts, and be clearer in our communications – all of which reduce the misunderstanding and mistrust that so often lead to stress.

For example, one of the classic conflicts between men and women is directly related to listening. When a woman is talking to her husband about the frustration of her day, he is busy trying to solve her problems. In all likelihood, all she wants is for him to really listen to her. She is quite capable of solving her problems; she simply needs him to listen to her, to give her his attention. The real message is, "Honey, I need your attention," not, "Please solve this problem for me." Meanwhile, instead of really paying attention and listening, he is busy thinking about what she should have done. Worse, out of good intentions, he will probably tell her what she should have done. This can start a chain reaction where both are not listening to the other, and both frustrated with the other for not understanding.

Learning to listen with the whole mind is not difficult to do. The best time to practice is in social situations where there is no pressure to solve problems or gain information. The next time you find yourself chatting with someone, practice using Breath Awareness while she is speaking. Don't try to solve her problems, or add to her story, simply listen. Be aware of the thoughts and feelings that pass by as you listen. You might be surprised by how much you learn about that person in just a very short period of time.

When we listen with the whole mind we become aware of enormous amounts of information that we never noticed before. This information comes to us through all our senses, not just our eyes or ears. There are times when we enter a room full of people and the tension is so thick that you could almost see it. We don't go around assessing each person individually in the room to see if he or she is angry or upset. We feel the tension the moment we enter the room. Our kinesthetic sense warns us very quickly and accurately of trouble. And while there isn't an instrument in physics that can measure that atmosphere in the room, the mind knows it instantly and accurately. This sudden recognition is a powerful form of knowledge called instinct.

## Instinctual Knowledge: Nature's Gift

Peter Drucker, one of America's top management theorists, argues that the one reason executives fail to develop is that they rely too heavily on analytic skills and never develop the ability to perceive the Gestalt, to see the whole picture at once. What he is arguing for is a greater use of instinct, a powerful form of knowledge created in the mind.

Instinct is a perceptual event, not an analytic one. Instinctual knowledge doesn't come from thinking about something, but by being aware of what already is there. It is part of the primitive urge for self-preservation and makes us aware of potentially harmful or helpful elements in the environment. We don't have to analyze or think about instinct; it is embedded within the act of perception. The greater our perceptual sensitivity, the more effectively we use instinctual knowledge.

We are most familiar with instinct as that aspect of self-preservation that warns us of danger. We must be sensitive to any dangers that we face, and the sooner and more clearly we recognize dangerous situations, the more effectively we deal with them. But it isn't at all necessary to create imaginary dangers through worry and fear. Nor need we be fearful of danger once we recognize it. As we already know, this only interferes with our ability to act effectively.

We all experience times when instinct warns us about danger. We may be driving along and, suddenly and unexplainably, we have a strong sense that we had better slow down. As we slow our speed, the driver next to us suddenly changes lanes without any warning. In fact, the danger may not be a deadly one; it may only be to our pocketbook. How often have you had the feeling you need to slow down, and sure enough, there was a speed trap right over the hill in front of you. There was no danger to you physically, but there was a negative outcome waiting for you if you weren't attentive to your instincts.

We are often very instinctual about those who are emotionally close to us – our children, other family members, or close friends. We often know, without any logical reason, when something is wrong or that something has happened to them. But because of these close emotional ties to our children, our fears interfere, and often tell us to be concerned when no real danger exists. When this happens, we use our thinking to justify actions and decisions that often create problems that are unnecessary. We may not allow our children to participate in an activity, we may spend resources on protective gear, and we may even take unnecessary actions that have drastic outcomes.

One terrible example of this was the downing of an Iranian passenger aircraft by a missile fired by a United States naval vessel. This occurred during a time when there was a military action by the United States to "protect" oil shipments in the Persian Gulf. The ship was equipped with extremely sophisticated radar and other sensing equipment. The plane could have been an attack, and under war-like circumstances, the Captain had to make a decision as to how to protect his ship. He and the other officers only had moments to analyze the technical information available to them and make the right decision. He made a logical decision based on analysis of a vast amount of technical information. Unfortunately, he made the wrong decision, and a great many innocent people died.

Peter Drucker's warning about executive failure seems particularly and sadly relevant here. We can only speculate, but the outcome might have been different if the captain had been as well trained to use his instincts as he was to use his analytic skills. Instinctual knowledge, if it had been discriminated from his concerns about his ship and crew, would have told him clearly that there was no danger even as his instruments registered the airliner. Instinctual knowledge is always accurate, but our awareness of instinctual knowledge is often hidden by, and confused with, fears, worries, and desires.

Instinctual knowledge, based on sensory input, necessarily passes through emotional pathways. Our instincts are expressed as feelings, not thoughts. And these are often very subtle, easily camouflaged by a noisy, chattering mind. Consequently, we often confuse our fears, desires, wants, and needs with instinctual knowledge. But if we pay attention we can separate our worries from true instinctual knowledge. Just as any skill, we acquire this degree of self-awareness through time and practice.

When we become skilled at listening to the whole mind, we find that instinctual feelings are quite different from fear. Like anyone else, I can worry about my children being hurt. Recently, I had to leave town on a business trip the same day my oldest daughter participated in a canoe race on the river that runs through our town. The river level was high and the current very swift because of snow melt and spring rains. Since this was only her second time in a canoe, I was concerned for her safety. I agreed to her participation, but as I drove to my destination, my mind would occasionally return to worrying about her. After nearly thirty years of practice listening to my inner voices, it was quite obvious to me that my worry was rooted in my concern for her safety, not from an instinctual response to the reality of her canoe trip. With practice, we can learn to make the subtle differentiation between what our fears are telling us and what our instincts are telling us.

Instinct also provides us with an unerring sense of timing, and allows us to be sensitive to the subtle thoughts and feelings of others. In our communication with others, we often only hear the words, and not the unspoken, subtle messages that often reflect the other person's real intent or emotional state at the moment.

Instincts tell us when to take action, and when to refrain from taking action. Instinctual knowledge can be a powerful aid in making decisions *if* we know how to use it.

Unfortunately, most of us must relearn how to really listen to ourselves and trust our senses. The sensory mind and body act like a radio receiver, constantly pulling in and responding to information. As we take in information, the unconscious part of the sensory mind processes it and immediately communicates any vital data back to the conscious mind. Our instincts, tied to the primitive drive for self-preservation, communicate to the conscious mind through the emotional message path of our feelings. If we aren't sensitive to our feelings and sensations, we can't use our instincts effectively. They often become confused with the fears and desires that are also in our unconscious.

The more skilled we are with breath awareness, the more sensitive we are to these subtle feelings and sensations. We can use any activity, even the way we walk with someone, to gain insight into their personality and the nature of our relationship with them. Try the following Walking Exercise, then practice using it when you are with people. See what your feelings tell you about that person. This exercise provides an opportunity to practice listening with your whole mind, and helps you to become more sensitive to the subtle perceptions that form the basis of instinct.

## The Walking Experiment

The next time you go for a walk by yourself, be very sensitive to how this feels. The purpose is to establish a baseline of information about your own inner feelings. Do this several times, noticing the difference in how it feels to walk in different situations, e.g., when you are in a hurry, when you are relaxed and comfortable, or when you are worried about something.

After establishing a baseline about your inner feelings, use it as a reference to study what you feel when you walk with someone else. As you walk with this person, be aware of how you walk, how you hold your body, what it feels like to walk with him. How does it differ from when you are walking by yourself? How do your feelings differ? Are you more tense or less tense? Do you have feelings of anticipation or of lowered energy? What are the differences between walking with this person and walking by yourself?

Do this with different people. How do your inner feelings and reactions differ from person to person, or from when you walk by yourself? What does this tell you about how you feel about each of these individuals, about how they react to you, or about the nature of your relationship with them? Does anything else come to your mind?

You might think you walk differently with other people because they have a different stride. But they also walk differently with you than by themselves or with someone else. After your walk, write down your feelings and any insights you might have had during your walk. Use this record to see which feelings gave you accurate information, and which ones mislead you. Doing this allows you to recognize the difference between your emotional projections and genuine instincts.

Instinct and creativity are natural resources of the sensory mind. If we learn to keep the mind clear of the noise and distortions created by fear and self-hatred, we discover an increased ability for creative problem solving, understand people more completely, find that our instincts are more refined, and have a more effective sense of timing. When we are under attack from the dragons, the noisy chatter of our mind buries these resources. The more calm and focused we become, the more information and knowledge we have, and the better choices we make. As we make better choices, we create fewer problems and less stress for ourselves.

## THE NEXT STEP: REACHING FOR THE POWER

By taking control of the sensory mind, you begin to take control of your life. You can use an almost endless number of techniques – language and reframing, imagery and affirmations, the RARE model to control conflict, or creativity techniques for effective problem solving – to redirect the creative force of the mind. The more sensitive you are to the subtle perceptual events of your mind, the easier it is to use your instincts, and the better decisions you make.

As we become more fearless and less abusive to ourselves, we must turn to the final dragon, loneliness. It takes more than balance and clarity to vanquish this dragon. We must travel beyond the busy sensory mind, beyond the limitations of habits and language, beyond the influence of emotions, to the most subtle dimension of the mind, and cross this barrier into the unlimited spiritual Self.

To solve the problem of loneliness, we must be strong enough to take on the ego, the most powerful and generalized function of the mind. To do this, we must tap into and refine the power behind the creative force of the sensory mind. We do this through our conscious ability to pay attention, to concentrate. Unless we develop and refine our inner concentration, we cannot access and use our inner strength and wisdom as conscious tools, nor can we reach into the experience of the spiritual Self. These are our next steps, to move from balance and clarity into power, and from power into strength and wisdom.

# MOVING FROM POWER TO WISDOM

*"Tell me Master, what is the great secret?"*
*"Attention," said the old man. "Attention, attention, attention!"*
—Zen Story—

Of all the different personal qualities that you bring to your work – creativity, experience, knowledge, communication skills, sense of humor, organization skills, persistence–which one would you choose as the most important? What is the one skill or quality that makes you successful in your work?

I have asked thousands of people this question, and the answers vary from person to person. Less than one-tenth of a percent ever reply, "my ability to pay attention." No matter how creative you are, how well you communicate or manage others, or how well you solve problems, the day you go to work and cannot focus your attention, you cannot do anything well. *The single most important skill that we have as a human being is the ability to focus our attention, to concentrate.* When we concentrate, we coordinate mind and body, think more clearly, work more efficiently, and achieve peak experiences. Our ability to learn and to remember depends entirely on concentration. Through concentration we alter our experience of time and space and become more sensitive to our environment. The greater our power of concentration, the more effective we are at everything we do.

We depend on this all-important power of the conscious mind for everything; yet, very few of us ever systematically train this crucial skill. Nor is concentration training part of formal education. The failure to recognize and train this critical skill is one of the greatest defects of our educational system. For most, concentration is a haphazard event. Sometimes it happens and sometimes it doesn't. Consequently, our ability to concentrate varies from day to day, even moment to moment, and whatever skill we have is accidental. And yet, it is critical to everything we do.

## MIND POWER: SYNCHRONIZED ENERGY

Most scientists, including psychiatrists and psychologists, think that the mind is nothing more than the neuronal activity of the brain. This unrealistic and limited view doesn't allow them to explain concentration, or any of the more subtle functions of the mind. What pill can you take, for instance, that will enhance concentration, increase your wisdom, give you a strong will, or allow you to experience love? But if we recognize, as the tantrics do, that the mind is a subtle field of energy, then we have powerful ways of understanding concentration, as well as all the other subtle functions, knowledge states and experiences of the mind. We also gain a clear understanding of meditation and how and why it works. More importantly, we also have effective methods to develop and enhance concentration and meditation, as well as all the other resources of the mind.

Energy is not a foreign concept to us. We live with all kinds of energy fields – sound, electrical, magnetic, bioelectric – just to name a few. In fact, as elementary physics points out to us, everything is made of energy, including us. The most common form of energy is light. Both mind and light are forms of energy, and both can be either scattered or focused. We can use light as an analogy to understand how concentration occurs in the mind.

The difference between a distracted mind and a concentrated mind is like the difference between a normal light bulb and a laser. Light consists of subatomic particles of energy called photons. These photons are given off by a light source and travel through space until they strike a surface. When they strike a surface they bounce off, illuminating the surface. In a normal light bulb, these photons scatter and weaken as they interact with other subatomic particles on their journey through space. By the time they strike our skin, they have traveled a long distance (at least it's long for subatomic particles) and they are so weak we don't feel them. Hold out your hand. Do you feel the light in the room? Highly doubtful! In fact, if someone walked into the room claiming, "I feel the light!" the first thing you do is button up the pocket that has your wallet in it.

But if you put your hand right next to the light bulb, the photons are strong and cohesive enough to cause heat when they strike the skin. Or, if you take a magnifying glass on a sunny day, you can collect and organize enough photons that you can produce heat with them, and burn a piece of paper or start a fire. The bigger and more powerful your magnifying glass, the more photons you can collect and organize, and the more heat you can generate.

If we collect and synchronize all the photons from the light, compress them into a cohesive flow, and make them move in the same direction at the same time, we create a light called a laser. Depending on how we build the laser, these synchronized photons become a light so powerful that it can penetrate steel plate, or so delicate and precise that it is used for eye surgery. The power of the light depends on synchronized energy. If we can synchronize photons and create a powerful light, why can't we synchronize our *mentons* (just for fun, let's call the individual units of mental energy "mentons") and create a laser-like mind?

As we interact with the environment, our mentons (mental energy) are modified into different forms – thoughts, images, and sensations (feelings) – which we experience as knowledge. These patterns stimulate others and the mind constantly moves from thought to thought, from image to image. The more distractions we have, the more difficult it is to keep focused on any one thing for a period of time. Recall one of those days when everything was falling apart, and everyone was demanding something different. Our thoughts ran here and there and we couldn't keep our focus and think clearly. We were so distracted we couldn't get anything done. At the end of the day, we were stressed out!

If we could take an energy picture of our mind on that day, it would probably look something like Figure 8.1.a. We have mentons going in all directions, with very little cohesiveness in the flow of our mind's energy. Since we couldn't organize our mental energy, we couldn't organize our work or anything else. We are no longer *homo sapiens,* we have become *homo haphazardous!* And remember, every thought has an impact on the body. Mind and body were no longer coordinated, and it's no wonder that we felt stressed out.

But then, something comes along and grabs our attention. At least on a conscious level, we organize our mentons, and direct the mind's energy toward whatever attracted our attention. We can see in Figure 8.1.b how the energy is beginning to organize and flow in a synchronized manner. Since we are just beginning to pay attention, we can still be easily distracted. We don't have enough synchronized energy flow to be very strong. As you can see, the energy in the unconscious mind is still fairly disorganized.

But as we become more fascinated by the object of our attention, more and more of the total mind becomes synchronized. This is reflected in Figure 8.1.c. Now we have greater synchrony and a stronger mind. At this point we have begun to concentrate. The more synchronized the energy, the stronger our concentration. Notice in Figure 8.1.c that the line between conscious mind and unconscious mind is broken and no longer solid. That indicates a greater flow of information back and forth between our conscious perceptions and our unconscious knowledge. Since the conscious mind is more organized, sensory information is less distorted by emotions and other distractions. Consequently, the input into the unconscious mind has greater clarity and is more useful to the unconscious. More importantly, the information flow from the unconscious is facilitated, and we have greater insight, solve problems more effectively, and feel more balanced. And, you know from your own experience that the more concentrated you are, the more effective you are at whatever you are doing. This is because of the increased coordination and communication between the conscious and unconscious mind.

When we refine attention, we create concentration. When we refine concentration with a focus on an inner point, we create meditation. Figure 8.1. d shows the whole mind synchrony that characterizes our meditation. The only interruptions of the synchrony are subtle breaks in the unconscious mind. The conscious mind is totally synchronized. At this point, the barrier between conscious and unconscious mind almost disappears, and the communication between conscious and unconscious is unhampered. As we discuss later, this refined inner concentration, characterized by a high degree of synchrony, is the defining characteristic of meditation. This powerful state of refined inner concentration opens the subtle resources of the mind to conscious awareness.

When we refine meditation, we create a very special condition of the mind where we achieve complete synchrony of the energy. Figure 8.1.e shows a condition of perfect synchrony. Even subtle distractions have been resolved. This perfection characterizes what is known in the Western world as a mystical experience, and in tantra yoga as *samadhi*. The mind has achieved a state of perfect unitary consciousness in which the entire mind field is synchronized. At this point, awareness transcends the mind and we experience the spiritual Self as our true identity. Just one experience of this unique, powerful reality is life changing. And as we shall see later, this spiritual experience brings about the end of loneliness.

These energy conditions of the mind flow from one to the other as we refine our ability to focus attention. As the mind becomes more synchronized and less distracted, we perceive more effectively, think more clearly, and understand more completely. In other words, the greater our power of concentration, the more powerful the mind. We solve problems easily, we engage others more effectively, and at the end of the day, we feel satisfied and ready to be with our family. The more cohesive our mental energy, the better we do and feel. From the very beginning there are powerful benefits to refining the power of concentration. The greater our skill to concentrate, the more effective and penetrating the mind becomes.

## Relaxation: The Deepest Level

The first and most immediate benefit of concentration is enhanced inner balance. As we concentrate, we minimize the cross-currents of the conscious and unconscious mind. This reduces demands on the body that, in turn, creates a deeply relaxed body. The stronger the concentration, the greater the coordination between mind and body, and the deeper our physiological balance and harmony. This is why the deepest level of relaxation is created through concentration.

One of the most important relaxation exercises is called "61 Points." It creates a deep and profound state of relaxation, which is why we use it to control high blood pressure. No other relaxation exercise can reduce vascular tension as completely. In this exercise, you concentrate on 61 points within the body, visualizing a blue star or blue flame at each point. If you have difficulty visualizing, concentrate on feeling a point of warmth at each point. The exercise is very systematic and easy to learn. Figure 8.2 shows the 61 points, and detailed instructions for taping are provided in Appendix D.

## Figure 8.1

**a: DISTRACTED MIND**

**b: PAYING ATTENTION**

Mind energies scattered as the mind reacts to any stimulus; the body in stress as it reacts to mind chatter; the subtle skills of the mind are hidden by the noise of the chatter.

Mind energies begin to synchronize and focus; less chatter, more awareness of immediate environment; body less pressured; thoughts have more clarity.

**c: CONCENTRATION**

**d: MEDITATION**

Mind energies more synchronized with greater focus; body becomes calm; mind skills more available, greater clarity of thought; intuition more available; enhanced perceptual sensitivity.

Mind completely focused; concentration effortless and flowing; enhanced awareness of environment and inner skills; unconscious mind and its power available to conscious access; body in deep, restful condition.

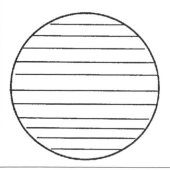

**e: UNITARY CONSCIOUSNESS**

Total concentration; super state of awareness; mystical knowledge and experience; complete mind/body consciousness; all resources of mind available for conscious use.

## Expanded Awareness: The Foundation for Choice

It's easy to see how concentration creates relaxation and balance. The more focused we are, the fewer instructions are sent to the body, and the more relaxed we become. But relaxation is only the tip of the iceberg. An even greater benefit of concentration lies in its ability to expand the power of the conscious mind through enhanced awareness.

Recall from Chapter 3 that the power of the mind lies in the unconscious mind, and that the conscious mind is usually only an excuse maker for what is decided by the unconscious. You might also recall that the one tool of the conscious mind is the ability to direct attention. Concentration is a conscious, intentional action. Through concentration, the conscious mind accesses the power functions that lie in the unconscious. Once we are aware of these functions, through practice we can turn them into conscious skills and the conscious mind now becomes a powerful tool. Daydreams, trance states, subliminal learning, even hypnosis have limited value. They do not synchronize mental energy and they do not strengthen the conscious mind. Only by consciously focusing our attention do we achieve this.

There are any number of reasons why we pay attention to something, but they can all be subsumed under two headings: interest and fear. We pay attention when something interests us – we expect to find pleasure or avoid pain, earn money, solve a problem, meet someone interesting – the list is endless. As Figure 8.3 (page 230) illustrates, when we are interested in something, our awareness expands, and we become more sensitive to everything related to the object of our attention. The more interested we become, the more intensely we pay attention, and the more synchronized the mind's energy becomes. As the mind becomes stronger, our awareness continues to expand, and we find even more to be interested in. We initiate a positive cycle of interest, awareness, focus, and more interest, leading to deeper and deeper states of concentration, increased awareness, knowledge, and skill.

For instance, writing is part of my profession. When I start an article, or work on a book, it takes me a while to get into what I am doing. If I get distracted in the first half-hour or so, it takes longer. But if I can really focus on my work, and don't get distracted by a phone call or someone in my family asking questions, I become more and more involved. After an hour of focused work, it takes much more to distract me. My writing begins to flow, I make connections and think of examples more easily, and I am much more productive. I become more and more fascinated by the subject, and more interested in expressing my thoughts as clearly as I can. Once I become really focused, even my breaks become productive, creative times when I let my mind explore alternatives and create new ways of expressing my subject. At the end of the day, I am in a great mood, ready to interact with my family or do whatever else is on the agenda.

On the other hand, whatever we fear (or whatever we worry about) also grabs our attention. But fear has a dramatically different impact on the mind. As you can see in Figure 8.3, fear focuses our attention, but it constricts our awareness. The greater the fear, the more we become fixated on the problem, and we find it harder and harder to come up with creative solutions and alternatives. We suffer from "tunnel vision" and all we can see or think of is the problem itself.

## 61 POINTS EXERCISE

Concentrate on either a blue flame or a blue star at 61 different points in or on the body. Choose one or the other, but don't switch them around. The star should look like an actual star in the sky, while the flame should look like the small blue flame used in natural-gas commercials on television. The color blue provides a restful focus for the mind. Do not substitute colors; doing so will change the effect. If you cannot picture any light at all, concentrate on a point of warmth, about the diameter of a pencil.

1. Begin by clearly deciding to remain awake. Then lie on your back on a pad or carpeted floor. Place your feet about twelve to eighteen  inches apart, and your arms and hands slightly away from the body, palms facing up. Use a small pillow to support the curve of your neck.

2. Concentrate on smooth, even diaphragmatic breathing. Picture your body like a hollow reed, breathing as if you are inhaling through your toes and filling your body with breath to the top of your head. Then exhale back down to the toes. Continue this until you can feel as if your whole body is expanding when you inhale and contracting when you exhale. (This is the Sweeping Breath Exercise, page 190).

3. Visualize a blue star or flame at each of the 61 points as shown in the accompanying diagram. Begin with the first point and let the star or flame be as clear, as small, and as perfect as your mind will allow it to be. Hold the image in your mind for ten to fifteen seconds. (As you become more skilled, gradually increase the time to at least twenty seconds.) Then visualize this star or flame at each of the other sixty points in the body as shown in the accompanying figure, focusing on only one point at a time and spending the same amount of time on each one. Follow the diagram and instructions exactly, as this is a very precise exercise.

4. Finish with the Sweeping Breath, and be aware of your body. Before opening your eyes, slowly bring your hands up, being aware of every movement from the inside out. Then, holding the palms of your hands about four inches from your face, open your eyes to the palms of your hands. After your eyes are open, you can bring the hands back to your side, and get up whenever you are ready.

## Figure 8.2

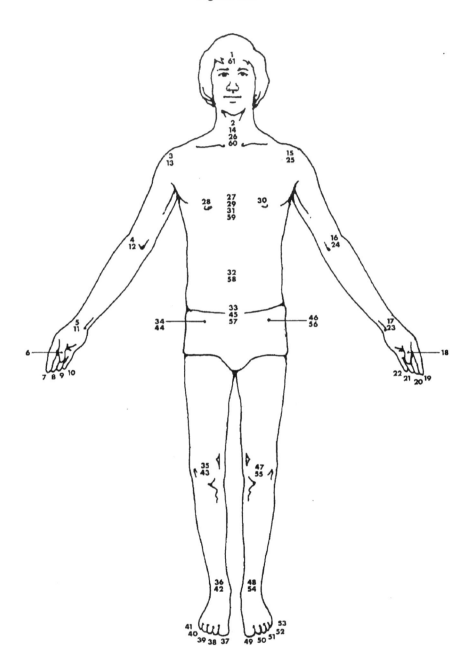

All of us experience times when we were so worried about something that we just couldn't seem to find a way out. Then someone else says, "Why don't you do this?" The answer to our difficulties was right before our eyes, but we couldn't see it because our awareness was so limited to the problem

Fear literally destroys concentration. While the conscious mind becomes very focused, the unconscious mind becomes a disaster. Instead of calming the mind, fear intensifies the emotional cross-currents in the unconscious mind. Instead of synchronizing the subtle energies of the mind, fear disrupts them, preventing genuine concentration. We end up with pseudo-concentration – the conscious mind is focused, but the unconscious mind is increasingly disorganized. In pseudo-concentration, the body becomes tense; thinking is clouded and grows more rigid; we behave in compulsive and erratic ways; and even our physical movements become awkward, jerky, and unbalanced.

The greater the fear, the more limited our awareness, the stronger the fight-or-flight alarm reaction, and the greater our stress and unhappiness. If you want to damage your effectiveness, or anyone's productivity, create fear in the workplace. Fear is a mind-killer. It creates a thousand little deaths, and each death inhibits abilities, damages health, limits creativity, and takes away joy.

While not as dramatic, self-hatred is just as destructive to our ability to concentrate. Self-hatred prevents concentration by reducing the energy available to concentrate. Depression and withdrawal significantly reduce the energy available for concentration to occur. The more depressed we feel, the harder it is to think about anything, let alone do it properly. We get stuck in a vast, gray, and formless world, unable to focus on any useful task.

By eliminating fear and self-hatred and being interested in what we are doing, we create a positive energy condition for ourselves. The greater our concentration, the more calm and sensitive we become, and the greater the power of the mind to penetrate and understand the realities we face. The bridge between the resources of our inner world and the challenges and demands of the outer world is secure. The greater our awareness, the more effective we become.

### Intuition: Developing Inner Wisdom

Through concentration we access and command the deeper, more powerful inner resources. Concentration is particularly important for the most powerful and useful of the three knowledge states, intuition. As we refine our inner concentration and expand our inner awareness, we access the power of discrimination, the fourth dimension of the personality. You will recall from Chapter 1 that discrimination is the mind's ability to discern subtle cause/effect relationships, and understand the true nature of things. In tantra yoga science, this dimension is referred to as *buddhi,* or pure intellect.

The power of discrimination is subtle, involving the core of how the mind forms knowledge. Although discrimination is the basis for rational analysis, it is not an analytic function. Pure discrimination is a process of discernment, or illumination. This dimension of the mind is free of the limitations of time/space and pain/pleasure that shape the patterns of the sensory mind. The power of discrimination and the knowledge it forms is unaffected by conditioning or habits. It is also free of the powerful influence of the emotions. Because of this, its voice is subtle and quiet, easily buried beneath the noisier, more demanding distractions of our habits and emotional reactions.

When we use the power of discrimination with the sensory function, we think things out, analyze, and make conscious decisions. The more skillfully we use our discrimination, the greater our capacity for rational thought, and the more clearly we think about things.

The real power of the pure intellect, however, lies in the fact that it is not dependent on sensory information and its limitations. Through discrimination, we discern subtle critical elements as they now exist, as well as their outcomes. We experience this as intuition, the ability to "see into the future." This is not fortune telling, nor is it intelligent guessing, but a *clear recognition* of subtle cause/effect relationships. This is the basis of visionary skills so highly regarded in business, in politics, in every human endeavor.

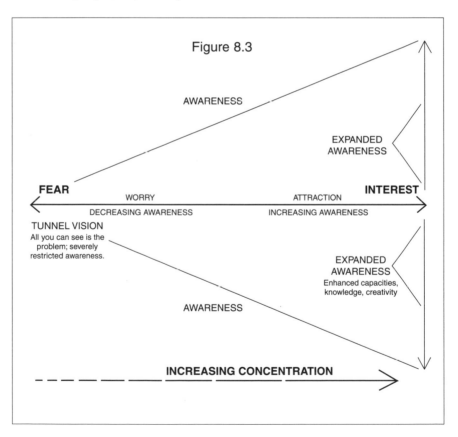

Figure 8.3

There are many different techniques to develop intuition, and all depend on the ability to concentrate. When we pay attention to something, it is as though we've inserted a disc into a computer to copy a program on it. If extraneous data, such as a computer virus, slips in during copying, it interferes with our ability to run the program. When we are distracted, we add extraneous data to our inner programs. The more distractions we have, the more difficult it is to form accurate knowledge. The more concentrated we are, the more perfect the knowledge.

Simply collecting information does not lead to intuitive insight. We need focused involvement – concentration – to generate knowledge. *The quality of our concentration is far more important than the amount of information we gather.* Studies of executive decision-making clearly showed that successful executives made decisions based on far less information than executives who aren't so successful. Likewise, studies of scientific insight show that reverie and daydreaming are more important than the amount of information. Information is useful, but more important is our ability to discriminate and comprehend intrinsic connections and cause/effect relationships. To quote Albert Einstein, "There comes a leap in consciousness, call it intuition or what you will, the solution comes to you and you don't know how or why. ... The truly valuable thing is the intuition."

An essential element to using intuition skillfully is the ability to witness the subtle thoughts and images in the mind. This is called reflective attention. Letting the mind focus in an untroubled manner on the problem and then clearing the mind completely allows the unconscious processes to form knowledge. Learning to listen, to focus without strain, without the struggle of "trying," takes a degree of skill. The more relaxed you are and the less troubled your mind, the greater your ability to concentrate, and the more sensitive you are to your own innate intuitive wisdom.

Along with reflective attention, the following crucial elements help develop and enhance intuition:

• **Self-Awareness:** Perceptual sensitivity and skill: the ability to quiet the thought processes and become aware of the more subtle skills of the mind and body. Through this we gain sensitivity to subtle feelings and thoughts as sources of information, and an enhanced awareness of inner strength and knowledge.

• **Fearlessness:** a calm, tranquil mind, free of fears and anxieties; non-judgmental attitude, skilled in the practice of non-attachment. Genuine self-confidence.

• **Concentration:** Committed, fully involved and concentrated on the task; inner concentration leads to direct awareness of spiritual knowledge; external concentration leads to task absorption, visionary skills, and enhanced performance.

• **Playfulness:** Willing to experiment, learn from mistakes; creative, open to new ideas, new ways of doing things.

• **Incubation Periods:** Stillness is very necessary for inner awareness and developing intuitive knowledge. A busy and/or a stressed mind is rarely, if ever, intuitive.

• **Flexibility:** Physical, mental, and emotional flexibility lead to enhanced intuitive knowledge and personal effectiveness.

• **Openness, Receptivity, Courage, and Love:** Respecting oneself and others; compassion; a willingness to listen and learn from others; a sense of humility.

The Insight Exercise that follows is a very useful technique for developing intuitive insight. Like many exercises of this type, it involves becoming relaxed and being receptive to whatever your mind presents.

## Things to Watch For

Becoming skilled with intuition takes some practice. You can be misled by subtle fears or desires, mistaking them for insight, or you can have an intelligent hunch, which is still not using your intuition. Be aware that the following factors can mislead you:

• **Not everything that we think, imagine, or feel is an intuition.** A close friend of mind woke up with a clear thought about betting on a particular horse. He kept thinking about that horse the entire morning. Finally, he rushed over to the track just in time to bet on the horse. He lost. Not everything that comes to the conscious mind is wisdom. Maybe it's just a desire, some need or want. This is particularly difficult to distinguish when you are just beginning to develop your intuitive sense. As my friend discovered, the mind is quite capable of fooling us. You can quickly train yourself to differentiate between real intuition (and instinctual knowledge) and everything else by taking notes. Every time you think that you have an intuition, write it down. Note everything you observe about intuition – how you felt; whether it was an image, thought, or feeling; what was your reaction; how strong or clear it seemed. Then, later on, indicate whether or not it was accurate, and note any benefit you gained from the insight. This forces you to pay attention, and it's attention that develops sensitivity to genuine insight.

• **Imagery may not be clear.** Because the images that come from our unconscious are almost always symbolic, they must be interpreted and understood in context. Always cross-check your understanding of your insights by checking out how they feel to your body. Was the insight comfortable or uncomfortable? Was there an emotional component? If so, be careful. True insight is free of emotional content, and feels like a simple statement of fact. We may get excited after the insight, but the insight itself is characteristically clear. However, we can often validate the thoughts and images the mind generates by consulting our feelings about them.

• **Intuition does not always give a complete answer.** Often, intuition only points us in the right direction. We will not always know how things will turn out. But if we continue to pay attention as we act on our insights, we self-correct and take advantage of new insights and developments. Periodically check your feelings and thoughts about your direction. This helps keep you on the right track, even when your intuition is incomplete and partial.

It isn't difficult to develop your power of discrimination and intuition. It simply takes practice. A number of excellent books, such as Philip Goldberg's *The Intuitive Edge,* and Frances Vaughan's *Awakening Intuition,* provide a variety of techniques to help access intuition.

## DEVELOPING CONCENTRATION

There are a number of ways to develop and enhance concentration. One way to start is by using the body to train the mind. There are good reasons for this. First, we are usually more familiar and more comfortable working with the body than the mind. Secondly, the body needs exercise and stretching to minimize muscle tension and maximize flexibility. At the same time we are minimizing stress in the body, we can be training the mind in concentration. Again, Eastern traditions lead the way in using the body to develop concentration.

Traditional schools of martial arts, such as karate, taijiquan, and aikido, use the body and breathing to train concentration skills. Traditional approaches focus on self-development through concentration and self-discipline. The goals are self-respect and respect for others. A genuine martial artist is guided by the principle, "Never fight; but if forced to fight, never lose." The training develops mind and body as a way of eliminating fear, and developing awareness of the underlying unity of life.

The most sophisticated approach to using the body to train the mind is hatha yoga. The postures are designed to work with the body to expand awareness of both mind and body. It systematically proceeds from physical exercises to breathing exercises to mental exercises – all to achieve a higher level of awareness. In particular, the balancing postures, which require your full attention to accomplish, help refine your concentration. Be careful, the current vogue is to teach hatha yoga as power yoga, or aerobic exercise. Unfortunately, most yoga teachers, even those who are "certified," know hatha yoga only as a physical culture, and are not knowledgeable or skilled in how to use hatha as a tool for the mind.

The best way to develop concentration is to use what is most natural to the mind. That's why Breath Awareness is such a useful tool. Sitting quietly, focusing on the feeling of the breath, and not allowing your attention to wander is a very simple way of training concentration. We are using the kinesthetic sense to train the mind to be one-pointed. You don't have to sit still to use Breath Awareness to help you focus. The practical usefulness of this tool is that anyone can use it anytime or anywhere to refocus the mind.

When Sam was only twelve, he learned to use his breathing to focus his mind during basketball. Like his two older sisters, Sam loved to play basketball. Very early in his life, Sam was taught how to use his breathing to focus his attention. When he was five years old, he also began training in Washin-Ryu Karate.

Because of his karate training, Sam has a great deal of poise and balance. He is an aggressive player, and when he plays basketball, he is a good defensive player, and rebounds well. His shooting skills, however, took a bit longer to develop.

About halfway through his eighth-grade basketball season, Sam discovered that he could use breathing and concentration to improve shooting foul shots. Normally, he would make about fifty percent of his foul shots. But after his discovery, when he came to the line you could see him briefly close his eyes, focus on Breath Awareness, and then concentrate on the ball going through. His foul shooting average shot up to eighty-five percent. This change gave Sam a great deal of confidence in his ability to solve any problem through concentration. He

---

## INSIGHT EXERCISE

Use this simple exercise after you have already come to some conclusions, but are not sure which one would be best. The key is to empty the mind completely, allowing your conscious effort to be submerged into the imagery of the exercise, clearing the mind of all conscious thoughts and concerns about the problem. The quietness of the mind will allow a greater wisdom and a new perspective to develop.

Sit back comfortably in your chair, closing your eyes and relaxing as completely as you can. Let your breath become smooth and even, and picture your forehead as smooth as a piece of silk. Now visualize a beautiful blue mountain lake, surrounded by evergreens and snow-capped mountains. Focus on the blueness of the lake, until you feel that you are completely surrounded or submerged into that blueness. Let yourself experience the depth, quietness, and wisdom of this ancient lake.

Now focus your attention on the base of the largest snow-capped mountain. Imagine yourself becoming that mountain emerging from the lake. Your seat is the base of the mountain. Slowly bring your attention up to the top of your head as you visualize yourself at the snow-capped peak. Allow your arms to be the slope and sides of the mountain. Experience the strength of the stone of the mountain, and the great breadth of vision that can be seen from the top of the mountain. Let yourself become the mountain, with the deep blue lake before you. Allow yourself to feel the depth, quietness, and wisdom of the lake and the strength and vision of the mountain.

Spend at least a few minutes just enjoying the stability, tranquility, and peace of the mountain and the blue lake before you. After a few minutes, gently bring your attention to the problem you face, and examine the different choices you see. The best choice will most likely feel that way to you. An obvious choice may be apparent, but if not, choose the one that seems to fit with the strength, vision, stability, and peace of your mind.

used this same concentration to teach himself to play guitar, become skilled in tennis, and earn the district scholar-athlete award in high school.

We can also use vision to train concentration. Since we depend so heavily on the sense of sight, it is a natural tool for training the mind. In yoga science, this is called *trataka,* or gazes. When we hold a gaze, the eyes are not allowed to move off the target object or even blink, and the body is very still. We focus all of our attention on the object, ignoring all other thoughts and sensations, until our eyes begin to water, or concentration is involuntarily broken by blinking. At that point, we can close our eyes and rest, or visualize the object internally.

One of simplest exercises is a candle gaze (page 236). The human mind is naturally attracted to light. We can use this natural attraction to strengthen concentration. We can either focus directly on the flame, or gaze at a reflection of the flame in a mirror. Gazing at a direct light creates a heating sensation in the eyes, while an indirect or reflected light creates a cooling sensation. If you are light sensitive, you may wish to use reflected light. The goal is to slowly increase your capacity to gaze at the light without blinking or distraction for increasingly longer periods of time. Don't wear glasses or contacts when you practice a gaze.

## MEDITATION: FROM POWER TO WISDOM

Where there is peace and meditation, there is neither anxiety nor doubt.
—St. Francis of Assisi—

Concentration leads to a powerful mind. But even a powerful mind can be tormented by loneliness and grief. We cannot escape from ourselves through power, but we can use it to discover the spiritual Self. We must take the final step and find a way to live in today's world with inner strength and wisdom – a way in which we can stay balanced, use our power to fulfill our obligations and desires, and access our wisdom to create the joy, peace, and fulfillment that we have always known is possible.

We are citizens of two worlds: the external reality and our inner reality. To be effective in the world without destroying ourselves in the process, we must bridge these two worlds successfully. We can do this if we develop inner strength and utilize our deepest resources. But we must use the whole mind, not just part. Once we know how to create inner balance and power, we must continue to expand our awareness, and discover our more subtle resources – intrinsic wisdom, genuine self-confidence, and the unlimited power of the spiritual Self – and become skilled in using the innate powers of the spirit. If we are skilled only with the resources of the body and mind, we remain incomplete human beings. It is the spiritual Self that completes life and makes it whole.

Meditation is the bridge between our internal and external realities. It is the finest tool we can use to develop concentration, and awareness of our inner strengths and the resources of the mind. Meditation is a practical, systematic method based on refined concentration that allows us to:

- become aware of and understand all dimensions of our personality;
- understand our environment completely, without emotional bias;
- eliminate and prevent inner conflicts, distortions, and disturbances;
- create an alert, tranquil mind that is fearless, loving, joyful, and compassionate.

Meditation is not an act of magic, but a process to access and refine the resources of the mind and access the power of the spiritual Self. Meditation is systematic, unfailing, and developmental. It is a process of inner growth, and does not happen overnight. If you put the in the time and effort, you will develop and command the power of the mind. With it, you will achieve whatever you choose, and do it without creating unhappiness, stress, and disease.

## CANDLE GAZE EXERCISE

Do this exercise in a dark, quiet room. The candle should be an even-burning dinner candle, placed approximately an arm's length in front of you. The flame should be level with your eyes so you can hold your head steady and gaze straight ahead. To use reflected light, place the candle behind you so that you see the reflection in a mirror directly in front of you, at the proper height.

1. Sit quietly, and for a few moments close your eyes and focus on Breath Awareness to clear your mind and steady your concentration.

2. Open your eyes and gaze without blinking at this steady flame (or reflection). If you blink within a few seconds after beginning the gaze, ignore it and continue to gaze. Focus your attention on the flame, ignoring all other thoughts, sensations, and feelings. Keep your gaze steady and unblinking.

3. When you blink, or your eyes begin to water, stop the external gaze. Close your eyes and visualize the flame in the center of your mind as long as you comfortably can. The smaller, clearer, and more defined the image of the flame, the better the training for concentration. Don't worry if at first the image of the flame is undefined or vague. With practice, the image will become clearer and more defined. By internalizing the image, you change the exercise from a concentration exercise (external orientation) to a meditation exercise (internal orientation).

Keep a daily practice, and let your capacity slowly expand until you can hold the external gaze for at least twenty minutes. If at any time, you get a headache, reduce the time you spend gazing. Headaches are an indication that you are pushing too hard and going beyond your natural capacity. After reaching this twenty-minute capacity, maintain at least a weekly practice of twenty minutes. You might notice an increase in both the intensity of your dreams and your ability to recall them.

## Misperceptions and Misapprehensions

In the past twenty-five years, much of the silliness first attached to the term "meditation" has dissipated. Still, many people think of meditation as strange and foreign, and are misinformed about what it is, prejudiced about its origins and ignorant of its power and simplicity. They often associate it with a foreign religion, or funny-looking people who shave their heads and wear orange-colored clothes, or misguided people trying to float in the air. Others simply confuse meditation with hypnosis, or closing the eyes and fantasizing about New Age angels, guides, and other spirits. Unfortunately, many of those who practice, and even teach meditation, have only fragmentary knowledge about it.

One of the most common mistakes is to confuse meditation and religion. Meditation is not a religion, nor is it a philosophy. It is a tool that has been used by all major religions, including Christianity, as well as by agnostics and atheists. Likewise, meditation has no intrinsic link with any particular culture. Meditative techniques are found in all areas of the world. Eastern methods, particularly yoga science, have been more completely and systematically developed than others, and thus they often serve as models.

Many people mistakenly think of meditation as a kind of trance state or hypnosis. It is neither, although all three share one basic characteristic – you must be relaxed to do them. The similarity stops there. In trance states, you lose awareness as you surrender to a sensual experience. In order to be hypnotized, you must focus your attention on a suggestion (either your own or the hypnotist's) and comply with it. Unfortunately, most of us are already hypnotized, in the sense that we are always following others' suggestions (we call it peer pressure or advertising).

Meditation, on the other hand, is a process of *conscious observation,* a condition of heightened awareness; it is self-directed and can never be other-directed. Concentration on a single point such as the breath, or a mantra should not be confused with suggestion, for suggestion implies action taken. Observation means only observing – there is no judgment or action. The difference between suggestion and observation is like the difference between watching a particular horse (observation) and getting up on the horse and riding away with it (hypnosis), or focusing on the pleasure of the ride (trance). They are different actions, and they have radically different outcomes.

In hypnosis you surrender control to the suggestion, and in trance, you surrender to the feelings. In meditation you expand conscious self-control and awareness. Research shows that there are no significant changes, either physically or psychologically, after the long-term practice of hypnosis, other than what you can achieve by simply practicing relaxation.* On the other hand, if

---

* Changes resulting from hypnosis are specific to the hypnotic suggestion only, and are not lasting. This includes the use of hypnosis as a part of therapy, for in this case hypnotherapy is part of the overall process that induces personality changes.

you practice meditation over a period of time, you significantly reduce the physiological parameters of stress and significantly increase psychological maturity.

New hypnotic techniques now blend observation and hypnosis and appear to approach the meditative state. However, if suggestion is followed, it is still hypnosis and thus limited in scope and power. Only when you change your perspective from involvement with the hypnotic suggestion to pure observation does meditation occur.

Meditation and drug usage are not at all compatible. So-called teachers who advocate the use of psychedelic drugs to enhance meditation are ignorant of the meditative process. Drugs don't expand awareness; they explode it, and the collapse that inevitably follows leads to confusion rather than clarity. Meditation is a systematic, controlled expansion of consciousness that takes place totally under your own control. Drugs are antithetical to the development of self-control and lead ultimately to internal chaos.

Another common misconception concerns the lifestyle necessary to do meditation. First of all, meditation does not create instantaneous personality change. Change occurs naturally as we become healthier and more mature, and we make better choices for ourselves. There is no meditative profession or lifestyle, but there are lifestyles that prevent you from meditating. These also prevent you from growing in any direction. Meditation is as useful to the executive as it is to the plumber, as it is to the housewife, as it is to the student. Meditation is a tool; it is not a way of life. Everyone can benefit from it. Not everyone will (or can) utilize the same form of meditation, but there are many different methods – and, for the most part, they all work. This tool can be adapted to any personality with any reasonable lifestyle, at any time.

Finally, there is confusion between meditation and certain brain wave patterns. Many people, especially research professionals, associate meditation with particular brain wave patterns, such as alpha or alpha/theta waves. Researchers identify certain brain waves that arise when you sit quietly with your eyes closed, focusing your attention inwardly. The psychological states of reverie produced during alpha and theta wave, as beneficial as they are, are not necessarily part of meditation. They are generally desirable states, associated with creativity, inner balance and peacefulness, and produce healthy and beneficial outcomes. But meditation is not a psychological state or a physiological event; it is a *conscious process* which leads to a fourth state of consciousness beyond the three familiar states of waking, dreaming, and sleeping.

Highly skilled meditators can meditate in any of the three states, including deep sleep. Meditation is a process that involves expanded awareness and a condition of high potential energy created through concentration. These conditions are not dependent on any particular brain wave pattern.

Recently, researchers Andrew Newberg and Eugene G. d'Aquili at the University of Pennsylvania studied which parts of the brain are active or not active during meditation by measuring blood flow. They found that frontal lobes which determine concentration are more active during meditation, and that the parietal lobe becomes "a quiet oasis of inactivity – a fact that could explain the borderless spiritual communion felt by the faithful for the millennia." The issue is not about whether or not physiological changes occur; they certainly do, and are expected. The issue lies in how we interpret these facts, in where we assign the causal factors.

Most scientists want to believe that the brain is the cause of the feelings of oneness. The great masters say, "No, the brain simply does what is necessary to achieve what has been decided by the mind." Just as there are different conditions that constitute meditation, there are different conditions or levels of *samadhi*, different experiences of the Divine. Brain conditions will necessarily change relative to these different conditions. We should explore all these conditions to understand more completely the role of the brain in meditation.

## Meditation as Refined Concentration: Creating the Laser Mind

So what is meditation? In three words, it is *refined inner concentration*. If you understand why concentration is so important, it is easy to see why meditation is such a critical tool. By intensifying concentration, we create an even more powerful mind. As we refine concentration, we synchronize more and more of the mind's energy until we are deeply concentrated. Now the mind becomes like a laser, burning away any remaining distractions. Any distractions left are inactive, and no longer influence the mind.

We make the conscious mind strong through the discipline of deep concentration. We have seen how unconscious emotional habits and patterns can create fear and other problems for us. But they have little power against the "laserstrong" power of a trained conscious mind. This is the consequence of the practice of meditation. It takes away the power from the habit function, and through enhanced awareness, gives it back to you as the ability to choose.

Refined concentration is not easily achieved. Nor is it something that anyone else can do for you. Like any skill, it takes effort and practice. But neither is it something magical or esoteric. It is practical, available to anyone who puts forth the effort, and requires only sincere effort and the right techniques. It does not require a college degree, a particular religious belief or subservience to a teacher.

## The Elements of Meditation

Relaxation, often confused with meditation, is only the first step toward meditation. It is a very important step, however, for unless mind and body are relaxed, concentration becomes difficult, and meditation is impossible. Of course, the more concentrated you become, the more relaxed you become.

Proper breathing is another critical element in meditation. We know that we must breathe with the diaphragm if we want to balance the autonomic nervous system and eliminate stress. But there are other subtle aspects of breathing that are important if we want to refine concentration. We must also create balance between the two hemispheres of the brain. This balance is indicated by an even, steady flow of breath through both nostrils. Recall from Chapter 6 that ordinarily we breath primarily through one nostril, and that nostril dominance shifts on a cyclic basis. When the flow of breath is even through both nostrils, we create balance between the two hemispheres of our brain. This balance is necessary if we are to deepen concentration. We accomplish this through the application of *sushumna* mentioned in Chapter 6. Without this balance, meditation cannot occur. With a little effort, we can consciously control the flow of air. The Alternate-Nostril Breathing Exercise given in Chapter 6 develops the ability to consciously control nostril balance.

After we calm the body, stabilize the breath, and establish neurological balance, the next step is to calm and focus the mind through inner concentration. This final element in the process of developing meditation is often mistaken for meditation itself. In yoga science, inner concentration is the necessary stage before meditation, and if properly developed, leads to meditation.*

Most of us can concentrate to some degree if we focus on an object in the external world. We can concentrate on our work, our play, or a book, particularly if it captures our interest. But if we have to concentrate on an internal process, most of us quickly we find that we have little capacity for it. We are a determinedly materialistic culture, focused almost exclusively on what the senses tell us.

Our culture is not familiar with the inner world, nor does it encourage much exploration. Our education and training involve the external world of facts, figures, and objects. We are taught to study the objects of our senses but not the filter mechanism – the mind in which that sensory data is collected, organized ,and given meaning. Science itself is deterministic and materialistic. Its greatest weakness is that it systematically and purposefully excludes the subject of cognizance, literally the fact that all data, all theory, all knowledge – literally, all meaning – is achieved through and by the human mind. As Shimon Malin points out in *Nature Loves to Hide*, this objectification is the Achilles' heel of science. It is no wonder that we can focus easily on the external world, but find it difficult to do so inwardly.

When we first try to meditate, we find we have very little skill. Our attention is pulled here and there by competing thoughts and feelings, and we seem to have very little conscious control. For instance, if we are worried about something, our mind returns to the problem over and over, generating even more fear. When we want to sleep, our mind chatters on and on, preventing us from falling asleep. The harder we try to focus, the more insistent the disturbances become.

---

* Most of the research on "meditative" states has really been made on inner concentration, not meditation. This does not deny the usefulness of the research, it only points out an incomplete state of knowledge about meditation.

All of us suffer from this monkey mind to some degree. Very few of us have the ability to choose the focus of our mind, to choose what and when to think. As a consequence, very few experience genuine tranquility and calmness.

Remember, control doesn't mean that we suppress or repress our thoughts. This only leads to even greater dis-ease and stress. Real control is the ability to consciously choose which thoughts we think, to use our emotional energy in the way that benefits us, and direct the activities of the brain to achieve what we wish to achieve. As we saw in Chapter 7, we began this process of choice by controlling the inner dialogue of the mind.

But the ability to choose depends on how aware we are of our habits and other patterns in the mind. This awareness comes from the ability to focus attention, to concentrate on an inner point. If we aren't skilled at inner concentration, we have little ability to choose which thoughts and feelings we want. Our choices are made by our unconscious habits and emotional reactions. As we become more and more skilled in meditation, as we focus our attention on one thought, image or sound, all others are brought under control and become quiet.

Meditation expands inner awareness. Picture the mind as a large, very hard block of ice. We can easily see what's on the surface and just below the surface of this block of ice. But the deeper we go, the less we can see. This is the same with the mind. Remember, the conscious mind consists of what we are aware of at any moment. We are also aware of thoughts, feelings, memories that are just below our normal awareness, but the deeper parts, the unconscious mind, remain unknown to us. We have a sense that something is there – emotional habits, knowledge, feelings – but we aren't conscious of what that something is or how it affects us.

Like the deeper part of the mind, we can't see into the center of this large block of ice. We know something is buried in the center, but we can't quite see what it is. In order to get to the object buried in the ice, we must break through it. If we take a flat, wide board and beat on the ice, the force of our blow is dispersed over the flat surface, and we have very little power to penetrate the hard ice. It is the same with the mind. We have very little power to penetrate the unconscious because all sorts of thoughts, feelings, sensory inputs, and reactions distract our attention. On the other hand, if we use a sharp ice pick so that all the force of the blow is focused on a single point, we can very quickly break through to the buried object. If we train our concentration to be one-pointed, like the ice pick, we can penetrate the unconscious and be aware of our habits.

We often speak of the unconscious mind as if it were a permanent reality, with no way to directly apprehend, or understand it. Western psychiatry and psychology, with their focus on pathology, have promulgated a fear of the unconscious that is both unreasonable and ill-founded. The unconscious mind is neither foreboding nor forbidden. In reality "unconscious" simply means that we haven't paid attention. We can indeed know the total mind, with all of its habits and talents, if we use our attention to penetrate it. This is the task of inner concentration and meditation.

If you want to understand the spiritual Self, there is no alternative to inner concentration, to sitting very quietly, still, and focused. Systematic methods for training inner concentration and meditation are given below. Once you become skilled in relaxation, you shouldn't spend more than five minutes on this preliminary stage. The more time you devote to training your power of inner concentration, the better. The concentration itself leads to deeper relaxation. As you become more focused and develop greater awareness, you increase your command of the inner resources. More importantly, as you become more skilled in inner concentration, you prepare yourself to use the most sophisticated tool for self-knowledge and self-control available – meditation.

## Meditation: Pathway to Freedom

Meditation is not a state or a condition, but a process by which we achieve ever-expanding (greater, deeper) levels of awareness. There are an infinite variety of meditation techniques, but there are only two basic forms of meditation – classical or exclusive meditation and meditation in action or inclusive meditation – which are like two sides of a coin. We use these two terms for categorical convenience, as both involve concentration and observation. The primary differences between the two lie in the focus points and in their application.

The classical form of meditation is what most people think about when they hear the word meditation. To become skilled at meditation, the mind must first become still and calm. To accomplish this requires consistent daily practice – sitting quietly, closing the eyes and bringing full attention to the flow of the breath, then to a particular center, and then observing the flow of your mind chatter. Sitting quietly, with eyes closed, you focus concentration on a single point. When other thoughts, feelings and sensations arise, simply allow them to pass and return your attention to the focus point. In this way you gradually train the mind to remain focused on a single point by excluding all other thought forms.

Classical or inclusive meditation is a very specific process. According to the masters of yoga science, meditation is actually a technical term indicating a highly refined inner process of concentration. *Meditation is a continuous stream of effortless concentration, on a single point, over an extended period of time.*

The phrase "continuous stream" indicates an uninterrupted flow of concentration. Attention never wavers or wanders. This also characterizes the breath that must flow evenly, without pause. Pauses and stops in the breath actually reflect pauses and halts in the mental processes going on in the mind. Uneven breathing means uneven attention. The entire process of meditation is directly related to an even, steady flow of breath. Until you have learned breath control through diaphragmatic breathing and breath awareness, you cannot meditate.

Effortless concentration defines the quality of the inner concentration – the flow of concentration must be effortless, without any struggle. If there is a struggle, if you are *trying* to meditate, you aren't. For example, you are concentrating on the breath and suddenly your mind begins to wander off. You immediately restrain the mind and bring your attention back to the breath. The very effort required to refocus your concentration prevents meditation from occurring. Meditation is not thinking about meditation, or trying to meditate; it is the process of the concentration flow itself. The word "effortless" also points to another difference between concentration and meditation. Concentration evolves into meditation when the faculty of attention is so highly trained that effort is no longer required to focus it.

The next phrase, "on a single point" means that the mind does not wander here and there but remains focused on the object of observation. This is more difficult than you might suspect. Try for a few moments to concentrate only on the word *blue*. What happens? If you observe carefully, you will see all sorts of thoughts come into your mind, associations based upon the word *blue*. Or, you might have felt an itch somewhere on your body, or moved in order to get more comfortable. It takes time and practice to create single-minded, one-pointed concentration, and gain mastery over the wandering monkey mind.

The phrase "on a single point" also differentiates between meditation and contemplation. In contemplation you focus on a word or concept and then attempt to understand and experience it in all its aspects. The mind is trained to fully understand its core meaning as well as all its relational meanings. In the meditation process, on the other hand, all relational (and, of course, non-relational) aspects of the focus point are purposefully and systematically excluded. You do not "think about" anything. You focus only on the one thought, image, or sensation in order to make your concentration one-pointed.

Finally, the phrase "over an extended period of time" indicates that the flow of effortless, uninterrupted and one-pointed concentration must be more than momentary. Concentration must be unbroken and maintained for some time. This is difficult; even two or three minutes are quite an accomplishment. This requires absolute stillness of both body and mind. Sitting absolutely still is not easy, and takes more than a little practice. Even the slightest movement can create a distraction for the mind and interfere with meditation, particularly when meditation is just beginning. But once the mind becomes very focused, stillness arises naturally in the body.

Don't be alarmed or discouraged about how difficult this might seem. It takes time and effort to develop and refine your power of inner concentration, but the dividends are great. The journey itself is rewarding and brings about many of the changes you need to achieve self-mastery. If you look upon the practice of inner concentration and meditation as an investment in personal growth, then you minimize both your impatience and discouragement.

As you gain skill with inner concentration, it slowly expands itself into meditation. Even as a beginner, you will have rewarding moments. The process is evolutionary. The more skilled you become, the more benefits you have, and the better you feel. When your skill becomes sufficient, and your inner concentration becomes effortless, unbroken and sustained, then you will feel the full power of meditation. You will have no question about whether or not you are meditating; the process is complete in and of itself. You will know through your experience.

## Focus Points in Classical Meditation

There are three types of content in the mind: thoughts, images, and sensations. Any one of these can serve as the focus point. In meditative traditions, when thoughts are used as the focus point, they are called mantras. A mantra is a syllable, sound, word or set of words, that has a particular effect on the mind. Different sounds create different effects. When you are initiated into a particular meditative tradition, the mantra is chosen through the intuitive skills of the teacher to fit your particular nature. All mantras calm the mind and allow awareness to penetrate into deeper levels of the mind at a gentle, controlled rate. As you become more aware of the subtle dimensions of the mind, you gain access to its powerful functions, such as intuition and inner strength.

Images serve as another focus point for meditation. Light, such as a candle flame or a white light, are common focus points in all meditative traditions because the human mind has a natural affinity for it. If you are walking down a street, and someone strikes a match or shines a light, it immediately draws your attention. We can use this natural affinity to train the mind in meditation. In yoga science, *yantras* are often used as meditation focus points. *Yantras* are mathematical symbols that represent different energy patterns in the mind. They may be very simple such as an upward pointing triangle or very complex, such as the *Sri Yantra,* which consists of interposed triangles, circles, and squares.

Still other focus points are sensations, such as Breath Awareness, focusing attention on the feeling of the breath as it passes in and out of the nostrils. As you concentrate more deeply on Breath Awareness, you gradually become aware of more subtle sensations, until you achieve awareness of the energy (*prana, chi,* or *ki*) within the breath.

Often breath is the focus point while the meditator simply observes without interacting with, or reacting to, all other thoughts, images, and sensations as they pass through the mind until nothing is left but the breath and the awareness.

Care is used in choosing a focus point because many of these can lead to negative states. Not all thoughts are beneficial, nor are all sensations and images helpful. An anxious person concentrates on his thoughts, but they only lead to more compulsiveness, pain, and suffering. Concentration on the wrong images can easily lead to fear. All of us know someone who concentrates on the wrong sensations – like the hypochondriacs who take hours to answer the question, "How are you?"

In all meditative traditions, such as yoga science, the mantras, images, and sensations have been researched and verified for their usefulness for thousands of years. They are carefully selected for their known effect on the mind.

Meditation in Action

In inclusive meditation, the focus point is the stream of consciousness itself. No object, perception, thought, feeling or image is excluded. All the activities of the mind are included in the observational field. The critical factor here is that you as the observer remain an observer. You don't allow yourself to be caught up in the mind's events. Everything that happens in the mind is noted with the same neutral equanimity that you would experience when watching the flow of water under a bridge. When you get caught by a thought or emotion, then concentration is broken.

You get caught when you identify with the thought or emotion. Instead of observing the mind feeling anger, and noting it, "I" get angry. Of course, once "I" get angry, "I" also experience all the feelings, disturbances, and tension that accompany the anger. Instead of remaining calm, "I" get excited and upset. By losing awareness, by no longer remaining a witness, you become the emotion and must travel with it wherever it goes.

The primary tool for meditation in action is Breath Awareness. The purpose of meditation in action is to gain complete knowledge of the mind and its contents, and to place yourself in a position of choice rather then be controlled by the mind's compulsive habits. By remaining an observer, you can actually experience what the mind is doing. You don't have to figure the mind out; it presents itself to you directly. It's like sitting on a fence watching all the horses in a corral. If you continue to sit on the fence, eventually you see all of the horses in the corral as they come by. In this way, you come to know the entire contents of the corral. But if you become attracted to a particular horse, jump on that horse and ride away, you no longer see the other horses in the corral. By learning to watch the mind, you will eventually know its patterns and habits. This gives you a greater opportunity for choice.

Both inclusive and exclusive meditation are needed if we want to understand the mind's power and use it effectively. If the mind is cleared for thirty minutes each day with exclusive concentration, then muddied up with uncontrolled or habitual reactions for the next twenty-three and a half hours, the odds of developing self-mastery are not favorable. But if we practice both forms of meditation, we gradually develop the skill to maintain equanimity for twenty-three and a half hours. Then thirty minutes of deep, one-pointed concentration quickly evolves into meditation, and we access the power of the mind and spirit.

## LEARNING TO MEDITATE: METHODS AND TECHNIQUES

Many effective techniques train the mind and open the door to the inner resources. But all require that we enhance concentration and develop the skills that lead directly to meditation. Many of the techniques we have already learned, such as "61 Points" can easily be used to develop concentration. After several months of practice, the Alternate Nostril Breathing exercise (page 195) can evolve into a sophisticated Breath Awareness exercise. To do this, stop using the fingers to control the flow of breath and use only your attention. This takes some skill and practice, but it is a powerful technique for enhancing concentration. To begin, the simplest concentration exercise is Breath Awareness. It is easily used, and reinforces your skill for meditation in action.

## Success Insurance: Knowing How to Practice

The purpose of practice is to gain skill. We want to become skilled human beings, in control of our resources. Trying to use the mind in a sophisticated way without a systematic approach involving all dimensions of the personality is like trying to play championship tennis without learning how to serve. All concentration and meditation practices should be done systematically. We build success from preparation. The stronger the foundation, the easier it is to develop the power of the mind. Following are a number of foundation builders that we must consider:

**1. Commitment: Dedicating Time to Personal Growth and Development.** Find and dedicate one fifteen-minute period a day to developing your internal skills. It should be a time, and place, when no one will disturb you. Early morning is an excellent time to practice. Your mind is fresh and rested, and concentration is easier. However, any time that is free of distraction and allows you to practice regularly is fine. Avoid times when you are tired or have just finished eating. Concentration takes energy and alertness, and if you are tired or digesting food, you will not be very successful in your efforts.

**2. Start From a Position of Balance:** Concentration requires a mind free from worries, anxieties, and fears. If you are uptight or upset, it is difficult to clear the mind and focus your attention. Practice relaxation and diaphragmatic breathing before each meditation practice. The more skilled you become at relaxation and inner balance, the easier it is to increase concentration. Once you are skilled, never spend more than five minutes maximum practicing relaxation. The time is far better spent in concentration exercises.

**3. Sit Comfortably in a Correct Posture:** Posture can either facilitate or interfere with concentration. If you slump while seated, or walk with your shoulders hunched, it creates a neurological imbalance and interferes with diaphragmatic breathing. All of this creates noise in the mind. For practicing concentration, the most helpful posture is an erect, seated one, with the head, neck, and trunk in proper alignment. A natural S-curve of the spine keeps the trunk of the body erect without any muscle tension. This upright posture allows you to breathe easily with the diaphragm, properly aligns the neural pathways of the spine, and allows the muscles of the upper body to relax. With few exceptions, such as the 61 Points exercise, always practice concentration in this erect, seated posture.

**4. Make Transitions Gently:** Whenever you close your eyes to practice an inner exercise – relaxation, imagery, concentration, or meditation – do not open your eyes abruptly when you are finished. Doing so creates a subtle shock for the nervous system, similar to awakening to a shrill alarm clock. The sudden rush of sensory data to the mind also creates a momentary confusion. Instead, before opening your eyes, slowly bring your hands up, being aware of every movement from the inside out. Then, holding the palms of your hands about four inches from your face, open your eyes to the palms of your hands. This eases the transition from one level of awareness to the other, and prevents any shock to your nervous system.

**5. Consistency is More Important Than Length:** Sit every day for a comfortable length. Don't struggle with the mind. When you feel like you have sat long enough, sit for one more minute, and then get up. Gradually build your capacity so you can sit easily for sixteen to twenty minutes, focusing on your concentration point.

**6. Enjoy Your Practice Time:** Remember, concentration is guided by interest. If you make meditation a chore, you won't gain any skill. If you pay close attention to your focus point, watching carefully all the subtle changes it goes through, your practice will steadily improve. Gradually you will come to value this time of mind clearing and focusing.

## Breath Awareness as a Meditation Exercise

As mentioned above, Breath Awareness can also be an effective concentration technique. To practice, sit in the erect, seated posture. Relax the body and focus the mind by using the Alternate Nostril Breathing exercise (page 195). Then focus your attention on the feeling of the breath as it enters and leaves the nostrils. For the first few moments, just center your attention on Breath Awareness. Then, by paying attention to the feeling of the breath going in and out of the nostrils, determine the dominant, or open, nostril. This is the one through which the air flows most easily. Don't use your fingers; use only your sensitivity to determine which nostril is dominant. After determining the dominant nostril, focus your attention on it for several breaths.

Now switch your attention to the passive, or closed, nostril, the one where the air flow is blocked or diminished. Concentrate on this nostril until you begin to feel the air moving freely through it, and it becomes the dominant nostril.

After the air flows freely through this nostril for several breaths, bring your attention back to the first nostril, the one originally open. When you begin to feel the air flow freely through this first nostril, shift your attention to the center between both nostrils. Concentrate on the air flowing freely through both. (Remember, air flowing freely through both nostrils indicates complete balance in both the autonomic nervous system and between the hemispheres of the brain. During this time, your concentration can deepen and intensify.)

Whenever the mind wanders to thoughts or other distractions, bring your attention back to the feeling of the breath. Pay attention: can you notice how far the breath travels outwards as you exhale, or from how far out you pull air into the nose when you inhale? The more interested you become, the stronger your practice. Sit very still, maintaining this focus, for as long as you comfortably can. When you are ready to finish, gently wriggle your toes and fingers. Slowly raise your hands to your face. Holding the hands about four inches from your face, open your eyes to the palms of your hands.

## A Meditation Practice

Once you become skilled in using Breath Awareness, shift the focus point from the breath to a deeper mental image. You can begin by using the image of a candle flame as a focus point. It is easy to begin with the Candle Gaze (page 236), which is concentration exercise. It will help develop this natural focus point. After a few minutes of doing the gaze, close your eyes and visualize the flame in the center of the mind, directly behind the point between the eyebrows. This is known in yoga science as the Ajna Chakra, or mind center. Creating an internal image turns this concentration exercise into a meditation exercise.

For many, using the flame is often a good way to begin practicing meditation. But for others, it is easier to focus on the heart center, known in yoga science as the Anahata Chakra. Instead of flame, use a soft white light as the focus point at the heart center. But eventually, you should learn to use thought as the focus point in either the mind or heart center. This leads to the most subtle levels of the mind. When using thought as the concentration point, the key is to learn how to listen to the thought, and not "think" it. The thought becomes a sound of the mind.

Listening trains your power of observation as well as your power of concentration. As you become skilled at observation, concentration becomes effortless and evolves into meditation.

You can use the sound of the breath to provide a useful, neutral thought. If you listen carefully to the breath, you can hear the sound *So* on the inhalation and *Hum* on the exhalation. Converting these sounds to thought, focus on the thought *So* during the inhalation and *Hum* during the exhalation. These two thought forms, *So* and *Hum*, are neutral to the mind, free of any unconscious associations. They provide a useful focal point for training the mind at the most subtle levels of the unconscious.

We will break the meditation practice into two steps. The first step is a Centering Exercise that brings you to the fifth dimension of the mind, the Balanced Mind, a center of quietness and stillness. Centering is a crucial step in meditation, but it can also be used as a first step in a number of different exercises, such as regaining self-confidence and resolving emotional conflicts with others. The second step consists of a meditation exercise using the words *So* and *Hum* as the mantra.

When you first begin, you will be thinking So and Hum. After some months of practicing, learn to listen to the mind think instead of doing the thinking yourself. At this point, do not coordinate the So and Hum with the breath. Forget about the breath and focus only on listening to the mind think the So and Hum for you. Remember, meditation is not thinking, it is a perceptual process. You have to shift from thinking about So and Hum to listening, which is a perceptual process. In this way you train yourself to become the observer of what the mind does instead of being the one who thinks.

Sit for as long as you comfortably can, letting your own capacity be the determining factor. But do so on a daily basis, for regularity is essential in order for you to increase your capacity. It will also help if you select a specific time, and do your practice at that time every day. This helps establish the habit of sitting to meditate, and the time becomes associated with a relaxed, peaceful state of mind. If you have difficulty using a mantra, use the Candle Flame or Breath Awareness as your focus point.

With these exercises you can begin practicing inner concentration. If you practice them systematically and consistently, you will find them very effective. It is very helpful to find a competent teacher or guide, and learn the basics of meditation. An experienced, skilled teacher can point out the pitfalls and provide the fundamental skills and tools you need to refine the process. Remember though, that your goal is independence and freedom. A teacher or guide cannot do your meditation for you, nor can they be responsible for your health, your choices, or your life. Only you can do that. *You must create and take your own response-ability!*

## PRACTICAL APPLICATIONS

During meditation, don't try to solve problems or work out personal issues. Keep meditation reserved only for meditation, concentrating on your focus point. As you become more skilled, you will find that practical benefits of meditation happen outside of the meditation process. But you can and should use the Centering Exercise for a number of different inner-work exercises, such as creative problem solving, imagery exercises to develop insight and intuition, and even conflict management.

One of the most powerful applications is to use it to resolve disputes and conflicts that leave you feeling upset and disturbed. The steps are very direct and simple. The key to using centering as an effective conflict tool is to remember that you cannot control someone else's behavior, but you have unlimited opportunities to choose other behaviors for yourself.

## Resolving Emotional Conflicts

Use the Centering Exercise to establish a clear, calm mind after being drawn into a conflict situation that was not resolved and left you feeling angry and/or upset. Once centered, use the calmness of the mind and your ability to observe and minimize your emotional disturbance and find effective ways to achieve your goals. Two principles are involved: First, when we operate from a clear, calm mind, we operate from strength. When we are emotionally upset, we operate from weakness. Second, it is far easier to create options for your own behavior than try to change the behavior of another. By changing your behavior, you create different outcomes. When you find yourself upset owing to a conflict situation, take the following steps:

**1. Centering Exercise:** find a quiet time and do the Centering Exercise (page 253) to create a calm, clear mind free of emotional upset.

**2. Observe:** Once you are centered, re-create the situation in your mind. Observe both your behavior and the other person's behavior with a clear sense of detachment. If you feel any emotional hook as you review the incident, return to your Breath Awareness and repeat the Centering exercise until your mind is calm and clear. Then again review the incident. Continue to re-center yourself whenever necessary until you can review the entire incident without any emotional attachment and without any judgment about what occurred in the incident.

**3. Review:** Study your behavior in the situation, but do so without any emotional attachment and without any judgment about right or wrong. Is there anything you could have done differently to create a positive outcome? It is important that you not justify your behavior or criticize the other person's.

**4. Visualize:** See yourself performing these alternative behaviors, and experience the positive outcome that the new behaviors are designed to bring about. Practice the new behaviors and the positive outcome in your mind until you are confident that you will use these new behaviors at the next opportunity.

**5. Observe:** Review the other person's behavior with particular attention to their emotional compulsion. Understand how their emotional reactions determined their behavior and they had no real choice. If you feel any negative emotional reaction, any hint of anger, clear your mind with Breath Awarenes,s and again re-center yourself. When your mind is then calm and clear, again review the situation until you can watch the other person's behavior without any negative reaction.

**6. Visualize:** Visualize this person's face surrounded by golden light or a blue light, whichever comes easier, until you feel a sense of compassion for this person.

**7. Centering:** Return to the clear, calm center of your mind, then practice Breath Awareness for a few moments, and open your eyes to the palms of your hands. Now you can resolve this conflict from a position of strength rather than weakness brought on by your emotional reactions.

You can use the Centering exercise in a number of different ways. The more you use it, the more skilled you become. But it cannot and should not replace the consistent practice of meditation. Without the refined concentration established by the practice of meditation, other mental exercises lack power and effectiveness. The effectiveness of any mental exercise *depends* on the quality of your concentration. The most important example of this relationship between meditation and centering exercises is found in the access and use of our innate self-confidence.

## Unlimited Confidence

Underlying much of our fear and unhappiness is a subtle lack of self-confidence. We hold ourselves back, feel anxious, delay decisions, avoid difficulties, and accept unnecessary limitations – all because of self-doubt. When push comes to shove, most of us lack genuine self-confidence. Even those who appear confident, when faced with the possibilities of failure – losing their job, not making enough money, having their boyfriend or girlfriend "fall in love" with someone else – are racked with anxiety, indecision, and self-doubt.

Most of us build self-confidence by being successful in the world. As long as we are successful, we feel confident. But what happens when we aren't successful? By depending on success, we depend on what happens in the world around us. No matter how much effort we expend, we can never control all the events in the world around us. No one can ever be certain that they will succeed. When we rely on success to build confidence, we build on a bed of shifting sand. Even when it works, the uncertainties leave much to the imagination, and confidence is never complete.

You don't have to live very long before you experience a fundamental rule of life, the 10-80-10 Rule:

- 10% of the time no matter what you do, you are successful.
- 80% of the time your ability to influence events varies. You have some input or control over what happens, but the outcome is indefinite.
- 10% of the time no matter what you do, you fail.

As a consequence:

- 10% of the time you have absolute self-confidence.
- 80% of the time you are insecure because you aren't sure just what will happen. This, of course, clouds your confidence with doubt.
- 10% of the time you have no confidence at all.

When we rely on success to build self-confidence, we unknowingly stack the odds against ourselves. At the subtle level of the discriminating mind, we unconsciously recognize that success is fickle, and that we really don't have control, no matter how much insurance we buy, how many contracts we sign, or how much money we save. We all feel the insecurity that being subject to the fickle finger of fate creates. We see ourselves as victims and talk about chance and luck, hoping that the fates will be kind.

Negative self-concepts are even more destructive to self-confidence. In early childhood, the pain of "failure" – people laughing at us, calling us names or telling us that we are inadequate, not good enough, hearing constantly words such as "no, don't," and "you can't" – have a stronger impact on the mind than whatever success we achieve. By the time we enter adulthood, these patterns exert a powerful influence. Even though we may compensate by making a large fortune or being the "big shot," our inner world is full of self-doubt and stress because we really don't feel genuinely confident. There are ways to help unwrap your confidence:

1. Use Breath Awareness to clear your mind whenever your mind chatter starts "bad-mouthing" you. Don't allow the mind's habit of name-calling and criticizing to remain unchallenged.

2. Take control of your language. There is no such thing as failure, only premature quitting. Reinterpret the situation in terms of cause/effect. Whenever you take any action, you always get some results. Instead of labeling them as "good" or "bad," "successful" or "unsuccessful," examine how they came about. Spend your time and effort understanding cause/effect relationships instead of creating mind pollution.

3. Evaluate how you produced these particular results and modify, if necessary, your actions. Then take the necessary actions to produce different results, using what you have learned from the last time.

4. Any time you find yourself focusing on what you can't do, immediately clear your mind with Breath Awareness. Refocus your attention on what you can do. Keep doing this until it becomes your mind's habit.

All of this will help, but it still won't lead to unlimited self-confidence. Genuine, unshakable self-confidence has nothing to do with the world at all. It is a natural part of every human mind. Unfortunately, we are so busy talking to ourselves, feeding our dragons, and paying attention to outside events that we ignore this inner reality.

The problem we face with self-confidence isn't one of acquisition. We already have everything we need, including unlimited self-confidence. The problem is one of access. It has nothing to do with "positive thinking." In fact, it has nothing to do with thinking at all.

Remember the experience of "God's in His Heavens – All's right with the world?" This sense of genuine harmony and contentment is the natural expression of the Balanced Mind, the fifth and most subtle level of the personality. This inner balance is the source of our genuine self-confidence. We access it through a deeply quiet and calm mind, the kind of mind created by meditation.

*The most effective and efficient method of achieving unshakable self-confidence is the consistent practice of meditation.* The more skilled at it you become, the more confidence you gain. You will experience this as:

## CENTERING EXERCISE

Begin this exercise in the erect, seated position with your eyes closed. For the first few moments, mentally scan the body, relaxing any tension you may find. Then for a few minutes, practice Breath Awareness until you feel both nostrils open. After a few moments of concentrating on both nostrils flowing freely, follow the next inhalation up as if you are following it into the center of your mind. It is as if you are turning your eyes inward and looking toward the very center of your brain. Then picture yourself sitting in the middle of the mind, watching the body breathe around you. At this point, experience the body like a shell around you. After a few more moments, be aware of the center of the mind, and the inner space around it. Notice that there is an inner space where thoughts, images, and sensations seem to be, and an outer space, outside the skin of your body. Your body is like the dividing line between the outer space and this inner space.

Within this inner space, right where thoughts first seem to arise, you will find a center of quietness. When you become aware of this center, your body will become effortlessly still, and the mind very calm. You will notice that thoughts, images, and sensations now seem to revolve around this center, but within the center itself, it is very quiet and peaceful. Enjoy this calm center for a few moments. Learn to watch the thoughts and other activities passing by. You are only the observer, the witness to these activities of your mind. Don't get involved in thinking, just observe, and enjoy the calmness of this center.

- an increase in mental calm and clarity, the ability to focus on what's important, and to ignore distractions;
- increasing emotional stability – things just don't bother you as much;
- clearer thinking, greater perception, understanding cause/effect relationships more clearly;
- greater effectiveness as you focus your energies more efficiently and waste less time disturbing yourself.

Meditation leads to a gradual overall increase in the ability to access your innate self-confidence. As you become more aware of this subtle core within the balanced mind, you can use the Centering Exercise to access this experience and train your mind to remain calm and confident whenever difficult situations arise.

## MEDITATION: USING POWER TO GAIN STRENGTH

Meditation is the finest tool we have for personal growth and development. Through meditation, we systematically expand inner awareness and become conscious of our true inner potential. In this way we gradually transform the entire

## CONFIDENCE EXERCISE

Begin with the Centering Exercise (page 253). When you feel centered, observe whatever thoughts arise in your mind. Notice how these thoughts appear around the center of your mind, but never occur in the center. Then direct your attention towards the problem you face. As disturbing thoughts or feelings arise, clear your mind with Breath Awareness and re-center yourself. Keep returning to the problem until you can watch your mind think about the problem without feeling disturbed or worried. As you remain calm, you will notice that you feel more confident about handling the problem. Once you can observe without any emotional reactions, let your mind play with the problem, allowing whatever creative solutions to arise without judgment. You can now use the creative force of your mind to find a solution. After choosing the solution you want, visualize yourself solving the problem, and allow yourself to feel the success of the solution. Now you are programming the unconscious mind for success. Then clear your mind with Breath Awareness, open your eyes to the palms of your hands, and go to work.

## MEDITATION EXERCISE

When you are centered, bring your focus of concentration to either the space between the two eyes, the mind center, or to the space between the two breasts, the heart center. If you are more intellectual than emotional, you should center your focus on the mind center. If you are more emotional than intellectual, you should focus your concentration on the heart center. Either concentration or focus should be on the space within the body, not on the surface skin area. Now focus your attention on the sound of the breath. On the inhalation you will hear the thought (sound) of *So,* on the exhalation the thought (sound) of *Hum.* Try to focus on exactly where the thought arises in your focus space (mind center or heart center). Don't try to anticipate or remember, but stay focused on the thought itself, as it exists at this moment. All sorts of thoughts will come to your mind. Let them come and go. Whenever you find your thoughts wandering, or off on a tangent, bring your attention back to the *So* and *Hum.* Don't struggle or fight with your mind, simply come back to the focus point. When you are ready to finish, direct your attention to the flow of breath through the inner space of your body. Follow the next exhalation out the nostrils, and focus your attention on the feeling of the breath for a few moments. Now wiggle your toes and fingers gently. Slowly, being aware of every inner movement of the body, bring your hands up to your face. Holding your hands approximately four inches from the face, open your eyes. The first things you should see are the palms of your hands. Maintain the inner calm and stillness you feel as long as possible throughout the day.

personality. Meditation enhances and promotes the evolutionary growth process, and since this takes place as a natural consequence of our own efforts, it remains under our control. As we grow in inner strength and independence, we are able to give more freely to others without resentment, without fear, and without manipulation.

The consistent practice of inner concentration and meditation provides specific benefits to our physical, mental, and social health:

- A gradual change in the physiology of the body reflecting a significant and permanent reduction of stress – a slower pulse rate, a lower and more stable blood pressure, a more stable galvanic skin response, deeper and more even breathing patterns, and lower blood lactate levels;
- A corresponding increase in self-confidence and self-acceptance as well as an overall increase in measure of self-actualization (a strong indication of increasing maturity and personal fulfillment);
- Less need for and less use of alcohol and drugs of all types – prescribed and non-prescribed;
- A gradual change from compulsive and rigid behavior (which results in negative outcomes) to more helpful, thoughtful behaviors which are more satisfying and productive;
- Increased powers of concentration leading to greater personal effectiveness.

But the most important benefit is the change in how we experience ourselves. Meditation is an introduction of ourselves to ourselves. Our personal sense of "I-ness" undergoes a gradual transformation as we slowly become aware of the deeper resources of the mind – our innate strength and wisdom, and the very essence of life, the spiritual Self. We begin to view the world from a dramatically different perspective. Change no longer frightens us, and we no longer need to be perfect or punish ourselves for not being perfect.

As we grow in mastery and knowledge, we gradually dis-identify with those aspects of ourselves that we considered for so long essential to our sense of identity – our thoughts and ideas, our emotions, our body and behaviors, our roles and social attachments. As we develop skill in inner concentration and meditation, we put the old self into a new and more useful perspective. We grow out of self-imposed limitations, and as we gain emotional distance, we see things with greater clarity, become less reactive to stressful situations, and take command of our habits and actions. As we refine our mind power, we increase an evolutionary movement that leads us to our most potent resources, an unlimited inner strength that we experience as a genuine self-confidence.

But most importantly, we experience the spiritual Self, the unlimited core of our humanity. We do not reach this transpersonal Self through therapy, drugs, reading books, or even having wonderful parents. It cannot be gained through intellectual discourse or by going to college. It is already deep within us; it is who we already are. With meditation, we access and refine the power of the mind. With this refined power, we take the final step to access our spiritual strength and free ourselves from the dragon of loneliness.

# SPIRITUAL STRENGTH: THE END OF LONELINESS

*The most beautiful thing we can experience is the mysterious.*
*It is the source of all true art and science.*
—Albert Einstein—

Our success and self-confidence shouldn't depend on external forces we cannot control, but on the inner ones we can. As we practice meditation and refine the power of the mind, we experience our real inner strengths. Self-mastery is not a matter of becoming or acquiring something, it is a matter of being conscious of the strengths we already have. It is a process of transformation, not change. With the proper tools – diet, exercise, relaxation, and breathing – we transform a weak, rigid, and stressed body into a balanced, flexible, strong, and stress-free body. By developing and using our natural resources, we end up with a powerful body. The same is true of the mind. With the proper tools – breath awareness, imagery, reframing, and concentration – we transform a fearful, self-hating mind into a clear, flexible, creative, and insightful mind. By developing and using our natural inner resources, we end up with a powerful mind.

With a healthy body and a powerful mind, we complete the journey to self-mastery. As we refine concentration to achieve meditation, we refine meditation to achieve awareness of the spiritual Self and experience yet another transformation – one that is deeper, more profound, and complete. It is the blossoming of spiritual knowledge and strength, and the resolution of all loneliness. This experience is often called a mystical experience, yet it is the most practical way of life. It is called mystical because the intellect cannot quantify or qualify the experience. Any words we use to define or explain the experience are not the experience itself, but only a shadow of the truth that we experience. What the mind does not comprehend, the heart knows completely. This is not the physical heart, but the spiritual heart, the soul-Self that lies at the core of the personality. It is practical because it completely frees us from the dragons of the mind and the limits of the ego, and returns to us our full capacity to love.

This experience is called by different names. In Zen it is called *satori,* or enlightenment, in Taoism it is referred to as living the *tao,* and in tantra it is called *samadhi.* In Western traditions, it is referred to as a mystical experience. Whatever the name, it is this experience alone which completely frees us from loneliness and the other dragons of the mind. And it does this through love.

We may have a powerful mind, even a powerful will, but unless we reach into the core of our being and experience the spiritual Self, we have not yet completed the journey to self-mastery. How we first experience this Self varies from person to person. There are, however, universal qualities – timelessness, unsurpassed peace, a blissfulness that transcends any experience of pleasure – that are part of almost every mystical experience. For many, it is a timeless experience of an indescribable light. Listen to the words of the mystical poet, T. S. Eliot:

> *At the still point of the turning world. Neither flesh nor fleshless;*
> *Neither from nor towards; at the still point, there the dance is,*
> *But neither arrest nor movement. . . .*

> *I can only say, there we have been: But I cannot say where.*
> *And I cannot say, how long, for that is to place it in time. . . .*

> *The inner freedom from the practical desire.*
> *The release from action and suffering, release from the inner*
> *And the outer compulsion, yet surrounded*
> *By a grace of sense, a white light still and moving. . . .*

For some, it is a recognition that this Self is eternal, a part of the Universal One, free of all disease, all suffering, and all limitations. For others it is timeless, an experience of Christ Consciousness, or the moment of awakening.

Each person must try to explain this unexplainable mystical experience with concepts and words limited by culture, beliefs, and traditions. There can be no argument about which explanation is correct, as they are all "correct." For these are all only explanations. The mystical experience is achieved by stilling the mind, by going beyond all thought. Comprehension is direct, not mediated through the intellect. Consequently, the intellect has no logic to explain it. At best, the mind approximates the experience through different words. The only way to understand, to comprehend the experience is to have the experience itself. This mystical experience is the core of all meditative and spiritual traditions. Without it, we cannot know our full capacity for love, and we cannot be completely free from loneliness and the other dragons.

Although a mystical experience can happen spontaneously, these events are rare. Consequently, the great traditions of self-mastery systematically develop the capacity for mystical knowledge through the consistent practice of meditation. In tantra, the task is to refine meditation so that all the power of the mind is focused on a single point. Like the point of an ice pick penetrating the block of ice, the sustained inner concentration of the meditator penetrates the dense veil of the mind and opens awareness into the spiritual realm. This awareness of the spiritual Self frees our identity, or sense of "I'ness," from the grasp of the ego function, and we no longer identify with physical and mental limitations.

## The End of Ignorance ...

This singular experience need only happen once, and the entire personality is transformed. You don't become a different person, you experience a new identity. You no longer think of yourself as the habits and patterns of the ego-dominated mind. However brief this one experience may be, you know beyond a shadow of any doubt that this personality that represents you to the external world is not who you really are, but simply your tool. The ego can no longer claim to be the owner of the personality. The tantrics have a saying: "If a fool enters into deep sleep, he awakens as a fool. If a fool enters into *samadhi*, he awakens a sage."

In tantra yoga, this mystical experience is considered to be the beginning of the end of ignorance. In other words, the real journey has just begun. Recall from Chapter 3 that in the meditative traditions, ignorance means to ignore, to be unconscious of. When we are unconscious of the spiritual Self, we identify with the ego-self, the material personality. Instead of seeing the mind and body as the tools they are, we believe that our mental and physical experiences are all that we are. Consequently, we define ourselves by whatever thoughts and feelings come to mind. This confusion of identity lies at the root of all loneliness, fear, and self-hatred.

When we finally experience the spiritual Self directly, this experience awakens us to the fact that we are much more than thoughts and feelings, much more than a physical presence. It is not an understanding, but a realization. No matter how intellectual we are, or how many degrees we earn, thinking about the spiritual Self is not at all the same as having the experience. Just as thinking about eating is not the same as eating, reading about mystical experiences is not the same as having one. The proof of the pudding, the power of the experience, is in the experience itself.

Although our first mystical experience is indescribably powerful, it does not mean that we have the skill to sustain this spiritual awareness. In fact, we will probably spend time agonizing why we cannot get back to the mountaintop. The task we face after achieving *samadhi*, or the mystical experience, is to become skilled at maintaining that awareness. This is precisely why there are traditions of self-mastery. They provide the systematic methods that not only lead us to the mystical experience, but also develop the ability to maintain this spiritual awareness and knowledge as the foundation for the rest of our lives.

## ... And the Opening of Love

The power of this mystical experience lies in a simple reality called *love*. For the tantric masters, love is considered to be the most ancient of all travelers. It is the power of Consciousness itself. Or, said in more Western terms, it is the very nature of God, and consequently, of every spiritual Self. Nearly every account of a mystical experience speaks of this transcendent experience of love as the core quality of the experience. But it is always spoken of as a force that flows through and from the spiritual Self, not something that is received. This is quite different than the emotional experience that we often call love in poetry and love songs. There is no longer a sense of "me" or "mine," no sense of a small ego-self taking something in. It is self-less. It is this defining quality of selflessness that puts an end to the dragon of loneliness.

This makes sense if we understand something about emotions. When we examine the nature of emotions and emotional energy carefully, we see why this change of identity from the personality to the spiritual Self brings about an end to the emotional disturbances that we suffer.

## EMOTIONAL ENERGY: A SOURCE OF POWER

Much of the power that we command through concentration and meditation has its source in emotional energy. When we don't understand this energy, we unknowingly use it to create conflict and disturbance, harming ourselves and others. Out of ignorance, we even believe that an emotional person is a weak person when, in truth, emotional energy is the power behind our actions.

All the exercises we have learned are designed to help us balance and direct emotional energy. But how is this energy channeled into emotions? What are emotions anyway, and how do we create them? Unfortunately, modern psychiatry and psychology have only a superficial view of emotions. They do not have a systematic science or technology that provides the tools we need to command and direct this powerful energy. They do know how to label emotions. There are diagnostic manuals that have labels and categories for any and all behavior. In fact, if you look at these books you begin to think that everything we do can be labeled as some emotional disorder. But we don't find a clear understanding of emotions and how they arise in the mind and body. Since emotions impact every aspect of our lives, it is foolish not to have at least some way to think about or understand how we create emotional disturbance.

## The Four Primitive Drives

In yoga science, there is a clear distinction between negative emotions which lead to imbalance, stress, and suffering, and positive emotions, which lead to freedom, balance, and harmony. These two categories of emotion have two very different sources. Negative emotions are a distortion of powerful and primitive drives which are part of the physical body. Yoga science points out that there are four instinctual urges, or primitive drives, inherent in our biological structure: self-preservation, hunger, sleep, and sex. (As was discussed in previous chapters, self-preservation is the most powerful of these primitive drives. And, distortions within self-preservation create the dragons of fear and self-hatred.) We share these four primitive drives with all other members of the animal kingdom. The purpose of these primitive drives is to ensure both the survival of the individual and the continuation of the species. These drives motivate us to protect ourselves from danger, seek out food for nourishment, give ourselves adequate rest for revitalization, and participate in the creation of new life so that the species may continue. These innate drives are not the emotions. They are the primary structures that direct the flow of energy for the emotions.

When one of these primitive urges is stimulated, such as self-preservation when we face danger, it generates energy. This energy is quickly directed to a specific action, goal or object that in the past has satisfied the underlying urge or drive. When this energy is given a specific direction, or goal, it is called desire, and becomes a powerful motivating force. All behavior is motivated by a desire of one kind or the other. We may have lots of wants and wishes, but we won't be moved to action until there is a desire, enough energy to move us toward achieving some goal.

From a yogic perspective, animals are controlled by their nature. Whatever primitive urge is strongest at the moment dominates the actions of the animal. It will eat any food available, run or fight if threatened, find a den when rest is needed, and engage in sex during the mating season. Unfortunately, human beings can also be dominated by urges and desires. But we can also refrain from acting, no matter how strong the desire. Through the power of *reflective awareness,* human beings can step back and observe their urges, they can postpone their desires, and they can go halfway around the world to pick a mate, or find a specific food. In other words, we can complicate our world. We can find a seemingly endless number of objects that can satisfy (at least temporarily) any one basic urge. As a consequence, we can, and have, created an almost endless number of desires.

Notice that the phrase is "reflective awareness," not "thinking." Thinking is a different process. Thinking is using the mind to collect sensory data, to analyze, to discriminate however well we may. Animals also clearly think. They solve problems, they use language, and they also show emotions. But there is no evidence that animals know they are thinking. It is this power of reflective awareness, the ability to observe the mind work that provides us with response-ability, the capacity to free us from the compulsion of the primitive drives, the freedom to choose something different. This is the human difference – not that we think, but that we can step away from the mind and its compulsions, to put things into a perspective and "see things from a distance," even from the perspective of the spiritual Self. This is why meditation is so necessary – it develops the capacity for reflective awareness.

If the object of our desire satisfies us in any way, the connection between the urge and the particular object is reinforced, and the desire becomes stronger. It's as if desire is a channel of energy that deepens if the chosen object satisfies the desire. Every time we satisfy a desire, it becomes stronger, and we increase the probability that this particular channel will be utilized again. Soon, that particular choice becomes a powerful habit in the mind. If our choice is painful or uncomfortable in any way, we quickly learn to avoid it. Then avoidance becomes the habit. In many ways, pain conditions the mind even more powerfully than pleasure. We act as much or even more from the need to avoid unpleasantness or pain as we do to find pleasure.

The more often we successfully use the object, person, or situation to satisfy a desire or avoid pain, the stronger the connection becomes. This connection between the desire and the object becomes so strong that the desire and the object come to be seen as one. At this point, we are dependent on that particular object, convinced that only that object (person, event, belief) will make us happy, secure, fulfilled, satisfied, and/or protected. By this time, we have developed a very strong habit in the mind.

This is where we begin to get into trouble. Up to this point, we are in harmony with ourselves. Neither the basic drive nor the desires, in and of themselves, create imbalance and unhappiness. The danger lies in how we create our relationship to the objects of our desires.

Let's take a simple example. When the body is running short of fuel, we suffer from nutritional deficiency. At this point we begin to feel hungry. But we don't stay with a vague sense of hunger for long. We quickly begin to think about specific foods that will satisfy us. While there may be plenty available, we begin to "hunger" for a particular dish – cherry pie, for instance. Hunger, the urge, is now directed to a particular object; we desire the cherry pie even though it may not provide the nourishment we really need, the absence of which is the real cause for the hunger.

Let's say that you had a long morning at work, missed taking your break, and by the time twelve-thirty or one o'clock rolled around, you were really hungry. What made you even more hungry and eager for lunch is that a colleague with a reputation as an excellent baker had left a message that there was a piece of homemade cherry pie waiting for you in the staff refrigerator. It was yours to have on your break or at lunch.

Your mouth watered as you thought about that piece of pie. You quickly shuffled papers off your desk and went immediately to the staff lounge. As you walked into the lounge, you saw a colleague, someone you didn't like very much, eating the last bites of a piece of cherry pie. You opened the refrigerator, and all you saw was an empty paper plate with your initials on it, and an apple sitting next to it.

What do you think your reaction would be? It would depend very much on how much you wanted that piece of pie. If the desire was strong, your sense of frustration at seeing the empty plate would be strong. Add your dislike of the individual in the room, and there is a high probability that this other person, finishing "your" piece of cherry pie, is definitely in danger. Notice that in your mind the piece of cherry pie that he was eating became the one you were supposed to eat. Of course it was, how could it be any other way? The apple could certainly assuage your hunger just as well as the cherry pie, and in fact, would do a much better job of it. But under the power of your attachment to the pie, you would look at the apple and not even see it.

It wasn't your hunger that caused the emotional reaction. It wasn't even the desire for a piece of cherry pie. What made you angry was your "need to have" that piece of cherry pie. It is the "need" for a specific object that leads to a negative emotion. In *Creative Use of Emotions,* Swami Rama and Swami Ajaya state, "It is in seeking to obtain and keep objects of our desire that we become emotional in one way or another. Thus it is said that desire is the mother of all emotions." Emotional disturbance always involves a dependency relationship to an object in the external world. Not a single negative emotion has an exclusively internal source; it always arises from a dependency, an attachment, to a desired object, situation, or person.

It doesn't have to be a piece of cherry pie. We get attached to just about everything – belief systems, ideas, people, causes, automobiles, gems, income, spouses, children – the list is as endless as our desires. And every dependency has the power to create a negative emotion.

We can become emotionally disturbed whenever any desire is unfulfilled, blocked, or somehow threatened. When someone or something prevents us from fulfilling our desire, or threatens to take away, change, or even attack an object of our desire, we become disturbed. This emotional disturbance creates patterns in the mind that distort perceptions and thinking, inhibit the creative force, and force us into more rigid forms of behavior that lead to imbalance and stress. Even though we may express our emotion, such as anger, and relieve some pressure, the damage (internal imbalance) has already been done. The best we can do now is to clear the mind and rebalance as quickly as possible.

As we have already seen, fear and self-hatred are distortions of the urge for self-preservation. We set the conditions for these dragons whenever we feel that our physical self and/or our ego-self (our sense of self-worth, importance, financial well-being, and so on) depend upon a specific event or condition, object, or person. After all, our greatest attachment is to our lives, which certainly includes our physical body. When we *anticipate* harm to the body, or to the ego-self, through loss, a change in events, or the inability to gain what we think we need, the inevitable outcome is fear. And when we don't measure up to expectations and standards, we turn on ourselves and create self-hatred. As the authors of *Creative Use of Emotions* point out, "Without the habit of dependency there could be no fear." Each and every negative emotion is based on an attachment, a condition of dependency. And all of them are powerful habits in the mind.

## Building Helpful Habits

Satisfying every desire, even if it were possible, is not the answer. It doesn't take long before we realize that sometimes satisfying a desire leads to even greater difficulty. For example, greed, another negative emotion, arises when we already possess the objects of our desire. But this possession only feeds the desire further. Instead of just one piece, now we want the entire pie. Many of us never have enough no matter how much we get. Life becomes a rat race, a futile attempt to get enough to make us happy. This is the hidden trap of materialism. We always want something a little bit better. We always strive to raise our standard of living. We must have a little more than last year or we think we are not doing well. We lose any sense of sufficiency as we become driven to have more and more and more.

As we become focused on satisfying desires, we lose sight of any consequences until after they happen to us. For example, eating the piece of cherry pie might satisfy our desire, but what would happen to the digestive system? The pie, loaded with refined sugar and white flour, creates an imbalance in the digestive process, and we end up with another kind of problem. Or we "fall in love," marry, and find out that the person we married is definitely not the person we thought we married. How many times have you heard that love is blind? That isn't true at all. Love isn't blind, it is undemanding. What is blind is emotional attachment.

Nor do we gain much ground by trying to regulate each emotion or reaction. Negative emotions are symptoms, information signals that tell us that something is out of harmony. Negative emotions are the result of misdirected energy. To take control, to consciously direct energy skillfully – enhance concentration, create a strong will, live joyfully without stress – we must discriminate between the emotion (such as anger or fear) and the emotional power behind it. By regulating and directing the emotional power (the primitive drive), we free ourselves from emotional disturbances and the problems and stress they create.

If we have a body, we have emotional energy. The challenge we face is to channel it constructively. If we remain unconscious and allow our old habits to continue to direct this energy, we continue to suffer from negative emotions and related diseases. But if we take charge, develop new patterns and channels, new habits of thinking, speaking and behaving, this energy flows smoothly, satisfying the primitive urges, and leading to healthy, creative living, and a powerful will.

Regulating the expression of emotional energy by building helpful habits is the first level of self-mastery. For instance, we already know that fear is a distortion of self-preservation, and that by taking charge of our mind chatter, we prevent fear. We also know the impact of diet and the necessity of regulating the "what, when, and how" of food intake. We satisfy this primitive urge by taking nutritionally useful food at proper times and in a proper way. By regulating food intake, we control the difficulties related to food intake (such as compulsive eating, indigestion, and obesity) as well as associated emotional disturbances (such as guilt, fear, and self-hatred). Practicing good dietary habits also leads to the desire for healthy food, thus channeling this urge constructively.

Knowing how to sleep is as important as knowing how to eat. If you regulate sleeping habits and train yourself to sleep properly, your life force is revitalized, and you don't feel tired and cranky at the end of the day. Too many of us simply collapse into bed and fall asleep. Even if we sleep through the night, our sleep is disturbed from tension. The key is to systematically relax before going to sleep, and prepare both the mind and body for a restful sleep. The Sleep Exercise (page 209), for instance, quiets the unconscious and allows for deep and peaceful sleep. You will spend less time sleeping as the quality of your sleep increases. In this way sleep becomes truly revitalizing – an important element in a healthy lifestyle.

The fourth and final primitive urge, sex, is different from the other three. In yoga science, both the primitive drives of food and sleep are considered to be subservient to the primary drive of self-preservation. Sex, however, is considered to be unique, and serves a unique function. Contrary to popular opinion, you can live your entire life without engaging in sex, and you will survive. Your quality of life may suffer, but you will certainly live. The sex drive is for the preservation of the species, not the survival of the individual. But because sex is extremely pleasurable (or painful) both physically and emotionally, it creates very strong attachments. In addition, since it involves another person's needs and moods, its satisfaction becomes highly unpredictable. As a consequence, sex is extremely fertile ground for developing negative emotions such as jealousy, greed, anger ,and fear. Therapists will tell you that sexual conflicts are by far the most prevalent emotional disturbance in any society.

Yoga science has studied sexuality as intensively as it has studied all inner events. In yogic traditions, sexual management doesn't necessarily mean abstinence. But it does require that we take control of both the mental as well as the physical aspects of sexual activity. The word control does not mean to suppress or repress sexual energy. This inevitably leads to disease and emotional pathology. Control means *conscious, skillful choice*, not compulsive action.

There are a number of steps we can take to make sex a very powerful and satisfying experience. Two essential elements are to limit the frequency of the sexual act and to develop a stable sexual partnership. This is not a moral position, but recognition of the specialness of sexual energy, and the need to develop its full power and potential. If we simply react every time we feel the desire, we only build the habit of reaction. Sex becomes commonplace and habitual. Along with this comes a whole host of problems – guilt, fear of loss and rejection, disappointments, even disease – leading to ever-increasing dysfunctional states of mind. The attention created by specialness is lost as quantity replaces quality. Having a stable partner does much to eliminate both the risk of disease as well as insecurity.

The purpose is to make the sexual act very special, and to free it from compulsion and guilt. One of the most productive ways to do this is to consciously fix the time and place for sexual expression with a chosen partner. This makes sex very special, which, in return, generates even greater attention and concentration. It also leads to control of this powerful source of energy. The greater our control, the greater our use of sexual expression to gain genuine union. As we alter our attachments to old patterns of behavior, our control over the expression of this energy flow also increases.

In tantra yoga science, there are a number of physical and mental exercises that gradually lead to highly disciplined and skilled control of sexual functioning. The consequence is enhanced ability to direct energy into healthy, satisfying expression and away from destructive, troublesome patterns of behavior. We become more involved physically, emotionally, and spiritually with our partner. This leads to greater understanding, communication, and satisfaction. At the same time, breathing exercises and meditation help maintain clarity and allow for increased self-awareness at all levels. Through practice and discipline, the sexual urge becomes an extremely important ally in creative work, loving relationships, and expanded levels of consciousness.

## NON-ATTACHMENT: THE END OF OWNERSHIP

If we accept that the root cause of negative emotions is dependency, then building healthy habits can help regulate emotional energy. But the key to self-mastery is to put an end to dependencies. That doesn't mean that we can't satisfy our desires, or that we no longer have any pleasure. Obviously we aren't going to stop eating, sleeping, having sex, or protecting our selves. Nor does it mean that we become passive and accept whatever happens to come our way. Through self-mastery we put an end to dependency and the suffering it causes by being more skillful in creating happiness, having pleasure, and satisfying our desires.

The process for letting go of dependencies is called non-attachment. If you were non-attached to that piece of cherry pie, you could have still enjoyed it if it had been there for you. But you would not have had the emotional reaction when you found it missing. Instead of being angry about someone eating your piece of cherry pie, your mind would have appreciated having the apple to eat. Sure, you would have liked to have the pie, but you wouldn't be disturbed by its absence.

Non-attachment doesn't mean non-involvement. It means that our involvement is clear of dependencies that muddle our thinking and prevent us from understanding the reality around us. Non-attachment means that we don't "need" a particular thing, person, or event in order to be content and secure. It stems from recognizing that things and people do not make us secure or happy, and realizing that the source of our happiness, joy, security, and strength is within ourselves.

We cannot achieve this realization as long as we remain locked into identifying with the ego-self. Here again, we discover the power of the mystical experience. But even before we reach this level of awareness, we experience increasing degrees of freedom from the need to have things. Close your eyes and do the Centering exercise (page 253). Once you feel centered, then explore what it feels like to be in the center of your mind. Do you find any disturbance there? Is there anything wrong with you? Is there anything lacking here at the center?

Notice that if any negative thoughts do arise, they seem to come up around that center, but not from the center itself. Be aware of the contentment you feel in the center of your mind. This brief experience of contentment is just a taste of what we experience as we gain freedom from the need to have objects.

When we are so focused that we penetrate the veil of the mind and experience the eternal spiritual Self (in other words, have a mystical experience), we find that we are already complete and whole, that nothing more is needed. Non-attachment arises naturally from the recognition of the spiritual Self as our true identity and the experience of our own wholeness.

As we become skilled in accessing the spiritual Self, there is a corresponding decrease in our dependency on things in the world to make us feel whole, complete, and secure. This is true non-attachment. Until we have this realization of the spiritual Self, and the inner strength that it brings, we are not yet free.

## SPIRITUAL DESIRE: THE WELLSPRING OF INNER STRENGTH

We know that desire is powerful, the motivating force of all actions. Not all desires, however, spring from the four primitive drives. Yoga science points to another desire which does not stem from the primitive drives – the desire for higher knowledge. This potentially all-powerful drive has its roots in our spiritual nature. It leads us to explore both the external universe and internal truth, and it can become so strong that even the primitive drives will come under its control.

The desire for higher knowledge lies at the heart of a meditative discipline. It provides an unlimited source of emotional energy, giving us the strength to complete our journey. Meditation is the release mechanism for this force. As our meditation deepens, the positive emotions of love, joy, and tranquility emerge without effort, and we experience their power to change our life. With this driving force gathering strength behind our meditation, we achieve the mystical experience and complete the process of transformation.

### Love: The Freeing Force

The first and most powerful positive emotion is love. Love plays a vital role in all life, but most of us have a limited view of what love really is. We aren't talking about the emotional attachment of so-called love songs. This form of love is polluted with emotional need and attachment to someone who satisfies our needs and desires. Listen to the words of love songs. They are all about what you do for "me," how miserable "I am," and you belong to "me." Everything is about I, me and mine. These songs and poetry are not about love; they are about emotional attachment. And the stronger the emotional attachment, the more pain we experience. We often hear that love hurts. This is absolute malarkey. What hurts is emotional attachment.

Whenever we experience pain, we experience a boundary or a limit. Ask someone who has a headache where it hurts, and they will always point to a specific location. All pain has boundaries, or limits. If you eliminate the boundary or limits, pain disappears. (Recall the Disappearing Headache exercise in Chapter 1.) Often chronic pain patients are taught psychological techniques to minimize and eliminate these boundaries in order to minimize and eliminate the pain. Many of the emotional habits, beliefs, and self-characterizations that we learn in early childhood are boundaries and limits that we place on ourselves. By refusing to accept these limitations, we begin to free ourselves from them. But the greatest limitation is the ego. If we believe that all we are is our personality, then we are stuck with whatever habits constitute it. It's easy to gauge the degree of neuroticism and unhappiness a person feels. Simply count the number of times he or she uses the words "I," "me," or "mine" in a conversation. The equation is very direct: the more self (ego)-centered you are, the more pain you create for yourself. This attachment to the ego (ego-centeredness) is the sole cause of loneliness.

A friend and I were in a deep discussion about her life. She was very unhappy and dissatisfied with the way her life was going. She was in another relationship that was not meeting her emotional needs. Kae had been practicing meditation for several years, and I knew that her greatest fear was being alone. I asked her to name a famous individual that she felt would be free of the loneliness that so plagued her. After several moments of thought, she said, "Mother Teresa."

I was a bit surprised because that was the choice that I had in my mind. So I asked, "Why did you choose her?"

"Because she gives so much love that it must always come back to her."

Kae's answer reflected her own need to have someone love her. If she could only love enough, then someone would love her back. And if that happened, then she wouldn't be lonely anymore. So Kae would always find someone who needed a lot of love and set off to make him her life's work. Unfortunately, these people were unable to give enough love back to make the relationship really work for her. When the relationship ended, Kae would declare, "I always seem to choose the wrong person."

I asked Kae who was it who was getting love back? She looked at me rather peculiarly, probably thinking that somewhere I had lost a little bit of my sense. "Mother Teresa was getting it back," she replied.

"No, no, who was there to get it back?"

"Mother Teresa. If she was giving that love, it was all coming back to her."

"Look Kae, if Mother Teresa was giving love, there was no little ego there to demand love back. There was no little "self" to be lonely. Her strength doesn't lie in all the love she receives, but in all the love that she gives."

In its pure form, love is the expression of selflessness, the ability to give to another. Love is the spiritual force that flows from us, and releases us from the limitations of the ego. The more loving we are, the less limited we are, and the less pain we experience in life. The secret of spiritual strength is that we are able to transcend ego needs. Literally, when we truly love, there is no little ego, no sense of "me," to be lonely. Love allows us to break free from the boundary of the small self and experience the great Self, the spiritual Self that is unlimited, timeless, and universal.

When we love, we aren't even thinking of ourselves. Just remember the time you were shopping for gifts during the holiday season. Suddenly, you saw the perfect gift for someone. You could feel their surprise and happiness as you imagined them opening the gift. Just look at how this simple act of giving made you feel. No matter how pleased they were, you already had the real benefit. You were free, however momentarily, from the ego.

To become skilled at loving, practice selflessness. This doesn't mean sacrifice. Selfless service doesn't mean resentful giving. If you have a martyr complex, you are not loving. If you feel like you are making a sacrifice, you are not loving. Graham Greene once described a martyr in the following way: "Alice lived her whole life for others. You could tell 'the others' by the haunted look in their faces." We all know, or have met, someone who lives only to help you, and you damn well better be grateful. This isn't loving, it's manipulation. Doing favors to gain favor, using guilt to ensure payback, or creating dependencies, have little to do with genuine love.

When we are truly selfless, we feel free, not imposed upon. Others feel our compassion and love; they don't feel haunted and smothered. They experience the same freedom we experience as we love. The more we practice selflessness in daily life, the more freedom we all gain.

## Joy: The End of Expectation

Joy, the second positive emotion, is what we experience when we love. Joy arises out of a natural and unrestrained expression of who we are. Spontaneous and unrehearsed, it is found in the experience of being one's self without pretense or apology. The greater our integrity, the more consistent our inner thoughts, beliefs, and values are with our outer behavior, the more joy we experience. It is joy that both reflects and maintains our inner and outer harmony in life.

We increase our joy through laughter and our sense of humor. Simple, spontaneous laughter is one of the best techniques for stress management available to us. If we understand laughter, we understand joy. We laugh at a joke because the punch line is unexpected. The third or fourth time we hear the joke, it's no longer funny. It is the unrehearsed, spontaneous punch line that breaks through our expectations that creates our laughter.

Now, let's take the analysis one step further. The opposite of life is death, right? Wrong. Death is the opposite of birth. Without birth, there is no death. In this world of duality, the one reality that has no opposite is life. It changes form, it changes from gross to subtle, from seen to unseen, but life continues on and on. Life is complete in and of itself. Life itself is joy. But when we impose expectations on life, we miss the punch line. When we greet life as it is, without expectations and demands, we experience joy. Expectation is the mother of suffering. The more dearly we hold on to expectations, the more dearly we suffer.

Our joy, as it expresses itself in laughter, is the light that illumines our path through life. We cannot cultivate joy by seeking our own happiness, but we will always find it as we help others find theirs. When we love, when we express ourselves without limitations, when we stop creating expectations, when we accept life as it is, we cannot help but experience joy. When we stop disturbing ourselves, when we stop being ego-centered, joy is spontaneous and natural. Like love, joy is the natural expression of who we are when we are truly free.

## Tranquility: The Calm of Self-Acceptance

The third positive emotion, tranquility, or inner peace, is the expression of complete self-acceptance. Just as we experience joy when we lose our expectations of life, we experience tranquility when we lose our expectations of ourselves. This doesn't mean we become passive or apathetic. It is rather, a state of tranquility that characterizes a balanced mind. This inner peace allows us to fully enjoy and engage the turns and tumbles of the world without being disturbed. Instead of withdrawal from the world, we enjoy complete and skillful participation in it. It is a calm, peaceful mind that comprehends the absolute fullness of life and can participate in it. The deeper our inner concentration, the deeper our inner balance and tranquility. *Meditation is the most powerful tool to achieve inner peace and tranquility.*

Some people seem to think that if you meditate and achieve inner peace that you become some kind of zombie, never reacting to the challenges and difficulties and don't experience the intensity of life. This is far from true. Meditation leads to inner strength, and you engage life more completely and more effectively. The fortunate few who achieve tranquility face difficulties with a clear, calm mind, and are far more effective than those who react emotionally, and as a result, don't think clearly or effectively. Being established in tranquility doesn't mean you don't experience pain and pleasure, sadness, and happiness. It means that you don't create or participate in the unnecessary drama, the soap opera that many people make of life.

The spiritual desire for higher knowledge is our most powerful aid in becoming free from the dragons of the mind. In the final analysis we alone are the source of our suffering. We are also the cure. Only we have the power to alter those habits of behaving, perceiving, and feeling that result in fear, self-hatred, and loneliness. They were not acquired overnight, nor will they be magically altered overnight.

There are no fast and easy answers, only the promise of continued evolution and growth. In the mastery of skillful living lies our freedom. Self-mastery and inner strength are the consequence of skillful living, and just as any skill development takes time and training, learning to live skillfully requires patient self-training.

## WILL: DIRECTING THE POWER OF THE MIND

As we touch upon the strength of our human spirit we discover all the elements of a powerful will: a relaxed, calm mind, free of stress and disturbance; an enhanced power of concentration; the ability to resolve conflict; and access to our inner strength.

Using will is quite different than using what we call willpower. When we get caught up in conflict, we typically try to use willpower to solve the problem. This is particularly true when we deal with inner conflict. One part of the mind wants one thing; another part wants just the opposite. We get into a battle with ourselves, and try to overpower any resistance. Unfortunately, what we overpower is only another part of our own minds. Instead of focusing on possible solutions, we are involved in a struggle. No matter which side wins, we lose since the mind becomes the battlefield. The only sure outcome is misery, stress, and more conflict.

Before I was really able to stop smoking, I quit a thousand times. I would throw away whatever cigarettes were left in the pack, and tell myself that I would not smoke again. Ten minutes later, I would remind myself that I quit smoking. And again, a little later on, I would tell myself again that I quit smoking. I would tell myself at least 100 times a day that I quit. But I really wanted that cigarette. The more I told myself that I quit, the more I wanted the cigarette. I became preoccupied with not smoking, so smoking was always on my mind. Finally, I would find a cigarette, light up, and say to myself, "Maybe next month." I wasn't really ready to quit, and all I did was create conflict for myself. And when I did finally give in and smoke, no matter how much I rationalized, I felt like a failure.

Will is the conscious ability to focus all the energy of the mind toward a single direction. We use will when our thoughts, emotions, and actions are then consistent. When this happens, our determination is complete (no internal conflict), and our mind's energy is one-pointed. I was able to quit smoking when I was sensitive to the pain that smoking caused for me, and decided that I had nothing to do with cigarettes, one way or the other. I never allowed my mind to even think about quitting. I kept my focus on anything else but smoking or stopping smoking. Since there was no conflict in my mind, stopping was very simple. With willpower, we have only partial commitment, whereas when we use the will we have total commitment. We convert doubts and worries to motivation, and we direct all of our desires toward achieving our goal.

To create a powerful will, our values and beliefs must be fully in accord with our actions. Those who have a powerful will are committed to their value system. They function with integrity; there is no conflict between their inner thoughts, emotions, and beliefs, and their outer actions. They are true to themselves.

One of the most subtle and unrecognized causes of stress is when our actions are inconsistent with our true beliefs. This causes a subtle (often unconscious), but powerful conflict in the mind, that if not remedied, leads to feelings of guilt and powerlessness, and damages the will. Along with refining concentration, meditation plays a powerful role in developing our integrity in two ways:

1. Through meditation we gain the self-awareness and knowledge necessary to realize and examine our values and beliefs, and the sensitivity to realize when we are inconsistent with ourselves.

2. Through meditation we gain awareness of the spiritual Self and the innate harmony and values that arise from it. This leads to enormous strength of character and integrity, which in turn provides for a powerful will.

Most of us spend very little time thinking about the purpose of our lives, or seriously examining our beliefs and values. All too often, we simply repeat what we learned as children, incorporating the values and beliefs of the culture in which we grew up. Unfortunately, much of what we learn is inconsistent with our real nature, and includes contradictions, fallacies, and mistakes that often lead to cynicism, inner conflicts, and self-doubt. These all become incorporated at an unconscious level into our personal values and belief systems. As a result, our personal philosophy becomes a source of weakness instead of strength, of stress instead of harmony, and of conflict instead of will.

As we become more skilled at meditation, the increasing awareness of our inner resources and the experience of the spiritual Self allow us to create a personal philosophy consistent with our true nature. When we act with integrity, when we are consistent both inside and out, we are in harmony with ourselves and with the world around us. We may not be understood, we may not be in agreement with some of society's beliefs and values, but we will be in harmony with our own nature.

The difficulties in life cannot affect us. This is self-mastery – to live life fully and completely, to become a complete human being and experience the love, joy, and tranquility that is our spiritual Self.

## SELF-TRAINING: DEVELOPING PERSONAL RESPONSIBILITY

A world-class personality requires world-class training. We know that to develop into a skilled tennis player, surgeon, or musician takes a great deal of training. But what does it take to become a skilled human being? We seldom, if ever, even think in terms of becoming a skilled human being, and yet, freedom and personal fulfillment demands exactly that.

The training we need is self-training. Externally imposed discipline is based on suggestions and information from others. This can be useful, and we can gain a great deal of information, methods, and techniques through it. But if this is all we do, it leads to an "ignorant" or "blind" mind because it doesn't require that we fully understand what we are learning. This training builds habits, but they remain unconscious and unexamined. When we are asked only to accept, believe, and/or behave in a certain way, no matter how beneficial the intent, it leads to a constriction of awareness, dependency, and inner conflict. As a result, we lack genuine self-confidence, and suffer from indecision, which leads to conflict and stress. Then, when the mind is divided and our habits in conflict, we end up doing what we really don't want to do, and rarely do what we want. The mind is too scattered, awareness is limited by the suggestions we accept, and the will is weakened.

Self-training, on the other hand, is based on the expansion of awareness and the increasing ability to guide or direct that awareness. In self-training, you do not accept suggestion (someone else's experience) as the basis for decision. Instead, you seek to discover your own inner reality through directing and examining your own experience. In this way you gain self-confidence and develop the power of will, the ability to discriminate, to decide and to carry through that decision in thought, speech, and action. Self-training involves all aspects of your life, from self-study and relaxation to regulation of the four primitive drives.

Relaxation training provides a concrete example of the two different approaches to training. As we noted earlier, external training utilizes suggestion and autosuggestion to create a state of relaxation. This method, usually used by psychologists, psychiatrists, and other therapists, is effective to a limited degree. In self-training we use the relaxation posture, diaphragmatic breathing, and observation of a smooth, even flow of breath. We direct attention towards what is taking place in the body. This expands our awareness and provides greater control. You can easily tell the difference between relaxation based on suggestion and relaxation based on diaphragmatic breathing and direct awareness. The first leads only to a state of relaxation; the latter leads to a state of inner knowledge and balance – as well as a much deeper state of relaxation.

The purpose of self-training is to develop the self-mastery that comes from self-knowledge and self-control. In this way we increase our capacity to consciously direct the mind, speech, and actions. Through self-knowledge, we eliminate the indecisiveness, and the inner conflicts it creates. We now have the ability to control and direct the flow of emotional energy and achieve balance. Once we free the mind of the dragons, we can use our inner resources to become more successful, gain deeper knowledge, and develop our creative abilities.

There are several positive attitudes that are not only essential for good health, but facilitate our efforts at self-training. There are certainly more than discussed here (and you can add as many as you wish), but the following play a major role in determining success. They are not moral absolutes, but practical guides to day-to-day life.

## Self-Responsibility

By now you should realize that you have sole responsibility for yourself and your world. This doesn't mean blame. As we discussed in Chapter 1, responsibility is really response-ability. There is no room for blaming others and becoming a victim, or blaming ourselves and becoming depressed. Practice taking response-ability for your feelings and actions without blaming yourself for mistakes. Remember, when we make mistakes, we pay close attention and learn the most.

The outstanding characteristic of self-responsibility is personal strength. The choices we make for ourselves allow us to go through life without feeling resentment towards others. Those who interact with us feel comfortable and enjoy our company because they know that they won't be blamed for how we feel. Even if they disagree with us, they respect us because we act with integrity and responsibility.

## Self-Acceptance

Self-acceptance doesn't mean a pat-on-the-back, "I'm OK no matter what" attitude, nor is it self-serving egotism. True self-acceptance allows us to look at all aspects of ourselves and to recognize their fundamental unity. It is the recognition that mistakes and failures are opportunities for learning and growth, not whipping posts for self-punishment. It is also the recognition that one's intrinsic value is never altered by petty, or even great, stupidities.

To the degree that we condemn ourselves, we create unnecessary suffering. To the degree that we condemn ourselves, we also condemn others. Self-acceptance leads to acceptance of others. The biblical commandment, "Love thy neighbor as thyself" is not a hopeful injunction, but an accurate description of reality. You can only love and accept others to the extent that you can love and accept yourself. This isn't an egotistical and selfish concern for your personality; it is a deep and abiding respect for the universal consciousness, the spiritual Self that is inherent in all of us.

Both self-acceptance and self-responsibility are extremely practical. Most of us focus on only part of the truth about ourselves, the part that satisfies our emotional need or condition at a given time. It's very easy to focus on negativity when we feel depressed, or "down on ourselves." Then all we can see are our mistakes, our petty faults and stupidities, and the consequence is more suffering and depression. Or, perhaps we do something marvelously well, and we swell with pride and become egotistical. Both attitudes are based on a partial understanding, an incomplete awareness of the truth about ourselves.

Through meditation, we begin to see ourselves in a calm, detached way; we observe the personality and the workings of the mind and body from a neutral viewpoint. This sharpens discrimination, our ability to discern clearly cause and effect without judgment. Judgment implies a right or wrong, good or bad value placed upon the cause/effect relationship, and this leads to emotional involvement. To understand inner workings clearly, we must be able to experience them directly without interference from our emotions and defense mechanisms. This awareness enables us to alter the habits and patterns we decide are not helpful. If we judge instead of discriminate, we obscure this knowledge by an emotional attachment to a "good" or "bad" outcome. It is very probable that our judgments would then be wrong, as they would be based on inaccurate information.

Self-acceptance, on the other hand, allows us to experience the truth about ourselves. The very practical consequence of this knowledge has been stated in many ways, and for thousands of years. In the Western world it is reflected in the biblical statement, "The truth shall set you free." In the Eastern world it is reflected in the Vedantic statement, "Knowledge is that which liberates."

The outstanding characteristic of self-acceptance is humility. Genuine humility has little relationship to meekness, or passivity. It arises from inner strength and health. It has its origin in the sense of awe that we experience upon the birth of a child, when we look at the starry heavens on a clear, dark night, or experience the power of a thunderstorm. When we see all of the personality, and the spiritual Self that lies at the heart of it, we experience an inner sense of awe as we recognize that we are one small but integral part of a reality that is far larger, more profound, and mysterious than the ego. This natural sense of humility stimulates our curiosity and allows us to learn, to appreciate other ways of living, and to be attuned to the rhythms of life around us.

## Equanimity in the Face of Evil

Many people think that self-mastery, meditation, and living life in harmony and balance is a cop-out. They say that there are terrible things that happen in the world, that there is evil, and we should be disturbed by that evil. Otherwise, we do nothing, and all will be lost.

There is no question that "evil" and "terrible" things happen. Cancers grow in the body, people inflict violence on others, innocent children are harmed, innocents suffer from terrorist attacks, governments support dictators, religious wars are fostered, the environment is polluted for monetary gain – the list is as long as the history of humanity. These are all real events in the world around us. But the question is whether we react with emotional disturbance or we respond with clarity and effectiveness. If I react to disturbance by being disturbed, I increase disturbance in the world. If I respond to hate with hate, I create more hate in the world. If I respond to violence with violence, I add more violence to the world. Is that being responsible to myself or to my community?

Of course we have a responsibility to ourselves, to family, friends, and neighbors – to all living creatures – to create and live with harmony and balance. That responsibility will only be realized if we remain clear and focused. Otherwise, our emotional disturbances prevent us from understanding the real nature of the problem, and we take actions that only lead to greater problems. When there is a cancer on the body – whether it is an actual cancer on a person, or a terrorist attack on a community – we must eliminate the cancer. But at the same time, if we don't clearly understand how that cancer came to be, and rectify the conditions that lead to this terrible disease, the only outcome is more cancers. Only if we remain steady, with a clear mind, confident in our strength, and compassionate in our resolve, will we understand, address, and resolve the underlying issues.

In tantra yoga, there is a saying that one should be indifferent to evil. This does not mean to ignore evil. Rather, the statement reflects the knowledge and wisdom that clarity, compassion, and inner strength are the only real antidotes to evil. The great masters are powerful, forceful human beings, but they are not violent. Strength is necessary, and sometimes force is the only intelligent response. But violence is the overuse of force, and we create violence when we are dominated by fear, hatred, or any emotional disturbance. Self-mastery means that we have the inner strength to remain undisturbed so we can focus our best intellectual efforts, our emotional power, and our love to solving problems, rather than adding to them.

## Skeptical Curiosity

If you really want to learn about yourself, develop a very healthy, skeptical curiosity. Obviously, curiosity is necessary. If it only feeds a superficial analysis, it will impede your ability to discriminate, to observe the mind with detachment and dispassion. You need to be skeptical about whatever answers the mind presents to you. The mind never tells you the truth, it only tells you what it needs to say to maintain its own integrity and patterns.

If you remember that your purpose is not to find answers, but only to observe, you facilitate the natural evolutionary process of inner transformation. Direct, experiential knowledge does not require that the mind analyze itself; it requires only that you become aware of what the mind is doing at the time it is doing it. Constantly free yourself from preconceived notions about what should be. This will be done easily as you develop your skill with breath awareness.

Remember that beliefs are guidelines, not gospel truth. They are structures that help us organize our experience. But when they become rigid, when we allow ourselves to be trapped into "only one way" thinking, we stop growing and create fear. As long as we remain flexible, willing to entertain new ideas, alternative ways of viewing life and the world, we continue to grow and expand.

These attitudes – self-responsibility, self-acceptance, equanimity in the face of evil, and skeptical curiosity – are integral to achieving self-mastery. The practice of meditation develops and strengthens them. When you practice you set in motion a circular reinforcement system. Self-training and meditation help develop these attitudes and these attitudes strengthen your practice.

## BUILDING SKILLS

You have the basic knowledge and tools, now you must establish your own self-training program. There is no other way to gain mastery, strength and freedom. Only you can do the necessary breathing and relaxation, as well as practice concentration and meditation. Only you can regulate your diet and exercise. Remember, the whole person needs to be trained. If you do a partial job, you only obtain partial results. To this end there are a few points that you should keep in mind when establishing your own program:

**1. Begin with the practice of Diaphragmatic Breathing.** Proper regulation of the breath is of primary importance in stress management. In fact, you must breathe diaphragmatically in order to eliminate unnecessary levels of arousal in the body. If your breathing rate is "normal," (if it is between sixteen and twenty breaths per minute), you can be sure that you suffer from stress.

A minimum practice is ten to fifteen minutes twice daily. This can easily be done when you go to bed at night, and right as you awaken in the morning. This gradually re-establishes Diaphragmatic Breathing as your habitual pattern. It will also reduce the accumulated stress in the body, and prepare the mind for concentration exercises.

**2. Begin your self-training program very gently.** Don't expect yourself to start an all-out program, spending an hour or two every day on it. You will tire of this superficial discipline very quickly – and decide to stop doing anything. The most successful programs are those that are built slowly and methodically. Decide what you can do on a daily basis that will not interfere with your essential duties. Then make sure that you practice according to that schedule every day.

When an exercise, or period of practice, becomes habitual, then add to it. For example, once you have become accustomed to spending five or ten minutes on Diaphragmatic Breathing every morning, add five minutes of concentration on Breath Awareness. Then slowly expand that period of concentration to your capacity. If there are times when you feel that you can't concentrate, simply practice breathing. Keep practice time for practice. Don't do something else with the time you have set aside for it.

Apply this same method of scheduling to your physical exercise. If you do five minutes of stretching, slowly expand the time and the amount you exercise after the first five minutes has become routine. Self-discipline is a matter of slowly acquiring the habits you want to have. It should not be self-punishment. Avoid sudden and dramatic changes, as these most often lead to resistance and problems. Study yourself; learn to understand your needs, and gradually shape your behavior to satisfy those needs in a systematic and regulated way.

**3. Be consistent.** Even if you do only five minutes of diaphragmatic breathing daily, do that every day. Consistent practice develops skill. The more systematic you are, the greater will be your progress. It definitely helps if you set aside a specific time every day in which to practice. This helps establish the habit. You will also find that this daily time period becomes a stimulus for inducing a state of relaxation and calm. The same is true if you select a certain room or place to do your practice. This place becomes associated with relaxation and further reinforces your practice. In this vein, it is important that the place be quiet, clean, and well ventilated. Don't expect to gain skill in inner concentration and relaxation by practicing in the corporate cafeteria or some other noisy place.

**4. Be flexible and work within your own capacity.** Your goal is increased awareness, not a particular state or exercise ability. Learn to let your concentration flow; it should not be forced (forced relaxation or concentration only creates tension). You only create more tension when you try to beat the clock or set some kind of record. Remember that you are an explorer, discovering the truth about yourself at this moment; you are not trying to become an expert at anything. By working consistently and systematically within your own unique capacity, you will definitely expand it.

**5. Be patient. Allow time for progress to take place.** Be gentle with yourself; trust in your innate capacity for growth. Trees, flowers, plants, and animals all grow to fulfill innate potential. You have that same capacity. You create tension when you try to control instead of allowing your innate capacity to unfold in its own natural, inevitable way. Trusting yourself helps you grow and creates minimum stress. Above all, your program must be practical. Each time you practice, it is an excursion into awareness and tranquility. So enjoy what you are doing.

I strongly recommend that you work with a competent meditation teacher, preferably one with years of training in breathing and meditation techniques. While this book gives you sufficient information to begin your practice, meditation is best learned directly from a good teacher.

When selecting one, examine both his training and experience as well his students. The biblical phrase, "By their fruits shall ye know them" definitely applies in this situation. The teacher should be inspiring and exhibit some degree of self-awareness and self-control. Real teachers aren't hunting for mindless followers; they work to instill independence and self-respect in students. Real teachers will be demanding, pushing you to your limits, testing your strengths, and helping you become stronger. But most of all, does the particular path really appeal to you? Does it fit your heart?

## BEING FULLY HUMAN

Of all the sources of stress, fear, self-hatred, and loneliness are the most destructive. These are the "will-killers" that cripple us, prevent us from being creative, and destroy our human potential. When we objectively examine the dragons of the mind, we discover an untapped capacity for life that we had only vague notions and dreams of before. Just as the calm depths of a lake lie hidden beneath its turbulent surface, so does our true potential lie hidden by the sound and fury of the dragons.

It is not by accident that the same tools, which eliminate the dragons, also lead us to experience, directly and consciously, our true selves. In a very real sense, self-mastery, taking charge of the personality, is also Self-Mastery, the fulfillment of our spiritual heritage. This has been known to yoga science for thousands of years. By learning to regulate your breath and develop your powers of inner concentration and meditation, you take the first steps on a wonderful journey to fulfilling your inner potential.

Each step, however small, brings greater understanding and increased capacity for living life in all its fullness and richness. The dragons only allow us to be partly human. To become fully human is to discover the peace within and to live using our full capacity.

We call this personal empowerment. Empowerment doesn't depend on external conditions. It can't be earned through university degrees or granted by government decree. Many of us think that if we become rich and famous, we'll be happy and content, and personally fulfilled. It doesn't work that way. Personal empowerment is exactly that – personal. It arises out of the innate resources found in every one of us. When we discover these inner resources and turn them into conscious skills, we empower ourselves, become effective human beings, and create the life we choose.

Throughout the book, we speak of various innate abilities, such as instinct, intuition, and genuine self-confidence that emerge from within the different dimensions of the personality. Now we will put them all together to see what the road map of personal empowerment looks like.

The ultimate skill is refined concentration that we achieve through the practice of meditation. When we use meditation we achieve awareness and skill in the following areas:

**Balance:** We develop health and wellness. These are the skills of *body/mind balance, optimism/joy,* and *contentment* that lead to a healthy mind and body, free from stress and disease. Through self-control, we face the world with equanimity, free from fears, worries, and compulsive wants and needs. Optimism and joy are inner qualities that arise naturally from a balanced mind.

**Perceptual Sensitivity**: We develop *instinct, creativity,* and *imagination.* As we have already seen, our instincts are powerful sources of information. As we weave the patterns of our life, our creativity not only solves problems, but also adds color and beauty. When we remove the dragons from the mind, the imagination becomes a powerful tool to direct our creativity, and the power of the mind to accomplish what we choose.

**Insight:** We develop *intuition, reasoning,* and *decisiveness.* These visionary skills allow us to create our future. Intuition, the knowledge of cause/effect relationships, provides both insight and wisdom. It is the true conscience, telling us what will benefit us, and what we should avoid. The power of critical thinking, or reasoning, allows us to understand and solve the problems we face. When we come to trust the mind, making decisions is not any more difficult than paying attention. We already know what to do, and even how to do it. Decisiveness is a natural function when we eliminate self-doubts, anxieties, the fear of making mistakes, or of what others will think of us.

**Power:** We develop genuine self-confidence, will, and *self-discipline.* Through self-confidence, we turn any obstacle into an opportunity. When we act with integrity, when we are consistent with who we are, we develop a strong will, the ability to consciously direct the power of the mind. Above all, life demands self-discipline. For those who understand the mind, self-discipline is simply doing what you really want to do. The mind has an infinite capacity to form habits. By taking charge of this capacity, we can consciously build the habits we choose, and act in the ways we want to act.

**Harmony:** We develop a sense of *wholeness and community,* and the spiritual skills of *cooperation, humility,* and *love.* We know that fear and self-hatred are two of the greatest sources of stress. But there is another, even greater, and that is loneliness. Of all the conditions we face as human beings, the greatest misery is loneliness. We make friends, get married, have families, and yet, we remain lonely. The only solution to this deep-seated isolation is to discover the friend and lover within, the spiritual Self. The experience of this spiritual Self allows us to be whole, and ends loneliness forever.

Spiritual skills arise from the successful practice of meditation. As we discover the power of the human spirit, we realize that the fundamental law of life is not "survival of the fittest," but cooperation. Our personality is a cooperative effort. All levels, functions, and systems of the personality work together, doing whatever is necessary to maintain the personality. Each part, organ, and function serves the whole. The personality is a model of interdependency and cooperation. When these don't cooperate, the result is stress and disease.

When we realize the spiritual Self, we understand that all living creatures are a part of the whole. We experience a sense of community that destroys all vestiges of mistrust, isolation, loneliness, and fear. In its place is the natural awe and humility that spiritual realization brings. The final skill, love, is the expression of the spiritual Self in our daily life. The more we give of ourselves, the greater we become. If we give respect, we gain respect. If we give power, we gain power. By giving of ourselves, we overcome all self-imposed limitations.

## FULFILLING THE PROMISE

Why be content with just a little relaxation or a healthier coronary-vascular system? These you can have – and much, much more. Experience your true nature directly. Calm the body; then calm the mind through self-training. Allow no movement of body or mind to disturb the clarity of your inner perception. Meditation will lead you to fulfill the most meaningful question of all – "Who am I?"

It is important to remember, however, that we are talking about self-mastery – not religious ritual. They should not be confused. Meditation is a practical technique for understanding human nature at all levels. This is the most important thing we can do. The great sages of all cultures have been very practical men and women who, through meditation, have sought for and discovered genuine and lasting release from fear and suffering. What they discovered is found in many languages, in many religions, in many cultures. It is found in Sophocles' statement, "Know Thyself"; it is "Be still and know that I am God" in the Jewish tradition; it is "The kingdom of God is within" in the Christian tradition; and in the Vedantic tradition it is, "That I am." Every culture expresses this one great truth in some way. It is the same truth that you must, and will discover in your own practice.

Nothing is more practical than the freedom of self-mastery. Nothing is more powerful than the direct and joyful experience of the inner spiritual Self, and the discovery that it has always been there. As T. S. Eliot said at the end of his last and greatest work, *The Four Quartets:*

> *We shall not cease from exploration*
> *And the end of all our exploring*
> *Will be to arrive where we started*
> *And know the place for the first time.*

Addendum

# ON THE WAY TO SELF-MASTERY: STARTING YOUR SELF-TRAINING PROGRAM

*If you always do what you always done,
you always get what you always got.*
—Anonymous—

To build a successful self-training program takes commitment, care, and attention. When we were children, we were told what, when, and how to do things. As adults, we often find the same conditions – either someone telling us what, when, and how, or we struggle with conditions that dictate to us our what, when, and how. Self-training programs are different. You are in charge; you and you alone decide what is to be done or what is not to be done.

The great beauty of self-training is that you get out of it exactly what you put into it. You alone decide how important it is to develop your inner strengths. You alone decide the amount of time and effort. You have the freedom to make excuses; you can find any number of valid reasons for not taking the time to practice. But in the end, it is your life and what you make of it is up to you. You end up with what you take the time to create.

## Inspiration and Commitment

Obviously, the key is your commitment to self-mastery. What you need to know is that commitment is an emotional process based on inspiration, not facts and information. As we saw in Chapter 9, desire is the motivating force. Very little desire comes from facts. My master always spoke of progress as being ninety percent inspiration and ten percent perspiration. When you are inspired, effort becomes effortless. You can do a number of things to maintain your commitment to your own self-mastery:

**1. Maintain a high level of inspiration.** Read books, talk with others who are engaged in developing self-mastery, listen to inspiring lectures, do whatever you need to keep your level of interest high in your practice and in your goals.

**2. Enjoy the exercises you do.** We make a great mistake when we look upon self-mastery disciplines as "work." It isn't. It is experimentation, it is exploration, and it is having fun with your mind. When it becomes a burden that you "must do" along with all the other things you "must do," then your practice is definitely in danger.

**3. Strive to create "beginners mind."** Don't let routine dull your attention. In karate, students strive to achieve "beginners mind." When we first learn something that we are interested in, when we are beginners, our attention is really focused. As we become more familiar, we lose this capacity for attention, and we lose our capacity to learn. In doing your exercises, don't let them become routine. Pay attention; learn to watch for the subtle changes that are always there.

**4. Use affirmations.** Your mind can provide powerful motivation and encouragement through affirmations. An affirmation is a mental/emotional confirmation of your own power, or of the reality you want to bring about. You create affirmations with thoughts, images, or feelings. The greater your concentration, the more effective the affirmation. To be effective, affirmations must be made with a strong desire and in accordance with what you really believe and value.

There are no magic affirmations; there are only thoughts or images that the mind empowers. Below are affirmations that I have found particularly helpful:

• I must do it, I can do it, I will do it.

• I am full of confidence, free of worry and doubt.

• I am responsible, able to learn from any situation.

• Fear (doubt) is a thought. I will face my fears, let them pass through without resistance, and when they have passed, I will remain.

To do an affirmation, begin with the Centering exercise (page 253). Then focus your attention on the affirmation. Allow the entire mind to be filled with the affirmation until you actually feel the confidence and calm indicated by the words. Once you feel the emotional aspect of the affirmation, clearly picture yourself going through the day, doing your tasks in this calm and focused state. If the affirmation is specific to a particular task, clearly picture yourself completing the task.

Some Basic Principles:

• Build with simplicity: Keep your program very simple and direct.
  Make only one or two small changes in your daily routine, and
  practice these changes until they become habits.

• Don't try to change the world or yourself in a day. Make a reasonable
  time commitment. Keep in mind what you earn depends on what you

invest. A five-minute investment is not a large investment. Progress demands that you make at least one fifteen minute commitment where you only work on building inner skills.

- Consistency is important. A fifteen-minute commitment done consistent ly provides real benefits whereas an hour done haphazardly will lead to little skill development. Every day do something to become stronger, wiser, more capable, and more loving.
- Persist until you have the habit or skill established. If you finish the smallest of tasks, you strengthen your will. If you do not finish a self-assigned task, you subtly weaken your will.
- Build on a strong foundation and continue to build it. You won't be able to meditate if you can't breathe properly and have chronic tension in your body. Start at the beginning, build your skill at relaxation and establish diaphragmatic breathing as your moment-to-moment breathing pattern. Then your practice at concentration and other exercises will be success ful.
- Develop an attitude of experimentation and playfulness with your self-training program. Once you begin to work with your mind, you will discover a wide array of exercises. Some you will like and some you won't. Don't be afraid to try new ways of gaining insight, or developing your instincts, or solving problems.

## Getting Started

The exercises from the book are summarized in Appendix A. There are exercises, such as meditation or concentration exercises, which must be done every day and require an investment of time to do. There are also exercises and techniques that are incorporated as part of your day-to-day activities, such as Breath Awareness and the RARE technique for conflict management. These do not require any separate time to do.

Then there are exercises which take some time to do, but can be done whenever you have the need, such as the Insight exercise from Chapter 8.

The absolutely essential techniques are:
- Diaphragmatic Breathing
- Relaxation, particularly Deep-State Breath Relaxation and 61 Points
- Breath Awareness
- Concentration (such as the Candle Gaze exercise)
- Meditation

You will find that your ability to work successfully with any mind technique will depend on your ability to concentrate. Of course, the more you use any technique, the more skilled you become.

## The Essential Elements

**Make a Commitment:** Set aside one period of time during the day that you dedicate to developing self-mastery skills. Pick a time when you can leave all other concerns and duties behind. This time should become sacred to you, and don't allow anything to intrude or postpone it. A reasonable beginning time is fifteen minutes. Once you make the commitment, always find a time to fulfill it. It's best if that time is the same every day, but there may be times when you can't be that consistent. Then be practical, and take the time when you can.

Different exercises are best done at different times. It might be best to practice relaxation right after you come home from work. After you are skilled in relaxation, that fifteen minutes should be given over to concentration and meditation exercises. These are often best done in the early morning before your mind is distracted and disturbed by the day's events.

**Build the Foundation:** The first techniques should be Diaphragmatic Breathing and Relaxation skills. Use the practice period to work on relaxation. Start by learning muscle relaxation. Then shift to the Deep-State Breath Relaxation. After mastering this exercise, move on to the 61 Points exercise. Once you are skilled in relaxation, never spend more than five minutes doing deep relaxation unless it is the 61 Points exercise. Make sure you don't allow yourself to fall asleep during relaxation training. Go back periodically and do a long relaxation just to maintain a high degree of skill.

At the same time, re-establish Diaphragmatic Breathing as your moment-to-moment breathing pattern. Establish a habit of practicing for at least ten minutes right before falling asleep. Focus on even breathing for the first five to eight minutes, then switch over to 2:1 Breathing to create a deeper state of rest. Practice Diaphragmatic Breathing during the day as often as you can remember to do so. The more you practice, you stronger your habit becomes. Continue to practice even after Diaphragmatic Breathing becomes your habit. After thirty-one years, I still practice Diaphragmatic Breathing right before falling asleep.

**Incorporate Breath Awareness Into Your Day-to-Day Activities:** Breath awareness is a key skill. It can be done anywhere, at any time. All you have to do is remember to do it. Leave notes for yourself, use the alarm on your wristwatch as a reminder to practice; do whatever you need to do to remember to practice breath awareness. This exercise is the most practical and important mind-management technique you have available to you. Use it, use it, use it, every chance you have.

Taking two minutes to clear the mind with Breath Awareness minimizes chronic stress and fatigue and clears the mind for the next task you face. Using Breath Awareness during traffic keeps you free from traffic stress. Whenever I travel on a plane, I spend at least part of the time focusing on breath awareness. This minimizes travel fatigue and leaves me ready to work when I arrive at my destination.

Table A.1

SUGGESTED DAILY SCHEDULE
FOR EFFECTIVE SKILLS DEVELOPMENT

Morning:

15 minutes of diaphragmatic breathing immediately upon awakening. Use an
    8–10 pound sandbag to strengthen the diaphragm.
Shower or bath to loosen muscles and clear the mind.
5 minutes stretching exercises.
5–10 Sun Salutations: Begin with 2 or 3, gradually increase number over a peri
    od of weeks until doing 12 or more.
10–15 minutes of concentration training, using Breath Awareness or the Candle
    Gaze exercise.

During the day:

2 minutes of breath awareness each hour to clear tension, refocus the mind.
Breath awareness as often as you can during the day.
Take a 10-minute relaxation or concentration break in the morning and in the
    afternoon; you will be surprised at how it helps clarify thinking.
Use imagery techniques, the RARE model, other applications any time during
    the day for effective problem solving.

After work:

Relaxation or concentration exercise right after you come home from work.
    This clears the mind of work-related tensions, increases your energy, and
    facilitates interaction with friends and family.

Evening:

5–15 minutes of stretching exercises. This removes tension and allows for a
    more peaceful sleep.
15 minutes of Diaphragmatic Breathing (even or 2:1 breathing) in bed before
    going to sleep using the 10-pound weight.

**Develop Concentration Skills:** Once you are skilled at relaxation, use the fifteen-minute period to practice concentration exercises. When you practice concentration and meditation exercises, sit in an erect, relaxed posture with your neck, head, and trunk properly aligned. This allows the mind to come to a deep state of focus, and the body to be very relaxed without falling asleep. Continue to practice deep relaxation once or twice a week, but use breathing techniques or the 61 Points exercise.

**Build a Solid, Consistent Meditation Practice:** After six to eight weeks, you should be sitting at least once a day to train the mind in concentration and meditation. Try to maintain at least a fifteen-minute period, but don't force the mind. On days when the mind won't focus on the meditation technique, switch to Breath Awareness for that period of time. But gradually, train the mind to stay focused on the image of a flame or the *So Hum* of the meditation exercise. This will refine your power of concentration, develop your intuition, and gently lead to the mystical experience that has so much power. Once you establish a meditation exercise, don't keep switching the focus point. Maintain a consistent practice so the concentration becomes refined.

**Incorporate Techniques Into Your Day-To-Day Activities:** Develop the habit of using mind exercises and techniques whenever you have the opportunity. It takes very little time to use the Centering exercise for creative problem solving or to minimize an emotional reaction. By using different techniques, you build powerful habits for problem solving in the mind. You will find that even a short five-minute meditation or concentration practice during a hectic day will pay large dividends in your ability to maintain a calm mind and solve problems in a creative way.

**Find Time to Stay Flexible:** Stretching exercises are best done in the morning for general health, and in the evening to increase flexibility. It is often very useful to spend a few minutes stretching in the morning before practicing meditation. You will find the sun salutation to be very helpful in the morning for taking the kinks out of the body and energizing your mind. Do a minimum of six every morning for the best effect.

## A Personal Self-Training Program

This section includes a suggested daily schedule (Table A.1) for a self-training program. Use it as a guide to help establish your own unique program based on your schedule, needs, and goals. Remember, you have to fit your needs and goals into the program.

You can establish your own unique program. Grab a pencil and a piece of paper, and let's outline a program. This will help clarify your goals and what steps you need to take in order to accomplish them. We will look at four areas: goals, steps to accomplish your goals, possible interference, and specific steps to take.

Concentration or meditation exercises should be practiced at least once a day for 10–15 minutes. Gradually increase the time as you gain greater control over concentration. Using Breath Awareness as often as you can during the day will gradually increase your ability to stay calm and relaxed. This schedule is only a guide. Evolve your own schedule and slowly increase the time spend on concentration and meditation exercises. The key is to be consistent!

**1. Goals:** Decide what you would like to accomplish in the next month, six months from now, one year from now. Write out your goals. You can project as far as you want, but keep it practical.

**2. What will help me accomplish my goals:** List the specific things that you must do to accomplish your goals. This will include setting up a time to practice the exercises, noting changes in your diet, setting up reminders in your computer or on your desk, and so on.

**3. Interference and counter measures:** We all have habits and patterns that create resistance. Identify these habits and the steps you can take to minimize their impact on you.

**4. Specific steps:** Decide what practical steps to take in order to reach your goals. Be very specific about how much time you will commit, when you will do it, and even what exercises you are going to do.

Below is a sample program to give you an idea of what your outline could look like. This program is for concentration.

*1. Goals:* Increase my power of concentration. To accomplish this I first need to lower my stress levels and then learn to focus my mind more effectively. So I will need to learn deep relaxation, make sure my breathing is done with the diaphragm, and practice concentration exercises. By the end of:
- First month: Establish Diaphragmatic Breathing as my normal breathing pattern.
- Second month: Become skillful at Deep Relaxation.
- Third month: Practice Candle Gaze exercise after doing relaxation.
- Sixth Month: Sit comfortably and still for fifteen minutes, focusing on breath awareness.

*2. What will help me accomplish my goals:* I will do the following to help me achieve my goals:
- Set up a specific time for practice; For the first two months I will take 15 minutes to practice relaxation right when I come home from work.
- Reduce intake of stimulants (coffee) and depressants (alcohol), particularly at times when they might interfere with practice.
- Practice being more patient with myself and others, use Breath Awareness to help me be less reactive; set up notes to remind me be to use breath awareness.
- Take time to read materials that interest and inspire me.

*3. What will interfere with program:* Taking the time to do the exercises; I hate to follow a schedule; laziness; not seeing any progress; boredom with the exercise routine. Solutions:

- Set up and commit to a specific time for practice that has minimal chance for interference.
- Don't allow myself to become a fanatic. Be flexible, vary my schedule and don't be overly restrictive about my diet.
- Reward myself when I feel I have accomplished a degree of ability to relax, stay calm during conflict situations, or become more focused.
- Keep sight of my goals.
- Add a new exercise or focus point when I become bored.

*4. Specific Steps:*
- First step: Read more about stress, make or buy a relaxation tape; practice breath awareness during the day as often as I can remember, work with diaphragmatic breathing for fifteen  minutes before going to sleep, and as often as I can during the day. Length of time: one month.
- Second Step: Practice relaxation exercise at least once a day lying in the relaxation posture. Be aware of breathing as often as I can during the day; take breath breaks at work. Length of time: one month.
- Third Step: Begin practicing Candle Gaze after relaxation period. Length of time: one month or until I reach fifteen minutes on the gaze.
- Fourth Step: Begin practicing inner concentration using *So-Hum* for at least fifteen minutes every day. Begin to work with the Centering Exercise to solve problems; use the insight exercise to help make decisions.

Don't be discouraged if you aren't enlightened after five days, or five weeks, or five months, or even five years. Self-mastery is a lifetime of exploration, experimentation, and expression. With honest and consistent effort, you cannot fail. After all, you already are the power; you already are the spiritual Self. The only thing left is discovery.

# APPENDIX A
## SUMMARY OF EXERCISES

*Awareness Exercises:* These exercises are designed to increase self-awareness and your sensitivity to the events and relationships within the different dimensions of the personality.

| EXERCISE | CH | PAGE | PURPOSE AND VALUE |
|---|---|---|---|
| Shrinking Headache | 1 | 20 | Use awareness to eliminate head pain. |
| Traveling | 1 | 29 | Become aware of the different levels of our personality and the power functions operating at each level. |
| Mind/Body Awareness | 3 | 89 | Develop sensitivity to the impact of our thoughts on the body. |
| Butterfly Image | 3 | 90 | Gain awareness of how images in the mind can control a physical event in the body. |
| Green Frog | 3 | 93 | Develop awareness of how language can provide invalid information; gain objectivity toward our thoughts and images. |

*Desk Exercises:* Simple stretching exercises for the head, neck, and shoulders to help minimize and eliminate chronic stress in these areas. These exercises are easily done while sitting at your desk, or at anytime during the day.

| EXERCISE | CH | PAGE | PURPOSE AND VALUE |
|---|---|---|---|
| Shoulder Rotations | 5 | 150 | Loosen shoulder muscles |
| Neck Rotations | 5 | 150 | Loosen neck muscles. |
| Forehead and Sinus | 5 | 151 | Reduce tension in face, eye muscles. |

*Balance Exercises:* Simple, easy-to-do exercises to increase the coordination between the left and right hemispheres of the brain.

| EXERCISE | CH | PAGE | PURPOSE AND VALUE |
|---|---|---|---|
| Hand to Knee | 5 | 152 | Mental and physical balance, increased alertness. |
| Elbow to Knee | 5 | 154 | Mental and physical balance, increased alertness. |
| Elbow to Knee, Cross Pattern Front to Back | 5 | 154 | Mental and physical balance, increased alertness. |

*Relaxation Exercises:*Designed to help create deep relaxation, reduce chronic levels of tension, stress, and emotional reactivity, and to systematically build skills in deep relaxation.

| EXERCISE | CH | PAGE | PURPOSE AND VALUE |
|---|---|---|---|
| Relaxation Posture | 5 | 128 | A posture that allows all the muscles of the body to achieve a state of relaxation; helpful in learning deep relaxation. |
| Muscle Relaxation | Appendix B | | Systematic exercise to learn deep relaxation on the structural level. |
| Sweeping Breath | 6 | 189 | A simple, easy-to-use relaxation exercise often used as a preliminary exercise for other relaxation techniques or concentration exercises. |
| Deep-State Breath Relaxation | 6 Appendix C | 188 | A sophisticated breathing exercise that creates a deep state of relaxation by manipulating the autonomic nervous system. |
| 61 Points | 8 Appendix D | 227 | A sophisticated concentration/relaxation exercise that provides a profound state of relaxation, useful in preventing hypertension. |

*Stretching Exercises:* A series of stretching exercises based on hatha yoga to improve flexibility, enhance glandular and neurological activity, calm the mind.

| EXERCISE | CH | PAGE | PURPOSE AND VALUE |
|---|---|---|---|
| Side Stretch | 5 | 154 | Increase circulation and breathing capacity, |
| Simple Back Stretch | 5 | 156 | build flexibility for the spine and limbs, |
| Angle Posture | 5 | 156 | develop arms and chest, |
| Torso Twist | 5 | 156 | and reduce abdominal fat. |
| Sun Salutation | 5 | 157 | A sophisticated, integrated series of 12 spinal positions, each stretching various joints and ligaments and moving the spinal column. |

*Breathing Exercises:* Designed to develop healthy breathing patterns, increase capacity and energy levels, reduce stress and stabilize emotional reactivity.

| EXERCISE | CH | PAGE | PURPOSE AND VALUE |
|---|---|---|---|
| Diaphragmatic Breathing | 6 | 172 | The natural moment-to-moment breathing pattern; absolutely essential for balance in the body. |
| 2:1 Diaphragmatic Breathing | 6 | 176 | Creates a deeper state of balanced rest in the body by increased stimulation of the parasympathetic nervous system. |

| | | | |
|---|---|---|---|
| Alternate Nostril | 6 | 178 | Calms and focuses the mind; increases lung capacity and control over autonomic nervous system; can be extended into a sophisticated concentration exercise. |
| Nasal Wash | 6 | 187 | Clean and rejuvenate the mucous membrane, alleviating congestion and sinus problems; eliminate sinus headaches, reduce the symptoms of allergies, prevent colds and sore throats. |
| Complete Breath | 6 | 190 | Increase level of energy, reduce fatigue and reduce muscle tension. |
| Sweeping Breath | 6 | 189 | A simple, easy-to-use relaxation exercise often used as a preliminary exercise for other relaxation techniques or concentration exercises. |
| Deep-State Breath Relaxation | 6 | 188 Appendix C | Sophisticated breathing exercise that creates a deep state of relaxation by manipulating the autonomic nervous system. |
| Two Minute Breath Break | 6 | 190 | Simple relaxation/mind clearing exercise to use any time to rebalance, clear the mind and refocus attention. |
| Sleep Exercise | 6 | 191 | A simple-to-learn and effective sleep exercise that leads to a deep, restful sleep and minimizes, even eliminates insomnia. |

*Mind Control Techniques:* These techniques are direct methods to strengthen conscious control over the mind and to develop different mind skills.

| EXERCISE | CH | PAGE | PURPOSE AND VALUE |
|---|---|---|---|
| Breath Awareness | 7 | 196 | Direct control of mind chatter. When used skillfully, provides absolute control over emotional reactions. It is the most important tool available for taking charge of the mind and mental clarity . |
| RARE | 7 | 201 | A very effective model for conflict management based on self-control and eliminating opposition. |
| Scanning Exercise | 7 | 202 | A technique for a quick check and release of muscle tension. |
| Three Strategies to Control Fear | 7 | 207 | To minimize and eliminate worry and fear. |
| Four Strategies to End Self-Hatred | 7 | 209 | To minimize self-hatred, access inner strength. |
| "Should" Stopper | 7 | 212 | Disrupt the habitual pattern of the mind to rely on "should" and "should not" as a method of self-punishment. |

| | | |
|---|---|---|
| Creative Thought Exercise | 7 216 | Demonstrates the creative force of our sensory mind to either help us or create problems for us. |
| Walking Exercise | 7 219 | Develop sensitivity to subtle feelings in your body as you react to others. Develop awareness of instincts as well as insights into other people's personality and your relationship with them. |

*Concentration and Meditation Exercises:* These exercises are designed to enhance your powers of concentration and lead to the ability to meditate, and to enhance insight and develop self-confidence.

| EXERCISE | CH PAGE | PURPOSE AND VALUE |
|---|---|---|
| 61 Points | 8 227 Appendix D | Sophisticated concentration/relaxation exercise which provides a profound state of relaxation, useful in preventing hypertension. |
| Insight | 8 234 | Develop insight into which solution or direction is the best one to take to resolve a particular prob lem or choice point. |
| Candle Gaze | 8 236 | An efficient concentration exercise combining an external and internal focus point. |
| Breath Awareness as Meditation | 8 247 | Breath Awareness to train concentration and develop meditation skills. |
| Centering: Resolving Emotional Baggage | 8 250 | The Centering exercise paired with another exercise to resolve emotional conflicts and free the mind from the burden of anger. |
| Centering | 8 253 | Establish a steady point of internal awareness. Use at the beginning of any meditation exercise, and for exercises involving other inner skills, such as intuition, imagery work, and conflict resolution. |
| Meditation | 8 254 | Lead the mind to one-pointed concentration. |
| Confidence | 8 254 | Establish a pathway to the balanced mind, the fifth level of our personality, and the source of our inner strength.Useful technique to enhance problem-solving abilities. |

## APPENDIX B
## DETAIL OF MUSCLE RELAXATION EXERCISE

Begin by lying in the Relaxation Posture. Close your eyes and focus your attention on your breath ... breathe easily and gently with the diaphragm, with no jerkiness, stops or pauses ... let your breath be very smooth and even, without any effort on your part ... picture yourself breathing in relaxation and exhaling all the tension out of your body ... let your breath be very easy and gentle, with no strain or effort. ... You are breathing in peacefulness and quietness, exhaling all thoughts of the past, all concerns for the future ... just bring all of your attention to your breath as it flows in and out of your body ... now picture your forehead as smooth as a piece of silk ... as if you are looking into the mirror of your mind and seeing all the bumps and wrinkles melting away in your forehead ... you can feel the muscles in your forehead relaxing down into your face, relaxing your eyebrows and your eyes ... relaxing your cheeks ... the corners of your mouth, your lips, and even your tongue ... relax your lower jaws and your ears ... and relax your neck muscles, front and back. ... Picture the muscles in your neck as being very warm, very heavy, and so loose they can't even hold your head up.

Again, bring your attention back to your breath, breathing in relaxation and exhaling tension ... easily, gently, no strain or effort ... let your body do all the breathing for you. ... Relax your shoulders, letting go of all tension from your shoulders ... relax your upper arms and your forearms, picturing the muscles in your arms as being very warm and heavy ... relax your hands, your fingers, and even your fingertips. ... Again, bring your attention back to your breath, and imagine yourself inhaling down into your fingertips and exhaling all the tension out of your arms ... very easy, very gentle, no effort ... let your body do all the breathing for you. ... Relax your fingertips, fingers, and hands ... relax your forearms and your upper arms, picturing the muscles as being very warm and heavy ... and, relax your shoulders. ... Again, bring your attention back to your breath ... let the inhalation merge into the exhalation, merge into the inhalation ... smooth and even, the breath is like a large wheel moving effortlessly through the body. ... Relax your chest muscles ... relax your stomach and your abdominal muscles ... relax your hips ... relax your thighs, picturing the muscles as being very warm and heavy ... relax your calves ... your feet, toes, and even the tips of your toes. ...

Again, bring your attention back to your breath ... imagine your body to be like a hollow reed, and you are breathing in through your toes, inhaling to the top of your head, filling the body with breath ... then exhaling from the top of your head to your toes, completely emptying the body of breath ... all very easily and gently, and without any effort. ... You are only the witness, allow the body to do all the work ... in your mind you can feel the entire body breathing in and breathing out ... expanding on the inhalation and contracting on the exhalation. ...

Relax your toes and your feet ... relax your calves and thighs, picturing the muscles in your legs as being very warm and heavy ... relax your hips ... relax your abdominal muscles and your stomach ... relax your chest muscles ... and relax your shoulders. ... Let your whole body become warm and heavy, give up all control over the body, and trust that the floor will support you completely. ... Again, bring your attention back to the breath ... let the inhalation merge into the exhalation merge into the inhalation ... very easy, very gently ... breathing in and out very smoothly, without any effort on your part. ...

Relax your neck muscles, front and back ... relax your lower jaws and your ears ... relax your lips, the corners of your mouth, and even your tongue ... relax your cheeks ... and your eyes ... now picture your forehead as smooth as a piece of silk ... now right in the center of your mind, where all your thoughts seem to begin, on your next exhalation, relax that mind center.

Gently wriggle fingers, toes. Being aware of every movement, slowly raise your arms and hold your hands about four inches in front of your face. Slowly open your eyes to the palms of your hands, then gently lower your hands. Remain as relaxed as you can throughout the day.

During the day, take a few moments to picture your forehead becoming very smooth and even. This will help you stay more relaxed. Don't forget to use diaphragmatic breathing to also keep you more balanced. The greater your skill at muscle relaxation, the more relaxed you stay throughout the day.

APPENDIX C
DETAIL OF DEEP-STATE BREATH RELAXATION EXERCISE

Lying in the Relaxation Posture, focus on even, diaphragmatic breathing ... let the body do all the breathing for you, you are only the witness to the breathing ... let your breath become very smooth and even ... breathe in relaxation and exhale all the tension from your body. ... Breathe in peacefulness and quietness, exhale all thoughts of the past, and all concerns for the future. ... Now picture your body like a hollow reed, and breathe in from your toes, fill your body with breath to the crown of your head, and exhale back down and out your toes. ... Let your conscious mind travel up your body with the inhalation and back down with the exhalation ... easily, gently, without any effort and strain, let your body do the breathing for you. ... Inhale from your toes to the crown of your head and exhale down to and out your ankles, then inhale as if you are breathing in through your ankles back to the crown of your head ... easily, gently, letting your conscious awareness travel between the two points with the inhalation and exhalation. ... Inhale from the ankles to the crown of your head and exhale down and out your knees ... inhale through your knees to the crown of your head and exhale down and out the tip of your spine, and inhale from the tip of your spine to the crown of your head, filling only the trunk, neck, and head with breath. ...

Easily and gently, letting your conscious thought travel up and down with the inhalation and exhalation between the two points ...inhale from the tip of your spine, up the spine to the crown of your head and exhale down and out your navel ... Inhale through your navel to the crown of your head, filling only the stomach, chest, neck and head with breath ... easily and gently, without any effort or strain ... Inhale from the navel to the crown of your head and exhale down and out your heart center, the center of your chest, then inhale from your heart center to the crown of your head, filling only the chest, neck and head with breath. ... Breathe as quickly as you need to be comfortable, but very easily and gently ... without any strain, or effort. ... Inhale from your heart center to the crown of your head and exhale down and out the base of your throat, then inhale to the crown of your head filling only your neck and head with breath ... Notice that your breath is becoming very shallow, hardly any motion of the lungs at all. ... Inhale from the base of your throat to the crown of your head, and exhale down and out the nostrils, then inhale from the opening of the nostrils to the point between the two eyes, and exhale back down and out your nostrils, filling only the nose with breath ... breathe as quickly as you need to feel comfortable, but very gently, very easily, you shouldn't have to pant. ... Now there is really no breath going at all down into the lungs, just an exchange of air in the nose. Your breath should be extremely shallow and light at this point. ...

Now inhale through the tip of your nose to the crown of your head, and exhale from the crown of your head down and out the base of the throat. Then inhale through the base of the throat to the crown of the head, filling the neck and head with breath. … Let your conscious thought travel up and down between the two points with the inhalation and exhalation, very easily, very gently. … Inhale from the base of the throat to the crown of the head, and exhale down and out the heart center in the center of the chest, then inhale again to the crown of your head filling the chest, neck and head with breath. … Remember, there should be no strain or effort, you are only the witness, letting your body do all the work … inhale from your heart center to the crown of your head and exhale down and out your navel, then inhale from your navel to the crown of your head, filling the stomach, chest, neck and head with breath … easily, gently, without any strain or effort … inhale from your navel to the crown of your head and exhale down your spine and out the tip of your spine, then inhale from the tip of your spine, up the spine to the crown of your head, filling the entire trunk, neck and head with breath. … Let your conscious thought travel up and down between the two points. … Inhale from the tip of your spine, up the spine to the crown of your head and exhale down and out your knees, then inhale through your knees to the crown of your head … filling your body from the knees to the crown of your head with breath … easily, gently, let the body do all the work for you. … Inhale from your knees to the crown of your head and exhale down and out your ankles, then inhale as if breathing through your ankles, filling the body with breath to the crown of your head. … Let your conscious thought travel up the body with the inhalation and back down with the exhalation, easily, gently … inhale from your ankles to the crown of your head and exhale down and out your toes, completely emptying your body of breath. … Then inhale, from the toes, filling the body with breath, peacefulness, and quietness to the crown of the head, exhaling from the crown back down and out the toes, completely emptying the body of breath, leaving only the peacefulness and quietness behind. … In your mind you can feel your whole body breathing, as if every pore and cell were breathing in and out.… The entire body expands on the inhalation and contracts on the exhalation … every easily, without any effort … for a few moments, concentrate on this feeling of expansion and contraction … .

Gently wiggle fingers, toes. Being aware of every movement, slowly raise your arms and hold your hands about four inches in front of your face. Slowly open your eyes to the palms of your hands, and then gently lower your hands. Remain aware of inner calmness and energy that flows within you, and remain calm and aware throughout the rest of the day. After you become skillful with this exercise while lying in the Relaxation Posture, you can do it sitting. Our minds have difficulty going around corners, so change the base point from the toes to the tip of the spine. You still begin with a deep and complete gentle breath, but then work your way up the spine. The imagery helps make the exercise effortless so you do not become tense from trying to control your breath. Once you can change the motion without effort or strain, you no longer need to use imagery. At this point, each breath should be either more shallow or deeper than the one before it, depending on which way you are going.

## APPENDIX D
## DETAIL OF 61 POINTS CONCENTRATION EXERCISE

Lying in the Relaxation Posture, close your eyes and concentrate on making your breath very even, very steady, and very smooth. ... You are not trying to fill your lungs completely, or trying to empty them. Breathe easily and gently, letting your body do all the work for you. Your breath should be smooth and even, letting your inhalation and exhalation be smooth and even. ... The pressure of the flow of the breath should be even, having the same flow or pressure at the end of the exhalation as you do at the beginning and in the middle. Don't allow any pauses, jerks, or shakiness in your breath. Even minimize the pause between the inhalation and the exhalation.

Now mentally scan down through the body, checking for any excess muscle tension ... wherever you find tension, simply release the tension in the muscles ... now using your imagination, picture your body as being a hollow reed. Breathe as if you are breathing through your toes, filling your body with breath to the crown of your head, and exhaling back down and out your toes again. Breathe easily and gently, no strain and no effort. ... Again, you aren't trying to fill your lungs, or empty them completely, just an easy deep, slow and gentle breath ... breathing in through the toes to the crown of your head and exhaling back down and out the toes. In your mind, you can feel your whole body expanding when you inhale and contracting when you exhale, as if every cell in your body was breathing in and breathing out ... easily, gently, no strain, no effort. ...

And now bring your attention to your mind center, the space between your two eyebrows. Picture as clearly as you can a small blue star or flame inside the space between the two eyebrows. Let the star or flame be as perfect, as small and as clear as your mind will allow ... and now at the base of the throat, the throat center, picture a small blue star of flame ... in the center of the right shoulder joint ... in the center of the right elbow joint ... in the center of the right wrist joint, a small blue star or flame, as clear and as perfect as your mind will allow ... on the tip of the thumb on the right hand ... on the tip of the forefinger on the right hand ... on the tip of the middle finger ... on the tip of the ring finger on the right hand ... on the tip of the small finger, a small blue star or flame, as clear or as perfect as your mind will allow. ... Again in the center of the right wrist joint ... in the center of the right elbow joint ... in the center of the right shoulder joint, a small blue star or flame ... again, at the base of the throat, the throat center, visualize a small blue star or flame. ...

Now in the center of the left shoulder joint, let the star or flame illuminate the entire center of the joint ... in the center of the left elbow joint ... in the center of the left wrist joint ... now on the tip of the thumb on the left hand ... on the tip of the forefinger of the left hand ... on the tip of the middle finger of the left hand ... on the tip of the ring finger ... and on the tip of the small finger of the left hand, a small blue star or flame, as perfect and as small as your mind will allow it to be ... Again, visualize the star or flame in the center of the left wrist joint ... in the center of the left elbow joint ... in the center of the left shoulder joint ... again at the base of the throat, the throat center, a small blue star or flame. ...

Now visualize the star or flame in the center of the chest, between the two breasts, the heart center ... on the nipple of the right breast, visualize a small blue star or flame ... back again to the heart center ... now on the nipple of the left breast ... back again to the heart center ... Now visualize the star or flame at the navel center, just behind the navel. ... Now visualize a small blue star or flame at the pelvic center, in the center between the two hip bones ... in the center of the right hip joint, let the star or flame illuminate the entire center of the joint ... in the center of the right knee joint ... in the center of the right ankle joint ... at the tip of the large toe on the right foot, a small blue star or flame ... on the tip of the second toe ... on the tip of the third or middle toe of the right foot ... on the tip of the fourth toe ... and on the tip of the small toe of the right foot, a small blue star or flame as clear and as perfect as your mind will allow it to be ... Again, in the center of the right ankle joint ... in the center of the right knee joint ... in the center of the right hip joint. ... Now visualize a small blue star or flame at the pelvic center ... in the center of the left hip joint ... in the center of the left knee joint, let the star or flame illuminate the entire joint area ... in the center of the left ankle joint ... At the tip of the large toe on the left foot ... on the tip of the second toe ... on the tip of the third toe of the left foot ... on the tip of the fourth toe ... and on the tip of the small toe, a small blue star or flame, as perfect and as clear as your mind will allow it to be. ... Again, in the center of the left ankle joint ... in the center of the left knee joint. ... in the center of the left hip joint ... and again at the pelvic center, a small blue star or flame. ... At the navel center ... at the heart center in the middle of the chest ... at the throat center at the base of the throat ... and in the mind center, the space between the two eyebrows, let the star or flame be as clear, as perfect and as small as your mind will allow it to be. ... Now using your imagination, picture your body as being a hollow reed. Breathe as if you are breathing through your toes, filling your body with breath to the crown of your head, and exhaling back down and out your toes again. Breathe easily and gently, no strain and no effort ... Again, you aren't trying to fill your lungs, or empty them completely, just an easy, deep, slow, and gentle breath ... breathing in through the toes to the crown of your head and exhaling back down and out the toes. ... In your mind, you can feel your whole body expanding when you inhale and contracting when you exhale, as if every cell in your body was breathing in and breathing out ... easily, gently, no strain, no effort. ... Gently wiggle toes. Being aware of every movement, slowly raise your arms and hold your hands about four inches in front of your face. Slowly open your eyes to the palms of your hands, then gently lower your hands. Remain aware of inner calmness and energy that flows within you, and remain calm and aware throughout the rest of the day.

# INDEX

Affirmation: 95, 220, 283
Aikido: 233,
Ajaya, Swami: 263
Animal:
    instincts and urges, primitive: 57, 261
Antahkarana: 78
Avidya: 115

Bach, Richard: 209
Balance:
    dynamic: 65-66, 116
    emotional: 116
    harmony: 24, 116
    mental: 36, 126
    physical: 116
    social: 116
Bandler, Richard: 94
Beginners Mind: 283
Behaviors:
    acceptance: 203, 211, 255, 274
    avoidance: 208, 262
    behaviorism: 107, 114
    training for essential hypertension: 184
    decisiveness: 27, 118, 280
    determination: 28, 82, 116
    distress: 48, 61
    forgiveness: 211-212
    patience: 116, 211
    passive volition: 129
    playfulness: 232, 284
Benson, Herb: 54
Biofeedback: 69, 110-116, 147
Blood sugar: 136-139
Brain wave patterns: 238
Brain gym system: 149
Breathing
    autonomic nervous system and: 162-164,
    chest: 166-171, 173
    diaphragmatic: 126, 166-172
    mid-cycle rest dangers: 175
    respiration processes: 165
    thoracic: 166
    two-minute breath break: 190
    2:1 breathing: 175-176
Bua, Swami: 148
Buddhi: 230
Burnout: 59-60, 63
Butterfly image: 90

Cannon, Walter: 58

Chakras: 34-35, 248
Chopra, Deepak: 144
Commitment: 246, 272, 282-285
Commoner, Barry: 131-132
Concentration:
    See also: meditation
    development of: 221-224, 233
Conflict management: 201, 250, 284
    RARE model: 201,286
Conscience: 87, 280
Contemplation: 243
Cottle, Maurice: 180
Coulter, David: 165
Creativity: 24, 27, 213-216
Critical Thinking: 41

D'Aquili, Eugene: 239
Decisiveness: 27, 118, 273, 280
Dennison, Paul: 149, 152
Dependency: 140, 263-264, 266-268
Depression:
    disease link, as: 53, 62, 63
    nostril activity, and: 186
    possum reaction, and: 62
    relation to stress: 60, 62
    treatment for: 176
Diet:
    additives 130, 134, 139, 140, 142-143
    digestion 134, 141-142
    food quality: 130-132, 143-144
    genetic engineering: 131, 135
    self-mastery, and: 142
    compulsive eating: 265
    eating discipline: 139-141
    hunger: 109, 141, 261-263
    indigestion: 1441-142, 185, 186, 265
    irradiation: 135-136
    fat: 132, 139, 143
    fiber: 133, 140
    microwave cooking: 135
    caffeine: 138, 182
    convenience foods: 138
    protein: 143-144
    snacks: 144
    soft drinks: 139
    sugar: 136-139, 143
    water: 143
Dis-ease: 47, 68, 75, 148
Distress: 48, 61
Drucker, Peter: 217, 218

Drugs: 39, 55, 99, 116, 119, 125, 144,
    180, 195, 238
Dukas, Paul: 103

Eastern traditions: 233
Efficiency: 113, 126, 136, 163, 168, 181
Ego: 18-19, 43, 73-75, 85-86, 97, 99-
    102, 258-259, 265, 267-269, 274
Einstein, Albert: 231
Eliot, Robert: 54
Eliot, T. S: 281
Emotion:
    controlling: 264-266
    negative types: 260-261
    nostril activity, and: 186-187
    positive types: 267-271
    reactivity, and: 21-23, 38
    sensory mind, and: 40
Empowerment 279
Energy level: 26, 29, 135-136, 291
Eustress: 48, 61
Exercise, physical: 144-147
Exercises:
    alternate nostril breathing: 178-180
    angle posture: 156
    auto-hypnosis: 156
    awareness: 144
    back stretch: 156
    balance: 152
    candle gaze: 236
    centering: 253
    complete breath: 190
    confidence: 254
    creative thought: 213-216
    desk: 150
    flexibility: 144
    green frog: 93
    imagery: 127
    insight: 234
    meditation: 254
    neck: 150
    relaxation: 127
    relaxation posture: 128
    scanning: 202
    should-stopper: 212
    shoulder: 150
    side stretch: 54
    61 Points: 227, 298
    sleep: 191
    stretching: 154
    sun salutation: 157-159
    sweeping breath: 189
    torso twist: 156

traveling: 29
walking: 219

Experience:
    mystical: 44, 74-75, 224, 257-259
    peak: 44, 195, 221

Fatigue: 59, 60, 188
Fear:
    cause of stress: 50
    concentration inhibitor: 229
    controlling: 207-209
    language of: 34, 88
    mental dragon: 68
Fearlessness: 231
Flexibility: 144, 146, 150, 232
Fliess, Wilhelm: 186
Freud, Sigmund: 78, 186
Friedman, Mayer: 54
Future: 85

Galway, Timothy: 145
Gelberman, Rabbi: 117
Goldberg, Philip: 233
Green
        Alyce: 36
        Elmer: 36
Greene, Graham: 269
Grinder, John: 94
Gupta, D. S.: 183

Habits:
    health, and: 38, 104
    emotions, and: 38-39, 42, 94, 98, 105
    poor breathing: 170
    channeling power of: 104
    self-awareness of: 108-110
    self-discipline and mastery of: 20-21
    sensory mind, and: 38
    unconscious, and: 80, 106-108, 113
Harmony: 27, 66, 68, 136, 193, 280
Harvey, John: 88
Havel, Vaclav: 43-44
Health:
    cancer risks: 53, 59, 63, 106, 130
    insulin: 137-138
    immune system, and: 24, 52-53, 61
        87, 127, 130
    ulcer problems: 49, 53, 198
Heart:
    problems: 24, 31, 49, 52, 53, 168,
        183
    rate: 33, 57, 59, 61, 66, 83, 162, 176

Helplessness: 62, 209
Herring-Breuer reflex: 173-174
Homeostasis: 33, 59
Humility: 232, 275, 280
Hymes, Alan: 180-181, 183
Hyperactivity: 186
Hypertension: 36, 54, 128, 164, 180,

Ignorance: 73-75, 100, 115, 259
Imagination: 279-280, 298
Inhibition: 33, 60, 66-68
Inner conflict: 92, 203, 236, 271
Inner strength: 19, 28, 42-45, 75
Inner wisdom: 40, 229
Inspiration: 116, 282, 283
Instinct: 24, 41, 127, 217
Intimidation: 51
Intuition: 40, 41, 229-233

Judgment: 18-20, 206, 250, 275

Karate: 126, 207, 233-234, 283
Koshas: 25

Language:
    effective choice, and:88, 94
    of fear: 34, 88
    of self-hatred: 88
    reframing: 94, 95, 220
    sensory mind, and: 38
Laughter: 65, 111, 270
LeShan, Lawrence: 209
Life force: 24, 34, 37, 142, 265
    ki, chi: 34, 244, 192
Loneliness:
    controlling: 75, 99
    spiritual strength, and: 81, 99
Lurie, Oded: 211

Malin, Shimon: 240-241
Mantra: 237, 244, 249
Massage:
    forehead: 151
    sinus arrhythmia: 162
Masters:
    spiritual: 69, 71, 123, 125, 133, 142,
    189, 239, 276
    tantric: 44, 71, 73, 111, 118, 125,
    180, 260
Meditation:
    beginner level practices: 246
    benefits: 236
    breath awareness: 247

concentration: 222-224
diaphragmatic breathing: 167
elements of: 240
emotions: 250
exclusive: 244
exercise summary: 172
focus points: 244
in action: 245
inclusive: 242
misunderstandings about: 237
practical applications of: 249
relaxation, and: 224
suggested daily schedule: 248
teachers: 238, 278
Mental dragons:
    fear: 68
    loneliness: 73
    self-hatred: 72

Nadis: 34
Nasal wash: 187-188
Neural plexus: 35
Newberg, Andrew: 239
Non-attachment: 231, 266

Observation: 237-238
O'Brien, Justin: 136, 143
Ornish, Dean: 55, 132, 139
Overmeir, Bruce: 209

Pain killers: 31, 55
Peale, Norman Vincent: 94
Perception: 35-36, 213, 281
Persistence: 116, 221
Prana: 34, 244
Prayer: 141, 142, 158, 160
Problem solving: 80, 287
Psychoneuro-immunology: 53
Psychosomatic disease: 52-53

Rama, Swami: 36, 159, 263
Reality:
    external: 235
    inner: 30, 49, 235, 252, 273
Reasoning: 40-41, 68, 98, 280
Relaxation:
    autonomic, breathing: 127
    concentration: 128
    conflict management, and: 250, 284
    deep relaxation: 68, 126-128
    muscle: 127
    pain, and: 20
    posture: 128, 154

stress, and:126
structural: 127
Richter, C. P.: 209
Rosenman, Ray: 54

Samadhi: 74, 224, 239, 258
Sanskaras: 71-72
Self-:
    acceptance: 255, 270, 274
    awareness: 18-19, 75, 113, 205, 231
    confidence: 42, 82, 251-256
    criticism: 62, 87, 93, 199
    discipline: 17-20, 103, 115-116, 280
    esteem: 72, 117, 144
    hatred: 72-73, 86-88, 97-102
    knowledge: 17, 29, 123
    language of: 88
    mastery: 18, 21, 31, 45, 120
    as birthright: 120
    culture of: 119
    distilling power of: 18
    empowerment, and: 279
    science of: 21, 114
    preservation: 50, 57, 72
    respect: 44, 72, 73, 95, 210
    selflessness: 260, 269
    training: 120, 123, 184, 273
Scligman, Martin: 62, 209
Selye, Hans: 58, 60
Shakespeare: 94
Simonton, O. C.: 209
Skill:
    conscious mind's role: 113
    self-awareness, and: 18, 54, 72, 75
Skinner, B. F.: 107, 108, 115
Sleep apnea: 180-183, 185
Sophocles: 281
Sperry, Roger: 69
Spiritual:
    desire: 271
    non-attachment, and: 231, 266-267
    Sclf: 25, 74, 81, 99-102, 235, 258-267,
    280
Stage:
    activation: 63
    adaptation: 59
    alarm: 59, 62
    atrophication: 63
    fatigue: 59
    termination ("good-bye"): 59, 63
Stream of consciousness: 245
Stress:
    autonomic balance, and: 66, 162-163,

176, 173, 183
    defined: 47
    diet and: 130
    dynamic balance: 65-66
    fight or flight reaction: 33, 47, 49, 57-
    59, 62, 83
    good versus bad: 49, 60, 68
    mind's role in: 52
    myths about: 47-52
    possum reaction: 61, 65, 87, 117, 193
Sushumna: 187, 240
Swar swarodayam: 163
System:
    central nervous system: 31-32
    closed: 23
    endocrine: 59, 186
    enteric: 32, 33
    energy: 65
    immune: 73, 87, 127, 130
    limbic: 69, 173, 184
    living: 24
    nervous: 36, 67, 68
    autonomic: 32-33, 35, 62, 63, 68
    parasympathetic: 61, 62, 162, 176
    sensory motor: 31, 66
    sympathetic: 32, 33
    open: 23-24, 31

Tai chi: 192
Tantra yoga:
    energy dimension: 34, 71, 75, 266
    spiritual power mastery: 75, 222, 276
    tradition: 21, 44, 125
10-80-10 rule: 251-252
Trance states: 226, 237
Tranquility: 27, 42, 270
Trataka: 235
Trauma: 62, 103, 170
Twain, Mark: 81

Walton, Ralph: 130
Western traditions: 258
Wholeness: 19, 58, 278
Willpower: 109, 271-272

Yantra: 244
Yin and Yang: 68
Yoga:
    hatha: 112, 126, 148, 233
    masters: 36, 69, 71 (see also Masters)
    science: 34, 71, 162, 186-187, 236, 260
    tantra: (see Tantra yoga)

## ABOUT THE AUTHOR

With a doctorate in psychology, Phil Nuernberger has spent a lifetime studying with the great masters of personal excellence. He uniquely and skillfully combines the wisdom and knowledge of the East with the science and practicality of the West to train business executives in the personal skills of leadership mastery, emotional integrity, and spirituality.

Dr. Nuernberger has been a pioneer and innovator in bringing self-mastery disciplines to executive training. He has taught the integration of mind, body, and spirit, and made meditation and spirituality an important part of corporate executive training for over thirty years. A pioneer in the integration of inner human resources beginning in 1970, he was one of the first to:

- Develop, practice, and educate professionals in holistic health;
- Direct a successful clinical biofeedback program;
- Provide stress management training to corporate executives;
- Introduce meditation and spirituality into executive training;
- Develop and teach an MBA course in self-mastery disciplines.

Dedicated to the pursuit of personal excellence, Dr. Nuernberger's commitment is as strong today as it was thirty years ago. As Director of Intelligent Integration Systems, he continues to provide innovative programs in leadership training and personal effectiveness to executives, corporations, and business schools. His leadership in the areas of performance excellence and practical spirituality has gained him a national and international following. Recent clients include J.P. Morgan Partners, Cargill, Verizon, and Bank of Nova Scotia.

For the past thirty-three years, Dr. Nuernberger has studied with the great tantra yoga master, Sri Swami Rama, both in the United States and in the Himalayan Mountains of India and Nepal. An accomplished tantric yoga practitioner, Nuernberger is also a black belt in Karate, and a student of Shao Lin Tai Chi. He currently teaches an MBA course entitled "Leadership and the Executive Mind" at DeSales University and is a visiting faculty member for executive education at the Aresty Institute, Wharton School of Business, University of Pennsylvania and the Institute of the Himalayan Tradition.

To contact Dr. Phil Nuernberger:
Intelligent Integration Systems
One Rock Ledge Drive, Honesdale, PA 19431
(570) 253-4754 • www.mindmaster.com • info@mindmaster.com

For more great books from Yes International Publishers:
www.yespublishers.com • www.ihtyoga.org